T0178454

Communications
in Computer and Information Science   1486

More information about this series at http://www.springer.com/series/7899

Audrius Lopata · Daina Gudonienė ·
Rita Butkienė (Eds.)

Information and Software Technologies

27th International Conference, ICIST 2021
Kaunas, Lithuania, October 14–16, 2021
Proceedings

 Springer

Editors
Audrius Lopata
Kaunas University of Technology
Kaunas, Lithuania

Daina Gudonienė
Kaunas University of Technology
Kaunas, Lithuania

Rita Butkienė
Kaunas University of Technology
Kaunas, Lithuania

ISSN 1865-0929 ISSN 1865-0937 (electronic)
Communications in Computer and Information Science
ISBN 978-3-030-88303-4 ISBN 978-3-030-88304-1 (eBook)
https://doi.org/10.1007/978-3-030-88304-1

This Springer imprint is published by the registered company Springer Nature Switzerland AG
The registered company address is: Gewerbestrasse 11, 6330 Cham, Switzerland

Preface

We are happy to present to you the proceedings of the 27th International Conference on Information and Software Technologies (ICIST 2021). This yearly conference was held during October 14–16, 2021, in Kaunas, Lithuania. The present volume includes three chapters, which correspond to the three major areas that were covered during the conference, namely, Business Intelligence for Information and Software Systems, Software Engineering, and Information Technology Applications. According to the four special sessions of the conference, the proceedings and the three areas are subdivided into the following sections:

 i. Intelligent Methods for Data Analysis and Computer Aided Software Engineering
 ii. Intelligent Systems and Software Engineering Advances
 iii. Smart e-Learning Technologies and Applications
 iv. Language Technologies

Conference participants not only had the opportunity to present their rigorous research in more specialized settings, but also had the possibility to attend high-quality plenary sessions. This year, we had the pleasure of hearing keynote presentations by Christian Grimme (University of Münster, Germany) on "Technical and Social Perspectives on Disinformation, Social Bots, and Social Media" and Martin Haagoort (Managing Director and Data Scientist at Intellerts, The Netherlands) on "Artificial Intelligence for Finance – A Hyped Trend? Overpromising and Underdelivering? How to get on track for This Journey?" We would like to express our deepest gratitude to the special session chairs Audrius Lopata (Kaunas University of Technology, Lithuania), Marcin Wozniak (Silesian University of Technology, Poland), Danguolė Rutkauskienė (Kaunas University of Technology, Lithuania), and Jurgita Kapočiūtė-Dzikienė (Vytautas Magnus University, Lithuania). We acknowledge and appreciate the immense contribution of the session chairs not only in attracting the highest quality papers but also in moderating the sessions and enriching discussions between the conference participants. The entire team working on organizing the conference is proud that despite the uncertainties of the COVID-19 pandemic period, the conference maintained and attracted the interest of numerous scholars across the globe. Every year ICIST attracts researchers from all over the world, and this year was not an exception – we received 79 submissions from authors in approximately 19 countries. This indicates that over the years the conference has truly gained international recognition as it brings together a large number of brilliant experts who showcase the state of the art of the aforementioned fields and come to discuss their newest projects as well as directions for future research. As we are determined not to stop improving the quality of the conference, only 30 scientific papers were accepted to be published in this volume (a 38% acceptance rate). Each submission was reviewed by at least three reviewers, while borderline papers had an additional evaluation. Reviewing and selection was performed by our highly esteemed Program Committee, who we thank for devoting their precious time to produce thorough reviews and feedback to the authors. It should be noted that this year, the Program Committee consisted of 47 reviewers, representing 29 academic institutions and 16 countries. In addition to the session chairs and Program Committee members, we would also like to express our appreciation to the general chair, Audrius Lopata (Kaunas University of Technology, Lithuania), who has taken the responsibility of steering the wheel of ICIST since the 25th anniversary of the conference in 2019. Moreover, we would like to thank the Local Organizing Committee and the Faculty of Informatics at Kaunas University of Technology; the conference would not have been a great success without their tremendous support. The proceedings of ICIST 2021 are published as a volume in the Communications in Computer and Information Science series. This would not be possible without the kind assistance that was provided by Springer team, for which we are extremely grateful. We are very proud of this collaboration and believe that this fruitful partnership will continue for many more years to come.

August 2021   Audrius Lopata
                                                             Daina Gudonienė
                                                             Rita Butkienė

Organization

The 27th International Conference on Information and Software Technologies (ICIST 2021) was organized by Kaunas University of Technology and was held in Kaunas, Lithuania (October 14–16, 2021).

Conference Chair

Rita Butkienė   Kaunas University of Technology, Lithuania

Local Organizing Committee

Daina Gudonienė (Chair)	Kaunas University of Technology, Lithuania
Rita Butkienė	Kaunas University of Technology, Lithuania
Edgaras Dambrauskas	Kaunas University of Technology, Lithuania
Romas Šleževičius	Kaunas University of Technology, Lithuania
Lina Repšienė	Kaunas University of Technology, Lithuania
Vilma Sukackė	Kaunas University of Technology, Lithuania
Gintarė Lukoševičiūtė	Kaunas University of Technology, Lithuania

Special Session Chairs

Audrius Lopata	Kaunas University of Technology, Lithuania
Marcin Wozniak	Silesian University of Technology, Poland
Danguolė Rutkauskienė	Kaunas University of Technology, Lithuania
Jurgita Kapočiūtė-Dzikienė	Vytautas Magnus University, Lithuania

Program Committee

Audrius Lopata (Chair)	Kaunas University of Technology, Lithuania
Daina Gudonienė	Kaunas University of Technology, Lithuania
Ilona Veitaitė	Vilnius University, Lithuania
Vytenis Punys	Kaunas University of Technology, Lithuania
Martynas Patašius	Kaunas University of Technology, Lithuania
Aleksandras Targamadzė	Kaunas University of Technology, Lithuania
Carsten Wolff	Dortmund University Applied Sciences and Arts, Germany
Dalia Krikščiūnienė	Vilnius University, Lithuania
Alexander Mädche	Karlsruhe Institute of Technology, Germany
Sanjay Misra	Atilim University, Turkey
Jurgita Kapočiūtė-Dzikienė	Vytautas Magnus University, Lithuania

Contents

Information Technology Applications-Special Session on Smart e-Learning Technologies and Applications

Information Technology Applications-Special Session on Language Technologies

Business Intelligence for Information and Software Systems-Special Session on Intelligent Methods for Data Analysis and Computer Aided Software Engineering

Agile Infrastructure for Cloud-Based Environments: A Review

Guillermo Rodríguez[1]([✉]), Fabio G. Rocha[2], Dawitt Barbara[2],
Igor M. Azevedo[2], Pablo M. Menezes[2], and Sanjay Misra[3]

[1] ISISTAN-CONICET, Tandil, Buenos Aires, Argentina
`guillermo.rodriguez@isistan.unicen.edu.ar`
[2] Tiradentes University and ITP, Aracaju, Sergipe, Brazil
[3] Covenant University, Ota, Nigeria
`sanjay.misra@covenantuniversity.edu.ng`

Abstract. The development of infrastructure capable of meeting current demands is increasingly becoming a determining factor in the technological environment. The following work discusses problems causing these demands and attempts to chart how the present scenario deals with integrating technologies to provide an agile infrastructure for cloud-based environments. Eleven primary studies were identified and added value to continue the study of microservice and container integration. As a result, we have found several insights about how approaches are being used, how microservice architecture is addressed, what the community is seeking, and what research line is being pursued integration. Thus, most of the surveyed works are paying considerable attention to the integration of microservices and containers. Moreover, Docker and Kubernetes are the dominant technologies for implementing containers and managing containers at scale, respectively.

Keywords: Agile software development · Cloud computing · Containers · DevOps · Microservice architecture · Systematic literature review

1 Introduction

The use of microservices has grown rapidly in the business environment in recent years. Companies such as Netflix, eBay and Uber have adopted this standard for the architecture of their systems to replace the monolithic architecture design [3]. However, the lack of consensus in defining what a microservice is and what methodology to adopt when migrating from traditional services to this new paradigm has created several challenges for IT teams.

Among challenges that we can highlight in the implementation of a microservice architecture, according to Fowler, is the complexity when it comes to an operational perspective [3]. So, with increasingly scarce time and resources, making services available quickly has become essential for IT teams [9]. Container

© Springer Nature Switzerland AG 2021
A. Lopata et al. (Eds.): ICIST 2021, CCIS 1486, pp. 3–15, 2021.
https://doi.org/10.1007/978-3-030-88304-1_1

technology has been commonly used in cloud infrastructure and edge computing systems as a tool of lightweight virtualization. Thus, among the practices currently adopted is the use of containerization technologies, as they consume few resources, are scalable and allow rapid migration between heterogeneous infrastructures.

While microservices have emerged in the software industry for the past decade and have been the focus of professionals, academic researchers have not kept pace [1]. Numerous systematic mapping studies have been conducted in the microservice and container fields [1,23]. However, the existing works built on these tools are limited to performance evaluations [16,22,25].

DevOps means a collaborative and multidisciplinary effort within an organization to automate continuous delivery of new software versions, while guaranteeing their correctness and reliability [19]. In this context, we aim at conducting the most challenging part of an agile infrastructure: integrating with the unpredictable operations process, crossing the non-project boundary, and sharing operational resources with projects.

The main contributions of this study include:

- a reusable framework for classifying, comparing, and evaluating solutions, methods, and techniques for deployment microservices;
- an up-to-date map of the state of the art in deployment with containers;
- an evaluation of the potential for industrial adoption of existing research results on deployment microservices with containers;
- an evidence-based discussion of the emerging research trends, patterns, and gaps, and their implications for future research on deployment microservices with containers within DevOps teams.

The reminder of this paper is structured as follows: Sect. 2 presents the background. Section 3 describes related works. The review is organised in Sect. 4. Results are discussed in Sect. 5. Section 6 concludes and outlines future lines of work.

2   Background

Agile methods focus on short development and delivery cycles to present to the software client the features developed in each cycle and improve the product with the feedback. To provide an agile delivery, practices such as DevOps were developed. DevOps is a combination of the development team and operation team, sharing goals, processes, and tools. Although agile software development is being more widely adopted to many organizations, they were not able to achieve the release of the software in the desired frequency, mostly because of the separation of departments and to improve this aspect, companies have moved to DevOps, also achieving an agile, continuous delivery.

One of the characteristics of an agile delivery is the ability to provide small, low-risk releases. To achieve this, it is possible to use microservice architecture. Microservice architecture focuses on using small and simple services, instead of big and complex systems [10]. This is also aligned with the agile principles since it provides a framework for small and incremental steps that can be done in a cycle.

Microservices require differentiated forms of infrastructure, here called agile infrastructure. Agile infrastructure consists of three layers: Technical, Project and Operations. Technical relates to hardware and software used in the environment. Project is about the process that introduces the changes into the environment. Operations is the process of keeping the environment working [8]. Within this paradigm arise new technologies such as containerization environments, automation of deliveries, among others.

The microservices architecture paradigm can be considered an approach to developing a single application as a set of small services, each working in an isolated process and communicating through mechanisms [18]. Along this line, microservices have their growth linked to the platform of container [24]. Containerization is a technology for virtualizing applications in a light way that resulted in a significant absorption in the management of cloud applications. How to orchestrate the construction and deployment of containers individually and in clusters has become a central problem [22].

Container technology allows for resource use to be separated and monitored, fostering a performance-sensitive benefit and maximizing hardware usage. It is a considerable evolution for developers since they no longer need to worry about what the host machine would look like, having to carry out lengthy tests in homologation environments. In particular, in the case of microservices and containers, there is no standard model for deploying an infrastructure where the container technology and microservice architecture can be combined, complementing both and creating a secure and agile environment for the teams.

3 Related Work

In this section, we reviewed research works that have made systematic mappings of literature in the use of containers for microservices architectures. In [26], the authors analysed the container technology and the service discovery challenge in microservice architectures and presented Serfnode, a fully decentralized open-source solution to the problem of service discovery of service. They examined the existing solutions to the service discovery problem and compared them with Serfnode.

In [11], the authors agreed that microservices would simplify the orchestration of heterogeneous cloud applications and emerging micro datacenters. However, the creation of such applications (for example, smart city and smart health IoT clouds) requires further research on scheduling and resource management algorithms and platforms to manage highly distributed microservices.

In [25] the authors analysed the edge cloud requirements and discussed the suitability of container and cluster technology to facilitate applications through multi-cloud distributed platforms distributed, from datacenters to small devices. As a result, the authors identified light virtualisation and the need to orchestrate the implementation of these services as the main challenge. In the same line of work, in [23] the authors aimed to identify, classify taxonomically and systematically compare the existing research body in microservices and its application in the cloud.

Later, the authors identified, taxonomically classified and systematically compared the existing research body in containers and their orchestration and, specifically, the application of this technology in the cloud. As a result, they noted the current concerns in cloud platforms, microservices and continuous development [22].

Although microservices have emerged from the software industry and have been the focus of professionals in the last decade, academic researchers have not kept pace [1]. The motivation for this review stems from the fact that there is a limited number of studies focused on the research of microservice architecture in combination with containerization demands.

4   Study Design

This review aims to provide a summary of the current state of research, as well as to identify research directions for container infrastructure in a microservice architecture. Thus, the results can identify gaps in the field of study that deserve attention in future works. The method chosen for the development of this work was the systematic mapping of literature, a method that aims to extract data based on evidence. The research protocol was formalized by the tool StArt. This tool facilitates the categorization is free and developed by the UfScar Software Engineering Research Laboratory. For this mapping, we used an extract from the PICOC criteria (Population, Intervention, Comparison, Outcome and Çontext) [18]. We completed the following criteria, as can be seen in Table 1: Population, Intervention and Outcomes (PIO). In this way, the research goal was formalized using part of the GQM model [4]: To analyze cases of microservices to characterize tools and techniques concerning container demands from researchers' point of view in the context of theoretical and applied research. To achieve our goal, five researchers were defined, P1, P2, P3, P4 and P5. All of them took part in the first step, P1 and P2 were in charge of the second step, P1, P2 and P3 of the third step; finally, all of them conducted steps 4 and 5. To meet the research protocol, we developed the following research questions (RQ):

Table 1. PIO criterial

Population	Microservice, container, Docker
Intervention	Tools, Techniques, Methods, Models
Outcome	Overview of techniques and tools related to the use of container in microservice architecture

- **RQ1** - How is the container infrastructure integrated and designed in microservice architecture?
- **RQ2** - What tools and techniques have been used to implement agile infrastructure, containers and software microservices?
- **RQ3** - How were the identified tools and techniques evaluated?
- **RQ4** - What factors have been investigated as conditioning factors for the use of containers in microservice architecture?

4.1 Search Strategy

The search strategy aims to find initial studies that address the research questions above-stated. Initially, an automatic search was carried out through the search sources that were selected. Thus, once the search engines executed the search string, research works obtained were available to the researchers. Figure 1 depicts the distribution of the results in the first step of the review in the function of the outcomes of the search engines. These articles were selected because they cover a significant number of conferences, workshops, and journals. The number of articles obtained in each step of the search process is summarized in Fig. 2. In total, we selected 11 primary studies.

Fig. 1. Distribution of retrieved papers from search engines.

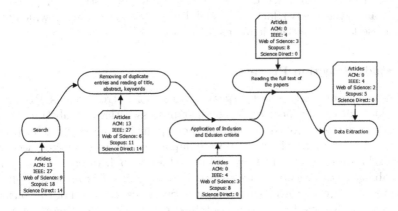

Fig. 2. Results obtained from the search process.

We defined the steps of our search process as follows:

1. **Step 1:** The search engines are utilized with the search string;
2. **Step 2:** By using StArt1, the metadata (title, abstract and keywords) resulting from Step 1 has been extracted, automatically removing duplicate articles;
3. **Step 3:** A qualitative analysis of the results was carried out based on the inclusion and exclusion criteria;
4. **Step 4:** A more in-depth analysis was conducted on the articles filtered in the previous step;
5. **Step 5:** The data from articles were extracted in order to answer the research questions.

We defined a period of search between 2016 and 2019. The search terms were constructed using Boolean OR to incorporate alternative spellings, synonyms or related terms, and Boolean AND to link the major terms:

(Microservice AND (docker OR container) AND (tools OR techniques OR methods OR models))

The scope of this work was defined based on the following guidelines:

- **Search engines:** Science Direct, Scopus, ACM, IEEE, and Web of Science;
- The review will consider articles published in international journals and conferences;
- The review will only consider works in English.

4.2   Study Selection Criteria

We defined inclusion and exclusion criteria for the studies returned by the search [18]. The **inclusion** criteria are: **(i)** the article analyses the techniques, methods, models and tools of container application in microservice architecture; **(ii)** the article discusses the process of using microservice architecture container. Whilst, the **exclusion** criteria are: **(i)** duplicate articles, **(ii)** articles that are not written in English, **(iii)** articles published only as abstracts or prefaces in journals and events, **(iv)** lack of availability of the article for download, **(v)** thesis, dissertations and academic monographs.

4.3   Study Selection Process

The first stage of study selection was carried out by researchers P1 and P2 and divided into two processes. In the first process, titles and abstracts of the articles were analyzed to assess whether they applied to our study. This process started with 84 articles, of which 10 were duplicates, 63 were rejected according to the exclusion criteria, and 11 were selected for Step 4. In order to guarantee the reliability of the selection process, we used a sample of 71 articles, excluding duplicates, to verify the level of agreement between researchers. For this purpose, we utilized the Kappa Test, and we obtained $\kappa = 0.912$, indicating a significant agreement level between researchers [12].

After step 4, 15 works met all criteria. According to [12], there is no a fair number of studies to be included in a systematic review. A possible factor that could have led to the reduced number of articles is that since 2013, we have a strong wave of widespread adoption of container technology with the advent of Docker. Therefore, as of this date, we observed an increase in academic research [12].

In addition, there is a selection of only six works [2]. We may, therefore, explain the fact that the number of 11 references does not impede this research; it merely shows that the academy has a large area to explore. Another important argument is that both the containers and the microservices are relatively fresh. The overlapping of such patterns is also much younger. The reduced number of references thus does not negate the quality of the work.

4.4   Data Extraction

As mentioned before, we used the StArt tool. The tool is divided into Planning, Execution, and Summarization. Planning comprises the protocol in which we define goals, the problem-question, the keywords, the inclusion and exclusion criteria, the languages of the works, the search engine, the qualitative classifier (example, bad, regular, excellent and excellent). Execution allows the to researcher define which works will be accepted or rejected; for that, it is necessary to fill a form with the keywords of each work, abstracts and some of the criteria defined in the protocol. Finally, Summarization allows for visualizing categorized information in graphs, networks and flowcharts. The tool was used for the organization of the references so that the research questions can be answered from the data extracted from each study.

5   Results and Discussion

According to **RQ1**, an extremely relevant issue is the fact that microservices and containers are treated as new architecture and technology for infrastructure. Therefore, we claim that methodologies that allow directing a way of integrating them are needed.

Although no methodologies have been found, it is worth noting that there is a trend in the use of Docker as a containerization tool for microservices, in addition, the provisioning and management of the environment has been conducted also by Docker and Kubernetes. The results indicate that one of the concerns of the researchers when using containers with microservices is the performance of the environment, along with scalability and high productivity.

As with **RQ2**, it could be seen that the community remains wary about using microservices and containers together. Of the various tools used in the articles we studied, we found performance measurement tools, performance improvement algorithms [15], a tool for provisioning analysis [17]. None of the tools deal with the implementation of microservices and containers in an integrated manner. Out of the 11 articles analysed, 7 used Docker as a tool for creating and managing the container environment. Among these 11 articles, the article [13] used, in addition to Docker, Kubernetes to manage the implemented environment. The use of Kubernetes stems from the fact that Docker fails to offer the appropriate management resources for the proposed environment. In only one article there was a mention to another tool for creating containers, named Rocket.

With regard to **RQ3**, among the 11 selected articles, all of them address the use of containers; however, the use of microservices was not mentioned in the same totality. Five different techniques or tools were mentioned. Two articles mention the use of the Non-Dominated Genetic Screening Algorithm (NSGA-II) [7] to check the resources that are being consumed by the container and carry out an evaluation if it was loaded optimally in terms of loading time, response and coupling. The results obtained after several tests, achieved a very reasonable value in a determined number of loading cycles.

Besides, in the research work presented in [6], the authors proposed to use the Open Cloud Computing Interface (OCCI) guidelines, to know how to implement container monitoring through communication plugins. However, when the environment is composed not only of containers, there is a divergence in the schedule that impacts on the results.

One article uses the open source benchmark tool for Web Services called Acme Air [27], verifying the best way to provide web services based on microservices or in a monolithic way and understand the best way to compose an infrastructure optimized for its use. The results showed that the high granularity of microservices demand a high coupling for communication between services. It was noticed that this demand for communication causes a negative impact in relation to the performance of the response time when compared to monolithic services. As a suggestion, the article suggests an optimisation in communication between services to potentially increase performance.

An article deals with the use of a model where it is possible to extract the architecture of a microservice, MicroArt [14]. Making it easier to extract and abstract the architecture model that was used in the analysed microservice, the test results were promising in the sense of allowing a microservice-based architecture to be refactored with a high percentage of cohesion.

Regarding **RQ4**, we realized that the driving factor for the use of a microservice infrastructure and containers is the attendance to the high productivity, which is allowed with this new methodology. Easy scalability, automated deployment, disaster recovery and elastic configuration achieved with its use, allows meeting the demand perceived in the organisations nowadays. Even with the caution perceived in the indications of the studies read, the consensus is that at the moment teams need integration instantaneous without physical limits and there is no time for the classic construction of an infrastructure. The use of containers and micro-services is gaining momentum, becoming a possibility and becoming ever more a reality in organizations. In [21], the authors have addressed the issue of redundant container deployment. Container technology has been commonly used as a tool of lightweight virtualization. However, in the resource pool scenario composed of multiple smart terminal devices, given these devices' limited resources and poor reliability, it is appropriate to divide the overall service into multiple microservices and install their backups in the respective containers. The authors used a meta-heuristic algorithm based on swarm intelligence, achieving outstanding results in comparison with state-of-the-art algorithms.

An efficient container resource scheduling approach not only satisfies user service requirements but also reduces running overhead and ensures cluster performance. In [20], the authors have proposed a multi-objective optimization model for container-based microservice scheduling, and proposes an ant colony algorithm to solve the scheduling problem. The algorithm takes into account not only the usage of the physical nodes' computing and storage resources, but also the number of microservice requests and the physical nodes' failure rate. The algorithm uses the quality assurance feature of the feasible solutions to guarantee the validity of pheromone updates and incorporates multi-objective heuristic knowledge to boost probability selection of the optimal path. Comparing with other similar algorithms, the experimental results show that the proposed optimization algorithm is superior in terms of cluster operation, cluster load balancing, and overhead network transfer.

Based on the above, 11 selected works, 5 were published in international conferences, 5 in international journals and 1 as a book, denoting the need for research, mainly experimental, to analyse the impact, performance, speed of integration and availability in adopting microservice integrated to container. It is also worth mentioning that the theme is relatively new, since the oldest article was published in 2015, being a field in progress.

Given the ability to create services with various interacting containers, which may execute on one or many nodes, complex applications can be synthesized by combining these services in interesting ways. In particular, as demand varies, the individual microservices can be replicated to scale with demand or reduced to fit current requirements. To support this adaptivity, the overall service must be architected to handle parallelism of individual microservices and to perform appropriate selection of the available instances to maximize performance [24]. To facilitate this adaptability, the overall structure must be architecturally designed to manage the parallelism of individual microservices and to select the appropriate instances to optimize performance.

In Table 2 the most targeted publication venues and relevant journals are reported. We can notice that researchers are mainly targeting specialized venues on deployment of microservices, cloud computing venues and software architecture venues. Researchers and practitioners can consider those venues and journal as their starting points for their exploration into the state of the art on agile infrastructure for cloud-based environments.

Figure 3 presents the distribution of publications on deployment of microservices using containers over the years. The period between 2019 and 2020 is only partial, as the search and selection process was performed in January 2020. The figure emphasizes a clear confirmation of the scientific interest on deployment of microservices using containers in the years 2015 through 2017 (in line with the research work [9]). A very small number of publications have been produced

Table 2. Publication venues and journals.

Venues and journals	Quantity
IEEE Access	2
IEEE Internet Computing	1
IEEE International Conference on Software Architecture Workshops	1
IEEE International Symposium on Workload Characterization	1
Procedia Computer Science	1
IEEE International Conference on Autonomic Computing	1
IEEE International Conference on Cloud Computing Technology and Science	1
Journal of Grid Computing	1
International Conference on Computational Science and Its Applications	1
International Conference on Software Engineering and Formal Methods	1
International Workshop on Science Gateways	1
IEEE Cloud Computing	1
Systems Modeling: Methodologies and Tools	1
Software Engineering	1
IEEE Software	1
IEEE Transactions on Cloud Computing	1
IEEE International Conference on Cloud Engineering	1
International Conference on Future Internet of Things and Cloud	1
International Symposium on Network Computing and Applications	1
International Conference on Cloud Engineering	1
International Conference on Cloud Computing and Services Science	1
International Conference on Service-Oriented Computing and Applications	1
International Andrei Ershov Memorial Conference on Perspectives of System Informatics	1

until 2015, which is actually the first year in which (i) microservices started to attract the interest of large organizations, and (ii) the term container as deployment unit was consistently used [23]. Year 2016 signed a booming in the research field of deployment microservices with containers, with the trend increasing in 2017 and still growing in the first months of the year 2019.

To sum up, we have found challenges and drawbacks faced by managers, engineers, and researchers that are not thoroughly handled by the current state-of-the-art:

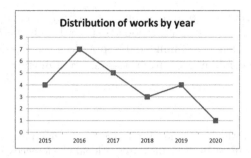

Fig. 3. Distribution of research works by year of publication.

- Definition of a process or methodology to re-design systems toward continuous delivery;
- Building of guidelines to deploy DevOps in an organization;
- Assessment of the quality of DevOps practices in organizations;
- Definition of criteria to qualify engineers for DevOps practice;
- Management of available resources in an automation environment;
- Avoidance of vendors' dependency in the containerization.

6   Conclusions

In this research, we presented a review and we were able to identify and analyse the research works concerning the use of the microservice architecture and the container technology for the development of an agile infrastructure. Starting with a set of 84 publications, we obtained a total of 11 accepted publications at the end of our systematic process. The gaps found during the mapping will serve as a starting point for the continuation of our work, after all, it is recognized that even with the great use and implementation of the studied architecture and technology, the integration of both is still on the academic research agenda.

We are convinced that our research can help communities that are interested in better shaping their methods and techniques according to the current state of practice on migration to microservices and how this process is carried out in other industrial contexts. Furthermore, this work sheds some light on the state of practice in communities that focuses on a topic still treated as recent; however, the demand is causing a considerable use of integration of microservices and containers [5]. The research lists the benefits that can be acquired with the implementation of an agile infrastructure with high availability, easy migration and resilience, as well as network latency and the need of a methodology for integrating microservice and container. Thus, this article already illustrated the points that must be analysed in the planning and execution of the implementation of the aforementioned integration.

As future work, we are planning the application of a survey aiming to evidence the use of microservices and containers tools. Firstly, our aim is to gather information about which are the most used tools, where and how they are used and integrated. Secondly, we aim to build a controlled environment, so that we can establish parameters and methods that we did not find throughout the research, helping to define recommendable practices for the deployment of an agile infrastructure combining microservices and containers.

References

1. Alshuqayran, N., Ali, N., Evans, R.: A systematic mapping study in microservice architecture. In: 2016 IEEE 9th International Conference on Service-Oriented Computing and Applications (SOCA), pp. 44–51. IEEE (2016)
2. Axelsson, J., Skoglund, M.: Quality assurance in software ecosystems: a systematic literature mapping and research agenda. J. Syst. Softw. **114**, 69–81 (2016)
3. Baresi, L., Garriga, M.: Microservices: the evolution and extinction of web services? Microservices 3–28 (2020)
4. Basili, V.R., Weiss, D.M.: A methodology for collecting valid software engineering data. IEEE Trans. Softw. Eng. **6**, 728–738 (1984)
5. Casalicchio, E.: Container orchestration: a survey. Syst. Model.: Methodol. Tools 221–235 (2019)
6. Ciuffoletti, A.: Automated deployment of a microservice-based monitoring infrastructure. Proc. Comput. Sci. **68**, 163–172 (2015)
7. Deb, K., Pratap, A., Agarwal, S., Meyarivan, T.: A fast and elitist multiobjective genetic algorithm: NSGA-II. IEEE Trans. Evol. Comput. **6**(2), 182–197 (2002)
8. Debois, P.: Agile infrastructure and operations: how infra-gile are you? In: Agile 2008 Conference, pp. 202–207. IEEE (2008)
9. Di Francesco, P., Lago, P., Malavolta, I.: Architecting with microservices: a systematic mapping study. J. Syst. Softw. **150**, 77–97 (2019)
10. Dragoni, N., Lanese, I., Larsen, S.T., Mazzara, M., Mustafin, R., Safina, L.: Microservices: how to make your application scale. In: Petrenko, A.K., Voronkov, A. (eds.) PSI 2017. LNCS, vol. 10742, pp. 95–104. Springer, Cham (2018). https://doi.org/10.1007/978-3-319-74313-4_8
11. Fazio, M., Celesti, A., Ranjan, R., Liu, C., Chen, L., Villari, M.: Open issues in scheduling microservices in the cloud. IEEE Cloud Comput. **3**(5), 81–88 (2016)
12. Felizardo, K.R., de Souza, É.F., Falbo, R.A., Vijaykumar, N.L., Mendes, E., Nakagawa, E.Y.: Defining protocols of systematic literature reviews in software engineering: a survey. In: 2017 43rd Euromicro Conference on Software Engineering and Advanced Applications (SEAA), pp. 202–209. IEEE (2017)
13. Florio, L., Di Nitto, E.: GRU: an approach to introduce decentralized autonomic behavior in microservices architectures. In: 2016 IEEE International Conference on Autonomic Computing (ICAC), pp. 357–362. IEEE (2016)
14. Granchelli, G., Cardarelli, M., Di Francesco, P., Malavolta, I., Iovino, L., Di Salle, A.: Towards recovering the software architecture of microservice-based systems. In: 2017 IEEE International Conference on Software Architecture Workshops (ICSAW), pp. 46–53. IEEE (2017)
15. Guerrero, C., Lera, I., Juiz, C.: Genetic algorithm for multi-objective optimization of container allocation in cloud architecture. J. Grid Comput. **16**(1), 113–135 (2018)
16. Kang, H., Le, M., Tao, S.: Container and microservice driven design for cloud infrastructure DevOps. In: 2016 IEEE International Conference on Cloud Engineering (IC2E), pp. 202–211. IEEE (2016)

17. Khazaei, H., Barna, C., Beigi-Mohammadi, N., Litoiu, M.: Efficiency analysis of provisioning microservices. In: 2016 IEEE International Conference on Cloud Computing Technology and Science (CloudCom), pp. 261–268. IEEE (2016)
18. Kitchenham, B., Charters, S.: Guidelines for performing systematic literature reviews in software engineering (2007)
19. Leite, L., Rocha, C., Kon, F., Milojicic, D., Meirelles, P.: A survey of DevOps concepts and challenges. ACM Comput. Surv. (CSUR) **52**(6), 1–35 (2019)
20. Lin, M., Xi, J., Bai, W., Wu, J.: Ant colony algorithm for multi-objective optimization of container-based microservice scheduling in cloud. IEEE Access **7**, 83088–83100 (2019)
21. Ma, B., Ni, H., Zhu, X., Zhao, R.: A comprehensive improved salp swarm algorithm on redundant container deployment problem. IEEE Access **7**, 136452–136470 (2019)
22. Pahl, C., Brogi, A., Soldani, J., Jamshidi, P.: Cloud container technologies: a state-of-the-art review. IEEE Trans. Cloud Comput. **7**(3), 677–692 (2017)
23. Pahl, C., Jamshidi, P.: Microservices: a systematic mapping study. In: CLOSER (1), pp. 137–146 (2016)
24. Pahl, C., Jamshidi, P., Zimmermann, O.: Microservices and containers. Softw. Eng. **2020** (2020)
25. Pahl, C., Lee, B.: Containers and clusters for edge cloud architectures-a technology review. In: 2015 3rd International Conference on Future Internet of Things and Cloud, pp. 379–386. IEEE (2015)
26. Stubbs, J., Moreira, W., Dooley, R.: Distributed systems of microservices using docker and serfnode. In: 2015 7th International Workshop on Science Gateways, pp. 34–39. IEEE (2015)
27. Ueda, T., Nakaike, T., Ohara, M.: Workload characterization for microservices. In: 2016 IEEE International Symposium on Workload Characterization (IISWC), pp. 1–10. IEEE (2016)

Creating Resilient Supply Chains Using Combination of Blockchain Technology and Different 4.0 Technologies

Anna Maryniak⬭, Yuliia Bulhakova$^{(\boxtimes)}$ ⬭, Włodzimierz Lewoniewski⬭, and Monika Bal⬭

Poznań University of Economics and Business, al. Niepodległości 10, 61-875 Poznań, Poland
{anna.maryniak,yuliia.bulhakova,wlodzimierz.lewoniewski,
monika.bal}@ue.poznan.pl

Abstract. The purpose of the paper is to assess the state of the art in the co-existence of blockchain technology with other 4.0 technologies that are used for supply chain management and to identify examples of solutions that can support the construction of resilient chains. The paper also aims to identify future research directions that are extensions of the primary objective. Therefore, a coalescence of coexisting 4.0 technologies that can support the construction of resilient supply chains is proposed.

For this purpose, secondary data from SCOPUS was used, as well as the author's program, jVectorMap library (https://jvectormap.com/), and data from collaboratively edited multilingual knowledge graph – Wikidata (https://www.wikidata.org/wiki/Wikidata:Main_Page).

Among other things, the authors identified four geographic clusters, in which blockchain coexistence with other 4.0 technologies is written about the most. However, only a few studies examined the synergistic effect between the two. It was also found that the least discussed attribute of resilient blockchains in the context of 4.0 technologies is supply chain agility. Moreover, other attributes like transparency, security and trust in supply chains can be further developed by using blockchain technology with the support of other technologies. At the same time, it was found that research on this topic is at a very early stage of development. Based on the identified research gaps, it can be concluded that science in the subject area is not keeping up with the needs of the economy.

Keywords: Blockchain technology · BT · Supply chain · Technology 4.0 · Industry 4.0 · Internet of Things · IoT · Resilience · Disruption

1 Introduction

Disruptions in the supply chains are caused by unintended natural and biological events such as climate change, volcanic eruptions, earthquakes, epidemics, as well as unpredictable events such as a missed offers, poor forecasts of the stock level, and returns due to product defects. Some disruptions are caused specifically by cyber intrusions into

© Springer Nature Switzerland AG 2021
A. Lopata et al. (Eds.): ICIST 2021, CCIS 1486, pp. 16–31, 2021.
https://doi.org/10.1007/978-3-030-88304-1_2

systems, counterfeiting of goods or consolidation of companies to establish dumping prices.

This is why it is so important to build high resilience in the supply chain. The level of resilience depends on inventory policy, reserve capacity, speed and scope of corrective measures, alternative suppliers, transportation routes, and the level of trust and cooperation in the supply chain.

One way to build resilience in a proactive system is to use blockchain (BT) and other Industry 4.0 technologies. Blockchain (BT) as a research area is relatively new, since the concept of BT and Bitcoin only emerged at the end of the first decade of 2000. The number of publications on this topic is increasing rapidly every year, nevertheless, even the review papers on research gaps [43] do not directly point out the need to extend BT research on the ground of mulitechnological approach to the creation of resilient chains [16].

There are emerging applications dedicated to the use of BT in other environments (e.g. P2P broadcast protocols, smart contracts, Botnet), applications to explore the essence of BT and identify fraud and possible security issues by tracking transaction flows (e.g. BitIodine, aBitcoin) or applications that focus on Bitcoin mixers. However, few studies address the use of BT in supply chain management and resilience. Based on models dedicated to the study of resilient chains and the literature on physical and intangible flows [3, 11, 42], it can be concluded that their basis is transparency (including tracking goods and documents), flexibility and trust, security. Thus, the study assumes that a resilient chain is a chain with a high level of visibility of the goods being moved that can adapt elastically to changes in the environment. It is also a chain in which the partners trust each other and care for the security of goods, transactions, and collected data. It is presumed that blockchain technology, with the support of other technologies, could allow for the development of the attributes of resilient chains.

2 Research Methodology

The study formulated four diagnostic and praxeological research questions.

RQ1: Which technologies most frequently co-occur in theoretical and empirical items? Mapping the co-occurrence of technologies across descriptions will help find niches for further research.

RQ2: What are the knowledge clusters of simultaneous use of several technologies in terms of geography and time. Knowledge in this area will allow identification centers of knowledge diffusion and will facilitate the search for cooperation partners in the field of science and consulting.

RQ3: How does the simultaneous use of BT along with other 4.0 technologies relate to building of resilient supply chains? Answering this question will help other researchers and practitioners better understand current research topics, reflect on the practical implementation of the technologies discussed and help to understand what the potential areas of application are in the context of immune chains.

RQ4: What might the underlying architecture look like for creating resilient chains using BT and other technologies? The proposed framework will facilitate hypothesis building and fill research gaps through verification.

The answers to the first two questions were obtained using statistical research of the literature included in SCOPUS with the use of the authors' search path allowing for deeper penetration of the database resources and with the application of various tools supporting research and visualization work. A detailed methodological description is provided in the relevant sections.

Answers to the third and fourth questions were obtained through qualitative studies of 339 selected records. Due to the volume limitations of the paper, an effort was made to select examples from different industries and of the different technological combinations. On this basis, the authors' indications of the relationship between particular technologies and creating resilient supply chains were proposed [2, 44].

3 Application of Blockchain Technology in Supply Chains

The literature repeatedly emphasizes that BT is an emerging research area that is just entering a phase of intense development [34, 37]. Ongoing review studies indicate that building of chain resilience is one of the fundamental research spheres that has potential [12, 31]. At the same time, it can be observed that the highlighted thematic clusters focused on BT [12, 22] can contribute to the strengthening of the chain through product traceability and monitoring of counterfeiting attempts, enhancing the security of smart contracts as well as ensuring privacy and cybersecurity.

The potential of BT in supply chain management is significant for many industries [4, 5].

Among others, the use of this technology facilitates the solution to food loss and waste [34]. Sharing information and monitoring of the subject flow will make the supply chain more resilient to market-type disruptions associated with a shortage or excess of fresh food in the supply chain. An example of this is the integration of this technology with Hazard Analysis and Critical Control Points (HACCP), which with the support of Internet of things (IoT) allows real-time tracking of food, thus boosting the resilience of chains by increasing their transparency, reliability, and safety [37]. Another interesting example is the use of BT by the coffee producer Smucker to track the origin and transportation of Colombian coffee beans [14]. Customers can scan a QR-code from the packaging and, via an app, learn where the beans were grown, processed and exported from, and can also donate funds to social programs related to farmers in the supply chain. Other examples of the implementation of this technology in the food industry include tracking the origin of marine fish, eliminating fraud in beef and dairy supplies, ensuring the transparency of ingredient information and brewing methods, and traceability in BIO and DOCG (Designation of Origin Controlled and Guaranteed) food supply chains [1].

The potential of BT is also demonstrated on the example of the pharmaceutical industry [6]. The new EU (European Union) regulation "Good Distribution Practice for Medicinal Products for Human Use", in force since 2016, imposes the need to monitor the temperature of each shipment. From a business point of view, BT and smart contracts allow to reduce the number of intermediaries and increase the automation of the record, which will reduce both operational costs and the risk of manipulation.

The described technology is also used by one of the largest container operators, Danish company Maersk, which has tested the use of BT applications in international logistics. Maersk uses the solution to track the shipping of containers using attributes such as GPS location, temperature, and moisture sensors. It is also helpful in documentation workflow, e.g. when the customs authorities sign a document, they can immediately send a copy with a digital signature. Then everyone involved – including Maersk and the government authorities – can see it. The cryptography used has made it difficult to forge virtual signatures [23]. By combining IoT and BT, information stored in the BT can also serve as a delivery log for container shipments. The movement of a container from source to destination is tracked by all actors in the supply chain, making it possible to track missing resources and reduce the risk of shipment delays [7].

It is also worth mentioning BT's potential in the humanitarian action supply chain, especially since logistics operations account for nearly 80% of disaster relief operations. The study argues that BT has a positive impact on supply chain resilience through increased transparency, trust, and collaboration [11]. In addition, humanitarian organizations are increasingly dealing with large amounts of sensitive information about their donors. The technology makes it easier for funds to reach the right victims at the right time by reducing transaction costs and publicly monitoring the flow of humanitarian materials, information, and funds.

Vinturas, a consortium of self-driving logistics providers in Europe, is also using this technology [17]. Using the IBM BT platform, Vinturas has built an open ecosystem that is accessible to all other players in the finished vehicle logistics (FVL) arena. Automakers are expected to reduce their costs by 10 percent or more as a result of improved supply chain transparency. For used car sales, it will prevent mileage manipulation. For new cars, it will help identify where damage occurs during transportation and determine the cause. Finally, this implementation of BT could help in identifying counterfeit replacement parts [40].

Studies highlight the benefits of the technology for supply chains [2, 23, 26, 33]. However, these proposals lack direct references to supply chain resilience.

4   The Co-occurrence of 4.0 Technologies in BT Supply Chains - The State of Research

In the following section, the coexistence of technologies in different research approaches is illustrated. For this purpose, out of 1207 documents containing the keywords "BT" and "supply chain" found in SCOPUS, those that co-occurred with a keyword concerning another 4.0 technology were generated. Ultimately, 339 records were identified. The search area was narrowed down to those items that contained the following words in the subject or keywords, in addition to the two basic keywords: Internet of things (IoT), Big Data (BD), Blockchain, Cloud computing (CC), Cybersecurity, Artificial Intelligence (AI), Additive Manufacturing (AM), Augmented Reality (AR), Autonomous Robots (Autorobots), and Autonomous Vehicles (AV). The selection of technologies was based on the most frequently appearing classifications [30]. Some technologies that appeared in such classifications were not included because a great number of articles in this field referred to solutions that cannot always be classified as highly advanced technologies (e.g. RFID, GPS). Nevertheless, it should be noted that in combination with other solutions they are an integral part of Industry 4.0. Some technologies, on the other hand, are components of others. For example, machine learning – and its components, namely deep learning technology and neural networks – are concentrically overlapping subsets of AI. Also, the research process took into account abbreviation notations (e.g. "IoT"), related words belonging to the same group of technologies (e.g., "autonomous transport", "drone"), and alternative spellings of the same technologies (e.g. "cybersecurity", "cyber-security"). Thus, the set of words and phrases was cleaned of repetitions. What is more, the authors identified those articles in which the same records were in the keywords and the title, so as not to duplicate the number of literature items. As a result of the work conducted, it can be concluded that the largest number of studies that concern supply chain and BT is related to IoT technology (241). The Augmented Reality technology (71) placed second, followed by Autonomous Robots (45), Artificial Intelligence (43), Big Data (39), Cloud computing (23), Cybersecurity (11), Additive Manufacturing (15) and Autonomous Vehicles (3) (Table 1).

Table 1. A matrix containing the number of publications (which were extracted based on keywords) on supply chain, block chain and at least one of the nine technologies.

	AM	AI	AR	A	BD	CC	C	IoT	AV
Additive Manufacturing (AM)	15	3	8	1	4	1	1	4	2
Artificial Intelligence (AI)	3	43	9	4	6	1	0	18	1
Augmented Reality (AR)	8	9	71	5	6	2	1	50	2
Autorobots (A)	1	4	5	45	2	0	0	15	0
Big Data (BD)	4	6	6	2	39	5	0	20	1
Cloud Computing (CC)	1	1	2	0	5	23	2	9	1
Cybersecurity (C)	1	0	1	0	0	2	11	6	0
Internet of Things (IoT)	4	18	50	15	20	9	6	241	1
Autonomous Vehicles (AV)	2	1	2	0	1	1	0	1	3

Source: [SCOPUS, downloaded on 2021.03.26].

As demonstrated, the literature on the co-existence and collaboration of 4.0 technologies in the supply chain is very scarce. As a result of the analysis of the acquired data, it was determined that there is an even greater research gap in studies concerning the cooperation of more than two technologies used for the optimization of the supply chain.

Given the needs of the economy, the diffusion of knowledge from this research area is necessary. There are not many studies linking BT with AV. On the other hand, publications on cybersecurity mention BT but they contain no references to other types of supply chain security technologies. Finally, there are few practical references to BT in publications on robots.

Based on the table and source data containing co-occurrence of more than three technologies, a grid of keyword connections was visualized using dynamic and browser based visualization library – vis.js[1] (Fig. 1). The size of the vertices on the grid depends on the number of publications in each area (e.g. for IoT – 241 items). The thickness of the lines shows how many publications are simultaneously embedded in two or more selected technologies (i.e., e.g., BT and IoT with AR - 50 items).

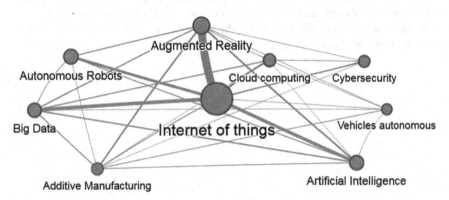

Fig. 1. A grid of keywords found in publications about supply chain, block chain and at least one other technology. Source: [SCOPUS, downloaded on 2021.03.26]. Interactive version: https://data.lewoniewski.info/supplychain2021/blockchain.html

To illustrate cities that are pioneering in combining the themes of "supply chain", "BT", and one of the previously mentioned technologies, an interactive map was produced (Fig. 2).

The map was generated using the jVectorMap library, which uses only native web browser technologies such as JavaS-cript, CSS, HTML, SVG or VML. To place an object (university or city) on such a map, its geographical coordinates must be known (latitude and longitude). For this purpose, data from a collaboratively edited multilingual knowledge graph – Wikidata – was used. This knowledge graph contains information about more than 93 million different objects (items), including scientific organizations and cities. Each item has its identifier in Wikidata. For example, the city of Kaunas is described as Q4115712[2]. To get information about hundreds or thousands of other objects, one needs to know their identifiers in Wikidata. The article focuses on the affiliation of authors who have written scientific papers on specific topics. The authors' affiliation can be marked in different ways: linguistically (for example, "Kaunas University of Technology" or "Kauno technologijos universi-tetas") or using alternative names of institutions ("KPI", "Kauno politechnikos institutas", "KTU"). Address can be written in different ways (with or without postal code, districts, provinces, counties, countries, etc.). Wikidata snapshots of entities as of March 2021 in JSON format (about 95 GB of gzip-compressed data) were used to find Wikidata identifiers for specific organizations and their geographical locations. First, affiliations were analyzed and only institution names with cities and countries were selected. Then, multilingual labels and alternative

---

[1] https://visjs.org/.

[2] https://www.wikidata.org/wiki/Q4115712.

names of over 90 million Wikidata items were analyzed, using a dump[3] file to find the necessary identifiers for institutions and cities. When there was no institution city data directly in the affiliation, related data from Wikidata was retrieved. At the same time, if an organization has buildings in different cities, its city data was extracted based on its headquarters. Finally, when the city information of each institution under consideration was extracted, the latitude and longitude data of these locations was also noted.

The map presents the cities in which the academic institutions researching in the considered fields are located (Fig. 2).

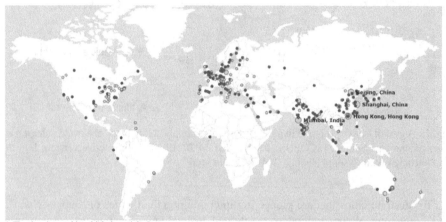

* The time interval in which the article first appeared in a given city from among a group of 339 items:
   ● 2016-2017   ○ 2018-2019   ● 2020-2021 (until 03)

Fig. 2. Academic centers that are pioneering publications on supply chain, BT and at least one other technology. Source: [SCOPUS, downloaded on 2021.03.26]. Interactive version: Maps (lewoniewski.info) (Color figure online)

The size of the dot indicates the number of publications in a given city. The largest size is for cities with more than 10 publications, the medium size is for cities with between 5 and 9 publications, and the smallest size is for other publications.

For example, in the city of Beijing (China), 17 publications had affiliations from academic units stationed in that city. In this case, these were: Beijing University of Posts and Telecommunications (7 items), Ministry of Education China (4), China Agricultural University (3), National Engineering Research Center for Information Technology in Agriculture Beijing (3).

The color indicates the period in which the article first appeared in the city from among the group of 339 items. For example, a red dot Darmstadt (Germany) means that the first publication appeared in this city in 2016 or 2017. If there are two or more scientific institutions in one city, they were treated as one common cluster (city). In such a situation, even if one publication was written by scientists from three research centers of the same city, it was counted as one publication for that city.

---

[3] https://dumps.wikimedia.org/wikidatawiki/entities/.

Based on the research conducted, it can be concluded that there are currently four main clusters in which the largest number of centers publishing on the topic in question are concentrated. They are located in central Europe, the east coast of the USA, India and eastern China.

The centers with the most publications include: Beijing University of Posts and Telecommunications (China), The University of Hong Kong (China), National Institute of Industrial Engineering (India), Khalifa University of Science and Technology (United Arab Emirates), Guangdong University of Technology (China). The 5 most productive authors include 5: Jayaraman, R., Li, Z., Tanwar, S., Bodkhe, U. and Dolgui, A. Among the most frequently cited publications are: "Blockchain's roles in meeting key supply chain management objectives" by Kshetri N., 2018 (368 citations); "Can blockchain Strengthen the Internet of Things?" by Kshetri, N., 2017 (310 citations); "The impact of digital technology and Industry 4.0 on the ripple effect and supply chain risk analytics" by Ivanov D., Dolgui A. and Sokolov B., 2019 (246 citations).

In the next stage of the research, it was investigated what research topics are being addressed within the coexistence of the described technologies. For this purpose, a keyword analysis was conducted.

In 339 scholarly publications we found 2481 unique keywords. Some of these keywords were reduced because of their generality (such as "supply chain", "Blockchain" etc.). Such words are too general and are not enough to distinguish between paper subjects within the considered collection of scientific works. Next, we unified groups of keywords which are related to the same topic (Fig. 3). For example, such keywords as "information use", "information flows", "information asymmetry" and others were unified to "information management".

Based on the data about publication date, it was possible to generate rankings of the most important keywords in each year from 2017 to 2021, based on the frequency of such words. 2016 has only one publication, therefore it was not considered. To compare importance of the same keywords the min-max normalization for frequency value in each year was used. Consequently, the value of importance of each keyword in each year falls within the range [0, 1]. The heatmap below shows the frequency of some of the important keywords. These keywords were selected based on the top 10 words from each year. If the minimum frequency of the words from the top 10 included other words in a given year, the overall frequency of these words in all years was also taken into account. For example, the relative frequency of the keyword "transparency" in 2020 is 0.26. In other words, it shows the value relative to the maximum keyword frequency within the same year.

Considering all the years studied, the topic of blockchain technology was primarily discussed in the context of information management. With each passing year, the topic of traceability and the application of BT in the food supply chain is increasingly being addressed. Digital storage and security is also an important research area. Considering the basic aspects of resilience, there is a research gap in relating the topic of supply chains to agility. There is also a lack of literature that holistically addresses the topic of BT in the context of resilience attributes.

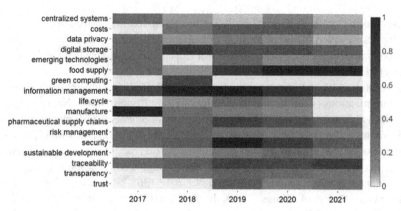

Fig. 3. Research areas for publications combining the topics of the supply chain, BT, and at least one other technology. Source: [SCOPUS, downloaded on 2021.04.22]. Interactive version: Important topics/keywords (lewoniewski.info)

5 Creating Resilient Supply Chains in a 4.0 Technology and Blockchain Environment

Existing descriptions and research results hardly comment on building digital resilient chains. Therefore, these relationships are illustrated by the example of the relationship between BT and other technologies.

Thus, for example, the integration of BT with AM is a response to the expectations of manufacturers and end-users to verify the authenticity and quality of individual parts, especially safety-critical products. One solution is chemical printing performed on a 3D component and combined with a BT record and QR code [21]. Combining unique chemical signature data with BT databases will significantly increase the cost of counterfeiting AM materials and increase the reliability of transactions between entities in the supply chain. In this process, nanomaterials are embedded in parts derived from 3D printing. With 3D printing, data is also encoded, the print template is identified, and the printing process is licensed, which ultimately increases job security [15]. Access to a particular print is then granted to those who have entered into smart contracts. This is particularly valuable for companies that apply lean management, as the traditional tools of the concept can increase supply chain vulnerability by reducing inventory. These technologies primarily affect supply chain pipelines and configurations. The use of AM in the production of parts strengthens the trend towards decentralized manufacturing which results in more agile and flexible supply chains and reduced logistics costs [25].

The collaboration of the two technologies thus generates the potential for creating an agile and secure environment that is adequate for resilient chains.

Another example is the use of digital twins integrated with BT in the aircraft manufacturing supply chain [18, 29]. Their integrations are used at virtually every stage: design, modeling, evaluation, monitoring, and manufacturing of aircraft components. Data is available in real-time in physical and virtual space in every corner of the world of cooperating teams. As a result, there are fewer errors already at the early stages of tasks, which affects the smoothness of production and quality of the final product. The digital twin is a combination of simulation, optimization, and data analysis completed in real-time in a new vision of supply chain disruption risk management. It is a BT model that can represent the state of the network at any time and enable full visibility of the entire supply chain to improve resilience and test contingency plans [20].

BT can also be applied with IoT, BD, and CC, for example in agriculture [20]. BD platforms are essential for handling the data generated by IoT. These technologies are used for intelligent crop analysis and planning, crop scheduling, precision agriculture. This affects the resilience of supply chains, as having accurate data makes it easier to plan the logistics process, hire rolling stock, assign logistics tasks. It also makes the chain less vulnerable because the integration of technology results in less crop loss and therefore less need for reverse logistics work.

The discussed technology also corresponds with AI, which can benefit from the availability of multiple BT platforms to perform machine learning algorithms and track data stored on decentralized P2P storage systems [36, 39]. This data is typically created using smart products connected to various sources such as IoT and swarm robots. The integration of AI and BT enable the creation of resilient chains, e.g. by quickly validating data transfers between different stakeholders. Working AI algorithms on secure data increase trust among all supply chain participants. For instance, the use of BT and AI together with remote sensing technology improves the collection and analysis of data in the supply of fresh eggs. Their location, movement times, temperature, and moisture levels are tracked. This data is reported back to the BT, creating a digital record to prove provenance, compliance, authenticity, and quality – contributing to the resilience of the entire chain [4].

Another example of a technology coexisting with BT is IoT. Such combination supports e.g. medical claims management, which includes billing, data filing, updating, processing related to diagnosis, treatment and prescribing medications for the patient. In this industry, IoT-backed BT can also be used to collect open research data for clinical trials available online-wide. BT combined with IoT can also have applications in healthcare, for example, by enforcing access control policies. This ensures the security and integrity of patient data [27]. Another application of the discussed technologies is in remote software update and vehicle insurance [10], which can be especially useful when using a large fleet of vehicles. With these technologies working together, supply chain partners gain increased transparency of information and improved integrity of IoT transactional data [34]. Thus, there is less disruption in both physical and information flows. Through the use of a "consensus mechanism" and encryption algorithm in BT, IoT security is improved. Furthermore, due to decentralization, there is a reduction in the risk of "Single Point of Failure" (SPF) [7].

In turn, use of the BT-based systems with IoT and BD can, for example, increase the resilience of aircraft supply chains by leveraging analysis of supply, demand and sources of availability of original spare parts for maintenance and repair [28]. A set of the same technologies can be used to monitor the supply chain for sustainability in a way that is resilient to data manipulation (e.g. on employee wages and contracts), which is especially important when locating suppliers with weak legislation [39], for life cycle assessment (LCA) and for assessing product impact and environmental performance [44].

6   Proposals for Future Research – The Concept of Coexisting Technologies to Support Resilient Supply Chains

To outline future research directions, a concept coexisting technologies to support resilient supply chains.

The first pillar is the technology perspective, where decisions are made regarding the coexistence of technologies. Knowledge of the potential of individual technologies is the key to creating parameters for their selection. The functionalities of each technology determine which features of resilient chains are exhibited.

The market perspective on the other hand requires looking for opportunities and using so-called disruptive innovations. This can include introducing disruptive technologies throughout the supply chain that significantly revolutionize the competitive landscape. Such innovations include the simulation of flows in augmented reality, preceded by the scanning of its most important links. For example, the international logistics company ID Logistics, together with the Economic Institute for Spatial Analysis (GIAP) in Poland, scanned the logistics center in Mszczonów using the M3 robot. Digital processing of the collected material produced a 3D model of the facility, accessible via the easy-to-use IndoorViewer web application, which will eventually be presented in virtual reality technology using VR glasses. The dynamic visualization of the chain makes a significant contribution to increasing cost efficiency and optimizing the timing and volume of flows, as well as speeding up the response to potential disruptions.

The third pillar is the relational perspective of supply chain participants, the essence of which is to create the so-called positive ripple effect. This effect is achieved by investing in technology across the supply chain and demanding digitization from potential new links in the chain. Thus, the resilience effect achieved at the link level spreads along horizontally integrated links. This is the opposite of the traditionally understood ripple effect [19].

The buckle that binds the different perspectives together is the BC technology. This is because the dynamization of chains from the point of view of their configuration and digitization will result in shifting the emphasis of building their resilience from physical to digital levels. This will consequently increase the security of digital objects and executed transactions. For example, the Chinese company Hangzhou Xiongmai Technologies, which produces webcams and related accessories, has recalled its products sold in the US. They were vulnerable to the Mirai malware (which hackers use). However, in a stagnant technology environment, it was difficult to track down the owners of the devices and execute the recall quickly. Therefore, in these types of cases, it is important to consider whether to rely more on cloud-based solutions or to support BC technology [23]. This is important because sensors and other devices are increasingly the focus of attackers [9].

The supply chain architecture thus created, in which various 4.0 technologies coexist, can be the ground for building resilient chains and blockchain can provide their protective umbrella (Fig. 4).

The result of this work will be the rise of so-called "coexisting tools 4.0" type AIoT (a technique based on the architecture of artificial intelligence of things, which combines the advantages of IoT and machine learning) [8]. For instance, by analyzing a large set of data available online artificial intelligence algorithms allow rapid response and prediction of machine failures before they occur, so that required spare parts can be ordered in advance. Thanks to this, production continuity is maintained.

AIoT can be used to monitor traffic between the main nodes of the chain. It leads to increased fluidity of goods streams. Increasing transparency by sharing information resulting from the trust of business partners and tracking flows has a positive knock-on effect. The use of BT, in this case, will strengthen the protection of data exchanged and received by all links. The ability to flexibly adapt to current needs by increasing process visibility leads to enhanced chain resilience.

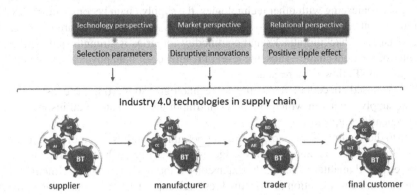

Fig. 4. The concept of coexisting technologies to support resilient supply chains. Source: [own elaboration].

Implementing the concept of coexistence of 4.0 technologies to support the construction of resilient supply chains requires companies to rethink the way they design supply chains. Other sets of co-existing technologies in the supply chain, such as research on BT IoT and 5G [32], unmanned aerial vehicles (UAVs) and RFID [13] BT, RFID or QR codes [41] or e.g. IoT, BT, and fuzzy logic [35, 38] should also be considered in the concept presented. Not only transformation is needed, but also discipline, planning, and commitment of top-down leadership [2].

In future studies, it is, therefore, reasonable to pose the following questions:

– Which technologies and in which sections of the supply chain should coalesce to develop resilience attributes like agility, transparency, trust, security in the supply chain?
– How can one position oneself in the marketplace by innovatively building resilience?
– To which links in the supply chain (on which paths) should a positive knock-on effect be directed first?

7 Conclusions and Limitations of the Study

Empirical research on the co-occurrence of 4.0 technologies in supply chain management is in its infancy [24] and is primarily descriptive of specific case studies. The technologies that are most often discussed in the context of BT include IoT and AR. Apart from IoT, empirical research on the coexistence of the other technologies represents a large research gap. The very topic of BT resilience in combination with any technology is also rare [11].

On the basis of analytical work, four clusters of knowledge in the field of the discussed topic were identified, however, the intensity of knowledge development does not depend on the places of first publications.

The result of the analytical work undertaken gives rise to the conclusion that the BT has great potential, which is not yet widely exploited. In combination with other technologies, it leads to the synergy of benefits. Numerous studies argue that with blockchain technology coalescing with other technologies, the supply chain becomes more flexible and transparent, goods are easier to track, documents and transactions are more secure and resistance to hacking attacks and commodity forgeries is strengthened. These are attributes of resilient chains. Thus, the level of resilience of both physical and intangible (financial and IT) flow is increased.

The proposed concept of coexisting 4.0 technologies supporting the construction of resilient supply chains in which BT plays an important role can be an inspiration for further scientific inquiries.

Due to the volume of the paper, it was not possible to address each of the items generated. However, to the authors' knowledge, this is the first such study to include both bibliometric and qualitative research. Extensions of the study may include methodological threads and consideration of identified research gaps. This could encourage process mapping in terms of the application of particular technologies at the supply chain level, combined with economic analyses. This is important because the state of the art in this area has not kept up with the needs of the economy.

Acknowledgments. "The project financed within the Regional Initiative for Excellence programme of the Minister of Science and Higher Education of Poland, years 2019–2022, grant no. 004/RID/2018/19, financing 3,000,000 PLN".

References

1. Antonucci, F., Figorilli, S., Costa, C., Pallottino, F., Raso, L., Menesatti, P.: A review on blockchain applications in the agri-food sector. J. Sci. Food Agric. **99**(14), 6129–6138 (2019)
2. Attaran, M.: Digital technology enablers and their implications for supply chain management. Supply Chain Forum: Int. J. **21**(3), 158–172 (2020)
3. Belhadi, A., Mani, V., Kamble, S.S., Khan, S.A.R., Verma, S.: Artificial intelligence-driven innovation for enhancing supply chain resilience and performance under the effect of supply chain dynamism: an empirical investigation. Ann. Oper. Res. 1–26 (2021)
4. Bocek, T., Rodrigues, B.B., Strasser, T., Stiller, B.: Blockchain is everywhere - a use-case of blockchains in the pharma supply-chain. In: IFIP/IEEE International Symposium on Integrated Network Management (IM 2017), pp. 772–777 (2017)
5. Bodkhe, U., et al.: Blockchain for Industry 4.0: a comprehensive review. IEEE Access **8**, 79764–79800 (2020)
6. Bumblauskas, D., Mann, A., Dugan, B., Rittmer, J.: A blockchain use case in food distribution: do you know where your food has been? Int. J. Inf. Manag. **52**, 102008 (2020)

7. Cao, B., et al.: When Internet of Things meets blockchain: challenges in distributed consensus. IEEE Netw. **33**(6), 133–139 (2019)
8. Chen, J.-Z.: The implementation to intelligent linkage service over AIoT hierarchical for material flow management. J. Ambient Intell. Humaniz. Comput. **12**(2), 2207–2219 (2020)
9. Chowdhury, M.J.M., Ferdous, M.S., Biswas, K., Chowdhury, N., Muthukkumarasamy, V.: A survey on blockchain-based platforms for IoT use-cases. Knowl. Eng. Rev. **35**, 1–23 (2020)
10. Dorri, A., Steger, M., Kanhere, S.S., Jurdak, R.: Blockchain: a distributed solution to automotive security and privacy. IEEE Commun. Mag. **55**(12), 119–125 (2017)
11. Dubey, R., Gunasekaran, A., Bryde, D.J., Dwivedi, Y.K., Papadopoulos, T.: Blockchain technology for enhancing swift-trust, collaboration and resilience within a humanitarian supply chain setting. Int. J. Prod. Res. **58**(11), 3381–3398 (2020)
12. Etemadi, N., Borbon-Galvez, Y., Strozzi, F., Etemadi, T.: Supply chain disruption risk management with blockchain: a dynamic literature review. Information **12**(2), 70 (2021). 1–25
13. Fernández-Caramés, T.M., Blanco-Novoa, O., Froiz-Míguez, I., Fraga-Lamas, P.: Towards an autonomous Industry 4.0 warehouse: a UAV and blockchain-based system for inventory and traceability applications in big data-driven supply chain management. Sensors **19**(10), 2394 (2019)
14. GBBC: Bbuild Back Better: Digital Updates for Today's Challenges. Annual Report, Geneva, London, Washington, DC, New York (2021). https://gbbcouncil.org/wp-content/uploads/2021/02/GBBC-2021-Annual-Report-Build-Back-Better-Digital-Updates-for-Todays-Challenges-1.pdf
15. Holland, M., Nigischer, C., Stjepandic, J.: Copyright protection in additive manufacturing with blockchain approach. Transdisc. Eng.: Paradigm Shift **5**, 914–921 (2017)
16. Hopkins, J.L.: An investigation into emerging Industry 4.0 technologies as drivers of supply chain innovation in Australia. Comput. Ind. **125**, 103323 (2021)
17. IBM: Blockchain brings visibility to the finished vehicle supply chain (2019). https://www.ibm.com/blogs/blockchain/2019/10/Blockchain-brings-visibility-to-the-finished-vehicle-supply-chain/?mhsrc=ibmsearch_a&mhq=BC%20supply%20chain%20benefit
18. Ivanov, D., Dolgui, A., Das, A., Sokolov, B.: Digital supply chain TWINS: managing the ripple EFFECT, resilience, and disruption risks by data-driven optimization, simulation, and visibility. In: Ivanov, D., Dolgui, A., Sokolov, B. (eds.) Handbook of Ripple Effects in the Supply Chain, pp. 309–332. Springer, Cham (2019). https://doi.org/10.1007/978-3-030-14302-2_15
19. Ivanov, D., Dolgui, A., Sokolov, B.: The impact of digital technology and Industry 4.0 on the ripple effect and supply chain risk analytics. Int. J. Prod. Res. **57**, 1–18 (2018)
20. Kamble, S.S., Gunasekaran, A., Gawankar, S.A.: Achieving sustainable performance in a data-driven agriculture supply chain: a review for research and applications. Int. J. Prod. Econ. **219**, 179–194 (2019)
21. Kennedy, Z.C., et al.: Enhanced anti-counterfeiting measures for additive manufacturing: coupling lanthanide nanomaterial chemical signatures with blockchain technology. J. Mater. Chem. C **5**(37), 9570–9578 (2017)
22. Kshetri, N.: Blockchain's roles in strengthening cybersecurity and protecting privacy. Telecommun. Policy **41**(10), 1027–1038 (2017)
23. Kshetri, N.: Blockchain's roles in meeting key supply chain management objectives. Int. J. Inf. Manag. **39**, 80–89 (2018)
24. Kshetri, N.: Amplifying the value of blockchain in supply chains: combining with other technologies. In: Blockchain and Supply Chain Management, pp. 67–88. Elsevier (2021)
25. Kurpjuweit, S., Schmidt, C.G., Klöckner, M., Wagner, S.M.: Blockchain in additive manufacturing and its impact on supply chains. J. Bus. Logist. **42**(1), 46–70 (2019)

26. Lezoche, M., Panetto, H., Kacprzyk, J., Hernandez, J.E., Alemany Díaz, M.M.E.: Agri-food 4.0: a survey of the supply chains and technologies for the future agriculture. Comput. Ind. **117**, 103187 (2020)

27. Liang, X., Zhao, J., Shetty, S., Liu, J., Li, D.: Integrating blockchain for data sharing and collaboration in mobile healthcare applications. In: 2017 IEEE 28th Annual International Symposium on Personal, Indoor, and Mobile Radio Communications (PIMRC), pp. 1–5. IEEE (2017)

28. Madhwal, Y., Panfilov, P.: Blockchain and supply CHAIN management: aircrafts' PARTS' business case. In: DAAAM Proceedings, pp. 1051–1056 (2017)

29. Mandolla, C., Petruzzelli, A.M., Percoco, G., Urbinati, A.: Building a digital twin for additive manufacturing through the exploitation of blockchain: a case analysis of the aircraft industry. Comput. Ind. **109**, 134–152 (2019)

30. Maryniak, A., Bulhakova, Y.: Benefits of the technology 4.0 used in the supply chain - bibliometric analysis and aspects deferring digitization. In: Abramowicz, W., Klein, G. (eds.) BIS 2020. LNBIP, vol. 394, pp. 173–183. Springer, Cham (2020). https://doi.org/10.1007/978-3-030-61146-0_14

31. Min, H.: Blockchain technology for enhancing supply chain resilience. Bus. Horiz. **62**(1), 35–45 (2019)

32. Mistry, I., Tanwar, S., Tyagi, S., Kumar, N.: Blockchain for 5G-enabled IoT for industrial automation: a systematic review, solutions, and challenges. Mech. Syst. Signal Process. **135**, 106382 (2020)

33. Pawlicka, K., Bal, M.: Blockchain in supply chain finance - a case study of Walmart. In: Cezayirlioglu Haluk, R. (red.) 18th Logistics and Supply Chain Congress: Conference Proceedings Book: The Importance of Digitalization in Industry an Logistics Sector, pp. 14–25. Istanbul Esenyurt University, Istanbul (2021)

34. Peña, M., Llivisaca, J., Siguenza-Guzman, L.: Blockchain and its potential applications in food supply chain management in Ecuador. In: Botto-Tobar, M., León-Acurio, J., Díaz Cadena, A., Montiel Díaz, P. (eds.) ICAETT 2019. AISC, vol. 1066, pp. 101–112. Springer, Cham (2020). https://doi.org/10.1007/978-3-030-32022-5_10

35. Rejeb, A., Keogh, J.G., Treiblmaier, H.: Leveraging the Internet of Things and blockchain technology in supply chain management. Future Internet **11**(7), 161 (2019)

36. Salah, K., Rehman, M.H.U., Nizamuddin, N., Al-Fuqaha, A.: Blockchain for AI: review and open research challenges. IEEE Access **7**, 10127–10149 (2019)

37. Tian, F.: A supply chain traceability system for food safety based on HACCP, blockchain & Internet of Things. In: 2017 International Conference on Service Systems and Service Management, pp. 1–6. IEEE (2017)

38. Tsang, Y.P., Choy, K.L., Wu, C.H., Ho, G.T., Lam, H.Y.: Blockchain-driven IoT for food traceability with an INTEGRATED consensus mechanism. IEEE Access **7**, 129000–129017 (2019)

39. Venkatesh, V., Kang, K., Wang, B., Zhong, R.Y., Zhang, A.: System architecture for blockchain based transparency of supply chain social sustainability. Robot. Comput.-Integr. Manuf. **63**, 101896 (2020)

40. Wang, K., Liu, M., Jiang, X., Yang, C., Zhang, H.: A novel vehicle blockchain model based on hyperledger fabric for vehicle supply chain management. In: Zheng, Z., Dai, H.N., Tang, M., Chen, X. (eds.) BlockSys 2019. CCIS, vol. 1156, pp. 732–739. Springer, Singapore (2019). https://doi.org/10.1007/978-981-15-2777-7_59

41. Westerkamp, M., Victor, F., Kupper, A.: Blockchain-based supply chain traceability: token recipes MODEL manufacturing processes. In: IEEE International Conference on Internet of Things (iThings) and IEEE Green Computing and Communications (GreenCom) and IEEE Cyber, Physical and Social Computing (CPSCom) and IEEE Smart Data (SmartData) (2018)

42. Wieland, A., Wallenburg, C.M.: Dealing with supply chain risks. Int. J. Phys. Distrib. Logist. Manag. **42**(10), 887–905 (2012)
43. Yli-Huumo, J., Ko, D., Choi, S., Park, S., Smolander, K.: Where is current research on blockchain technology?—A systematic review. PLoS ONE **11**(10), e0163477 (2016)
44. Zhang, A., Zhong, R.Y., Farooque, M., Kang, K., Venkatesh, V.G.: Blockchain-based life cycle ASSESSMENT: an implementation framework and system architecture. Resour. Conserv. Recycl. **152**, 104512 (2020)

Defining Beneficiaries of Emerging Data Infrastructures Towards Effective Data Appropriation
Insights from the Swedish Space Data Lab

Aya Rizk[1]([✉]) [ID], Cathrine Seidelin[2], György Kovács[1], Marcus Liwicki[1], and Rickard Brännvall[3]

[1] Luleå University of Technology, 97187 Luleå, Sweden
aya.rizk@ltu.se
[2] University of Copenhagen, 2100 Copenhagen, Denmark
[3] RISE Research Institutes of Sweden, 97347 Luleå, Sweden

Abstract. The increasing collection and usage of data and data analytics has prompted development of Data Labs. These labs are (ideally) a way for multiple beneficiaries to make use of the same data in ways that are value-generating for all. However, establishing data labs requires the mobilization of various infrastructural elements, such as beneficiaries, offerings and needed analytics talent, all of which are ambiguous and uncertain. The aim of this paper is to examine how such beneficiaries can be identified and understood for the nascent Swedish space data lab. The paper reports on the development of persona descriptions that aim to support and represent the needs of key beneficiaries of earth observation data. Our main results include three thorough persona descriptions that represent the lab's respective beneficiaries and their distinct characteristics. We discuss the implications of the personas on addressing the infrastructural challenges, as well as the lab's design. We conclude that personas provide emerging data labs with relatively stable beneficiary archetypes that supports the further development of the other infrastructure components. More research is needed to better understand how these persona descriptions may evolve, as well as how they may influence the continuous development process of the space data lab.

Keywords: Data infrastructure · Data lab · Beneficiary · Data appropriation · Persona

1 Introduction

One vision that has motivated the early calls for open data efforts and mandates was that making data accessible for all will enable data-driven innovation. Scholarly research has investigated this vision and the means by which the openness drives innovation in the public sector e.g. [1]. Since then, various governments and organizations in the public sector are doing efforts of digitalization, data collection and standardization for open data [2]. However, these are very complex and challenging tasks. Therefore, the efforts done

© Springer Nature Switzerland AG 2021
A. Lopata et al. (Eds.): ICIST 2021, CCIS 1486, pp. 32–47, 2021.
https://doi.org/10.1007/978-3-030-88304-1_3

to build the required data infrastructures, and corresponding data capabilities, towards the realization of data-driven innovation and evidence-based policy making have benefits that are yet to be realized [3]. Organizations, both public and private, are also struggling to identify and establish the data culture necessary in realizing those objectives, from commitment to data-based decision making, to the improvement of their data analytics processes and capabilities [4].

Data labs (also known as data hub, data factory, or policy lab) are currently being established as a result to the increasing amount of these open data initiatives. Data labs are initiatives that aim to help governments and other organizations make their collected data easily accessible and usable for evaluation, research and innovation [3]. In the United States, more than six data labs have been established over the past decade [3]. This paper focuses on a data lab initiative, which is situated in Scandinavia. In Sweden, the Swedish Innovation Agency is funding data labs and data factories to act as national resources in specific domain areas [5]. The objectives of funding theses labs range from lowering the barriers to data use to the use of data analytics, machine learning and Artificial Intelligence (AI) in to solve problems in said domains (ibid).

In order for data labs to be useful and value generating, it is crucial for these institutions to ensure that the data products and services they offer are relevant and appropriate for its intended beneficiaries. Beneficiaries are decision makers in organizations who decide on, and expected to benefit from, the adoption of data products/services offered by the data lab. Their buy-in is considered crucial for any data lab's establishment and survival [3]. Given the nascence of these initiatives, very little is currently known about how to identify and understand those beneficiaries so that this form of appropriation can be done [6]. In addition, in the early stages of establishment of data labs, there may be some ambiguity around key elements such as the core offerings (i.e. data product/service) and the talent required to deliver them [3]. With those ambiguous elements, the appropriation of data to the beneficiaries becomes even more challenging. Accordingly, we address the following research question: *How can the necessary appropriation of data for beneficiaries of data labs take place when the beneficiaries are undefined?*

We propose that developing personas can help us reach a preliminary understanding of beneficiaries and their needs. Hence, we also address the sub-question: *How can personas help identify and define beneficiaries of emerging data labs?* To address these questions, we designed a qualitative study in which we use the persona method [7, 8] in order to elucidate the beneficiaries of the Swedish Space Data Lab (SDL), as well as their characteristics as data infrastructure beneficiaries. Thus, the paper starts with reviewing related work on data lab initiatives, infrastructural challenges relevant to data labs and the status quo of earth observation data in Sect. 2. Section 3 describes the research method, followed by the findings in terms of persona variables and descriptions in Sect. 4. Finally, we discuss the implications of the identified personas on the SDL, as well as on the infrastructural challenges pertaining to data labs, before concluding in Sect. 5.

2 Background

2.1 Data Lab Initiatives

Data Labs are emerging in the public sector due to the need for data infrastructures that can support the technological development and its many possibilities for data-driven innovation [2]. The last decade's increase in wholesale digitisation has brought more citizens and organisations to make use of digital ways to connect with the public sector and vice versa (e.g., the healthcare system, their local municipality etc.). These new digital platforms have led to a vast collection of data on citizens' and organisations' preferences and behaviours, which are increasingly becoming more trackable and possible to access. Simultaneously, the developments in analytical techniques have created possibilities for understanding this data and applying it for different purposes and to varying actors [9]. However, despite the many promising possibilities for data analytics, governments are struggling with developing the infrastructures necessary for multiple stakeholders with varying interests to make use of relevant public data. These challenges pertain to, in part, the lack of understanding on how data drives development and innovation, as well as its associated mechanisms when such actors are from heterogenous knowledge backgrounds [10, 11]. Data Labs are emerging as a means to address this issue [3].

The Swedish Innovation Agency, who finances and supports national data labs, envisions data labs as national resources for their respective domains; a resource through which the domain's data is available, developed and used (e.g. for AI), and where different actors are encouraged and supported to use it for data-driven innovation [5]. A common goal of a data lab is "to improve public services using evidence-based decision-making which, in many cases, leveraged [administrative] data." [3, p. 7]. Various data labs are already established and have been serving their respective beneficiaries for years. California Policy Lab (CPL) provides analytics services that help different beneficiaries - at city, county and state level - evaluate and improve their public programs. UK-based Justice Data Lab helps organizations that work with offenders, gain access and make use of re-offending data, so that they can optimize their rehabilitation programs, predict and avoid re-offending. Even though these data lab initiatives have been ongoing for a few years, the scholarly literature is extremely scarce on them. A clear exception is Lyon et al.'s [12] evaluation of the Justice Data Lab.

Furthermore, more data labs are in the process of being established. At the time of writing this paper, the Swedish Innovation Agency has funded 16 data labs [5]. The Swedish Language Data Lab aims to develop the Swedish language reference dataset and models for Natural Language Processing (NLP). On the other hand, the Ocean Data Factory aims to "enable Sweden to be a global leader in sustainability and innovation in the digital blue economy" through the applications of AI in areas such as shipping and logistics, emissions both to air and water, and climate change [13].

2.2 Lessons Learned from Existing Labs

Existing data labs differ in their models around lab ownership, who the beneficiaries are, what services are offered, and the source of their analytic talent. Each dimension has its tensions. For instance, the decision of lab ownership has implications on its governance, data sharing agreements, the degree of buy-in required from various beneficiaries, and what projects, services or problems to pursue [3]. Furthermore, the relevant talent, that is able to generate insights and/or actionable recommendations from the analytical results, moderates these aspects and is often challenging to find. The CPL director notes the conundrum of data labs as follows: "Often the people most interested in research, do not have the relevant data, and the people charged with stewarding the data do not have the resources to pursue research." (Evan White, cited in Dinesh, 2017, p. 8).

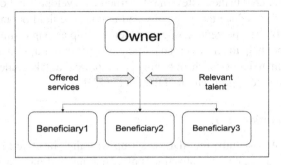

Fig. 1. Elements of a data lab

Accordingly, the four key elements (seen in Fig. 1) seem to be interdependent when defining and establishing a data lab. While the literature provides insights on identifying and the incentives to attract the relevant talent and build an appropriate data science culture [4], much less guidance is offered on how to define prospective beneficiaries and their needs. The current literature also assumes that the other three elements are fixed and known. However, if the beneficiaries are diverse, their needs and competences are unclear, it becomes problematic to define the other elements.

2.3 Infrastructural Challenges of Data Labs

The ability to share and reuse data can enable innovation [1]. However, it is a challenge to understand how data should be made available when the coordination and social practices pertaining to the data lab and its intended beneficiaries are at a very nascent stage. As a way to address this key infrastructural challenge, we include related work from the eScience and cyberinfrastructure streams to help us think about the emergent SDL. The eScience community is well-known for design and development of software pipelines that support data production, processing, and analysis within and across different scientific communities [14].

Previous research has investigated the development and use of such software pipelines and associated cyberinfrastructures, in particular with a focus on the organisational work it takes to create and maintain such infrastructures [15, 16]. Star and

Ruhleder [16] propose that infrastructure is inherently a substance for relations (i.e. between things and people) rather than a substrate. For example, Bietz et al. [15] look at how different stakeholders maintain the development of cyberinfrastructure. In this case, they explore how developers work to preserve a path that ensures continuous development of the infrastructure. The study shows that the developers do so by adjusting their own work to certain domain science projects and funding streams [15]. With the rise of the big data phenomenon, Demchenko et al. [17] proposed that we start considering the "data infrastructures" as distinct from the cyberinfrastructure due to their different physical and logical representations. Moreover, Lee et al. [18] propose the notion of "human infrastructure" which refers to different forms of organizing among stakeholders that overlap, might change over time, and might be used simultaneously to create and maintain a cyberinfrastructure. They propose several practical implications that should be considered in the context of infrastructure development. For instance, they argue it is essential to reduce the ambiguity and to embrace fluid organisational structures. Finally, the blurred perception of group membership among distinct stakeholders demands efforts that help to ensure broad participation from multiple stakeholders [18]. In this study, we aim to reduce such ambiguity and capture the stakeholders' perceptions in order to facilitate the appropriation of data in the SDL.

2.4   Earth Observation (EO)

The lab in focus of this study, the SDL, is set up with the objective to make EO data more accessible and usable for innovation, policymaking, and monitoring in Sweden. This data is obtained through the Copernicus program. The program launched a family of satellite missions, namely Sentinel-1 to Sentinel-6 [19], each containing two satellites in order to fulfil the revisit and coverage requirements. Data from the Sentinel missions are available in five cloud-based platforms, as well as in various download services. To be able to efficiently exploit this data, the SDL uses tools from the Open Data Cube (ODC) project [20]. ODC is an open source data management and analysis software project originally based on the Australian Geoscience Data Cube [21], designed to organise vast amounts of EO data into an efficient database structure. For the purposes of the SDL project, the Sentinel-2 data of Sweden from years 2017 and 2018 was batch-downloaded, and new data is continuously downloaded during the operation of the project, and as needed by the individual pilots.

Working with EO provides another dimension to this study, bringing the practical component of the research problem. It is not uncommon for domain experts who are not working with EO data to face challenges in making significant use of it for public benefit [6]. During a Copernicus networking event in 2019, various domain experts (e.g., on climate adaptation, forestry, etc.) expressed their interest to the Swedish space agency - one of the SDL consortium partners - in using the SDL data. However, it was unclear how and why they want to use it.

Taken together, these different perspectives highlight the challenges of emergent data infrastructures in terms of its ambiguity and fluidity of its actors and relations. The SDL can be viewed as an emergent infrastructure, and thus it becomes relevant to regard the above-mentioned challenges and recommendations, in particular, that there is no "one size fits all" solution. It is therefore important that the SDL takes into account the varying (data) needs of multiple different beneficiaries throughout the design process. We have created persona descriptions as a design tool to support the design team in creating a data lab that addresses the needs of various beneficiaries.

3 Research Method

The appropriation of data for the beneficiaries entails understanding the meanings they assign to data, their current mental models, their usage needs, and their expectations. As a way to develop a joint understanding of SDL's beneficiaries, we chose a qualitative approach to develop Personas, as this method is particularly useful for generating recognisable and distinct fictional character of typical user groups [22]. In this section, we first give a brief account on the Persona method, followed by a description of the SDL, which constitutes the research setting. Finally, we elaborate on our development of persona descriptions for this context.

3.1 The Persona Method

Developing a persona is a user-centred design method commonly used to understand user characteristics, needs, and goals in order to condense valuable insights that can inform a design process. The method emerged in the late 1990s as an attempt to communicate an understanding of the users to support IT system development [8, 23]. Personas constitutes abstract user representations, or character archetypes, which are most often developed by designers based on user data [8, 22].

> *"Personas are an efficient design tool because of our cognitive ability to use fragmented and incomplete knowledge to create a complete vision about the people who surround us. With personas, this ability comes into play in the design process, and the advantage is a greater sense of involvement and understanding of reality"* [8, p. 24].

Nielsen et al. [24] propose that the advantages of personas can be divided in three categories: mental models, data storage, and prioritization. The first category refers to how personas can support the creation of joint mental models, which can help to challenge assumptions, both on individual and organisational levels in design processes [25]. The second category emphasises benefits of how personas (and the information they hold) often are easy to access and communicate. Finally, the third category encapsulates personas' ability to prioritize audiences. Thus, as a design tool, personas aim to represent current and/or potential beneficiaries and users. This is highly relevant in our case.

3.2   The SDL Context

This study is conducted as part of the SDL project. The project was launched in June 2019 for two years. It aims to make EO data accessible and usable for public benefit and innovation. Representatives from four organizations make up the project consortium: the Swedish space agency, a university, a research institute and an NGO. When the project was initiated, it was a major challenge to pinpoint for whom the lab is developed. The project plan included five pilot projects with five different beneficiaries, however, it was not clear who these beneficiaries are and what their needs are. Therefore, the design decisions were informed as the project and pilots were ongoing, and the personas method facilitated such discussions.

3.3   Developing SDL Personas

Overall, we followed Goodwin's [7] guidelines to develop our personas. Eight individual in-depth semi-structured interviews and one workshop comprised our primary data collection. The interviewees were selected from current and potential pilot project leaders (beneficiaries) and each interview lasted between 45 and 70 min. An interview protocol was designed and guided the interviewers. Seven interviews were conducted in English and one in Swedish, albeit with English notes. All interviews were recorded. The workshop was conducted with five other prospective beneficiaries, in Swedish, and coordinated by one of the project researchers. The workshop had two sections: one where participants described their pain points when working with EO data, and the other where they were asked to describe a typical user for the SDL. The workshop was documented in notes organized by those sections.

   The interview data analysis was conducted in four phases. First, two interviews were listened to and analysed to extract the first set of persona variables. The analysis was largely inductive where the interviews were subject to thematic coding [26]. This yielded 9 continuous, 5 discrete and 3 demographic variables. Two of the researchers then read all the notes and met to discuss the variables. This resulted in the addition of 4 continuous, 2 discrete and the omission of one demographic variable. Second, all interviewees were mapped along the variables by two researchers, followed by the analysis of visible patterns. This process yielded 3 clear personas. During the mapping process, use case-specific missing data led to the exclusion of the following discrete variables (and including them with demographics in an ongoing questionnaire study complementing this one): user homogeneity and number of simultaneous users. Third, a description of each persona was written down in terms of behavioural descriptions and persona goals. The workshop notes provided triangulation and richness to the persona descriptions. Each description was written by one researcher and cross-checked by another, going back to the notes for consistency. Fourth, the personas were written in a résumé format (see example in the Appendix).

4   Findings

The variables identified from the analysis could be organized in different ways. The first categorization was structured according to whether they were discrete or continuous.

Then, they were also categorized based on whether they described the persona as an individual, their attitude in relation to a specific use case or scenario, or in relation to their organization. In this section, we report them along those two dimensions and describe the personas accordingly.

4.1 Persona Variables

These persona variables were identified and refined with the objective of pinpointing the beneficiaries' priorities and expectations engaging with space data and the SDL. Accordingly, rather than focusing on the demographics of individuals, we focused on their data needs, especially when it comes to spatial data and their (potential) use cases. Throughout the study, their goals from space data and current pain points were of main concern. Table 1 below summarizes the variables in focus that helped us develop the persona descriptions further.

Table 1. Persona variables.

	Continuous	Discrete
Individual	General technical proficiency GIS proficiency Attitude towards collaboration	Nature of role Interest in space data
Use case	Specificity of use case Temporal/feature coverage Temporal/spatial coverage Spatial/feature coverage Financial resources Dependency on SDL	Motivation for collaboration Anticipated benefits from SDL (with regards to domain, and data/information/knowledge) Most valuable aspect of SDL
Organization	Organizational/technical scope Level of outward data sharing Level of inward data sharing	Data sources Types of analyses

4.2 Persona Characteristics

Three clear personas were found among our beneficiaries. Table 2 shows the complete list of different personas characteristics, and a summary is provided thereafter to highlight the similarities and differences across the personas.

Table 2. Characteristics of beneficiary personas in the SDL.

	AB: the coordinator	CG: the consultant	ED: the GIO
Technical proficiency (remote sensing)	Non-technical	Technical	Technical
GIS proficiency	Basic to moderate	Advanced	Advanced
Role	Coordination	Operational	Executive
Interest	Brings opportunities - explorative	Neutral - business necessity	Must use it - legal compliance
Collaboration	Neutral	Follower	Leader
Use case specificity	Ambiguous	Clear	Clear
Coverage priorities	1. Temporal 2. Spatial 3. Features	Exhaustive	1. Spatial 2. Features 3. Temporal
Financial resources	Needs external financing	Full financing possible	Needs partial financing
Dependency on SDL	Direct service needed	Minimum support needed	Moderate support needed
Motivation	Exploration & innovation	Strategic business development & access to infrastructure	Legal compliance & operational efficiency
Anticipated benefits (domain)	Monitoring & responsiveness	Cost efficiency & service quality	Cost efficiency & service quality
Anticipated benefits (DIK)	Outsourcing of skills	Data quality & wider coverage	Accessibility (e.g. through SLAs)
Most valuable aspect of SDL	Data products & competence	Tools & infrastructure	Data products
Organizational scope	Geography- and domain-specific	Technology-specific	Domain-specific
Data sharing	Outward conditional Limited inward	Inward only	Outward Limited inward
Data sources	"GUI Maps" - readily computed models	LiDAR Radar National land survey Ground measurements Questionnaires Aerial photography Raster & vector	LiDAR Aerial photography Satellite imagery DEMs Land surveying Vector models

(continued)

Table 2. (*continued*)

	AB: the coordinator	CG: the consultant	ED: the GIO
Analyses	Temporal analysis Forecasting Change detection	Pre-processing atmospheric corrections Time series Fixing geometry	Pre-processing Fixing geometry Raster functions Overlays

The first persona (AB) assumes a coordination role in a county administrative board, mostly focused on specific phenomena (e.g., climate adaptation, flooding, etc.). Thus, they are primarily interested in their county's geographical area when it comes to data coverage. They also work with monitoring and preparedness and are interested in change detection and long-term temporal analysis for their respective phenomena. They often have elements of critical infrastructure within their scope; hence, they believe the data should not be entirely availed publicly. They have the least technical skills of all three personas, manifested in their ability to only work with readily computed "maps" accessible via a friendly user interface.

The second persona (CG) is a consultant and business associate who identifies as a "space actor", meaning they are familiar with the space vertical from satellite technologies to their end-user needs. They are focused on technology and have the most advanced technical (both on the programming and GIS) skills of the three personas. Their interest in the data coverage is paramount - the more data the better. The interest in the SDL and motivation for collaboration is strategic and regard the technical infrastructure as the SDL's main advantage.

The third persona (ED) assumes the role of a Geographic Information Officer (GIO), who is responsible for the acquisition, management and dissemination of geographic data for their agency. They also possess advanced technical GIS skills. The agency they work for oversees the use and management of natural resources all over the country, owned both by private and public entities. Thus, the GIO's interest in data coverage is wider than that of AB, but not as exhaustive as CG since they are interested in specific features. This also means that the areas they cover may be subject to some degree of confidentiality (for private owners) or protection (for certain protected areas).

5 Discussion and Conclusion

In this section, we discuss the insights which were generated through the development of the three personas and the usage of the descriptions as a tool to facilitate the establishment of the SDL, how the infrastructural challenge with its emergence is addressed, and implications on the SDL design of offered products and services.

First, the personas have elucidated the difference between beneficiaries, who are experts in specific technologies (e.g., remote sensing and space technologies) and application domains (e.g., forestry, climate change and sustainability, etc.) in their mental models, expectations and data needs, and motivations for collaboration. While the former group define themselves to be "space actors", the latter are relatively technology agnostic. EO data and the SDL provide a common language by which those different actors could communicate and a bridge between technology and domain. This presents yet another relation in the space of relations complementing Star & Ruhleder's [16] view of infrastructure. However, it also reveals that EO data users (and resulting personas) represent a continuum, rather than user/non-user distinction adopted implicitly in the literature [6]. It is difficult to draw the line between users and non-users, since data representations, granularities and media evolve from one user group to another, and from one infrastructure to another (i.e., from Copernicus, to ODC to the SDL).

Second, in the absence of fixed organizational structures and practices, ambiguity of products and services, and uncertainty of relevant analytical talent, the personas enabled the SDL to focus on relatively stable archetypes of beneficiaries as a starting point to address the other elements. In that way, the focus on the human infrastructure when the former elements are ambiguous or changing supports the development of the technical infrastructure [18], as well as the data infrastructure [17].

Third, the direct practical implications of the personas lie in the design decision taken by the SDL to shape the data lab's offerings. In the proposal to Vinnova, the SDL described the aim of offering access to the ODC and tools for analysis and visualization. These components were primarily designed for programmers. However, the design evolved to include three environments through which the SDL can be accessed and used, taking into account the skills and possible access to talent available to each beneficiary: a) analysis lab that enables Python programmers take full advantage of machine learning techniques and methods (most relevant to persona CG), b) a GUI that delivers readily computed data models (most relevant to AB), and c) integration services to allow connecting EO data with other software solutions (e.g. GIS) - most relevant to ED. The three environments are illustrated in Fig. 2 below.

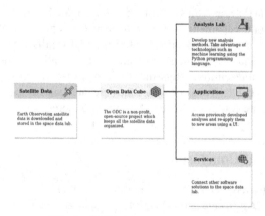

Fig. 2. SDL infrastructural design.

Another key implication is privacy and security measures related to EO data infrastructures. EO data is initially thought to contain no sensitive data, and thus should all be openly accessible. However, with increasing granularity and resolution, this notion is challenged. Personas AB and ED both highlighted the necessity to consider the implications of the open access on specific lands and properties that are critical in their respective domains, such as specific forests serving long-term measurements, properties that are part of critical infrastructures or locations that need to be protected for their biodiversity. Having data about these locations as open data poses risks to them. In addition, prioritization with regards to data selection, integration and selection of future pilots is considered based on the developed personas.

This study provides early insights on the infrastructural challenges with emergent data labs; in particular those of ambiguity of its various stakeholders, and how persona development can help tackling these challenges. Applying the persona method in the context of data infrastructures also revealed that the distinction between users and beneficiaries (typically referred to as customers in the persona literature) is not clear, since data usage represents a continuum of processing, analysis and use. The study also provides practical insights on how to identify beneficiaries of emerging data labs using the persona method, as a step towards lowering the entry barriers for them to be engaged in using its constituent offerings for public benefit [3].

However, the study has a few limitations. The personas developed are as representative of the interviewees as the selected variables, which were driven by their current practices rather than their future use of space data. The current study also does not account for the role of the different consortium members on the personas' characteristics, such as their motivation or attitude towards space data. Future work will address these limitations by testing the persona variables through a questionnaire to a wider sample of beneficiaries. This will enable us to also develop the tools to keep the personas as "live" representations of the beneficiaries. We will also observe how the inclusion and usage of personas influences the development of the data lab into the future. Further research is also needed to explore how the human, data and cyberinfrastructures notions may relate to one another and interact in the context of data labs.

Appendix

ED

EBBA DANIELSSON
GEOGRAPHIC INFORMATION OFFICER
BENEFICIARY | GOVERNMENTAL AGENCY

BRIEF PERSONA DESCRIPTION

Ebba is a geographic information officer in a governmental agency. She is responsible for the acquisition, management and dissemination of spatial data required for her organization to perform its function. Her role is of an executive nature and directly enables the agency's domain-specific operations. She often needs to make strategic decisions in relation to the three responsibilities mentioned earlier.

Ebba's decisions regarding GIS technologies are directly driven by her agency's needs. Her interest in space data grew when current surveying technologies impose limitations to their operations.

SKILLS

Technical background in remote sensing

Advanced GIS user, including data management & administration

ArcGIS, QGIS

USE CASE NEEDS

Ebba has detailed knowledge about applied use cases for space data. They have clear questions, data sets and ways to evaluate it in mind. In case compromise is required, wider spatial coverage is prioritized over longer temporal coverage. Detailed features (i.e. what is being measured) are also prioritized over longer temporal coverage, as long as specific change is detectable.

The motivation for her use cases is largely driven by enforcing regulations, complying with the law and enabling data-driven policies. Ebba anticipates benefits from SDL in terms of feasible wider spatial coverage and better SLAs (i.e. data availability).

To achieve these benefits, close collaboration and service from SDL is required. She is very motivated for such collaboration but will require (partial) external funding to help her realize those use cases. Ebba perceives SDL's data products as its most valuable aspect.

DATA SOURCES

The agency currently sources both vector and raster such as:
- LiDAR
- Aerial photography
- Satellite imagery
- DEMs
- Land surveying
- Vector data & models from other agencies (e.g. EPA)

ANALYSES

Ebba does not currently conduct analyses herself but prepares and manages spatial data for other users. She prepares it to be analyzed via:
- GIS systems (e.g. overlays)
- Raster functions

ORGANIZATION AND SDL

Ebba's organization operates all over Sweden. They are currently generating their own data from surveying, land measurements and area photography. The data is shared with county administrative boards and municipalities.
They have also started using satellite data for some time now, but are facing tremendous challenges regarding data quality, accuracy and availability.

GOALS

- Prepare data products for executive partners faster and with higher quality
- Enforce regulations in a more cost-efficient manner
- Activate data-driven policy making across their organization

EBBA SAYS...

"We have the pressure to manage a lot of [natural and financial] resources that depend on geographic data. It is very costly to do extensive manual surveying. And the European Commission is pushing for us to conduct area monitoring using Sentinel data. But it is also difficult to work with this data. We need an automated way of obtaining and using it... and also develop a decision support system that can help [our operations]. We were hoping that the Space Data Lab will solve these problems for us. That's why we became very interested in taking part in this" (Interviewee E)

References

1. Jetzek, T., Avital, M., Bjorn-Andersen, N.: Data-driven innovation through open government data. J. Theoret. Appl. Electron. Commer. Res. **9**(2), 100–120 (2014)

2. OECD: The Path to Becoming a Data-Driven Public Sector. OECD (2019). https://doi.org/10.1787/059814a7-en
3. Dinesh, A.: Building the smarter state: the role of data labs. Medium, 13 December 2017. https://medium.com/data-labs/building-the-smarter-state-the-role-of-data-labs-5b5428920f0f. Accessed 19 Nov 2019
4. Kremser, W., Brunauer, R.: Do we have a data culture?. In: Data Science – Analytics and Applications, Wiesbaden, pp. 83–87 (2019). https://doi.org/10.1007/978-3-658-27495-5_11
5. Vinnova: Datalabb och datafabrik som nationell resurs (2020). https://www.vinnova.se/e/datadriven-innovation/datalabb-datafabrik/. Accessed 07 Feb 2020
6. Yang, C., Huang, Q., Li, Z., Liu, K., Hu, F.: Big Data and cloud computing: innovation opportunities and challenges. Int. J. Digit. Earth **10**(1), 13–53 (2017)
7. Goodwin, K.: Designing for the Digital Age: How to Create Human-Centered Products and Services. Wiley, Hoboken (2011)
8. Nielsen, L.: Personas-User Focused Design. Springer, London (2019). https://doi.org/10.1007/978-1-4471-7427-1
9. Bright, J., Ganesh, B., Seidelin, C., Vogl, T.M.: Data science for local government. SSRN J. (2019). https://doi.org/10.2139/ssrn.3370217
10. Rizk, A.: Data-driven innovation: an exploration of outcomes and processes within federated networks. Doctoral thesis, Luleå University of Technology, Luleå (2020)
11. Rizk, A., Ståhlbröst, A., Elragal, A.: Data-driven innovation processes within federated networks. Eur. J. Innov. Manag. (2020). https://doi.org/10.1108/EJIM-05-2020-0190
12. Lyon, F., Gyateng, T., Pritchard, D., Vaze, P., Vickers, I., Webb, N.: Opening access to administrative data for evaluating public services: the case of the Justice Data Lab. Evaluation **21**(2), 232–247 (2015). https://doi.org/10.1177/1356389015577507
13. Vinnova: Datalabb och datafabrik som nationell resurs. Vinnova, Sveriges innovationsmyndighet, 2019–01038 (2019). https://www.vinnova.se/globalassets/utlysningar/2015-07023/omgangar/60709b5a-db86-421c-bb86-05616f1f2d1e.pdf932684.pdf. Accessed 24 Nov 2019
14. Paine, D., Lee, C.P.: Producing data, producing software: developing a radio astronomy research infrastructure. In: 2014 IEEE 10th International Conference on e-Science, vol. 1, pp. 231–238 (2014). https://doi.org/10.1109/eScience.2014.41
15. Bietz, M.J., Paine, D., Lee, C.P.: The work of developing cyberinfrastructure middleware projects. In: Proceedings of the 2013 Conference on Computer Supported Cooperative Work, pp. 1527–1538 (2013)
16. Star, S.L., Ruhleder, K.: Steps toward an ecology of infrastructure: design and access for large information spaces. Inf. Syst. Res. **7**(1), 111–134 (1996)
17. Demchenko, Y., Grosso, P., De Laat, C., Membrey, P.: Addressing big data issues in scientific data infrastructure. In: 2013 International Conference on Collaboration Technologies and Systems (CTS), pp. 48–55 (2013)
18. Lee, C.P., Dourish, P., Mark, G.: The human infrastructure of cyberinfrastructure. In: Proceedings of the 2006 20th Anniversary Conference on Computer Supported Cooperative Work, Banff, Alberta, Canada, pp. 483–492 (2006). https://doi.org/10.1145/1180875.1180950
19. ESA: Copernicus Overview. United Space in Europe (2020). http://www.esa.int/Applications/Observing_the_Earth/Copernicus/Overview4. Accessed 26 Jan 2020
20. Killough, B.: Overview of the open data cube initiative. In: IGARSS 2018 - 2018 IEEE International Geoscience and Remote Sensing Symposium, pp. 8629–8632 (2018). https://doi.org/10.1109/IGARSS.2018.8517694
21. Lewis, A., et al.: The Australian geoscience data cube—Foundations and lessons learned. Remote Sens. Environ. **202**, 276–292 (2017). https://doi.org/10.1016/j.rse.2017.03.015
22. Adlin, T., et al.: Putting personas to work. In: CHI 2006 Extended Abstracts on Human Factors in Computing Systems, pp. 13–16 (2006)

23. Cooper, A.: The Inmates are Running the Asylum. SAMS, Macmillan, Indianapolis, IA (1999)
24. Nielsen, L., Jung, S.-G., An, J., Salminen, J., Kwak, H., Jansen, B.J.: Who are your users? Comparing media professionals' preconception of users to data-driven personas. In: Proceedings of the 29th Australian Conference on Computer-Human Interaction, Brisbane, Queensland, Australia, pp. 602–606 (2017). https://doi.org/10.1145/3152771.3156178
25. Floyd, I.R., Cameron Jones, M., Twidale, M.B.: resolving incommensurable debates: a preliminary identification of persona kinds, attributes, and characteristics. Artifact 2(1), 12–26 (2008). https://doi.org/10.1080/17493460802276836
26. Gibbs, G.R.: Analyzing Qualitative Data, vol. 8. SAGE Publications, London (2007)

Design Workflows Graph Schemes Correctness Proof in Computer Aided Design Activity

Nikolay N. Voit$^{(\boxtimes)}$ (ID) and Semen I. Bochkov$^{(\boxtimes)}$ (ID)

Ulyanovsk State Technical University, Severnyy Venets Street, 32, Ulyanovsk, Russia
n.voit@ulstu.ru

Abstract. The authors substantiate the proof of the theorem about design workflows graph schemes correctness presented in visual languages form. In this work typical incorrect structures and techniques for constructing correct design workflows graph diagrams are described. Also, the meaning of design workflows graph scheme correctness is given. Definition of correctness is given and theorem on the design workflows diagram into algorithm diagrammatic form transformation and vice versa is formulated and proved. The results obtained provide, in scientific terms, the acquisition of new knowledge in the study of the complex technical systems behavior. In practical issue, the work will allow designers to avoid costly design errors in the complex products computer-aided design in the large industrial enterprise context at the mockup layout stage.

Keywords: Design workflows · CAD · Graph · Algorithm

1 Introduction

ISO 42010 standard defines computer-aided design (CAD) systems as complex software-intensive systems. In business process management theory, theoretical informatics, cyber-physical systems, development stages of such systems are represented by the design workflows, including algorithms, software-intensive business processes. The handling of such design workflows in the end-to-end digital design paradigm includes key design procedures such as analysis and synthesis, which are among the studies and seriously influences on the success of design and development. The problem of design solutions success in these theories has been studied for more than 30 years. This problem is caused by a high degree of development (design solutions) going beyond the planned time, financial and functional requirements. Reasons and methods for developing complex automated systems with improved efficiency are identified in above mentioned theory. However, according to the Standish Group [35], which is engaged in development in the field of successful automated systems development, currently only 40% have success.

This work develops the topic of processing design workflows in technical CAD systems [1–3]. We focus on one of the most important properties of any system namely correctness. Determining the workflow correctness is one of the most important problem in business process management. In theoretical informatics, correctness is one of the

A. Lopata et al. (Eds.): ICIST 2021, CCIS 1486, pp. 48–59, 2021.
https://doi.org/10.1007/978-3-030-88304-1_4

fundamental in the algorithms field. Correct workflows determine the success of an industrial enterprise, therefore, the proof of theorem on the workflow correctness, will allow designers to implement the theorem and avoid expensive design errors.

2 Related Works

Current works [4–33] analysis on the subject made it possible to compare the obtained results with the available ones, to determine the place and contribution of this work to the design workflows processing. The following is selection of articles on the design workflows analysis.

Repa et al. [4] describe a methodology for eliminating errors in the design workflows based on the state, hierarchy, details patterns definition but the method for identifying such patterns is not described. Amhad et al. [5] explore the possibilities of checking the design workflows of both atomic and complex events in the temporal automata (TA) context and temporal Petri nets (TPN), compare the semantics of simple and complex events with events in TA and TPN. Simple workflow events can be formalized using TA and TPN, but there are application restrictions for complex events. Jugel et al. [6] performed an interactive visualization of workflow patterns in order to increase visibility in demonstrating to stakeholders. Feja et al. [7] use the well-known model checking method to the logical rules describing the design workflows, and visual notations for algorithms. Pfeiffer et al. [8] demonstrate the model checking in design workflows validaton in software development, focusing on e-commerce. Mendling et al. [9] translate design workflows into a YAWL model, analyze them using the WofYAWL validation tool, and use logistic regression to show that the design workflows complexity has a significant impact on the error probability. In [10], it is proposed to simplify design workflows and then analyze them using Petri nets, taking into account only the reachability property. Van der Aalst et al. [11] describe the ProM 4.0 tool for analyzing the design workflows based on process mining, that is, extracting information about project activities based on recorded events, for example, a log file. Also they present [12] logical AND-free design workflows in the Petri net form and analyze them for errors with polynomial time.

Thus, the research shows that there are no theorems to determine the design workflows correctness with linear analysis complexity, therefore, in this work, a new theorem is presented and proved.

3 Formal Description

In this section we define the roles, variables and operations of design workflows choreography in the complex products computer-aided design with the logic algebra language.

Let Var_{Set} be the k, l variables set. Assume $\tilde{k}$ and $\tilde{l}$ the variables tuples respectively $\tilde{k} = \langle k_1, k_2, k_3, \ldots, k_n \rangle$ and $\tilde{l} = \langle l_1, l_2, l_3, \ldots, l_n \rangle$ where $k \in \tilde{k}$, $l \in \tilde{l}$. Assume $Operation_{Name}$ the operations names set, $Operation_{type} = \{one - way, request - response\}$ is the operations types set, where $one - way$ is one way operation, $request - response$ is request-response operation. Each operation is described with a name and type: $operation = \{(name, type)|name \in Operation_{Name}, type \in Operation_{type}\}$. $operation$

is an operations set where each element is uniquely identified by *name*. Assume $Role_{Name}$ a role names set, $Role_{Name} = \{\rho_i\}, i \in \mathbb{N}$, $Role = \{(\rho, \omega, V) | \rho \in Role_{Name}, \omega \subseteq Operation, V \subseteq Var_{Set}\}$ is roles set.

The choreography transition system state describes the variables values, it is described by the following function: $Function_{state} : Var_{set} \to Value, Value \in \mathbb{R}$. $Function_{state}(k)$ returns value of k in *state*, $Function_{state}(k) = \emptyset$ if k is undefined. Let $v \in Value \cup \emptyset$, then $St[v/k]$ means that a variable k of the system in the state St has the value v. Records with tuples $St[\tilde{v}/\tilde{k}]$ have the same meaning. Moreover, if $St[v/k] = St'$, then $St'(k') = \begin{cases} v & \text{if } k' = k \\ St(k') \text{ else} \end{cases}$.

Backus-Naur form of logical conditions for describing the variables constraints allows to set the initial state of the choreography transition system: $\chi ::= k \leq e | e \leq k | \neg \chi | \chi \wedge \chi$, where e is an expression containing variables and v value. If e is evaluated with the v value is St state, it is denoted as $e_{St} \to v$. If St meets χ condition, then $St \vdash \chi$. The rules for $\vdash$ are the following:

1. $St(k) = \emptyset \Rightarrow St \vdash (k \leq \emptyset \wedge \emptyset \leq k)$.
2. $e_{St} \to v, St(k) \leq v \Rightarrow St \vdash k \leq e$.
3. $e_{St} \to v, v \leq St(k) \Rightarrow St \vdash e \leq k$.
4. $St \vdash \chi' \wedge St \vdash \chi'' \Rightarrow St \vdash \chi' \wedge \chi''$.
5. $\neg(St \vdash \chi) \Rightarrow St \vdash \neg \chi$.

The rule 1 states that $St(k)$ has an empty value ($\emptyset$) if and only if $k = \emptyset$. Describe an *inter-role conversation* design workflow C with the following notation:
$$C ::= 0 | \eta | C; C | C \| C | \sum_{i \in N}^{\|L} (\eta_i \| C_i) | \sum_{i \in N}^{\oplus L'} \chi_i?(\eta_i, C_i), \eta ::= \left(\rho_A, \rho_B, operation, \tilde{k}, \tilde{l}, dir \right) | k ::= e, N \in \mathbb{N}.$$

In the notation, η is converted design workflow. $: : = (\rho_A, \rho_B, name, \tilde{k}, \tilde{l}, direction)$ means successful inter-role conversation between roles ρ_A and ρ_B, $name \in Operation_{Name}$. $\tilde{k}, \tilde{l}$ tuples serve conversation design workflows sending and receiving processes respectively. $direction \in \{\uparrow, \downarrow\}$ means design workflows sending ($\uparrow$) and receiving ($\downarrow$). $k := e$ means that e is assigned to k variable.

The conversation design workflows can have a value (0), base operator (η), sequence ($C; C$), parallelism ($C \| C$), non-conditional (parallel) or conditional (fork) choice ($\sum_{i \in N}^{\|L} (\eta_i \| C_i)$ or $\sum_{i \in N}^{\oplus L'} \chi_i?(\eta_i, C_i)$ respectively). Non-conditional choice is performed regardless of condition χ. L is a merge label for parallel workflows η_i, C_i. L' is a merge label for the workflows forked by the χ.

Describe the conversation action as $action_C = \{\mu | \mu = (\rho_A, \rho_B, name, \tilde{v}, direction)\} \cup \{time_{clock}\}$, where μ is workflow parameters set, $time_{clock}$ is a time value. $(C, St) \xrightarrow{action} (C', St')$ means that $action$ returned a single workflow C' and choreography system transits from St to St'.

Table 1. Design workflows and their view in WFGS.

No.	Design workflow	Graph
1	Sending	$S[v/\tilde{k}] \xrightarrow{\mu \quad \eta_{\uparrow\delta}} S'[\tilde{\delta}/\tilde{y}]$
2	Receiving	$S[\tilde{\delta}/l] \xrightarrow{\mu \quad \eta_{\downarrow v}} S'[v/\tilde{k}]$
3	Destination	$\xrightarrow{\tau} S'[v/l]$
4	Sequence	$\xrightarrow{} S \xrightarrow{\mu} S' \xrightarrow{}$ $I \qquad I' \qquad D$
5	Parallelism	$\xrightarrow{} S \xrightarrow{\mu} S'$ $I \qquad I'$ D
6	Choice 1 (parallel)	$\sum_{i \in N}^{\parallel L} (\theta_i \parallel I_i)$ $S \xrightarrow{\mu \quad \theta_i} S' \xrightarrow{\theta'_i} L$ $S \xrightarrow{I_i} S'' \xrightarrow{I'_i}$
7	Choice 2 (fork)	μ_θ : $S \xrightarrow{\theta_i} S' \xrightarrow{\theta'_i} L'$ $S \sum_{i \in N}^{\oplus L'} \phi_i ? \theta_i, I_j$ μ_I : $S \xrightarrow{I_j} S'' \xrightarrow{I'_j}$

4 Design Workflows Graph Scheme

Formalized *AM* model [1] is easily presented with design workflows graph scheme (DWGS): $G(AM) = (S, WF)$, where $S = \{s_i | i = \overline{1.N}\}$ is states set, $WF = \{wf_i | i = \overline{1.N}\}$ is design workflows set, $WF \subseteq S \times S$; $\sum^{\|}$ is parallelization states subset, $\sum^{\|} \subseteq S$; L is parallelized design workflows merge states subset, $L \subseteq S$; $\sum^{\oplus}$ is fork states subset, $\sum^{\oplus} \subseteq S$; L' is forked design workflows merge states subset, $L' \subseteq S$. Each wf_i matches one of the kinds of design workflows (see Table 1).

Below design workflows description is given:

- Workflow 1 *Sending* contains two roles (ρ_A, ρ_B), sending workflow $\lambda_{\uparrow \delta}^{\sim}$, initial $S[\widetilde{v}/\widetilde{x}]$ and final $S'[\widetilde{\delta}/\widetilde{y}]$ states;
- Workflow 2 *Receiving* contains two roles (ρ_A, ρ_B), receiving workflow $\lambda_{\downarrow \widetilde{v}}$, initial $S[\widetilde{\delta}/\widetilde{y}]$ and final $S'[\widetilde{v}/\widetilde{x}]$ states;
- Workflow 3 *Destination* contains a command τ for the assigning the x value v and final state $S'[v/x]$;
- Workflow 4 *Sequence* contains a command v, three sequential workflows I, I', D respectively;
- Workflow 5 *Parallelism* contains a command v, a couple of sequential workflows I, I' and parallel one D;
- Workflow 6 *Choice 1 (parallel)* contains outcoming design workflows I_i, θ_i in S state, conjunction $\sum_{i \in N}^{\|} \theta_i \| I_i$, command v, states S' and S'' with outcoming workflows θ'_i and I'_i respectively;
- Workflow 7 *Choice 2 (fork)* contains command v, workflows I_i, θ_i in S state, disjunction on ϕ condition of choosing next state, states S' and S'' with outcoming workflows θ'_i and I'_i respectively.

5 Workflow Graph Scheme Correctness

Definition 1. Workflow graph scheme (WFGS) $G(wf)$ is *correct* if the workflow wf_G matching the scheme satisfies the following conditions:

- wf_G is determined i.e. if wf'_G and wf''_G are different instances of design workflows then $\forall d_k \in D(wf'_G(d_k) = wf''_G(d_k))$. The determinism property assumes that the algorithm is described in such a formal language and presented in the form of such a clearly formulated system of rules that the results of its work do not depend on which system will implement these rules [13].
- design workflow duration is finite for any input data: $\forall d_k \in D(\tau\left(wf'_g(d_k)\right) < \infty)$.

Template configurations leading to the incorrect WFGS are the following:

1. *Deadlock* (Fig. 1, a) in state L: there is a couple of states S_i, S_j in WFGS so that they form the loop $S_i \rightarrow wf_j S_j$, $S_j \rightarrow wf_l S_p$, $S_p \rightarrow wf_l L$, $L \rightarrow wf_k S_i$, $\rightarrow wf_a L$, $wf_l \| wf_a$ and design workflows wf_i, wf_j, wf_l, wf_k, wf_a do not contain state $L \rightarrow$
$$\sum_{i \in N}^{\oplus L'} wf_l \oplus wf_a ? wf_k \, S_i,$$ where $\oplus$ is strict disjunction.
2. *Ambiguity* (Fig. 1, b): there is a couple of states S_i, S_j so that $[wf_i S_i] \| [wf_j S_j]$ and there is a state L' so that $S_i \rightarrow \sum_{i \in N}^{\oplus L'} wf_i \oplus wf_j ? wf_k L'$, $S_j \rightarrow \sum_{i \in N}^{\oplus L'} wf_i \oplus wf_j ? wf_k L'$.
3. *Freezing* (Fig. 1, c) in L state: there is a couple of states S_i, S_j so that $[wf_i S_i] \oplus [wf_j S_j]$ and there is a state L so that $S_i \rightarrow \sum_{i \in N}^{\| L} wf_i \| wf_j L$, $S_j \rightarrow \sum_{i \in N}^{\| L} wf_i \| wf_j L$.

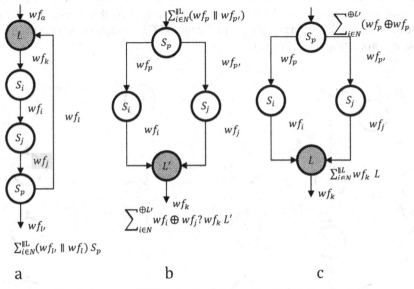

a   b   c

Fig. 1. Incorrect WFGS: deadlock (a), ambiguity (b), freezing (c)

There are situations in which there are no causal design workflows wf_1 and wf_2 between the two states S_1, S_2 which are parallel ($S_1 \| S_2$). In this case, it is unacceptable that $wf_1 S_1$ overlap in time with $wf_2 S_2$. These situations are usually caused by the need to use the same resource and are called *resource conflicts*. They can be eliminated by introducing priority and control mechanism, or *arbiter*. Priority setting for $wf_1 S_1$ and $wf_2 S_2$, means that the S_1 output is connected to the S_2 input by enabling two states of parallelization $\sum^{\|}$ and merging parallel design workflows L (Fig. 2a). An arbiter adds a new special state, which should correspond to the appearance of an arbiter in a real situation [14, 15] and should allow the prime execution of design workflow, for which the initial data were ready earlier, and prohibit the execution of the second workflow until the first one is performed (Fig. 2b).

The main difficulty in workflows design is building correct WFGS. The necessary techniques for constructing correct WFGS are defined in [16], and the fulfillment of the above conditions guarantees obtaining well-formed WFGS, or WF-networks, which have the following properties:

- any WFGS without cycles and loops is WF-network;
- below presented WFGSs (Fig. 3) are WF-networks;
- WFGS, obtained from the WF-network by replacing its elements with WF-networks, is a WF-network.

The WFGSs construction taking into account the mentioned techniques, ensures correctness, structuredness and facilitates the subsequent source code synthesis. However, the WF-networks class is a limited class of the correct WFGSs, there are many typical correct design configurations of the WFGSs (Fig. 4), but they do not belong to the WF-networks. For example, it is impossible to stay within the WF-network if it is necessary to set priorities, therefore the WFGS checking task is set broader than in [16]. It is solved on the basis of establishing a mapping between the WFGS correctness and the liveliness and safety properties of its Petri net.

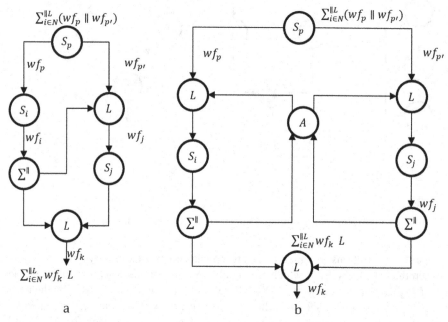

Fig. 2. Priority setting for wf_1 and wf_2 (a); adding an arbiter A (b)

In order to establish this mapping, it is necessary to convert the WFGS to an algorithm graph (AG) and use the proven theorem No. 2.1 [17] that each AG has a Petri net and such an AG is correct if and only if it has safety and liveliness properties, and, if possible, belongs to the WF-networks class with a good structure.

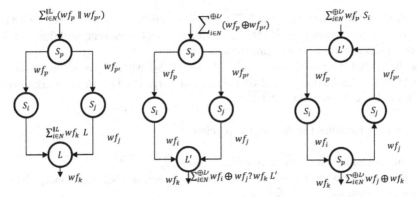

Fig. 3. Typical WFGSs from the WN-networks class

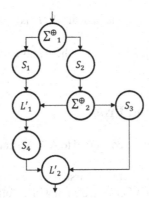

Fig. 4. Correct WFGS example

Convert the WFGS into the AG using the transition formulas [18], which have the following record in general form: $S \rightarrow \alpha S'$, where S is the system initial state, S' is the final state; α is logical expression of a condition. The transition formulas for the WFGS are as follows:

- for the sequential design workflows performing: $S \rightarrow I'S'$, where S is a source state, S' is a destination state, I' is a design workflow;
- for the parallel workflows (Workflow 6, see Table 1): $S \rightarrow \sum_{i \in N}^{\|L} \theta'_i S'_i$, where S is a source state of $G(AM)$, S'_i are destination states of $G(AM)$; $\sum_{i \in N}^{\|L}$ are parallelized design workflows, L is a merge label of current workflows, θ'_i are parallel workflows;
- for the parallel workflows θ'_i merging on label L: $S_i \rightarrow \theta'^L_i S_L$, S_i are source states of $G(AM)$, S is destination state of $G(AM)$, L is a merge label of current workflows, θ'^L_i are a parallel workflow items, $i \in \overline{1.N}$;

- for the fork (Workflow 7): $S \rightarrow \sum_{i \in N}^{\oplus L'} \phi_i ? \theta_i S_i$, where S is a source state of $G(AM)$, S_i are destination states of $G(AM)$, L' is a merge label of current workflows, ϕ_i is a fork logical condition, θ_i are parallel workflows;
- for the forked workflows merging: $\theta_i: S_i \rightarrow \theta_i^{L'} S_{L'}$ where S_i is a source state of $G(AM)$, S is destination state of $G(AM)$, L' is a merge label of current workflows, ϕ_i is a fork logical condition, $i \in \overline{1.N}$.

Transition formulas fog AG are listed below.

- for the sequential operators performing: $A_i \rightarrow A_{i+1}, i \in \overline{1.N}$;
- for the parallel operators: $A_i \rightarrow \wedge^L A_j$, where $\wedge$ is logical AND, L is a merge label of parallel workflows, $i, j \in \overline{1.N}$;
- for the parallel branches merging: $A_i \rightarrow L A_j$, where L is a merge label of parallel workflows, $i, j \in \overline{1.N}$;
- for the fork: $A_i \rightarrow \vee^{L'} A_j$, where $\vee$ is logical OR, L' is a merge label of forked parallel workflows, $i, j \in \overline{1.N}$;
- for the fork branches merging: $A_i \rightarrow L' A_j$, where L' is a merge label of forked parallel workflows, $i, j \in \overline{1.N}$.

6   Theorem Statement and Proof

Theorem 1. WFGS $G(AM)$ can be converted to AG, AG can be converted to the WFGS $G(AM)$.

■ The proof will consist of two stages. Firstly, we build conversion algorithms: from WFGS $G(AM)$ to AG and AG to WFGS $G(AM)$. It will be followed with pointers (*marks*) assignment to states and workflows. Secondly, we check the next conditions during pointers placement and accounting: $\sum_{i=1}^{n} Mark[S_i] + \sum_{j=1}^{m} Mark[wf_j] = 0$ ($G(AM)$ to AG), where $n \in \overline{1.N}$ is states count, $m \in \overline{1.N}$ is workflows count, $|Mark[S_i]| + |Mark[wf_j]| = 0$ after conversion; $\sum_{i=1}^{n} Mark[V_i] + \sum_{j=1}^{m} Mark[E_j] = 0$ (AG to $G(AM)$), where $n \in \overline{1.N}$ is edges count, $m \in \overline{1.N}$ is vertices count, $|Mark[V_i]| + |Mark[E_j]| = 0$ after conversion.

The AG model has the following view: $G = (V, E, TV, TE)$, where $V = \{v_i | i = \overline{1.N}\}$ is a vertices set, $E = \{e_i | i = \overline{1.N}\}$ is edges set, $E \subseteq V \times V$, TV is vertices types set, TE is edges types set. Restrict the input data so that AG can contain only one directed type of edge which matches a workflow in $G(AM)$.

The algorithm converting G to $G(AM)$ is described below:

1. **Define G to G(AM) vertices transition formulas.** It is necessary to define transition formula from G to G(AM) for each vertex and edge type: *Ftrans* : $V \cup E \rightarrow G(AM)$, based on the transition formulas. For each input edge e an input design workflow in G(AM) $wf\_in[N]$ must exist and for each ouput edge an output one $wf\_out[N]$ should exist.

2. **Forming AVN[N] set.** For each $v_i \in V$ and $e_i \in E$ construct conversion to G(AM) and obtain $VN : s_i \in VN$ and $AVN[N] = \{Ftrans(item_i) | item_i \in V \cup E\}$ sets, where *Ftrans* is a transition formula with marks placement. This process includes RVTI-based analysis procedures of G with linear complexity [34] which asynchronously places $Mark_i \in \overline{1.N}$ for each passed $v_i \in V$ and $e_i \in E$ and removes $Mark_i \in \overline{1.N}$ for each passed $v_i \in V$ and $e_i \in E$ if they match G(AM). G is converted to G(AM) with errors if the marks sum is not zero.

3. **Merging AVN[N] to G(AM).** Let $G(AM) = (\emptyset, \emptyset)$. Copy all design workflows and states to the $G(AM)$: $G(AM)[S] = \{s | \exists a \in AVN, s \in a[N][V]\}$, $G(AM)\left[wf\right] = \{wf | \exists a \in AVN, wf \in a[N][E]\}$, $G(AM)\left[\sum^{\|}\right] = \{s | \exists a \in AVN, s \in a[N][V]\}$, $G(AM)[L] = \{s | \exists a \in AVN, s \in a[N][V]\}$, $G(AM)\left[\sum^{\oplus}\right] = \{s | \exists a \in AVN, s \in a[N][V]\}$, $G(AM)\left[L'\right] = \{s | \exists a \in AVN, s \in a[N][V]\}$.

4. **Design workflows conversion in G(AM).** For each edge $e \in E$ connect states in G(AM) and search source v_1 and destination v_2 vertices and corresponding states $s_1 \in VN$, $s_2 \in VN$. Connect states with design workflows: $\exists wf\_in \in AVN, \exists wf\_out \in AVN, wf\_in[N][s_2] = e_i, wf\_out[N][s_1] = e_i$.

5. **Finish**

The output is G(AM) whose states are converted from G's vertices and design workflows from G's edges.

The algorithm converting G(AM) to G is described below:

1. **Define G(AM) to G transition formulas.** It is necessary to define transition formula from G to G(AM) for each vertex and edge type: *Ftrans* : $S \cup WF \rightarrow$ G. For each design workflow $wf\_in[N]$ an incoming edge $e\_in[N]$ must exist and for each design workflow $wf\_out[N]$ an outcoming edge $e\_out[N]$ should exist.

2. **AVN set forming.** For each vertex $v_i \in V$ and edge $e_i \in E$ in G construct conversion from G(AM) and obtain $VN : s_i \in VN$ and $AVN[N] : AVN = \{Ftrans(item_i) | item_i \in S \cup WF\}$ sets where *Ftrans* is a transition formula with marks placement. This process includes RVTI-based analysis procedures of G(AM) with linear complexity [34] which asynchronously places $Mark_i \in \overline{1.N}$ for each passed $s_i \in S$ and $wf_i \in WF$ and removes $Mark_i \in \overline{1.N}$ for each passed $s_i \in S$ and $wf_i \in WF$ if they match G. G(AM) is converted to G with errors if the marks sum is not zero.

3. **Merging AVN[N] to G.** Let $G = (\emptyset, \emptyset, \emptyset, \emptyset)$. Copy all AG edges e_i and vertices v_i to the $G(AM)$: $G(AM)[V] = \{v_i | \exists a \in AVN, v_i \in a[N][V]\}$, $G(AM)[E] = \{e_i | \exists a \in AVN, e_i \in a[N][E]\}$.

4. **Edges conversion in G.** Connect vertices in G based on the wf_n. For each design workflow wf_n find source $S_1 \in VN$ and destination $S_2 \in VN$ states and matching vertices $v_1 \in V$, $v_2 \in V$ in G. Find e_out edge in wf_out output workflows tuple for the selected workflow. Connect them: $v_1, v_2 : \exists e\_in[N] \in AVN, \exists e\_out[N] \in AVN, e\_in[N][v_2] = wf_n, e\_out[N][v_j] = wf_n$.

5. **Finish.** ∎

7 Conclusion

The paper presents theoretical foundations for determining the design workflows, software, business processes correctness in the technical systems computer-aided design. Design workflows correctness theorem has been stated and proved, so it makes possible for designers to use it in development. Design errors identification presented in the work will increase the design workflows, algorithms and business processes quality when developing such systems at the mockup prototyping stage, thereby providing an economic effect for an industrial enterprise, reducing financial costs for correcting errors in projects of technical systems, products etc.

Further research will be related to the design workflows, algorithms, business processes semantics and design procedures for design workflows analysis and synthesis in the computer-aided system design presented in the graphic languages basis.

The reported research was funded by Russian Foundation for Basic Research and the government of the region of the Russian Federation, Grant no: 18-47-730032.

References

1. Voit, N., Kirillov, S., Bochkov, S., Ionova, I.: Analytical model of design workflows organization in the automated design of complex technical products. In: Lopata, A., Butkienė, R., Gudonienė, D., Sukackė, V. (eds.) ICIST 2020. CCIS, vol. 1283, pp. 84–101. Springer, Cham (2020). https://doi.org/10.1007/978-3-030-59506-7_8
2. Voit, N.N.: The ensemble principle and analytical model of project workflow organization. Autom. Control Process. 61(3), 124–137 (2020). https://doi.org/10.35752/1991-2927-2020-3-61-124-137
3. Voit, N., Bochkov, S., Kirillov, S.: Temporal automaton RVTI-grammar for the diagrammatic design workflow models analysis. In: 2020 IEEE 14th International Conference on Application of Information and Communication Technologies (AICT 2020). IEEE (2020). https://doi.org/10.1109/aict50176.2020.9368810
4. Repa, V., Bruckner, T.: Methodology for modeling and analysis of business processes (MMABP). J. Syst. Integr. 6(4), 17–28 (2015)
5. Amjad, A., Azam, F., Anwar, M.W., Buttm, W.H.: Verification of event-driven process chain with timed automata and time Petri nets. In: 9th IEEE-GCC Conference and Exhibition (GCCCE). IEEE (2017). https://doi.org/10.1109/IEEEGCC.2017.8448053
6. Jugel, D., Kehrer, S., Schweda, C.M., Zimmermann, A.: Providing EA decision support for stakeholders by automated analyses. In: Digital Enterprise Computing (DEC 2015), pp. 151–162. Gesellschaft für Informatik e.V, Bonn, Germany (2015)
7. Feja, S., Fötsch, D.: Model checking with graphical validation rules. In: Proceedings of 15th Annual IEEE International Conference on Workshop Engineering of Computer Based System (ECBS), pp. 117–125. IEEE, USA (2008). https://doi.org/10.1109/ECBS.2008.45
8. Pfeiffer, J.-H., Rossak W.R., Speck, A.: Applying model checking to workflow verification. In: Proceedings, 11th IEEE International Conference and Workshop on the Engineering of Computer-Based Systems, pp. 144–151. IEEE (2004)
9. Mendling, J., Verbeek, H.M.W., van Dongen, B.F., van der Aalst, W.M.P., Neumann, G.: Detection and prediction of errors in EPCs of the SAP reference model. Data Knowl. Eng. 1(64), 312–329 (2008)
10. van Dongen, B.F., van der Aalst, W.M.P., Verbeek, H.M.W.: Verification of EPCs: using reduction rules and petri nets. In: Pastor, O., Falcão e Cunha, J. (eds.) CAiSE 2005. LNCS, vol. 3520, pp. 372–386. Springer, Heidelberg (2005). https://doi.org/10.1007/11431855_26

11. van der Aalst, W.M.P., et al.: ProM 4.0: comprehensive support for real process analysis. In: Kleijn, J., Yakovlev, A. (eds.) ICATPN 2007. LNCS, vol. 4546, pp. 484–494. Springer, Heidelberg (2007). https://doi.org/10.1007/978-3-540-73094-1_28
12. van der Aalst, W.M.P.: Formalization and verification of event-driven process chains. Inf. Softw. Technol. **10**(41), 639–650 (1999)
13. Napalkov, A.: Human Brain and Artificial Intelligence. MSU, Moscow (1985)
14. Plummer, W.: Asynchronous arbiters. IEEE Trans. Comput. **1**(C-21), 37–42 (1972)
15. Corsini, P., Frosini, G.: A model for asynchronous control networks. Digit. Process. **2**, 47–62 (1976)
16. Rumbaugh, J.: A data flow multiprocessor. IEEE Trans. Comput. **26**(1), 138–147 (1977)
17. Anishev, P.: Methods of Parallel Microprogramming. Nauka, Novosibirsk (1981)
18. Baranov, S.: Synthesis of Microprogram State Machines. Energiya, Leningrad (1979)
19. Virolainen, A.V.: Modeling business processes. Best Sci. Article 2019, 82–86 (2019)
20. Chernyshov, A.S.: Analysis of the methods of modeling automated systems. Information Technology and Control Automation, pp. 363–370 (2019)
21. Kopp, A., Orlovskyi, D.: An approach to analysis and optimization of business process models in BPMN notation. Inf. Process. Syst. **2**(45), 108–116 (2018)
22. Sergievskiy, M.V., Kirpichnikova, K.K.: Validating and optimizing UML class diagrams. Cloud Sci. **5**(2), 367–378 (2018)
23. Bohdan, I., Zadorozhnii, A.: The classification of errors on UML-diagrams occuring in the development of IT-projects. Tech. Sci. Technol. **1**, 68–78 (2018)
24. Kopp, A., Orlovskyi, D.: Analysis and optimization of business process models in BPMN and EPC notation. Tech. Sci. Technol. **4**(14), 145–152 (2018)
25. Anseeuw, J., et al.: Design time validation for the correct execution of BPMN collaborations. In: CLOSER (1), pp. 49–58 (2016)
26. Ramos-Merino, M., et al.: A pattern based method for simplifying a BPMN process model. Appl. Sci. **9**(11), 2322 (2019)
27. Claes, J., Vandecaveye, G.: The impact of confusion on syntax errors in simple sequence flow models in BPMN. In: Proper, H.A., Stirna, J. (eds.) Advanced Information Systems Engineering Workshops: CAiSE 2019 International Workshops, Rome, Italy, June 3-7, 2019, Proceedings, pp. 5–16. Springer, Cham (2019). https://doi.org/10.1007/978-3-030-20948-3_1
28. Lima, L., Tavares, A., Nogueira, S.C.: A framework for verifying deadlock and nondeterminism in UML activity diagrams based on CSP. Sci. Comput. Program. **197**, 102497 (2020)
29. Huang, H., Peng, R., Feng, Z.: Efficient and exact query of large process model repositories in cloud workflow systems. IEEE Trans. Serv. Comput. **11**(5), 821–832 (2015)
30. Aalst, W.M.P.: Everything you always wanted to know about petri nets, but were afraid to ask. In: Hildebrandt, T., van Dongen, B.F., Röglinger, M., Mendling, J. (eds.) BPM 2019. LNCS, vol. 11675, pp. 3–9. Springer, Cham (2019). https://doi.org/10.1007/978-3-030-26619-6_1
31. Barash, M., Okhotin, A.: Generalized LR parsing algorithm for grammars with one-sided contexts. Theory Comput. Syst. **61**(2), 581–605 (2016). https://doi.org/10.1007/s00224-016-9683-3
32. Bakinova, E., Basharin, A., Batmanov, I., Lyubort, K., Okhotin, A., Sazhneva, E.: Formal languages over GF(2). In: Klein, S.T., Martín-Vide, C., Shapira, D. (eds.) LATA 2018. LNCS, vol. 10792, pp. 68–79. Springer, Cham (2018). https://doi.org/10.1007/978-3-319-77313-1_5
33. Gorokhov, A., Grigorev, S.: Extended context-free grammars parsing with generalized LL. In: Itsykson, V., Scedrov, A., Zakharov, V. (eds.) TMPA 2017. CCIS, vol. 779, pp. 24–37. Springer, Cham (2018). https://doi.org/10.1007/978-3-319-71734-0_3
34. Afanasyev, A.N., Voit, N.N., Kirillov, S.Y.: Temporal automata RVTI-grammar for processing diagrams in visual languages as BPMN, EEPC and ASKON-Volga. In: ACM International Conference Proceeding Series: 5, Istanbul, pp. 71–75 (2019)
35. The Standish Group. https://www.standishgroup.com/

Financial Data Preprocessing Issues

Audrius Lopata[1], Rimantas Butleris[1], Saulius Gudas[1], Vytautas Rudžionis[1],
Kristina Rudžionienė[1], Liutauras Žioba[1], Ilona Veitaitė[1(✉)], Darius Dilijonas[2],
Evaldas Grišius[2], and Maarten Zwitserloot[3]

[1] Faculty of Informatics, Kaunas University of Technology, Studentų g. 50,
51368 Kaunas, Lithuania
{Audrius.Lopata,Rimantas.Butleris,Saulius.Gudas,
Vytautas.Rudzionis,Liutauras.Zioba,Ilona.Veitaite}@ktu.lt
[2] Intellerts, UAB, Studentų g. 3A-9, 50232 Kaunas, Lithuania
{d.dilijonas,e.grisius}@intellerts.com
[3] Intellerts B.V., Europalaan 400-7, 3526 KS Utrecht, The Netherlands
m.zwitserloot@intellerts.com

Abstract. Today the challenge facing every company is the enormous quantity
of data being captured, at yearly, monthly, weekly, daily and hourly levels and
how this data may be used. Despite the amount of data often this data is limited
regarding company processes and their analysis. This can be solved by preprocessing data, after its quality evaluation, for process mining activities. Prepared data
can be used for data dimensions' coverage and having dimension members filled
financial analyst may analyze this data from different perspectives for discovery
of certain patterns, anomalies and frauds. This paper presents primary results of
data cube dimensions fill according data of real organizations General Ledger
information. Provided examples help to illustrate the possibility cover majority
dimension members and give material for further researches.

Keywords: Process mining · Data preparation · Finance analytics · Process
discovery · Financial frauds · Financial anomalies

1 Introduction

Financial data analysis is challenging process, but it helps to evaluate company's performance and form possible trends. The major source of data are company's annual
reports, financial statements, balance sheet and/or general ledger. This data, explaining company's processes, may be collected in different ways by using different tools
or information systems. According collected data the analyst can choose different type
of analysis, in example: summary data, development trend, data comparison, composition, progress map and etc. It depends on main financial analysis purpose and from data
quality [1, 5, 12, 14].

Analyzing company's processes according stored data main issue is that companies
have limited data about how their processes run. Majority process data is stored in

© Springer Nature Switzerland AG 2021
A. Lopata et al. (Eds.): ICIST 2021, CCIS 1486, pp. 60–71, 2021.
https://doi.org/10.1007/978-3-030-88304-1_5

detailed log files, which are difficult to analyze. To make this analysis easier, process mining tools and methods are used [1–3].

Process mining is data analytics technology which main goal is to extract process-related information. Process mining is specifically focused on analysis of historical data of process implementation in the form of event logs [1–3]. There are many process mining technologies, tools and applications which can grant fact-based support process improvements and solutions. As it is mentioned, process mining is a tool that provides analysis of event logs extracted from the enterprise's information system [1, 2, 15]. Even though process mining has developed very quickly, it is quite new to the accounting literature and there are some challenges of its usage in this field, especially for fraud and anomalies detection [4–7, 9, 10].

Furthermore, business process mining is a comparatively new and expanding research field, which focuses on analysis of business processes by approaching diverse data mining and/or machine learning techniques on event data [2, 5, 11]. Such processes as modelling, management, analysis of business processes are currently mainly performed through process-aware information systems: Enterprise Resource Management Systems, Accounting Managements Systems, Finance Management Systems and etc. These systems collect all process events in particular form of event logs [4, 8, 10, 16]. Many recent discoveries in process mining research make it possible to discover, analyze, and improve business processes according event data. Of course, the growth of event data grants many opportunities: data analysis for forecasting and suggesting new solutions, detecting frauds, examining anomalies and etc., but also appoints new challenges related with data management, preparation and adaptation for further analysis [12, 14].

The process cubes were proposed in the [2] where events and process models are organized using different dimensions. A process cube is multidimensional space used to specify process models and event logs [1, 2, 13]. The process cube much like the data cube in which is applied in OLAP systems. Each cell corresponds to a set of events and can be used to discover a process model, to check conformance with consideration to some process model Even so, there are also meaningful differences because of the process-related format of event data. For instance, process discovery based on events is unmatched to computing the sum or average over a set of numerical values. Also, dimensions related to process instances (e.g. cases are split into various types of clients) or time (e.g., 2009, 2010, 2012, and 2014) are semantically diverse and it is challenging to slice, dice, roll-up, and drill-down process models efficiently [1, 2, 13].

In this paper data cube for financial data and difficulties of its covering are presented. Having particular financial data set, in example General Ledger there is quite challenging to evaluate its quality and to transform it for further process mining development. There are presented detailed data preparation process and as the main result of this usage of prepared data coverage of certain data cube dimensions.

Figure 1 present a meta-model of the research after receiving financial data about one company from the Netherlands. Type of financial data is general ledger, which consists of separate files such as general ledger account opening balance, journal, journal entry, ledger account, vat code and general ledger trail descriptions. Research process starts data quality evaluation. Then the process of data preparation begins. Data must be transformed to the more convenient structure for further analysis, in this case process

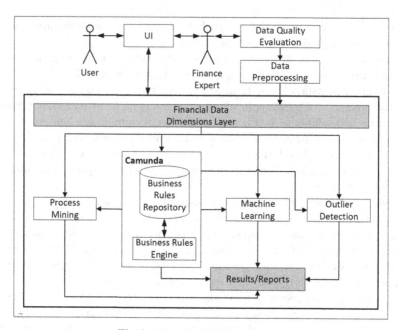

Fig. 1. Meta-model of the research

mining process. Prepared data is analyzed by using process mining algorithms and filling the data cube dimensions by certain data set fields. After process mining phase data is also processed by machine learning tools and techniques for outlier detection and etc. There are prepared reports of each phase, reports on statistics and all these results are presented for the user - financial analyst. The main focus of research described in this paper is to present data dimensions with their members, data preparation process and presentation on how data dimensions may be covered with certain financial data.

2 Financial Data Cube Dimensions

Financial data after the preparation process may be displayed as multi-dimensional array of data, early mentioned data cube.

Figure 2 present data cube dimensions and their members, which can be covered with particular data from General Ledger prepared for the analysis according transformation algorithms.

Table 1 presents dimensions, their members and possible data examples from general ledger (part of data fields are left in Dutch, because they are used for semantical analysis). For further presentation there are described some concepts:

- Financial Accounting Object (FO) – any name of the file field (data record field, i.e. the column name of the excel table), except for time attributes.
- Dimension – a type of FO (cluster) that corresponds to an aspect of financial accounting or performance management practices. There can be several dimensions of FO, it depends on the experts who provide the FO classification.

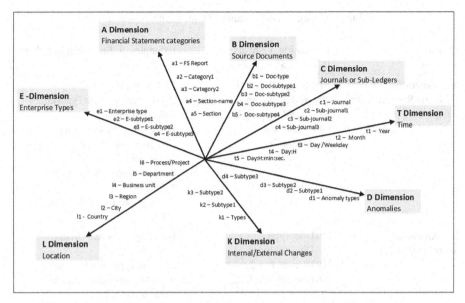

Fig. 2. Data cube dimensions and dimension members

- Each dimension corresponds to one axis of the Space of Financial Objects.
- Dimensions consist of dimension members that specify the hierarchical structure of the FO, i.e. identifies a more detailed classification of the FO type.
- Dimension members are assigned attributes (identifiers) that correspond to the data record fields (quantities, values or codes) and they may vary regarding provided data.
- Members of different dimensions can form combinations if they have at least one common attribute (identifier).

According a particular financial data a cube view defines which dimensions are visible and which events are selected. In order to apply standard process mining techniques, it is necessary to create an event log (to prepare financial data) for every cell in the cube view. At any point in time it is possible generate an event log per cell and compare the process mining results. To be able to apply process mining per cell, the classical requirements need to be satisfied, i.e. [1, 2]:

- events need to be (partially) ordered (e.g., based on some timestamp),
- one needs to select a case identifier to correlate events and an event classifier to determine the activities.

3 Financial Data Preparation

In this section financial data preparation and visualization possibilities are presented. The purpose of the experiment is to investigate applicability of Graph theory for General ledger data preprocessing for visualization and further analysis with process mining:

Table 1. Dimensions of Financial Objects with examples

Dimensions	Dimension members [Classification of FO]	Examples of dimension Members
A - Dimension: Financial Statement (FS) categories	a1-FS type (Report), a2-CreditCategory1, a3-CreditCategory2, a4-CreditCategory3, a5-SectionCode	FS Category (SysLedgerAccountTypeName): Balansrekening, Winst-en-verliesrekening... Category: Assets – Property, Liabilities... Section: MVA, IVA... OMZ, WIV... Sub-section: INCVR, DEB, CRE...
B - Dimension: Source documents	b1-Doc-Type, b2-Doc-Subtype1, b3-Doc-subtype2, b4-Doc-subtype3, ...	Doc-Type: Quotes, Orders, Invoices... Doc-sub-type: vendors quote, Sales (credit) quote, Purchase (vendors) invoice...
C - Dimension: Journals or Sub-Ledgers	c1-Journal, c2-Sub-Journal1, c3-Sub-journal2, c4-Sub-journal3, ...	Memoriaal, Inkopen Journal: Starting Balance, Adjusment Ledger, Inventory and Item Ledger... Sub-journal: Inventory accounting, Fixed asset accounting...
E - Dimension: Enterprise Types	e1-Enterprise Type, e2-E-SubType1, e3-E-SubType2, e4-E-SubType3, ...	There is separate table of general ledger trail descriptions
L - dimension: Location	l1-Country, l2-City, l3-Region, l4-Business Unit, l5-Department, l6-Process /Project...	Record fields may vary regarding provided data
T - dimension: TIME-period	t1-Year, t2-Month, t3-Day/week day, t4-Day: Hour: min: sec, t5-Hour: min: sec, t6-Period Beginning, t7-Period-Ending	Record fields may vary regarding provided data
D - Dimension: Anomalies	d1-Anomaly type, d2-subtype1, d3-subtype2, d4-subtype3, ...	Anomaly type: Sum anomaly, Time parameters anomaly, Anomalies of sum and time...

(continued)

Table 1. (*continued*)

Dimensions	Dimension members [Classification of FO]	Examples of dimension Members
K - Dimension: Changes: Internal/External	Internal Changes (IC): k1-types, k2-subtype1, k3-subtype2… External Changes (EC): k1-types, k2-subtype1, k3-subtype2…	IC types: infrastructure, management control method, workflow, roles, personalities… EC types: customers, vendors, banks, stakeholders, shareholders…

- Transform data into typical for:

  - graph format: Nodes table, Edge table (from node to node);
  - Dimensions coverage.

3.1 DP1. Rules for Data Preprocessing (SQL)

In order to simplify experiment, following pre-condition of the data will be used:

- Data for single company from the Netherlands with high level of data quality will be checked.
- For identification of the financial operation, following parameters (fields) will be used:

  - [JournalCode]
  - [JournalEntryNumber]
  - [InvoiceNumber]
  - [FinancialYear]
  - [FinancialPeriod]

- Only cases, which are "in balance" will be checked (amounts of debit operations and credit operations in case are equal).

3.2 DP2. Preprocessed Aggregated Data Results File/Table/View Name and Location

Data preprocessing:

- Stored Procedure: [PrepareData_JournalEntry] – Result: [JournalEntry_Full]
- Stored Procedure: [TransformData_FillTransformedData_table] – Result: [TransformedData].

Table 2. Table Fields descriptions

Field name	Description
[DebitSectionCode]	Section code, which has been debited during operation
[CreditSectionCode]	Section code, which has been credited during operation
[DebitAmount]	Amount, which has been transferred during this operation from Credit Section Code to Debit Section code
[CaseID]	Unique case identifier for business operation, based on [journalcode], [JournalEntryNumber], [InvoiceNumber], [FinancialYear], [FinancialPeriod]. One single business operation my have several Debit-Credit records
[FinancialYear]	Financial year for operations
[FinancialPeriod]	Financial period of the operation, typical means operation posting month and has values from 1 to 12
[JournalCode]	Journal code, which identifies accounting journal, which has been used by accountant to post operation
[SysJournalTypeName]	Type of the journal, which helps to identify operation type
[InvoiceNumber]	number of the invoice in case, if operation was related to the Purchase or sales
[JournalEntryNumber]	Operation identifier in journal scope

3.3   DP3. Rules for Aggregated Data Analysis (SQL)

Initial data contains set of debit and credit operations, one record for each funds transfer to/from account. Purpose of data processing – for every debit operation find related credit operations and store data in format Debit-Credit.

For accounts section codes instead of actual General Ledger accounts information will be used. Initial results will be stored in particular table and their descriptions are presented in Table 2.

Figure 3 presents transformation algorithm, where process of Transformation to Graph Edges starts; Data: List of Unique CaseID is provided; Process: Fetch CaseID; Decision: Is it end of the list, if yes - process ends, if no - process: Get list of debit operations for CaseID; Data: List of debit operations for CaseID is provided; Process: Fetch Single Debit operation: DebitSectionCode, DebitAmount, JournalEntryDescription; Data: DebitSectionCode, DebitAmount, JournalEntryDescription is provided; Decision: Is it end of the list, if yes - transformation is in progress, Process: Fetch CaseID, if no - Process: Get List of Credit operations for CaseID; Data: List of Credit operations for CaseID is provided; Subprocess: Process Credit operations.

Figure 4 presents transformation algorithm for credit operations counting, where Process of Credit counting operations starts: Process: Count Credit operations where JournalEntry description same as in Debit operation; Decision: if there is one operation - Subprocess: Process single Credit same JournalEntryDescription is counted, if no - Decision: if there are more than one operation - Subprocess: Process multiple Credit

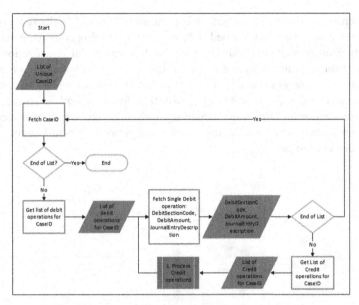

Fig. 3. Data transformation to Graph Edges algorithm

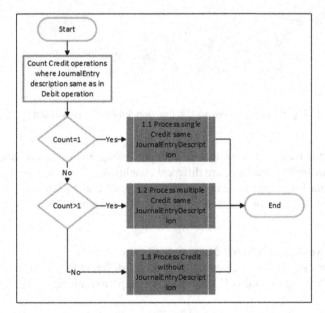

Fig. 4. Counting process of Credit operations

same JournalEntryDescription are counted, if no - Subprocess: Process Credit Without JournalEntryDescription is counted; Counting process ends.

Data preparation process takes thirteen Log transformations in total, to get necessary data for further analysis. Transformed data represents actual operations as they have been meant. Transformed data could be used for different useful visualizations based on graphs. However, transformation of initial data to graph nodes and graph edges is complicated and for other companies may not be possible due to the lack of data.

For visualization, R package library *networkD3*, function *SankeyNetwork*. Result of such visualization is html page containing flow diagram, which is presented in Fig. 5. Extremely helpful to visualize funds movement between General Ledger accounts (section codes in example).

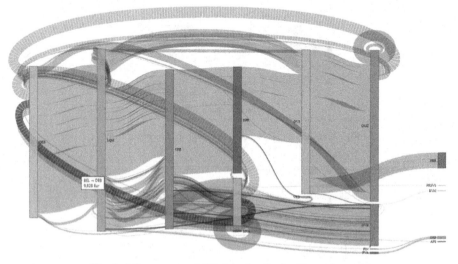

Fig. 5. Library networkD3, function *SankeyNetwork* result

Visualization result confirms, that data preprocessing was successful and it may be analyzed by an analyst. Furthermore different conclusions could be done by reviewing aggregated data for period (as example, for one year) and full transaction data. For additional analysis must be checked possibilities to add time dimension to such flow diagram:

- Could be investigated Alluvial diagrams application.
- Could be investigated use of additional node for different period in *SankeyNetwork* – add month index to section Code depending on period (month) of the operation.

SankeyNetwork should be checked as informative way of financial information representation.

4   Financial Data Set Fields

After all data preparation process, where financial company's data from general ledger was transferred to more convenient for analysis format previously described data dimensions and their members may be covered by certain financial company's data.

Table 3. Table dimensions and particular data set fields

Dimensions	Dimension members	Data set fields
A dimension (Categories)	FS Report	CreditStatementType
A dimension (Categories)	Category1	CreditCategory1
A dimension (Categories)	Category2	CreditCategory2
A dimension (Categories)	Section Name	CreditCategory3
A dimension (Categories)	Section	DebitSectionCode
A dimension (Categories)	Section	CreditSectionCode
B dimension (Source Documents)	Doc-Type	InvoiceNumber
C dimension (Journals)	Journal	JournalCode
C dimension (Journals)	Journal	SysJournalTypeName
C dimension (Journals)	Journal	JournalName
C dimension (Journals)	Journal	JournalEntryTypeID
C dimension (Journals)	Journal	JournalEntryDescriptionID
C dimension (Journals)	Journal	LedgerAccountCode
C dimension (Journals)	Journal	LedgerAccountName
T – Time dimension	Year	FinancialYear
T – Time dimension	Month	FinancialPeriod
T – Time dimension	Year/Month	EntryDate
T – Time dimension	Year/Month	EffectiveDate
E – Dimension	E-subtype2/3	CreditorCode
E – Dimension	E-subtype2/3	DebtorCode

Table 3 presents dimensions which can be covered by financial data set fields of analysed company's general ledger after data preparation process. According company's data dimensions A and C may be covered almost fully and dimensions B, T, E – partially.

As it is mentioned previously dimension members specify the hierarchical structure of the FO and also they are assigned attributes that correspond to the data record fields. This helps financial analyst evaluate relationship and meaning of particular processes.

As well as possibility that members of different dimensions can form combinations (if they have at least one common attribute) may help financial analyst to discover particular patterns, anomalies and even frauds.

5 Conclusion

Every company knows that they have quickly expanding amount of data. The challenge is it preprocess this data for further analysis to create competitive advantages. Ability to discover and identify particular patterns or anomalies according preprocessed data can make huge difference. Though, this may happen only if data will be prepared in the correct format.

Begining of the paper introduces main concepts for research implementation and presents meta-model of researh activities.

First part defines financial data cube dimensions, their members and basic concepts. Dimension members may be covered with information from company's financial documents such as general ledger.

Second part presents financial data preparation for further analysis: visualization solutions and possibility to cover dimensions presnted in the first part.

In the third part coverage of data dimensions is presented. There is delivered particular data set field which can cover data dimensions. Using these covered with prepared company's financial data dimensions analyst can identify different patterns, discover anomalies and even reveal frauds.

Acknowledgments. This paper presents primary results of research project "Enterprise Financial Performance Data Analysis Tools Platform (AIFA)". The research project is funded by European Regional Development Fund according to the 2014–2020 Operational Programme for the European Union Funds' Investments under measure No. 01.2.1-LVPA-T-848 "Smart FDI". Project no.: 01.2.1-LVPA-T-848-02-0004; Period of project implementation: 2020-06-01–2022-05-31.

References

1. Aalst, W.V.: Process Mining: Discovery, Conformance and Enhancement of Business Processes. Springer, Heidelberg (2011). https://doi.org/10.1007/978-3-642-19345-3
2. Aalst, W.M.P.: Process cubes: slicing, dicing, rolling up and drilling down event data for process mining. In: Song, M., Wynn, M.T., Liu, J. (eds.) AP-BPM 2013. LNBIP, vol. 159, pp. 1–22. Springer, Cham (2013). https://doi.org/10.1007/978-3-319-02922-1_1
3. Aalst, W.V., Kees M.V., Werf, J.M.V., Verdonk, M., Finance process mining Auditing 2.0: using process mining to support tomorrow's auditor. Computer **43**(3) (2010). http://www.pad sweb.rwth-aachen.de/wvdaalst/publications/p593.pdf
4. Adriansyah, A., Buijs, J.C.A.M.: Mining process performance from event logs. In: La Rosa, M., Soffer, P. (eds.) BPM 2012. LNBIP, vol. 132, pp. 217–218. Springer, Heidelberg (2013)
5. Alrefai, A.: Audit focused process mining: the evolution of process mining and internal control. Ph.D. thesis (2019). https://rucore.libraries.rutgers.edu/rutgers-lib/60514/PDF/1/play/
6. Das, K., Schneider, J.: Detecting anomalous records in categorical datasets. In: Proceedings of the 13th ACM SIGKDD International Conference on Knowledge Discovery and Data Mining, August 2007, pp. 220–229 (2007). https://doi.org/10.1145/1281192.1281219
7. Earley, C.E.: Data analytics in auditing: opportunities and challenges. Bus. Horiz. **58**, 493–500 (2015)
8. Debreceny, R.S., Gray, G.L.: Data mining journal entries for fraud detection: an exploratory study. Int. J. Account. Inf. Syst. **11**(3), 157–181 (2010)

9. Amani, F.A., Fadlalla, A.M.: Data mining applications in accounting: a review of the literature and organizing framework. Int. J. Account. Inf. Syst. **24**, 32–58 (2017)
10. Gally, F., Geerts, G.: Business process modeling: an accounting information systems perspective. Int. J. Account. Inf. Syst. **15**(3), 185–192 (2014). https://doi.org/10.1016/j.accinf.2014.08.001
11. Gehrke, N., Mueller-Wickop, N.: Basic principles of financial process mining a journey through financial data in accounting information systems. In: Association for Information Systems AIS Electronic Library (AISeL) (2010)
12. Gepp, A., Linnenluecke, M.K., O'Neill, T.J., Smith, T.: Big data techniques in auditing research and practice: current trends and future opportunities. J. Account. Lit. **40**, 102–115 (2018)
13. Mamaliga, T.: Realizing a process cube allowing for the comparison of event data. Master thesis. Eindhoven University of Technology (2013)
14. Mieke, J., Alles, M., Vasarhelyi, M.: The case for process mining in auditing: sources of value added and areas of application. Int. J. Account. Inf. Syst. **14**(1), 1–20 (2013). https://doi.org/10.1016/j.accinf.2012.06.015
15. Werner, M., Gehrke, N., Nuttgens, M.: Business process mining and reconstruction for financial audits. In: 45th Hawaii International Conference on System Sciences, pp. 5350–5359 (2012). https://doi.org/10.1109/HICSS.2012.141
16. Werner, M.: Financial process mining - accounting data structure dependent control flow inference. Int. J. Account. Inf. Syst. **25**, 57–80 (2017). https://doi.org/10.1016/j.accinf.2017.03.004

Information Technology of Decision-Making Support on the Energy Management of Hybrid Power Grid

Sergii Shendryk[1] , Vira Shendryk[2(✉)] , Sergii Tymchuk[3] ,
and Yuliia Parfenenko[2]

[1] Sumy National Agrarian University, 60 Herasyma Kondratieva Street, Sumy 40000, Ukraine
sergshen@ukr.net
[2] Sumy State University, 2 Rymskogo-Korsakova Street, Sumy 40007, Ukraine
{v.shendryk,yuliya_p}@cs.sumdu.edu.ua
[3] Kharkiv Petro Vasilenko National Technical University of Agriculture, 19 Rizdviana Street,
Kharkiv 61052, Ukraine
stym@i.ua

Abstract. This paper is devoted to the development of information technology for decision making support when controlling the parameters of the hybrid power grid (HPG), considering the meteorological forecast and changes in the required level electricity generation and consumption in the HPG. The problem of decision making in the HPG management is formed under conditions of uncertainty and incompleteness of input information, therefore, it cannot be considered as an optimization problem, but should be considered as a multidimensional and multiscale problem. In this study, models for the collection and preliminary processing of information, models for determining the level of generation from renewable energy sources (RES), models for forecasting electricity consumption, a model for assessing the quality of electricity and a decision-making model are formed, which constitute the algorithmic and information support of information technology for decision support. Management decisions are made using additional current information on the effectiveness of the established regime, as well as forecast information obtained based on the proposed models.

Keywords: Decision-making · Hybrid power grid · Information technology

1 Introduction

The innovative development of global energetics is characterized by increased requirements for the efficient use of available energy resources. This requires restructuring the infrastructure of electricity production, storage, distribution, and consumption. Thus, the importance of technological innovations aimed at energy saving, such as Smart Grid, is growing.

The Smart Grid is designed to provide real-time data on the almost instantaneous balance between electricity demand and its current level. The data management used to

© Springer Nature Switzerland AG 2021
A. Lopata et al. (Eds.): ICIST 2021, CCIS 1486, pp. 72–83, 2021.
https://doi.org/10.1007/978-3-030-88304-1_6

operate and maintain the Smart Grid requires data analysis and decision support tools to achieve grid reliability by reducing peak demands and increasing energy efficiency.

One way to increase the energy efficiency of the Smart Grid implementation is to integrate it with RES. It is economically and ecologically expedient to introduce distributed energy production from different types of RES. This approach to electricity generation has several advantages. Firstly, the usage of the HPG with RES reduces electricity losses during electricity transportation. Also, it is possible to generate electricity for consumers for their own use and give surplus energy to the centralized network [1]. Local RES can be used for electricity generation [2]. Distributed electricity generation is also characterized by low environmental pollution. The combination of different energy sources ensures the stability HPG operation, as the advantages of each RES complement each other.

Operation of the Smart Grid based on renewable energy requires the development of the HPG operation management tools such as decision support systems (DSS) for operation management, analysis of the possibility of energy production depending on constantly changing weather conditions and electricity needs of consumers.

2   The Analysis of Management Peculiarities of Hybrid Power Grids with Renewable Energy Sources

Many countries have begun to respond to the challenge of changing the concept of electricity generation, distribution, and grids reconfiguration. Thus, new markets for centralized and distributed renewable energy are emerging in all regions of the world. Over the last few years, the capacity and production of devices for converting energy from renewable sources into electricity has been growing. The estimated share of renewable energy in the total amount of produced electricity is also growing [3].

New generation electrical grids must become cyber physical system under integrated intelligent control. This transformation can provide opportunities for energy saving - for example, by changing the paradigm of "centralized" to the paradigm of "decentralized" electricity generation. This can be achieved by changing the logic of the process of electricity production and distribution and the usage of modern software that offers functional energy optimization. Therefore, the urgent problem is the digitization of the processes that accompany the energy life cycle. This can increase profits, and such a transformation aims to make better use of available energy resources, especially RES. Intelligent management of complex cyber physical systems focuses on the ability of systems to perceive information, obtain useful results and change their behavior, as well as to store knowledge gained from previous experience.

The Smart Grid can be divided into parts called MicroGrid. The key idea of Smart MicroGrid is the integration and coordination of operations of all network users, regardless of their generation. The flexibility of Smart MicroGrid control is achieved by introducing a large number of interconnections into the grid and the inclusion in the automated process of more intelligent decision-making methods that use current grid status measurement data. Typically, MicroGrid includes distributed power units with distributed generation units, distributed energy storage devices, and different types of end consumers [4]. Distributed energy sources are electrical energy sources that are not directly connected to a centralized power system [5].

To control the power grid, mainly local automatic regulation means are used, as well as periodic measures to maintain the grid efficiency. The presence of electricity additional sources at the level of consumers such as solar batteries, wind turbines greatly complicates the process of power supply management, especially in terms of coordination of operation modes of the distribution grid and subscriber power grid.

Optimal energy management of the HPG, in general, requires improvement and development of management and technical methods and tools. Today there are no effective management systems of the power grid on the consumer side. This necessitates the improvement of a methodological basis for energy management information support.

3 Problem Statement

The aim of the study is to increase the efficiency of decision-making in the management of the HPG with RES by developing models, information technology, and creating DSS to support energy management decision-making under uncertainty.

To achieve this goal, it is necessary to solve the following tasks:

- create a model of data collection and pre-processing to formalize the real-time data collection process, ensure data verification and completeness, pre-process data that is necessary to support decision-making on the HPG management;
- develop models for determining the level of electricity generation from different types of RES depending on the existing constantly changing forecast meteorological indicators in conditions of unclear input data;
- improve the model of short-term forecasting the electricity consumption level, create a model for assessing the quality of electricity produced in the HPG, develop a decision-making model that allows to choose the HPG operation mode for effective decision-making on the HPG management;
- develop algorithmic, information support of the decision-making process and information technology of decision support in the HPG management, design the architecture and develop the DSS software.

4 Decision-Making in the Management of Hybrid Power Grids with Renewable Energy Sources

Safe and efficient HPG operation is a multidimensional and large-scale problem. Typically, interactions at all operation stages affect the behavior of the entire power grid. Thus, the task of the HPG management on different stages of its life cycle can be represented by a number of interrelated activities. Information decision support in the HPG management should be described as a process that focuses on consumers who operate the HPG – end users.

The decision-making task on the HPG operation at each stage can be formalized by a tuple:

$$TDM = \langle A, E, O, D \rangle,$$

where A – a set of available alternatives of the HPG operation modes,

E – a decision-making task environment,

O – a decision-maker preferences,

D – actions on the set of alternatives.

Figure 1 shows the scheme of decision-making on the HPG management. The process of decision-making on the HPG management in BPMN notation is described in Fig. 1 [6].

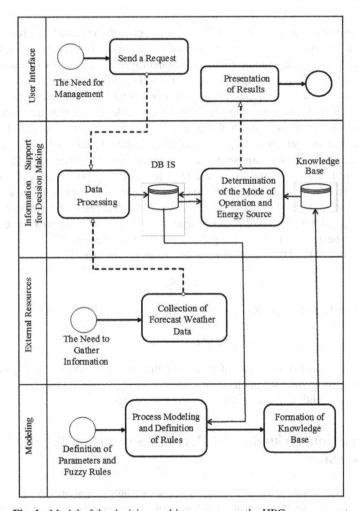

Fig. 1. Model of the decision-making process on the HPG management.

Analytical decision support on the HPG management is based on modeling. In the studied decision support process such developed models are used:

• the model of data collection and preprocessing;

- models for determining the level of electricity generation from different energy sources;
- the model for forecasting the level of electricity consumption, the model for assessing the electricity quality produced by the HPG;
- the model of fuzzy inference to determine optimal HPG operation, which provides a balance between power generation and consumption with a sufficient level of electricity quality, and gives recommendations for determining the energy source or a combination thereof.

To determine the decision on the HPG regime operation the knowledge base is used. It contains fuzzy rules, formulated on the basis of a survey of experts, and takes into account their experience with the HPG operational logic. As a result of data analysis in the process of choosing a solution in the user interface of decision-maker results and recommendations for the choice of energy source or a combination thereof are displayed.

Thus, decision-making is choosing from all available alternatives one variant that ensures effective HPG operation. In the general case, the management decision is based on defining the management goal, analysis of reliable data that characterize a particular management situation, and purposefully affects the object of management [7].

In this study it is proposed to use the DSS for modeling processes and determine sets of parameter values and fuzzy rules, to implement decision support processes on the HPG operation. To store data and organize access to them in the DSS have been created the database, which is essentially a set of interconnected data stored on a server, and is used to describe a subject area of the HPG operation management [8].

The process of the DSS functioning is described as follows:

$$Process \rightarrow O \times S_p \times Z \times D_S$$

The set of the DSS tasks Z is given as follows:

$$Z = Z_m \cup Z_{pg} \cup Z_{pu} \cup Z_f,$$

where Z_m is a set of tasks for information collecting and processing; Z_{pg} - a set of tasks for forecasting the level of electricity generation; Z_{pu} - a set of tasks for forecasting electricity consumption; Z_f is a set of decision-making tasks.

5 Information Technology of Decision Support on the HPG Management

Information technology used to manage complex technical systems, which is essentially HPG, is a set of methods and tools for collecting, processing, storing, transferring information and knowledge to solve management problems in the form of special software.

Information technology of the HPG management is a combination of models and algorithmic support of processes: collecting meteorological data and data on the current state of the HPG and each of its components, pre-processing of these data, determining the level of generation from RES or various RES combinations, forecasting the level of consumption, determining criteria for assessing electricity quality, as well as decision support for determining the effective mode of HPG operation, and data visualization.

The interaction of processes provided by the proposed information technology which consists of five stages is presented in Fig. 2 in the form of a functional model.

Stage 1. Data collection. At this stage, data are collected and validated. The collection of meteorological and sensor data is performed at three-hour intervals during the day. From the collected data set in the process of data pre-processing fuzzy data sets are formed.

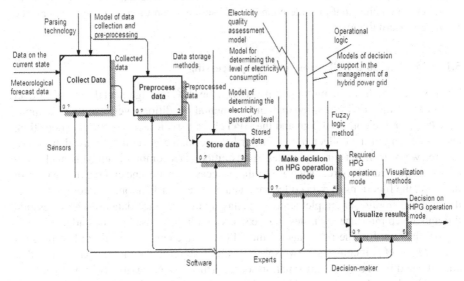

Fig. 2. Functional model of information technology of decision support on the HPG management

As a result of data extraction and sensor polling, the parameters of the HPG operation under current meteorological conditions are collected, as well as meteorological forecast data for the next three hours. This time interval is defined because usually the weather data does not change faster.

Stage 2. Preliminary data processing. At this stage, the sets of collected data are interpreted in the form of fuzzy sets for further use in models of power generation, consumption, and electricity quality assessment. Also, at this stage forms of interrelations between data are established.

Stage 3. Data storage. All collected and pre-processed data are stored in the database. The models used in the decision-making process refer to the collected and processed data. The results of the using models of determining the level of generation, consumption, forecasting and quality assessment are also stored in the database until they are used in the decision-making process.

Stage 4. The decision-making process. It carries out in accordance with the developed models and software. This process consists of subprocesses: determining the level of generation from RES or their various combinations in accordance with the forecast weather conditions, forecasting the level of electricity consumption for the next three hours, assessing the electricity quality, and the process of choosing an effective mode from possible available alternatives. The decision-making model takes into account the HPG operational logic. It uses a knowledge base consisting of fuzzy rules formed during a survey of experts. The result of this process is to determine the effective mode of the HPG operation, which is characterized by a balance between electricity consumption, and generation.

Stage 5. Results visualization. At this stage, the results are displayed for decision-makers in the user interface. Decision-maker receives recommendations for the management of the HPG operation in the form of concrete instructions for switching on or off specific switches that provide connection/disconnection of energy sources, balance load, and external network.

5.1 Model of Data Collection and Pre-processing

The first stage of the decision support process on the HPG management the real-time data collection of the HPG operation and environmental conditions, verification of compliance between the collected data and the HPG characteristics, erroneous data detection, and processing of the collected data for further use. In the general case, the data comes in three ways: from sensors and meters, transmitted via a communication channel; from external information sources such as weather forecast website, and entered by the user. In this case, the functions of data collection, data transfer, verification, preparation for further use and storage, are implemented. Displaying the collected data must be accessible through a web interface regardless of the software platform used by the end user.

All data used in the first stage of the HPG management can be described by a set $M_p = M_{po} \cup M_{pi}$. It consists of two subsets: subsets M_{po}, containing the parameters that are collected from external information sources (this data is variable over time) and are entered by the end user; subset M_{pi}, containing the calculated parameters.

Many of the parameters collected and entered by the end user M_{po}, can be represented as follows:

$$M_{po} = \{Mwo, Mres, Mg, MPl, M_{tech}\},$$

where M_{WO} is a data set of weather conditions forecast; M_{res} - a data set on the available HPG with RES configuration; M_{Pl} - a data set on the geographical location of the HPG with RES; M_g - a data set on the existing distribution networks in the area, to which it is planned to connect HPG with RES; M_{tech} - a data set that characterizes the current technical HPG condition (for example, the charge level of the battery).

Data M_{res}, M_g, M_{Pl} are entered once at user registration, data M_{wo}, M_{tech} are collected from external sources in the operational mode, affect the HPG current state, and are decisive for the management decisions support.

The successful management of the HPG with RES depends also on the possibility of timely receipt and processing of the necessary reliable meteorological data. The sources of data collection on the forecast and current weather conditions are web systems for forecasting weather, which provide ever-changing dynamic data. Therefore, it is necessary to ensure the collection, pre-processing, and accumulation of data that change over time.

The input dataset M_{wo} can be represented as a set of weather forecast data that is collected online. It is described by an ordered set of elements:

$$M_{wo} = \{(t, E, T, V)\},$$

where t – time interval for which meteorological indicators are provided on the weather website (hours);

E – level of insolation and precipitation in qualitative characteristics, (clear; partly cloudy; cloudy; cloudy and precipitation;

T – temperature, °C;

V – wind speed can also be represented by a range of values, м/c.

The set of time intervals t consists of three-hour intervals during the day, through which the monitoring indicators are collected:

$$t = \{time : time \in Z, 0 \le time \le 23\}.$$

The set of time intervals for collecting weather conditions T_w, through which they are collected, can be represented as follows:

$$T_w = \{time_n : time_n = 2 + 3(n - 1), 1 \le n \le 8\}|T_w| = 8.$$

Control for the correctness of the data extraction and storage processes lies in verification of received data, control of recording the meteorological parameters into the database, and providing a stable connection to the weather forecast website.

Information on the level of insolation and precipitation comes in qualitative characteristics described by linguistic variables, such as "clear", "weak cloudiness", "cloudiness", "heavy cloudiness". These data are characterized by additional non-uniformity in accordance with different periods (days, months, seasons). For further use, their quantitative values are determined [9].

5.2 Model of Determining the Electricity Generation Level

An efficient HPG operation mode is a balance between electricity generation and consumption. Therefore, the decision support process is to determine such a balance by choosing from the many available alternatives of HPG modes. The first stage of forming a set of alternatives of HPG modes is finding the possible level of power generation from RES under the predicted weather conditions, taking into account the HPG operational logic [10]. The object of this study is the HPG, which uses two complementary wind and solar RES for power generation.

The HPG operational logic is performed in the following sequence: the total generated electricity from solar panels and wind turbines in a certain time interval, the power demand of the consumer in this time interval are determined. It is also determined which of the RES has the highest performance under given climatic conditions. If the generated electricity amount is greater than necessary for consumption, the surplus electricity is sent to battery storage. If the battery is fully charged, the surplus electricity is sold to the external network. In case of an insufficient level of power generation, if the charge level of the total battery capacity is more than 50%, the battery uses as a power resource

[11]. The minimum battery charge is maintained to support the electricity supply in case of an emergency. The main principle of HPG operational logic is to maintain a balance between electricity generation and consumption in the autonomous mode without the electricity involvement from the external grid.

Developed mathematical models that determine the forecasted level of electricity generation depending on weather conditions are given in [12].

5.3   Model for Determining the Level of Electricity Consumption

To support decision-making in the HPG management, it is important to develop a model for electricity consumption forecasting, which will determine the effective mode of the HPG operation. It is known that electricity consumption depends on many variables (e.g., consumer load, environmental conditions, etc.). To solve this problem deterministic and probabilistic methods are used. The most common method today is regression analysis.

In most cases, information on electricity consumption may be incomplete, or it may be interval or fuzzy, so the usage of traditional methods of electricity consumption estimating and forecasting becomes a difficult task given the uncertainty and incompleteness of the information. Thus, the task of building a forecasting model of electricity consumption is related to solving the problem of input information uncertainty. One way to solve the uncertainty is to build forecasting models based on fuzzy regression analysis, which, unlike conventional regression analysis, is not based on probability theory but on possibility and fuzzy set theory.

In our case, it is obtained and investigated a regression dependence for long-term and short-term forecast of the HPG user electricity consumption. The input data are the results of electricity consumption measurements for the previous year. The developed forecast model is possible to obtain a daily schedule of electricity consumption for any day of the month of the following year, as well as an operational forecast for the next day with a breakdown into three-hour intervals.

In [13] the long-term forecast based on the results of power consumption data processing for the previous year was developed. The correction of this model for short-term forecast and its quality assessment were made on a sample of source data that were not used in long-term model development.

5.4   Electricity Quality Assessment Model

The main criterion for the ability to integrate the HPG with the centralized electricity network is the electricity quality. The term "electricity quality" is vague. Thus, a system of indicators and norms was introduced to assess the electricity quality [14]. The proposed technique does not contain complex mathematical calculations and can be easily implemented in the DSS software.

Generalized indicators of electricity quality can take values from the range [0, 1]. In this case, if you exactly follow the requirements of existing standards for assessing the electricity quality, then different from value 1 are clearly assessed as the lack of the required electricity quality. With a deeper implementation of the fuzzy approach in assessing the electricity quality, it is possible to avoid such a rigid differentiation due to the deterministic approach.

The developed methodology allows monitoring changes in the electricity quality even when the main HPG operation indicators are within acceptable values, to analyze the dynamics of changes in quality indicators, and to determine preventive measures to normalize the electricity quality. That is, it can be considered as the main criterion for managing the HPG operation [15].

The presented method of fuzzy assessment of conformity of quality indicators to the accepted fuzzy norms allows forming various integrated quality indicators taking into account features of loads in a power supply network.

The proposed method allows not only to assess the degree to which quality indicators meet the accepted standards but also to monitor changes in electricity quality even if the basic indicators do not exceed the allowable values, to form rules for managing modes of the HPG operation used in the DSS [15].

5.5 Models of Decision Support in the Management of a Hybrid Power Grid

The problem of decision-making in the HPG management is solved under conditions of uncertainty and incompleteness of the input information, which makes it impossible to formalize it in the form of an accurate mathematical model [11]. Different measurement scales with different levels of detail are used to assess the parameters that affect the HPG operation, so the decision to determine the effective mode of the HPG operation cannot be considered as an optimization problem but should be solved as a multidimensional and large-scale problem.

The task of decision-making is to find a rational solution that belongs to the set of alternatives. At the same time, there is a vagueness in the formulation of the problem, as it is present both in the description of the set of alternatives and in the criteria by which the effective solution is determined. In this case, it is advisable to use the fuzzy preference relation method [16]. If the fuzzy decision-making problem can be formalized in the form of a fuzzy mathematical programming problem (discrete programming) and the problem of achieving a fuzzy goal can be formulated, then the approach proposed by R. Bellman and L. Zadeh can be used to solve it [17]. According to this approach, the solution is considered to be the intersection of fuzzy sets of goals and possible alternatives.

The task of decision-making in the HPG management cannot be reduced to the problem of discrete programming, because it is much more complex and non-linear. Therefore, we propose to include in the solution only those alternatives that are not strictly dominated by others, fuzzy criteria and fuzzy constraints should be subsets of different universal sets. Due to the impossibility to formalize the decision-making task in the HPG management in the mathematical formulation, it is necessary to rely on the experts' knowledge about the real decision support process and take into account the operational logic of the grid. It is possible to describe the information on decision making in the form of the ratio of advantages to a set of alternatives, which can be obtained by interviewing experts, as experts have knowledge about the HPG operation, which cannot be formalized due to the complexity of these processes.

From the possible existing states of HPG operation, the one that allows achieving a balance between electricity generation and consumption with sufficient quality of generated electricity should be selected. The choice of decision from a set of alternatives should also be based on the operational logic of the grid. Therefore, in this case, an effective method of decision-making is fuzzy logic. This approach was chosen for decision support on the HPG management. It involves further development methods of the HPG control by using controllers with fuzzy logic.

The effective mode is determined taking into account the current HPG state and meteorological forecast data. It is designed to ensure effective HPG functioning in the next three hours [18].

6   Conclusions

The developed information technology provides data collection, processing, and storage that are necessary for effective HPG management. The main task of information technology is to support the decision-making on the reasonable selection of the effective mode of the HPG operation, which allows providing effective HPG management. Information technology does not affect the operation of automatic control and regulation devices but determines changes in the HPG operation mode in order to normalize the quality of electricity. It also allows efficient electricity consumption by prompt changes in the hybrid network structure by providing recommendations regarding switching off or on of RES, storage battery in the mode of charge or discharge, balance load to increase energy saving.

References

1. Daniele, M., Anna, P.: A method to improve microgrid reliability by optimal sizing PV wind plants and storage systems. In: 20th International Conference on Electricity Distribution, pp. 8–16. CIRED, Prague Czech (2009)
2. Shendryk, V., Shulyma, O., Parfenenko, Y.: The topicality and the peculiarities of the renewable energy sources integration into the Ukrainian power grids and the heating system. In: González-Prida, V., Raman, A. (eds.) Promoting Sustainable Practices through Energy Engineering and Asset Management, pp. 162–192. IGI Global, Hersey PA (2015)
3. Analysis of the market "day ahead" and the intraday market for 2019 (6 months). https://www.oree.com.ua/index.php/web/65
4. Menniti, D., Pinnarelli, A., Sorrentino, N.: A method to improve microgrid reliability by optimal sizing PV/wind plants and storage systems. In.: CIRED 2009 - The 20th International Conference and Exhibition on Electricity Distribution, Prague, Part 2, pp. 1–4 (2009)
5. Ali, A., Li, W., Hussain, R., He, X., Williams, B.W., Memon, A.H.: Overview of current microgrid policies, incentives and barriers in the European Union, United States and China. Sustainability **9** (2017). https://www.mdpi.com/2071-1050/9/7/1146/pdf
6. Object Management Group: A standard Business Process Model and Notation (BPMN). http://www.bpmn.org/
7. Dodonov, O.G., Putyatin, V.G., Valetchik, V.O.: Information, and analytical support for management decisions. Registration Storage Data Process. **7**(2), 77–93 (2005)
8. Schahovska, N.: Datawarehouse and dataspace information base of decision support system. In: 11th International Conference - The Experience of Designing and Application of CAD Systems in Microelectronics, CADSM 2011, pp. 170–173, 5744419 (2011)

9. Dotsenko, S.I., Tymchuk, S.O., Shendryk, S.O., Shulyma, O.V.: Calculation of capacity insolation for forecasting the production of electrical energy by photovoltaic panels. Bull. Petro Vasylenko Kharkiv Natl. Tech. Univ. Agric. **176**, 8–11 (2016)

10. Shendryk, V., Boiko, O., Parfenenko, Y., Shendryk, S., Tymchuk, S.: Decision making for energy management in smart grid. In: Diaz, V.G.-P., Bonilla, J.P.Z. (eds.) Handbook of Research on Industrial Advancement in Scientific Knowledge, pp. 264–297. IGI Global (2019)

11. Arcos-Aviles, D., Pascual, J., Marroyo, L., Sanchis, P., Guinjoan, F.: Fuzzy logic-based energy management system design for residential grid-connected microgrids. In.: IEEE Transactions on Smart Grid, pp. 530–543 (2016). https://doi.org/10.1109/TSG.2016.2555245

12. Tymchuk, S., Shendryk, S., Shendryk, V., Piskarov, O., Kazlauskayte, A.: Fuzzy predictive model of solar panel for decision support system in the management of hybrid grid. In: Damaševičius, R., Vasiljevienė, G. (eds.) ICIST 2019. CCIS, vol. 1078, pp. 416–427. Springer, Cham (2019). https://doi.org/10.1007/978-3-030-30275-7_32

13. Tymchuk, S., Shendryk, S., Shendryk, V., Abramenko, I., Kazlauskaite, A.: The methodology of obtaining power consumption fuzzy predictive model for enterprises. In: Ivanov, V., Trojanowska, J., Pavlenko, I., Zajac, J., Peraković, D. (eds.) DSMIE 2020. LNME, pp. 210–219. Springer, Cham (2020). https://doi.org/10.1007/978-3-030-50794-7_21

14. EN 50160:2010 Voltage Characteristics of electricity supplied by public distribution networks. https://infostore.saiglobal.com/preview/98699522296.pdf?sku=859794_saig_nsai_nsai_2045468

15. Tymchuk, S., Miroshnyk, O., Shendryk, S., Shendryk, V.: Integral fuzzy power quality assessment for decision support system at management of power network with distributed generation. In: Damaševičius, R., Vasiljevienė, G. (eds.) ICIST 2018. CCIS, vol. 920, pp. 88–97. Springer, Cham (2018). https://doi.org/10.1007/978-3-319-99972-2_7

16. Orlovsky, S.A.: Decision-making problems with fuzzy initial information. In: Science, p. 206 (1981)

17. Bellman, R.E., Zadeh, L.A.: Decision-making in a fuzzy environment. Manag. Sci. **17**(4), B-141 (1970). https://doi.org/10.1287/mnsc.17.4.B141

18. Tymchuk, S., Shendryk, S., Shendryk, V., Panov, A., Kazlauskaite, A., Levytska, T.: Decision-making model at the management of hybrid power grid. In: Lopata, A., Butkienė, R., Gudonienė, D., Sukackė, V. (eds.) ICIST 2020. CCIS, vol. 1283, pp. 60–71. Springer, Cham (2020). https://doi.org/10.1007/978-3-030-59506-7_6

Rule Driven Spreadsheet Data Extraction from Statistical Tables: Case Study

Viacheslav Paramonov[1,2](✉) [iD], Alexey Shigarov[1,2][iD], and Varvara Vetrova[1,3][iD]

[1] Matrosov Institute for System Dynamics and Control Theory, Siberian Branch,
Russian Academy of Sciences, Irkutsk, Russia
{slv,shigarov}@icc.ru
[2] Institute of Mathematics and Information Technologies, Irkutsk State University,
Irkutsk, Russia
[3] School of Mathematics and Statistics, University of Canterbury,
Christchurch, New Zealand
varvara.vetrova@canterbury.ac.nz

Abstract. Spreadsheet tables are one of the most commonly used formats to organise and store sets of statistical, financial, accounting and other types of data. This form of data representation is widely used in science, education, engineering, and business. The key feature of spreadsheet tables that they are generally created by people in order to be further used by other people rather than by automated programs. During spreadsheet creation, commonly, no consideration is given to the possibility of further automated data processing. This leads to a large variety of possible spreadsheet table structures and further complicates automated extraction of table content and table understanding. One of the key factors that influence on the quality of table understanding by machines is the correctness of the header structure, for example, position and relation between cells. In this paper, we present a case study of a tabular data extraction approach and estimate its performance on a variety of datasets. The rule-driven software platform TabbyXL was used for tabular data extraction and canonicalisation. The experiment was conducted on real-world tables of SAUS200 (The 2010 Statistical Abstract of the United States) corpora. For the evaluation, we used spreadsheet tables as they are presented in SAUS; the same tables, but with an automatically corrected header structure; and tables where the structure of the header was corrected by experts. The case study results demonstrate the importance of header structure correctness for automated table processing and understanding. The ground-truth preparation procedures, example of rules describing relationships between table elements, and results of the evaluation are presented in the paper.

Keywords: Table understanding · Data transformation · Table extraction · Table analysis · Spreadsheet · Table header · Heuristics · Case study · Rules

This work was supported by the Russian Science Foundation, grant number 18-71-10001.

A. Lopata et al. (Eds.): ICIST 2021, CCIS 1486, pp. 84–95, 2021.
https://doi.org/10.1007/978-3-030-88304-1_7

1   Introduction

Tables are one of the most general forms for representation sets of same data type. This form provides a convenient way to organise, present and distribute such data among humans. The number of spreadsheet tables presented on the Internet is estimated as more than 14 billion [3, 8]. Integration of tabular data received from different sources is frequently required to obtain the full value of information about an issue. Such data may be extracted from spreadsheet tables and stored in a database. In further, they also can be queried and joined with other data using database management systems [9, 19].

Spreadsheet tables are generally used for storing tabular data in electronic view. A spreadsheet is installed on most office and home computers. One of the popular spreadsheet software is Excel [14]. Spreadsheet tables refer to the majority of human life areas and play a significant role in business, education, science and other activities. Extraction and understanding data from spreadsheet tables is a significant challenge. Considering the huge number of tabular documents the task should be solved by software tools applying. Some of the spreadsheet tables structure and data organisation features could impede these processes.

1.1   Background

As pointed out above, normally spreadsheet tables are created specifically in a way that is easy to understand by people. Such human-centeredness of spreadsheets tables leads to the fact that arbitrary tables often may have too complex structure for machine-reading and processing, or might contain multi-format data representation, and "messy" text data (e.g. typos, non-standardised values, extra spaces) etc. [15]. It is also confirmed in [10] that tabular data formatted by people is usually different from tables that are directly generated for automated processing. Some studies estimated that more than 90% of all spreadsheets contain errors of some form [1, 11]. These errors are commonly associated with layout structure and incorrect data.

In general, tables consist of at least two main blocks: data and header [6, 8]. Automated data extraction from tables inextricably linked with correct reading and understanding of their headers. Table header may have a complicated multi-level structure with a visual merging of some cells. Visual perception, in this case, might be quite different from an actual physical structure of the cells [13]. On the other hand, table cells may have empty values,contain incorrect formulas or use different abbreviations [2]. All of the above might have a negative impact on automated table processing. Another common feature of tables that are formed by humans is the absence of metadata. This information is quite important for the interpretation of tabular information by software tools. In summary, such human-oriented data organisation leads to the difficulty of automated tables processing and data extraction.

Challenges of extraction data from spreadsheet tables by using software tools are relevant and investigate for a quite long time. There are some papers such as [2, 7] declare the approaches to tabular data organisation for increasing the efficiency of further automatic processing. Unfortunately, these recommendations in the most cases only remain as recommendations and authors create tables as these convenient for themselves. One of the treatments for improving quality of data processing results is automated table header correction. Thus the task of creating software tools for improving tabular data and the format of their representation is an actual challenge. It is assumed that quality of data representation directly affects on data extraction processes. Thereby it is also important to evaluate the influence of header correctness to table extraction and understanding processes.

1.2   Contribution

This paper presents an experimental performance evaluation of the software platform TabbyXL[1] [18] in the real-world spreadsheet data extraction scenario. The key feature of the platform is the ability for an user to create a set of rules that describe a relationship between elements of a table. This rule-set is then used for table processing. We defined a set of 18 such rules to extract tabular data from the following dataset and present them in a canonical form. These rules were developed by an expert. Note, that in a general case, different variations of rules can solve the same task. Dataset of statistical information SAUS200 and its two derivatives were used for the performance evaluation in this paper. The following sets of tables were utilised:

- tables as they are contained in the SAUS dataset;
- SAUS tables where machine-readable form of table header in Excel documents was corrected by HeadRecog tool [13] to its human-readable form;
- SAUS tables where machine-readable form of table header was corrected by an expert to its human-readable form.

We also specifically generated the ground-truth dataset. This dataset contains a canonical form of tables and their records of entries and labels. This ground-truth dataset might be useful for other researchers for further performance evaluation experiments.

2   Spreadsheet Data Preprocessing

2.1   Preliminaries

We consider real-world tables from SAUS (The 2010 Statistical Abstract of the United States) corpora. The collection[2] of 1369 SAUS tables were published by Chen & Cafarella [4]. Afterward, Nagy randomly selected 200 tables from them and shared their subset[3]. Our observations on the table properties are drawn from the study of Nagy's subset.

---

[1] https://github.com/tabbydoc/tabbyxl.
[2] http://dbgroup.eecs.umich.edu/project/sheets/datasets.html.
[3] http://tc11.cvc.uab.es/datasets/Troy_200_1.

The tables contain official statistical data of the US Census Bureau[4]. Many of them have some hand-coded modifications, such as manually split cells, messy data, hidden markup, or 0-width columns. Such artefacts can have a negative effect on automated processing of tables.

Characteristic	$del $del Selected characteristic $del	Total	Ever told had asthma	
			Number \1	Percent \2
Total \3	<chgrow;bold>Total \3	73,728	9,605	13.1
SEX \4	<1p;4q>SEX \4<c>			
Male	Male	37,686	5,550	14.8
Female	Female	36,042	4,055	11.3

Fig. 1. A fragment of a table with a hidden markup highlighted by the grey background.

Firstly, we assume that hidden markup columns can be removed without affecting the data completeness. Figure 1 shows a fragment of a table with a hidden markup. Secondly, all of 200 tables were copied to a single workbook and accompanied by tags $START and $END to be conveniently detected in sheets. The processed data are published as an archival material [17].

2.2 Tables Header Correction

We assume that the table header structure affects the performance of automatic table extraction and understanding. We define correctness here as a match between visual representation of the header (as it looks for a person and its physical form (as it is perceived by a machine) [12]. The physical layer of the table header ideally should not have empty cells (ideally each cell must contain some data) according to [2] for correct automated processing. HeadRecog was used here for the transformation of the physical layer of table headers [12,13].

An example of the visual representation of the table fragment is shown in the Fig. 2. Grey colour was used to indicate a data section of the table. Cells with white background belong to the header area. In this case, a person without any troubles would be able to identify which cells form the header section.However, in practice, a physical layer of the header often differs from a visual one. An example of this difference is shown in the Fig. 3 where the dash lines illustrate invisible for human borders of cells that form the physical layer. There are also some empty cells in the header of this table. Therefore, in this case, there is a need to transform the header structure on the physical layer to remove empty cells and preserve visual "links" between elements.

However, in practice, a visual layer often differ from a visual one. An example of this difference is shown in Fig. 3. The dash lines illustrate invisible for human borders of cells but forming the physical layer. There are some empty cells in the table header. It is need to transform header structure on physical layer to remove empty cells and preserve visual "links" between elements.

---

[4] https://www.commerce.gov/bureaus-and-offices/census.

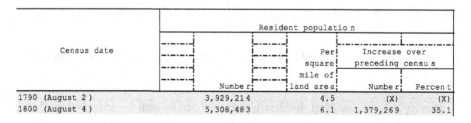

Census date	Resident population			
	Number	Per square mile of land area	Increase over preceding census	
			Number	Percent
1790 (August 2)	3,929,214	4.5	(X)	(X)
1800 (August 4)	5,308,483	6.1	1,379,269	35.1

Fig. 2. Visual representation of the table

Census date	Resident populatio n			
	Numbe r	Per square mile of land area	Increase over preceding censu s	
			Numbe r	Percen t
1790 (August 2)	3,929,214	4.5	(X)	(X)
1800 (August 4)	5,308,483	6.1	1,379,269	35.1

Fig. 3. Physical structure of the table before transformation

The HeadRecog algorithm [12,13] is used for the correction of the table header. Correction is consists of transforming the physical layer of the header to its visual one. As a result of applying this algorithm, the physical structure of cells presented in (Fig. 3) is automatically transformed to the structure which is perceived by a person (visual layer) (Fig. 4).

Census date	Resident population			
	Number	Per square mile of land area	Increase over preceding census	
			Number	Percent
1790 (August 2)	3,929,214	4.5	(X)	(X)
1800 (August 4)	5,308,483	6.1	1,379,269	35.1

Fig. 4. Physical structure of the table header after HeadRecog transformation

Analysing the content of cells, such cell style elements as borders and fonts, and cell position the decisions about cells merging are made. As a result, we got a header in which cells on a physical layer matching with cells on a visual layer.

In order to estimate the accuracy of the proposed header automatic transformation and correction by HeadRecog algorithm, each table from the SAUS dataset was also manually processed by experts. The manual processing consisted of adjusting the header cells by experts in such a way that their structure on physical and visual layers were matched. During the manual correction, experts only merged cells. As a result, we obtained a new dataset of statistical tables where machine-readable (physical) structure of the table header is equivalent to its visual structure.

It is worth to note that the manual correction is not always unique [12]. From 200 tables some abnormalities after automated correction were detected in the headers of 13 tables. Five cases of them related to choice of the left or right side of empty cells merging with non-empty cells. The results of dataset tables header structure automated transformation are shown in the Table 1.

Table 1. Results of header structure correction

Number of cells in SAUS200	8028
Cells after HeadRecog transformation	3795
Cells after manual transformation by experts	3768
Proportion of HeadRecog correctly identified cells	0.932
Share of HeadRecog incorrectly merged cells	0.025
Share of HeadRecog incorrectly tables headers structure recovery	0.045

The tables of SAUS dataset and the same tables but with automatically and manually corrected headers were used for evaluating the effectiveness of automated tabular data extraction process. We assume that the implemented method of table header correction may facilitate automated data extraction from hand-coded tables represented in spreadsheets.

3 Spreadsheet Data Extraction

In this Section, we consider the issues the data extraction from statistical tables driven by user-defined rules. The main ideas we exploit are as follows:

- Most tables are designed with a few common tricks of table layout, formatting, and content.
- People are able to use these tricks in order to understand tabular data correctly.
- The tricks can be set out as formal rules to analyse and interpret the tables.
- The rules enable to automatically extract data from the tables.
- Such rules can be user-defined, i. e. be explicitly separated from inference algorithms.

In our case study, we use CRL, a domain-specific language, to specify rules for recovering the table logical structure missing in the original source. In contrast to general-purpose rule languages, CRL allows expressing user-defined rules in terms of the table understanding [16]. CRL-rules are intended to map explicit features (layout, style, and text of cells) of an arbitrary table into its implicit semantics (entries, labels, and categories) [16,18]. Only 18 CRL-rules[5] allowed

---

[5] https://github.com/tabbydoc/tabbyxl/wiki/example-saus#ruleset.

us to process the most of source tables with an admissible quality. It should be noted that users may use both our set of CRL-rules and their own also. The functions of our set of rules are listed below:

- Rule #1 removes next line characters from the textual content of a cell.
- Rules #2-3 creates and categorise a label in a cut-in cell.
- Rules #4-5 creates and categorise a label in a stub-head cell.
- Rule #6 creates and categorise a label in a cut-in cell.
- Rule #7 creates and categorise a label in a head cell.
- Rule #8 creates an entry in a body cell.
- Rules #9-13 create a parent-child pair from two labels in stub cells (each rule for a for a separate layout trick used in a stub).
- Rule #14 associates a label originated from a stub cell with an entry.
- Rule #15 creates a parent-child pair from two labels in head cells.
- Rule #16 creates a parent-child pair from two labels in cut-in cells.
- Rule #17 associates a label originated from a head cell with an entry.
- Rule #18 associates a label originated from a cut-in cell with an entry.

Each rule consists of a left-hand side (LHS) specifying conditions and constraints on querying facts and a right-hand side (RHS) listing actions performed on these facts. For example, LHS of the Rule #2 has only one condition to query cells, which are placed on the top row (constraint 1), not blank (constraint 2), not matched to (\\u005c[0-9]+)|([Uu]nit indicator) by value (constraint 3). Its RHS includes 3 actions to annotate each cell by "STUB" tag (action 1), to create a new label from the text content of the cell (action 2), to associate this label with the category named "STUB" (action 3).

```
when
  cell c: cl == 1, !blank,
    !text.matches("(\\u005c[0-9]+)|([Uu]nit indicator)")
then
  set tag "STUB" to c
  new label c
  set category c.tag to c.label
end
```

TabbyXL enables automated translation of CRL-rules to Java source code. The generated Java classes are ready to be used without additional modifications. A snippet of the Java source code generated from Rule #2 is shown below.

```
@Override
public void accept(CTable table) {
  Iterator<CCell> cIterator = table.getCells();
  while (cIterator.hasNext()) {
    CCell c = cIterator.next();
    if ((c.getCl() == 1) && (!c.isBlank()) &&
      (!c.getText().matches("(\\u005c[0-9]+)|([Uu]nit indicator)"))) {
```

```
        c.setTag("STUB");
        c.newLabel();
        c.getLabel().setCategory(c.getTag());
} } }
```

TabbyXL also allows us to serialise Java file objects as Maven project that is ready to be built. As a result, we obtain an executable Java application including all dependencies. The application extracts data from statistical tables and stores them in a canonical form. This feature allows to users who are not familiar with the CLR-language to generate rules.

4 Experimental Results

4.1 Ground-Truth Preparing

To evaluate the effectiveness of the developed rules, we prepared referenced canonicalised tables as the ground-truth data, covering Nagy's subset. These tables were automatically generated from sources with manually corrected headers and colour annotation.

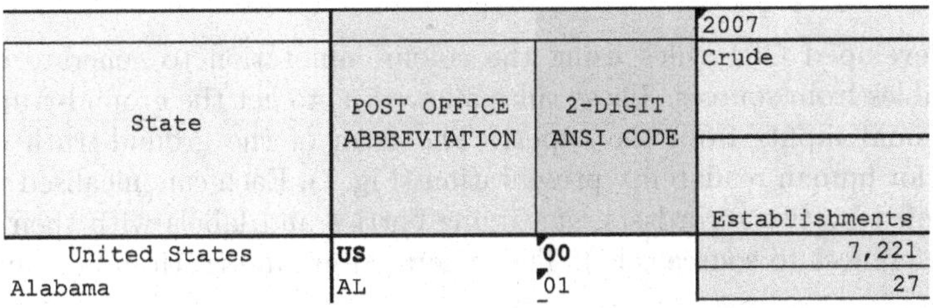

State	POST OFFICE ABBREVIATION	2-DIGIT ANSI CODE	2007	
			Crude	
			Establishments	
United States	US	00	7,221	
Alabama	AL	01	27	

Fig. 5. A fragment of a coloured table with 3 stub columns.

The experts manually assigned a predefined background colour to each functional region of cells in the following manner:

- the grey highlights data cells;
- the pink depicts head cells.

The green is used to designate cut-in cells: the dark and light shades correspond to parent and child relationships respectively. The shades of yellow correspond to stub head cells, each for a separate category (Fig. 5).

When there is a hierarchy of headings in a stub, then we use shades of blue to indicate levels of this hierarchy. We assume that any cell in a nesting level produces a child label for a parent label produced from the corresponding spanning cell. While top-level cells remain white, cells placed on the rest levels are designated by shades from light to dark blue depending on the nesting of their level (Fig. 6).

AWARD AND RECIPIENCY STATUS	2001			
	ALL CUSTODIAL PARENTS			
	Total		Mothers	Fathers
	Number	Percent distribut ion		
unit indicator	(1,000)		(1,000)	(1,000)
Total	13,383	(X)	11,291	2,092
With child support agreement or award \1	7,916	(X)	7,110	807
Supposed to receive payments in year shown	6,924	100.0	6,212	712
Actually received payments in year shown	5,119	73.9	4,639	480
Received full amount	3,099	44.8	2,821	278
Received partial payments	2,020	29.2	1,818	202
Did not receive payments in year shown	1,804	26.1	1,573	232
Child support not awarded	5,466	(X)	4,181	1,285
MEAN INCOME AND CHILD SUPPORT	(Dollars)			
Received child support payments in year shown:				
Mean total money income (dollars)	29,008	(X)	28,258	36,255

Fig. 6. A fragment of a coloured table with a hierarchy of headings in the stub.

We developed CRL-rules using the colour annotation to generate canonicalised tables from sources. These rules allowed us to get the ground-truth data with minimal inputs from the expert. The form of the ground-truth data is designed for human readability presentation (Fig. 7). Each canonicalised table is accompanied by two recordsets, specifying entries and labels with their provenance (references to source cells). The generated ground-truth data is available in [17].

DATA	HEAD	HEAD1	STUB
13 383	2001 | all custodial parents | total | number	unit indicator | (1,000)	award and recipiency status | total
(x)	2001 | all custodial parents | total | percent distribution		award and recipiency status | total
11 291	2001 | all custodial parents | mothers	unit indicator | (1,000)	award and recipiency status | total
7 916	2001 | all custodial parents | total | number	unit indicator | (1,000)	award and recipiency status | with child support agreement or award \1
(x)	2001 | all custodial parents | total | percent distribution		award and recipiency status | with child support agreement or award \1

Fig. 7. A fragment of a canonicalised table.

4.2   Performance Evaluation

We evaluated the performance of the application generated from 18 CRL-rules on two main stages of data extraction from spreadsheet tables, namely: (i) extracting entries and labels from cells, (ii) recovering relationships (entry-label and label-label pairs) of extracted data items. We considered 3 cases of the source data: (i) original tables without any correction, (ii) tables corrected automatically by HeadRecog algorithms, (iii) tables corrected manually by 3 experts.

The results of processing all three cases of the source data were compared with the ground-truth data (Table 2). For the performance estimation, the standard metrics in the information retrieval recall and precision were used [5]. The numerator in a fraction is a number of correct predictions of entries and labels, and their relationships (entry-label, label-label pairs).

The results confirm our initial assumption that the correctness of the table header increases significantly when the quality of data extraction is increased in Table 2. Concretely, recall for entries and relationships in the SAUS without any correction is much lower than recall after table headers were corrected by HeadRecog or experts.

The experiment also demonstrates the possibility of creating a set of rules that allow processing and data extraction from tables with a diverse data organisation structure. At the same time, the acceptable quality of data extraction is maintained.

Table 2. The results of the performance evaluation

	Entries	Labels	Entry-Label Pairs	Label-Label Pairs
Original tables				
Recall	0.8783 (120122/136766)	0.7544 (15155/20089)	0.6896 (267236/387499)	0.6392 (11471/17946)
Precision	0.8189 (120122/146695)	0.8207 (15155/18467)	0.7668 (267236/348509)	0.7007 (11471/16371)
After correction of headers by using HeadRecog				
Recall	0.8791 (120229/136766)	0.8617 (17310/20089)	0.8379 (324679/387499)	0.7557 (13561/17946)
Precision	0.8310 (120229/144682)	0.8571 (17310/20195)	0.8108 (324679/400435)	0.7716 (13561/17575)
After correction of headers by the experts				
Recall	0.9928 (135785/136766)	0.9360 (18804/20089)	0.9549 (370022/387499)	0.8391 (15058/17946)
Precision	0.9420 (135785/144148)	0.9446 (18804/19906)	0.9275 (370022/398967)	0.8636 (15058/17437)

5 Conclusions

This work focuses on approaches for extraction and canonicalisation data from spreadsheet tables with statistical information and evaluation of its performance. We utilised the TabbyXL platform here for performance evaluation of data extraction process from real-world datasets of tables. The set of 18 rules that allow to identify tabular elements was created. These rules could be adapted to a different case-study on an ad-hoc basis. Two derivatives sets were obtained from the SAUS: 1) A dataset where the structure of table headers were automatically corrected by HeadRecog; 2) with the structure of headers corrected by experts.

We generated a new ground-truth dataset which is a canonical form of the SAUS. This dataset and derivatives from the SAUS are utilised in the performance evaluation experiments. The results of the case-study experimentally demonstrate that the correction of the header structure improves the quality of the table canonicalisation. In addition, the ground-truth dataset, available in [17], might be of use to other researchers in order to estimate their own approaches for tabular data extraction and canonicalisation.

References

1. Abraham, R., Erwig, M.: Header and unit inference for spreadsheets through spatial analyses. In: Proceedings of the 2004 IEEE Symposium on Visual Languages and Human Centric Computing (VLHCC), vol. 00, pp. 165–172, September 2004. https://doi.org/10.1109/VLHCC.2004.29
2. Broman, K.W., Woo, K.H.: Data organization in spreadsheets. Am. Stat. **72**(1), 2–10 (2018). https://doi.org/10.1080/00031305.2017.1375989
3. Cafarella, M.J., Halevy, A., Wang, D.Z., Wu, E., Zhang, Y.: WebTables: exploring the power of tables on the web. Proc. VLDB Endow. **1**(1), 538–549 (2008). https://doi.org/10.14778/1453856.1453916
4. Chen, Z., Cafarella, M.: Automatic web spreadsheet data extraction. In: Proceedings of the 3rd International Workshop on Semantic Search Over the Web - SS@ 2013. ACM Press (2013). https://doi.org/10.1145/2509908.2509909
5. Dalianis, H.: Evaluation metrics and evaluation. In: Clinical Text Mining, pp. 45–53. Springer, Cham (2018). https://doi.org/10.1007/978-3-319-78503-5_6
6. Doush, I.A., Pontelli, E.: Detecting and recognizing tables in spreadsheets. In: Doermann, D.S., Govindaraju, V., Lopresti, D.P., Natarajan, P. (eds.) The Ninth IAPR International Workshop on Document Analysis Systems, DAS 2010, Boston, Massachusetts, USA, 9–11 June 2010, pp. 471–478. ACM International Conference Proceeding Series, ACM (2010). https://doi.org/10.1145/1815330.1815391
7. Ellis, S.E., Leek, J.T.: How to share data for collaboration. Am. Stat. **72**(1), 53–57 (2018). https://doi.org/10.1080/00031305.2017.1375987. pMID: 32981941
8. Koci, E., Thiele, M., Romero, O., Lehner, W.: Table identification and reconstruction in spreadsheets. In: Dubois, E., Pohl, K. (eds.) CAiSE 2017. LNCS, vol. 10253, pp. 527–541. Springer, Cham (2017). https://doi.org/10.1007/978-3-319-59536-8_33
9. Liu, Y., Mitra, P., Giles, C.L.: Identifying table boundaries in digital documents via sparse line detection. In: Proceedings of the 17th ACM Conference on Information and Knowledge Management, pp. 1311–1320 (2008)
10. McCallum, Q.E.: Bad Data Handbook. O'Reilly, Sebastopol (2013)
11. Panko, R.R.: Spreadsheet errors: what we know. What we think we can do. CoRR abs/0802.3457 (2008)
12. Paramonov, V., Shigarov, A., Vetrova, V.: Table header correction algorithm based on heuristics for improving spreadsheet data extraction. In: Lopata, A., Butkienė, R., Gudonienė, D., Sukackė, V. (eds.) ICIST 2020. CCIS, vol. 1283, pp. 147–158. Springer, Cham (2020). https://doi.org/10.1007/978-3-030-59506-7_13
13. Paramonov, V., Shigarov, A., Vetrova, V., Mikhailov, A.: Heuristic algorithm for recovering a physical structure of spreadsheet header. In: Borzemski, L., Świątek, J., Wilimowska, Z. (eds.) ISAT 2019. AISC, vol. 1050, pp. 140–149. Springer, Cham (2020). https://doi.org/10.1007/978-3-030-30440-9_14
14. Rahman, S., Mack, K., Bendre, M., Zhang, R., Karahalios, K., Parameswaran, A.: Benchmarking spreadsheet systems. In: Proceedings of the 2020 ACM SIGMOD International Conference on Management of Data. SIGMOD 2020, pp. 1589–1599.

Association for Computing Machinery, New York (2020). https://doi.org/10.1145/3318464.3389782

15. Shigarov, A., Khristyuk, V., Mikhailov, A.: TabbyXL: software platform for rule-based spreadsheet data extraction and transformation. SoftwareX **10**, 100270 (2019). https://doi.org/10.1016/j.softx.2019.100270

16. Shigarov, A., Khristyuk, V., Mikhailov, A., Paramonov, V.: TabbyXL: rule-based spreadsheet data extraction and transformation. In: Damaševičius, R., Vasiljevienė, G. (eds.) ICIST 2019. CCIS, vol. 1078, pp. 59–75. Springer, Cham (2019). https://doi.org/10.1007/978-3-030-30275-7_6

17. Shigarov, A., Paramonov, V., Khristyuk, V.: Spreadsheet data extraction from real-world tables of saus (the 2010 statistical abstract of the united states): Case study, April 2021. https://doi.org/10.6084/m9.figshare.14371055.v2, https://figshare.com/articles/dataset/Spreadsheet_Data_Extraction_from_Real-World_Tables_of_SAUS_The_2010_Statistical_Abstract_of_the_United_States_Case_Study/14371055/2

18. Shigarov, A.O., Mikhailov, A.A.: Rule-based spreadsheet data transformation from arbitrary to relational tables. Inf. Syst. **71**, 123–136 (2017). https://doi.org/10.1016/j.is.2017.08.004

19. Song, J., Koutra, D., Mani, M., Jagadish, H.V.: GeoFlux: hands-off data integration leveraging join key knowledge. In: Proceedings of the 2018 International Conference on Management of Data - SIGMOD 2018. ACM Press (2018). https://doi.org/10.1145/3183713.3193546

Semantic Interoperability of CV Builder: Problem and Practical Solutions

Svetlana Kubilinskiene[(✉)] [iD], Valdona Judickaite-Zukovske [iD], and Tatjana Liogiene [iD]

Vilniaus Kolegija, University of Applied Sciences, Saltoniškių str. 58, 08105 Vilnius, Lithuania
{s.kubilinskiene,v.judickaite,t.liogiene}@eif.viko.lt

Abstract. The article presents the results and practical solutions of the Operational Programme for the European Union Funds' Investments in 2014–2020 project "Automated CV Builder Based on Artificial Intelligence Module". The article discusses the problem of structuring curriculum vitae (CV) data, specifics of evaluation process, evaluation of candidate's technical and personal skills, data validity, and data presentation problems. The results of the carried out empirical research and the systematic review of the literature are described, and the new CV builder information model is presented.

Keywords: Curriculum vitae · Semantic interoperability · CV information model

1 Introduction

Widespread internet access has changed various aspects of our lives, including the search for job offers. Although, internet usage makes it easier to find job offers and send candidates their CVs, this has had an unfavorable impact on the work of HR managers handling the recruitment process. It has become difficult for HR managers to choose from an abundance of candidates those who best meet job requirements and should be invited for an interview. One stage in recruitment process management is the problem of structuring CV data.

The article presents the research results and practical solutions of the Operational Programme for the European Union Funds' Investments in 2014–2020 project "Automated CV Builder Based on Artificial Intelligence Module".

The paper is organized into the following interrelated sections. The systematic review of "Curriculum Vitae" and the review findings and the results of the comparative analysis are presented in Subsects. 1.1 and 1.2. Research methodology is presented in Sect. 2. Results of two empirical research are provided in Sect. 3, information of the personal characteristics of the candidate is analyzed in Subsect. 3.3 and proposed CV Information Model are provided in Subsect. 3.4 and the last Section presents the overall conclusion of the presented research.

© Springer Nature Switzerland AG 2021
A. Lopata et al. (Eds.): ICIST 2021, CCIS 1486, pp. 96–108, 2021.
https://doi.org/10.1007/978-3-030-88304-1_8

1.1   Systematic Review

In order to identify the information structure of the CV, basic systematic literature review method devised by Kitchenham [1] has been used. The systematic review was carried out in November 2019 via the Web of Science database. Only peer-reviewed articles in English published in 2014–2019 were chosen. Table 1 provides the protocol on the citation database Web of Science.

In the first stage, all the last five-year articles using the keyword "Curriculum Vitae" were found. As the result, 128 articles were selected.

Table 1. Search results in the database.

Result	Protocol
128	(TS = (Curriculum Vitae)) AND Language = (English) AND Document Types = (Article) Databases = SCI-EXPANDED, SSCI, A&HCI, CPCI-S, CPCI-SSH, ESCI Timespan = Last 5 years

The second stage was dedicated to the analysis of titles and abstracts subject to filtering by the mentioned criteria and 28 original articles were identified. However, due to the peculiarities of the research question, it was difficult to clear articles by analyzing only the summary. Therefore, it was decided to search for further information throughout the text. Finally, 22 articles were chosen.

1.2   Review Findings and the Results of the Comparative Analysis

This section analyses the results of the systematic review in order to answer the research questions. The selected scientific articles analyse the following aspects: 1. The problem of structuring CV data; 2. The specifics of CV information evaluation; 3. Data validity; 4. The problem of data presentation. Only the results of the first aspect are detailed in the article. The second aspect presents the methods of evaluating CV information, but is not analyzed in the article. The full review of all analysed aspects is provided in Appendix A of the project technical document.

The reviewed articles analyse CVs of different target groups: the researchers most analyse academic CVs (12 articles, 54.5%), CVs applying for web designer positions (1 article, 4.5%), medical career CVs (6 articles, 27.3%).

Review of CV Data Field Analysis

Only 7 articles analyse the structure of elements or present CV information.

The authors of the article [2] give recommendations to medical students on how to submit a CV application to Electronic Residency Application Service, ERAS.

The authors [3] analyse CVs collected from various sources and present the CV3 model, which divides the data into 7 categories. In this model, the authors [3] distinguish 4 types of data: (1) nominal data: general, personal, contact information, etc.; (2)

hierarchical data: professional skills and competences; (3) ordinal data: social skills and languages; (4) Spatio-temporal data: professional and educational history.

The authors of the articles [4, 5] recommend providing more information to medical staff when applying for various job positions or scholarships.

Table 2. Comparative analysis of the CV elements.

CV data element	Cover letter	Personal details	Contact Information	Career statement	Education and qualifications	Present position	Career history	Lectures	Research Experience	Voluntary/work experience	Audit and quality improvement work	Management and leadership	Prizes and awards	Certifications	Publications and presentations	Teaching experience	Training courses and educational symposia	Information technology skills	Professional and society memberships	Personal interests	Referees	Conflict of interest statement	Consultations	Service
[2]	-	+	A	-	+	B	+	+	+	-	-	-	+	+	+	-	-	-	+	F	-	-	-	-
[3]	-	+	+	-	+	-	+	-	-	-	-	-	C	C	D	-	D	E	-	G	-	-	-	-
[4]	+	+	A	+	+	+	+	+	-	-	+	+	+	+	-	+	+	+	+	+	+	+	-	-
[5]	-	+	A	-	+	-	+	-	-	-	-	-	+	+	+	+	-	-	+	-	-	-	+	+

A - Personal details; B - Career history; C - Professional qualifications; D - Education and training; E - Skill set self-evaluation; F - Partly, skills or interests; G – Other information.

The researchers from Pakistan [6] and [7] present ORCID (Open Researcher and Contributor ID) authors' identification system (http://orcid.org/) to promote this concept in developing countries. ORCID is a not-for-profit organization that has been trying to solve the problem of the identity of authors in various elements since 2012. ORCID identifiers are presented as 16-digit alphanumeric characters, e.g. http://orcid.org/xxxx-xxxx-xxxx-xxxx. A Web page is created for an author with a reference to a URL, e.g. http://orcid.org/0000-0002-3203-418X, where the following is given: (1) name, surname; (2) brief biography; (3) education (year, degree earned and main field of study); (4) work history (employer's name, date of employment and position); (5) funding section (type, name of project, brief description, amounts, dates and grant numbers); (6) contribution section (journal articles, books or book chapters, dissertations, conference presentations, intellectual property and datasets).

ORCID records may contain unique identifiers, such as digital object identifiers (DOI), "PubMed IDs", patent numbers, and many other external IDs. In their ORCID profile, researchers may have a peer review section for an additional fee, which avoids "fake" comments from reviewers.

The researchers from the Latin American region use the "CvLAC", also known as the "Curriculum Lattes" system, to manage academic CVs. The authors [8] have noted that CV standardization is insufficient. This is also noted by the authors of the article [9].

Table 2 presents the results of the comparative analysis of the CV elements described in the articles.

Review of CV Information Evaluation

Natural language processing methods [9], decision support systems (DSS) [9], multi-criteria decision support method [10], Semantic Web technologies [11, 12], innovative approaches using the relevance factor with vocabulary scoring [13], data visualization [3], comparison of CVs using calibration, branching out and repair methods [14], system of indicators [8] are used in order to evaluate CVs. The full review of methods is provided in Appendix A of the project "Automated CV Builder Based on Artificial Intelligence Module. Technical document".

Summarizing the Results of the Systematic Review of the literature, it can be stated that:

1. There is a need for ways and means to ensure more efficient CV creation and search, CV evaluation and recruitment of candidates.
2. There is no generally accepted standard of curriculum vitae. The quality of the CV and its structured presentation have a significant impact on CV evaluation and recruitment processes. HR managers find it difficult to find among all the candidates those who best match the requirements of the job and should be invited for an interview.
3. When analysing the structure of the CV, it is noted that the main information to be presented can be summarised in the following categories: (1) Contact details and personal information; (2) Education; (3) Work history. Less frequently presented elements: (1) Abilities; (2) Publications; (3) Certificates; (4) Awards.
4. When analysing the structure of researchers' CVs, it was noted that, to describe the qualifications and careers of researchers, which are analysed in the evaluation of both scientists and university science, technology and innovation results, more structured elements are needed: (1) Audit and quality improvement tasks; (2) Management and leadership; (3) Training courses and education symposiums; (4) Membership in professional and public organizations; (5) Referees; (6) Consultations; (7) Experience as a researcher; (8) Teaching experience; (9) Volunteering experience.
5. A variety of solutions and technologies are used for CV evaluation process. Decisions depend on how a CV is recognized. A generally accepted CV standard gives the possibility to store a CV in XML format that can be converted to OWL or stored as RDF files.
6. When analysing the presentation of CV data, it is noted that there is a convenient way to submit a CV using a portfolio managing and filling in a person's achievements. CV data is available at a unique URL where publications, and other resources that are mentioned in the CV can be submitted.

2 Methodology

2.1 Empirical Research

In order to highlight the basic information, the employer needs about the candidate for a particular position, empirical research was carried out in companies. The research was in English and Lithuanian. Countries such as Finland, Poland, Sweden, Denmark, Norway and Lithuania participated in the research.

A total of 1,347 responses were received, including the results of telephone and e-mail surveys of all countries. This represents 5.08% of the total number of respondents (the total number of respondents is 26,500). The responses were received from 79 Lithuanian companies and 1,268 foreign companies.

The analysis of the obtained survey data helped determine: (1) what information is missing in candidates' CVs; (2) how employee searches are conducted; (3) where employers post their job advertisements. This made it possible to establish the relationship between the real usefulness of CV tools and employers' needs.

After summarizing the results obtained, the following issues are not clear: (1) the structure of the CV, which best reflects the needs of employers and jobseekers, (2) compatibility of various CV structure tools.

Regarding the results of the employers' survey and the issues raised, the analysis of CV websites and systematic review of the literature were carried out.

2.2 Research of CV Websites

During the analysis of CV websites using the keyword "cv building tools", top tools were selected and 31 websites were reviewed: Canva, Visme, ResumeCoach, EuroPass, Venngage, Bitebale, Easy Prompter, CakeResume, VisualCV, Adobe Spark, Wordpress, Wix, Resumonk, SlashCV, CVmkr, ResumeGenius, ResumeCompanion, CraftCV, Zety, ResumeBuilder, MyPerfectResume, GreatSampleResume, Resume, Enhancv, Kick-Resume, ResumeMakerPro, Pongo, FreeResumeTemplates, CV-Template, Creddle, StudentJob.

CV information obtained from websites was organized according to the following criteria: 1. What types of CV builder tools are used; 2. Professional qualifications or other options for responsibility; 3. Language selection; 4. Adaptability to different regions of the world; 5. CV Europass support capability; 6. Targeting different target user groups; 7. Adaptability to screen size; 8. Ways to log in to a CV platform; 9. Ways to import a CV file; 10. CV format types; 11. CV storage format; 12. Types of elements used to fill in a CV; 13. Ways to submit a CV on a job search platform; 14. CV element groups.

3 Results and Discussion

3.1 Results of the Empirical Research

During the survey employers were asked: 1. What information do you lack in candidates' CVs? 2. What are the ways you are looking for employees? 3. Where do you post your job advertisements?

The results of the first question "What information do you lack in candidates' CVs?" are presented below (see Fig. 1).

The results of the survey show that employers most miss information about personality competencies in candidates' CVs. This represents 35.7% of employers in the EU countries and 20.5% of Lithuanian employers. Secondly, both groups of respondents (the European Union – 27.1%, Lithuania – 10.3%) want to see information about professional competencies in CVs. 27.7% of employers in the European Union report that candidates do not provide information about salary expectations. In addition, employers in the European Union lack information about candidates' education (17.4%) and they lack candidates' portfolios (25.2%). The special need to improve the content of CVs is seen in the countries of the European Union. In Lithuania, 48.7% of the respondents usually do not lack anything in CVs submitted by candidates, while in the European Union this index is only 0.1%. Such a situation in Lithuania may be influenced by the fact that 14.1% of candidates come directly to the employer.

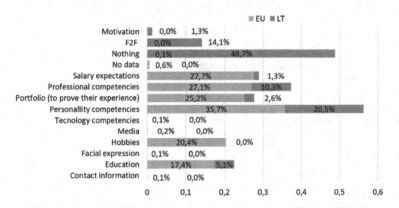

Fig. 1. Question "What information do you lack in candidates' CVs?"

The results of the second question "What are the ways you are looking for employees?" are presented below (see Fig. 2).

Most employers, both in the European Union and Lithuania, look for employees on job sites (40.9% and 24.4% respectively). Both groups of respondents take recommendations seriously (the European Union – 22.1%, Lithuania – 28.2%). In the European Union countries, it is also popular to contact recruitment agencies when looking for employees (27.2%) and use social network LinkedIn services (21.8%).

The results of the third question "Where do you post your job advertisements?" are presented below (see Fig. 3).

Most Lithuanian employers and the vast majority of employers in the European Union publish their job advertisements on social networks. Facebook is popular in Lithuania (23.1%), and Facebook (42.6%) and LinkedIn (41.6%) in the European Union countries. Lithuanian employers often publish their advertisements on job sites (12.8%), use labour exchange (24.4%) services or do not even publish their job advertisements anywhere (21.8%).

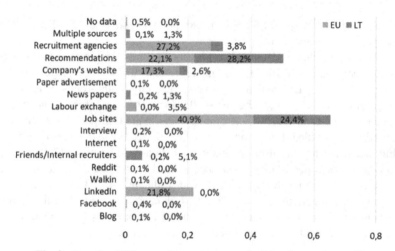

Fig. 2. Question "What are the ways you are looking for employees?"

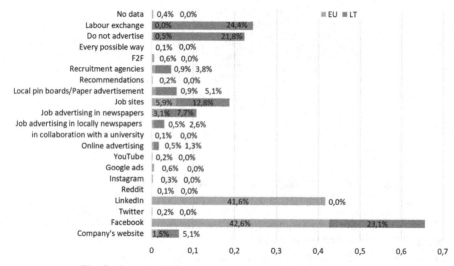

Fig. 3. Question "Where do you post your job advertisements?"

3.2 Results of the Research of CV Websites

After analyzing the CV websites, five types of tools were identified: 13 CV builder tools (41.9%), 2 video CV builder tools (6.5%), 3 tools (9.7%) that had the option of CV builder and job search. There are 2 CV website builder tools (6.5%) and 11 CV builder tools with a link to job search (35.5%). To sum up, the market is dominated by ordinary CV builder tools.

The classification of professional qualifications is included in the 12 tools examined (38.7%). The majority, i.e. the remaining 19 (61.3%) has no classification of professional qualifications or any other options for responsibility included. Almost half of the tools examined 15 (48.4%) have language selection, while the rest 16 (51.6%) do not.

There have been efforts to develop tools that apply to all regions, 23 tools 74.2%. 5 tools (16.1%) are applied to the US job market, 1 (3.2%) for European countries, 1 (3.2%) for the UK and 1 (3.2%) for Taiwan (Asia).

The vast majority of the tools examined do not rely on any CV builder standard. There are 26 (83.9%) such tools. The minority, i.e. only 5 tools (16.1%) offers the possibility to support the Europass CV form.

More than half of the tools (23 (74.2%)) are appropriate for the different target groups. One (3.2%) tool is IT sector-oriented, one tool (3.2%) is exclusively designed for graduates, students and schoolchildren, 2 tools are allocated to website developers (6.5%) and 4 tools (12.9%) are oriented towards users of design tools.

Most tools (22 (71%)) are adapted for desktop displays and only a third of the tools (9 tools (29%)) are adapted to work not only on desktop displays, but also on smart devices.

The three most commonly offered ways to log in to CV platforms are as follows: Facebook (19 tools. (31.1%)), e-mail (18 tools (29.5%)), Google (15 tools (24.6%)). Other ways to log in are: LinkedIn (6 tools (9.8%)), Twitter (2 tools (3.3%)) and AdobeID (1 tool (3,2%)).

Most of the tools analyzed do not allow importing CV files (20 tools 54.1%). 11 (29.7%) tools allow importing CVs from LinkedIn, 5 (13.5%) allow from PC and one tool allows importing files from GoogleDrive/Onedrive/Dropbox.

Almost all CV builder tools (29 tools, 93.5%) support A4 CV format. There various CV storage formats offered. Dominated by PDF (27 tools, 42.2%), TXT (11 tools, 17.2%) and XML (11 tools, 17.2%) formats.

Most tools (25, 80.6%) use structured data elements to fill in and only 6 tools (19.4%) are unstructured. There is a great number of ways to publish a CV. Most tools allow CV publishing on the website or providing a link to a CV (25 tools, 20%). 14 tools (11.2%) allow publishing on job platform, Twitter and FB. 11 tools (8.8%) support publishing on LinkedIn.

Less than half of the tools (14, 45.2%) publish CVs on various job search platforms. The most popular platforms are Livecareer, Indeed.com and ZipRecruiter.

The most popular CV element groups used in tools are shown in Fig. 4. Almost all tools have CV element groups such as contact information, personal data, career goals, education, work experience, skills and abilities, professional qualification, and additional information. The least important is a portfolio (4.2%).

Most CV builder tools are limited to a variety of self-assessment scales for skills and abilities. This carries the risk that a candidate may overestimate or underestimate his/her skills and abilities. In order to sidestep the issue, Europass suggests attaching a file, which can be a certificate or other proof of the specified skills and abilities. There are CV tools (e.g. KickResume, Creddle) built in with LinkedIn that take professional and personal data about a candidate from LinkedIn. The skills and abilities mentioned on LinkedIn are verified by testing a candidate. Several CV builder tools refer a candidate to other knowledge testing tools (e.g. Indeed, InterviewMocha, etc.) to test skills and abilities.

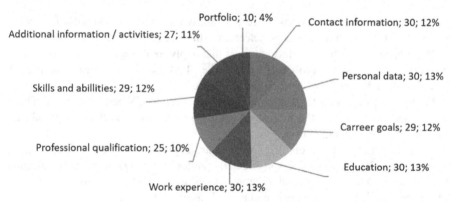

Fig. 4. CV element groups.

3.3 IBM Artificial Intelligence Tool for Personal Dimensions, Values and Needs Assessment

According to the results of the Empirical Research, it can be stated that when employers are looking for future employees, there is a lack of information about their personal characteristics. Thus, in the process of finding an employee, employers need to assess not only the subject-specific but also the personal characteristics of the candidate.

In psychology, a number of methods are developed for the assessment of personality skills. According to the source [15] in modern psychology, the most popular method for analysing personality skills is the Big Five dimensions of personality. The Big Five dimensions of personality model makes it possible to assess an employee's satisfaction with the work performed. The study described in the source [16] suggests that personality skills have an impact on professional success. According to [17], it is possible to assess a person using social networks, and only personal texts submitted on the social network are sufficient for this. The tool developed requires a large number of Twitter messages [17]. The source [18] describes a study of personality values based on messages in the social network Reddit. The authors say that the prediction of a person's values can be made on the basis of the consumption of words corresponding to values on social media. IBM has conducted a series of studies to assess whether personality characteristics from social media data can predict people's behavior and preferences. IBM offers a service "Personality Insights" for combined assessment of the Big Five personality traits, and values and needs, the API of which is described in the source [19].

3.4 Proposed CV Information Model

Based on the results in Sects. 3.1–3.3 and the results of the systematic review, the CV information model (CVim) has been proposed which will allow (1) effective organization of the needs of employers and job seekers; (2) realization of compatibility of different tools in CV saving CV in XML format.

The CVim is designed that a person's curriculum vitae provides sufficient information for an employer, which can be quickly assessed and visualized on several levels. The structure of the information model includes associated metadata acceptable for both humans and computers. Although, not all metadata is directly adapted to the end-user, it is possible to change the user interface, choose a more user-friendly form for filling in or submitting a CV.

The CVim provides data elements grouped by category. The CVim full elements set is a hierarchical structure of data elements that includes container (aggregate) data elements and simple data elements (leaf nodes of the hierarchy). Only leaf nodes have individual values defined through their associated value space and datatype. Container data elements in CVim do not have individual values.

For each data element, the following parts are defined in the CVim: (1) Name: the name by which data element is referenced; (2) Explanation: the definition of the data element; (3) Multiplicity: the number of values allowed; (4) Order: the order of the values only applicable for data elements with more than one value; (5) Note: some specific remarks using this data element; (7) Example. For simple data elements, the CVim also defines: (1) Value space: the set of allowed values for the data element; (2) Datatype: specifies whether the values are LangString, DateTime, VocabularyTerm, CharacterString or Undefined.

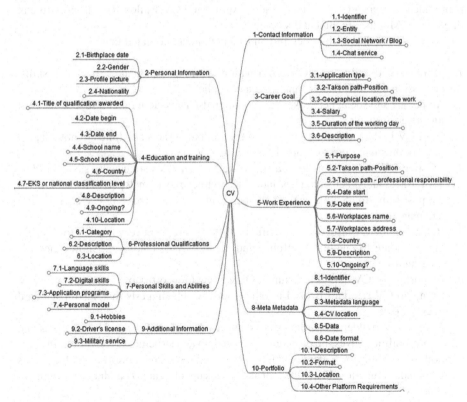

Fig. 5. Suggested CV information model.

The numbering of the data elements represents the aggregation hierarchy of data elements and their components. The information model groups' data elements into ten categories: (1) Contact Information, (2) Personal Information, (3) Career Goal, (4) Education and Training, (5) Work Experience, (6) Professional Qualifications, (7) Personal Skills and Abilities, (8) Meta Metadata, (9) Additional Information, (10) Portfolio. There are 119 elements in the CV information model of which 30 do not contain values but function as container elements that group value elements together. With the help of the mind map technique [20], the structure of the CV information model is visualized (see Fig. 5).

These elements are specified into three types: elements that must be filled in (mandatory elements), elements that are advised to be filled in (recommended elements). All other CV elements are non-mandatory.

4 Conclusions

The article aims to introduce the new CV information model that supports a variety of CV uses, including (1) Management, (2) Searching and finding, (3) Technical interoperability, (4) Evaluation. The full list of the elements of the CV information model is provided in Appendix A of the project "Automated CV Builder Based on Artificial Intelligence Module. Technical document".

Summarizing the results of empirical research, it can be stated that:

1. Employers usually lack CV information about a candidate's personal skills, professional abilities and cannot find a portfolio.
2. Ad portals and social networks are most often used to search for employees and post job advertisements.
3. Most CV builder websites support A4 format, but at the same time are not adapted to work on smart devices, thus complicating CV viewing.
4. Existing CV builder tools limit a candidate because CVs are usually saved in PDF, TXT, XML, and other similar formats. Meanwhile, only a small part of the tools gives the possibility to create a candidate's personal website increasing CV accessibility and management.
5. Regarding the CV structure, it is sufficiently structured, but very few CV tools allow the candidate to create a portfolio, and the survey of employers shows they are missing it.
6. In most tools, CV data is structured. Only a few tools offer to use the Europass CV form. No CV standard is used in other tools, which suggests that such a standard does not exist.
7. In some CV builder tools, the use of classification of professional occupations and responsibilities, gives the possibility to speed up and structure CV creation. In addition, some of the tools examined have integrated job search options, which expands the standard functionality of the tool and speeds up job search / candidate recruitment process.
8. An employee's personality skills can be evaluated using the most popular method in psychology–the Big Five personality traits. This method is successfully applied with the help of social media information, and artificial intelligence is used to process it.

Limitations of the research are the lack of verification of the CV information model. Currently, the implementation of a new CV information model in the automated CV platform is underway and validation studies of the CV information model are planned.

References

1. Kitchenham, B.: Procedures for performing systematic reviews. Joint technical report Software Engineering Group, Keele University, United Kingdom and Empirical Software Engineering, National ICT Australia Ltd., Australia (2004)
2. Woo, R., et al.: Writing the curriculum vitae and personal statement. J. Emerg. Med. **57**(3), 411–414 (2019).
3. Filipov, V.; Arleo, A.; Federico, P.; Miksch, S.: CV3: visual exploration, assessment, and comparison of CVs. In: Eurographics Conference on Visualization 2019, vol. 38, pp. 107–118 (2019)
4. Agha, R; Whitehurst, K.; Jafree, D.; et al.: How to write a medical CV. International journal of surgery-oncology **2**(6), e32 (2017)
5. Hicks, R.W., Roberts, M.E.E.: Curriculum vitae: An important tool for the nurse practitioner. J. Am. Assoc. Nurse Pract. **28**(7), 347–352 (2016)
6. Memon, A.R., Azim, M.E.: Open researcher and contributor identifier and other author identifiers: perspective from Pakistan. J. Pak. Med. Assoc. **69**(6), 888–891 (2019)
7. Vrabel, M.: Online registries for researchers: using ORCID and SciENcv. Clin. J. Oncol. Nurs. **20**(6), 667–668 (2016)
8. Amador, S.R., Pérez, M.D., López-Huertas Pérez, M.J., Font, R.J.R.: Indicator system for managing science, technology and innovation in universities. Scientometrics **115**, 1–13 (2018). https://doi.org/10.1007/s11192-018-2721-y
9. Alfawareh, H.M., Jusoh, S.: Intelligent decision support system for CV evaluation based on natural language processing. Int. J. Adv. Appl. Sci. **6**(4), 1–8 (2019)
10. Bazsova, B.: How can the company choose the best web designer? Decision-making application within a company. Int. J. Adv. Appl. Sci. **6**(2), 6–11 (2019)
11. Salinas, I., Lera, I., Guerrero, C., et al.: Towards a semantic research information system based on researchers' CV documents. Int. J. Qual. Res. **13**(1), 131–144 (2019)
12. Celik, D.: Towards a semantic-based information extraction system for matching resumes to job openings. Turk. J. Electr. Eng. Comput. Sci. **24**(1), 141–159 (2016)
13. Cabrera-Diego, L.A., El-Beze, M., Torres-Moreno, J.-M., Durette, B.: Ranking resumes automatically using only resumes: a method free of job offers. Expert Syst. Appl. **123**, 91–107 (2019)
14. Kaltenbrunner, W., de Rijcke, S.: Filling in the gaps: the interpretation of curricula vitae in peer review. Soc. Stud. Sci. **49**(6), 863–883 (2019)
15. Judge, T.A., Heller, D., Mount, M.K.: Five-factor model of personality and job satisfaction: a meta-analysis. J. Appl. Psychol. **87**(3), 530–541 (2002)
16. Roberts, B.W., Kuncel, N., Shiner, R., et al.: The power of personality: the comparative validity of personality traits, socioeconomic status, and cognitive ability for predicting important life outcomes. Perspect. Psychol. Sci. **2**(4), 313–345 (2007)
17. Arnoux, P.-H., Xu, A., Boyette. N., et al.: 25 Tweets to know you: a new model to predict personality with social media. In: Eleventh International AAAI Conference on Web and Social Media, pp. 472–475 (2017)
18. Chen, J., Hsieh, G., Mahmud, J., et al.: Understanding individuals' personal values from social media word use. In: Proceedings of the ACM Conference on Computer Supported Cooperative Work & Social Computing, pp. 405–414 (2014)

19. IBM Cloud Docs/Personality Insights Homepage. https://cloud.ibm.com/apidocs/person ality-insights. Accessed 12 Mar 2021
20. Li-Ren Chien, Li-R.; Buehrer, D: Using a typed mind map as data model in a TDD DICE system. J. Comput. Inf. Technol. **16**(4), 345–354 (2008)

Using Management Transaction Concept to Ensure Business and EAS Alignment in an Agile Environment

Karolis Noreika[(✉)] [iD] and Saulius Gudas[(✉)] [iD]

Institute of Data Science and Digital Technologies, Vilnius University, Akademijos 4, Vilnius, Lithuania

{karolis.noreika,saulius.gudas}@mif.vu.lt

Abstract. This paper presents a causal modelling-based approach for aligning information systems development and business strategy execution. The purpose is to ensure alignment between the business strategy of the organization and the way the information system is built. The suggested approach is based on the Agile frameworks such as Scrum, SAF'e, enterprise modelling framework MoDAF, modelling language ArchiMate 3.0, and the causal modelling concept of management transaction (MT). MT concept is the normalized structure to reveal business needs content and bridges MODAF and Agile concepts. MT is used to Agile process description on the level of themes, initiatives, epics, and user stories. Data from three real Enterprise Application Software projects over a one-year period were used to test the method.

Keywords: Enterprise application software development · Management transaction · Enterprise architecture · Agile software development

1 Introduction

Continuous process optimization is mandatory in a modern day business to stay competitive and takes a significant part in the business strategy of every enterprise. Software solutions like Enterprise Application Software (EAS) are used to organize, monitor and manage whole or part of processes in most modern day enterprises. Employees of the enterprise, that ensure the execution of the processes required to run the enterprise, use such systems daily in their work. This suggests that business and information system (IS) alignment is crucial to ensure process execution and in return, optimal business strategy execution.

Business strategy execution is often delivered by implementing various projects and most of them are IT related. However, the alignment of business management and IT solutions is now the result of human communication and collaboration that is not systematically orderly, not supported by any formal method of ensuring business and IS alignment.

We are looking for possible solutions integrating causal modelling and Enterprise Architecture development methods. Enterprise Architecture (EA) frameworks are the

© Springer Nature Switzerland AG 2021
A. Lopata et al. (Eds.): ICIST 2021, CCIS 1486, pp. 109–120, 2021.
https://doi.org/10.1007/978-3-030-88304-1_9

most widely recognized model-based methods to identify business strategy requirements and allows to transform them to application software architecture solutions. It is also a blueprint for how an organization achieves the current and future business objectives using information technologies [1]. Because of that, enterprise architecture solutions ensure the alignment of the process components in the enterprise to the supporting information systems and their components.

Development of EAS requires understanding of causality in the particular subject domain. Causal knowledge is a type of knowledge, next to declarative, procedural, and relational knowledge. Causal knowledge is described by Zack as a "description of causal links among a set of factors <...> which provides a means for organizations <...> how best to achieve some goal" [2]. The awareness of the specific domain causality is the prerequisite for discovering deep knowledge (i.e. regularities, laws) in a given domain.

Causal modelling is aimed for discovering causal dependencies of processes and information attributes in various real-world domains. Two levels of enterprise causal knowledge modelling were introduced by Gudas in [3]. The first level is the presentation of the discovered causation using the Management Transaction (MT) framework. At the second level, a deep knowledge structure of MT is revealed in a more detailed framework called the Elementary Management Cycle (EMC).

Agile principles and practices have been used for a while already for IT project management also having in mind business and IT alignment, and the usage of Agile frameworks is increasing [4], but their usage is often seen as sporadic, inconsistent and difficult to measure in terms of success, or the three classical project management constraints of time, scope and cost. The link between the task or user story in EAS project and strategic objectives of the enterprise is not clearly defined.

This paper is structured as follows: in the second section, the basic concepts of enterprise architecture, management transaction and Agile software development management are presented. In the third section related works are described. The fourth section explains the method to use management transaction to ensure business and IT alignment. In the fifth section, the case study using the suggested method is presented. Finally, conclusions cover the overview of results and summarize the case study.

2 Key Concepts

2.1 Enterprise Architecture Modelling

Business and EAS alignment issue is related to the modelling of complex systems (organizational systems, enterprises or cyber-social systems) summarized by the term systems of systems in the methodology of Enterprise Architecture (EA) frameworks.

EA has evolved over the years since it was mentioned for the very first time by Zachman [5] in 1987. There is no single definition of EA, but some authors as Kim et al. [6] describe it as "a holistic understanding of all aspects of a business, its drivers and surrounding environments, its business processes, organizational structures, information flows, IT systems, and technical infrastructures". More recent definition made in 2018 by Gartner [7] describes that EA is "a discipline for proactively and holistically leading enterprise responses to disruptive forces by identifying and analysing the execution of change toward desired business vision and outcomes. EA delivers value by presenting business and IT leaders with signature-ready recommendations for adjusting policies and projects to achieve target business outcomes that capitalize on relevant business disruptions". A properly defined EA allows businesses to identify and utilize their capabilities in executing business strategy.

Enterprise modelling is the initial stage (following model driven architecture (MDA) approach) of EAS in a wide range of industries, e.g. manufacturing, military, healthcare, energy, communication enterprises, and others. A captured domain causality is specified as the internal domain model, e.g. the cause-consequence rules, equations, ontology, meta-models. In our approach the discovered causation is specified using the Management Transaction (MT) framework as described in [3].

Business management frameworks (e.g. Deming's PDCA cycle [8]) have been formally referred to as the management transaction (Fig. 1) in [9] by Gudas and Valatavicius. The conceptual structure of the management transaction is presented in Fig. 1: Pi – basic physical (material) process (i – identifier), Fj – management function (j – identifier), A – Process State Attributes (raw data), V – Controls (impacts to P). Note that enterprise goal G is not explicitly stated in the description of MT, only marked with a dotted line in Fig. 1, but is considered by the analyst and affects the specification of MT.

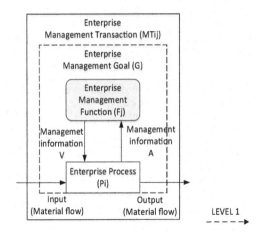

Fig. 1. Management transaction

2.2 Agile Software Development Management Concepts

Agile software development management practices were used already for a while before the commonly agreed Agile values and principles were described in Agile Manifesto in 2001 [10]. Over the years, the Agile frameworks such as Scrum, Extreme Programming (XP), ScrumBan, where Scrum is mixed with Kanban framework, Scaled Agile Framework (SAFe), Spotify model or hybrid versions of these gained popularity mainly because of adaptability to change and reduction of project costs [4]. One of the most widely used practice in Agile software development management for capturing business needs is "user story". A user story represents business requirements using natural language. There are research done by Luccasen et al. [11, 12] showing the benefits and some limitations of using user stories. But user stories on their own are not able to fully express the link from gathered requirements for information system to strategic objectives of the enterprise. Therefore, Epic, Initiative and Theme concepts are used and together with user stories they form a so called TIES structure [13] that help to semantically link the business requirements for information system from a user story to a strategic objective, see Fig. 2 below:

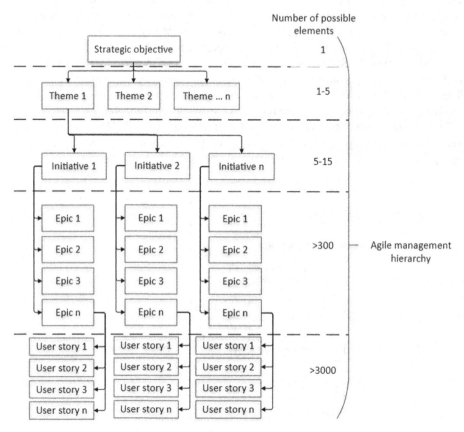

Fig. 2. Agile project management hierarchy

Agile project management hierarchy elements are considered as MT's (see Fig. 1) and therefore concepts of MT can be used to define elements in the TIES structure. The MT components mentioned in Fig. 1 are used as follows:

- F – management function: User-required data for processing tasks, data transformations, directing processes (P) according to strategy,
- P – basic physical (material) process: Enterprise strategy related activity or action, object of IT support,
- A – Process State Attributes: available raw data, i.e. parameters or characteristics of P (enterprise activity or action),

- V – Controls (impacts to P): directions for P - data processing and decision making outputs,
- G – Enterprise goal: strategy related description of why this specific MT (user story, epic, initiative) is needed, for what it is intended (Table 1).

Table 1. TIES specification template based on MT framework

TIES level	MT component				
	F	P	A	V	G
Theme	Business management	Business strategy execution	Performance metrics, KPI's	Legal, compliance requirements	Ensure strategic objective is reached
Initiative	Business management	Business process	To-be process; to-be performance metrics	Dependencies on related themes	Ensure theme goals are reached
Epic	Software development management	Software development	To-be process, performance metrics for part of full solution relevant to specific feature	Dependencies on related initiatives	Ensure initiative goals are reached
User story	Software development management	Software development	As-is process and performance metrics; To-be process and performance metrics	Dependencies on related software components	Ensure epic goals are reached

3 Related Works

The transformation of business strategy into digital solutions is the relevant problem and various solutions are known. We are looking for a solution to this problem in the Agile environment of business management and software development management. Here we will discuss some more interesting works on this topic.

Menglong et al. [14] for business and IT alignment proposed a coevolutionary framework that is containing four steps: EA design, sense of the misalignment, governance of the misalignment, and prevention of the misalignment based on Department of Defence Architecture Framework (DoDAF) [15], one of the best known EA frameworks. The authors indicate that "due to the absence of the IT executives in the IT strategy design process, the business executives may not understand the emerging information technologies" and therefore their framework is presented. However, the authors do not provide clear and repeatable steps how to monitor, recognize and measure sense of the misalignment between business and IT strategies and there are no clear steps provided to ensure the utility of the framework.

Weeger and Hasse [16] proposed to use Activity Theory to ensure business and IT alignment and their empirical examinations show that continually approaching emerging tensions within and between the two activity systems referring to business and IT respectively, and implementing changes enabled co-evolutionary processes of both systems. Activity theory is based on sociocultural development of humans [17]. The method is systematically well defined and applied in the medical field, but it is still abstract and does not contain any hierarchical structures. The authors state themselves that "further research has to approve the practical applicability of the framework" and that "the research is only providing "early evidence" on the validity and application" of the proposed approach.

Gerow et al. [18] identified 6 definitions of alignment, i.e.: Business alignment, Cross-domain alignment (business strategy to IT infrastructure and processes), Cross-domain alignment (IT strategy to business infrastructure and processes), Intellectual alignment, IT alignment, Operational alignment based on Henderson's and Venkatraman's strategic alignment approach [19]. The authors proved a relation between Henderson's and Venkatraman's strategic alignment model and improved financial performance by measuring financial indicators but did not provide details on how the alignment steps were executed.

Queiroz [20] empirical research using data survey of 120 companies focusing on Firm (or enterprise) level and on Process level of business and IT alignment showed different results applying the methods based on before mentioned approaches to IT and business alignment using EA.

The overview of related works clearly illustrates that the problem is actual and currently solved on the business management level. This situation requires a more practical structural approach, which is more directly related to IT software development management. Causal dependency investigation between aligned business and IT management processes is required when modelling the process content and this is missing in the works of authors mentioned in this section.

4 Using Management Transaction to Ensure Business and IT Alignment

An approach to business and IT alignment using Agile concepts from Scrum, Scaled Agile frameworks and Archimate as a tool for reference for missing information was presented earlier [21].

To detail the method, the elementary management cycle as a management transaction together with Agile management concepts of Themes, Initiatives, Epics, and User stories are used. This approach utilizes the concepts of MoDAF Strategic View (StV) and Operational View (OV) and concepts of Capability, Value stream, and Course of Action from Archimate modelling language. An example illustrating the as-is state where some of the information to ensure the link from strategic objective to a detail IT software development project requirement is presented in Table 2. "A flow" and "V flow" stands as MT interaction with Enterprise Process (as in Fig. 1), "-" stands for "No data".

Table 2. Requirements for Enterprise application project adherence to defined standard. Initial state (as-is).

Attribute	Agile project management concept				
	T	I	E	S	S
Management function	-	-	r100 – Software development management	r100 – Software development management	r100 – Software development management
ID	-	-	E01	S01	S02
Summary	-	-	Technical tasks	Technical architecture review	As a developer, I want log segregation
Description	-	-	-	-	-
A flow	-	-	Exists	Exists	Exists
V flow	-	-	-	-	Exists

By using the concepts from Gudas [3] the current as-is state of business and IT alignment can be projected to process space (Fig. 3).

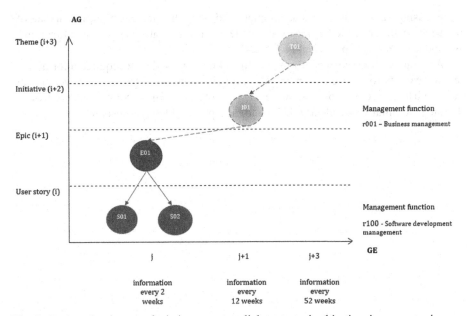

Fig. 3. Projected as-is state of missing user story link to strategic objectives in process universe

As it is clearly displayed, the levels of Initiative and Theme are not linking to the Epic and the User stories, although Epic has a link to User stories on its own. The dotted line represents that the link must exist, but it is not defined due to missing information. It means that by working on a single item from Epics or User stories it will not necessarily contribute to the strategic objectives of the enterprise.

Most widely used software development management tools (like i.e. "Jira") have vast customization capabilities, and some attributes to add additional information to items from the TIES structure, but these attributes are not defined completely and do not properly ensure the alignment from User story level to strategic objectives level. Some examples of attributes are mentioned in Table 3 below:

Table 3. Linking attributes for TIES structure in Jira

Line no	Attribute	Related to TIES structure element	Comments
1	Epic link	User story	Links user stories to single epic
2	Parent link (for initiative)	Epic	Links epics to single Initiative
3	Theme	Initiative	Links initiatives to single theme
4	Strategy		Potentially links themes to strategic objectives

By using Table 2 attributes as template and normalization function, the update of information must be added by the expert of the before mentioned management functions. An updated version is presented in Table 4.

As it can be observed, the information from Table 4 provides the required information and traceability to update and improve the requirements for EAS project development and could be projected to process space that is displayed in Fig. 4. Now the links between Theme and Initiative are clearly defined to the Epics and User stories level.

Table 4. Requirements for Enterprise application project adherence to defined standard. After normalization (to-be).

Attribute	Agile project management concept				
	T	I	E	S	S
Management function	r001 – Business management	r001 – Business management	r100 – Software development management	r100 – Software development management	r100 – Software development management
ID	T01	I01	E01	S01	S02
Summary	Exists	Exists	Technical tasks	Technical architecture review	As a developer, I want log segregation
Description	Exists	Exists	Exists	Exists	-
A flow	Exists	Exists	Exists	Exists	Exists
V flow	Exists	Exists	Exists	-	Exists

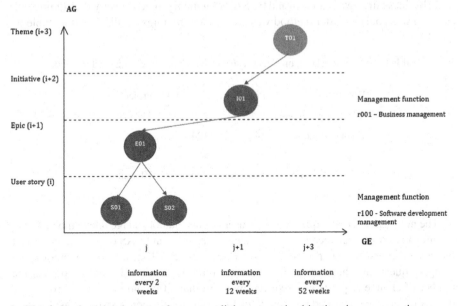

Fig. 4. Projected to-be state of user story link to strategic objectives in process universe

5 Case Study

Once delivering projects in an Agile environment there were observations done on 3 EAS projects. The projects were delivered in the financial domain and the detailed content of them is confidential. The input for project requirements is gathered from 4 different Nordic countries working on one core process for each project. From Agile perspective, Scrum is used as Agile software management framework. The requirements in the format of user stories (Initial requirements), change requests and bugs (considered as part of requirements for solution development) were analysed during the project lifecycle of 10 to 13 months. The results are displayed in Table 5.

Table 5. EAS projects requirement distribution.

Parameter	Project #1	Project #2	Project #3
Initial requirements	262	237	218
Change requests	168	219	53
Bugs	77	99	71
Project duration	13 months	10 months	12 months

Using the suggested method, a normalization of user stories and other requirements mentioned before was performed. Missing information was added and the information gap in business strategy execution and EAS development project delivery was minimized. The data was analysed after method was applied and findings are displayed in Table 6.

Table 6. EAS projects requirement distribution when using suggested method.

Parameter	Project #1	Project #2	Project #3
Initial requirements	262	237	218
Change requests	142	194	42
Bugs	68	85	63
Project duration	13 months	9 months	10 months

The number of initial requirements or user stories did not change due to the fact, that the information gap between business strategy execution and EAS development project delivery emerges during sprints or product development. But in other categories like change requests and bugs, the differences are quite significant. In the 3rd project the number of change requests was reduced by more than 20% and in the 2nd project the number of bugs was reduced by more than 14%. The results comparison is displayed in Table 7.

Table 7. EAS projects requirement distribution comparison.

Parameter	Project #1	Project #2	Project #3
Initial requirements	0	0	0
Change requests	−26; −15,48%	−25; −11,42%	−11; −20,75%
Bugs	−9; −11,69%	−14; −14,14%	−8; −11,27%
Project duration	0 months	−1 months	−2 months

6 Conclusions

The approach to ensure business strategy execution via developing relevant information systems is presented. The proposed approach to ensure business and IT alignment integrates currently used approaches of EA development, Agile frameworks and causal modelling concept of management transaction (MT).

The advantage of this approach is a normalization of specification of all Agile hierarchy elements (user stories, epics, initiatives, themes), and the systematization of the content of the elements using the MT framework. The usability of the MT framework in an Agile environment is illustrated. Therefore the analysis of interactions in the Agile hierarchy was formalized on the basis of MT, which enables business and IT alignment evaluation and monitoring.

The proposed method was experimentally tested on the basis of data from three real EAS projects. This has been found to save resources, as shown in the case study.

As the results of the case study shows, the proposed method to ensure business and IT alignment in an Agile environment, using TIES structure to link requirements of EAS projects described as user stories, change requests or bugs, to strategic goals of the enterprise, provides significant improvement to EAS project deliveries by reducing the number of change requests and bugs. Alignment of business and IT solutions is improved once missing information is added to enable the link of those requirements to strategic goals of the enterprise.

References

1. Dahalin, M.Z., Razak, A.R., Ibrahim, H., Yusop, I.N., Kasiran, K.M.: An enterprise architecture methodology for business–it alignment: adopter and developer perspectives. In: Soliman S.K. (ed.) Communications of the IBIMA, vol. 2011 (2011). doi: https://doi.org/10.5171/2011.222028
2. Zack, M.H.: If managing knowledge is the solution, then what's the problem? In: Malhotra, Y. (ed.) Knowledge Management and Business Model Innovation. Idea Group Publishing (2001). https://doi.org/10.4018/978-1-878289-98-8.ch002
3. Gudas, S.: Informacijos sistemų inžinerijos teorijos pagrindai. Publishing House of Vilnius University, Vilnius (2012). ISBN 978-609-459-075-7
4. Digital.ai Software, Inc.: 14th Annual State of Agile Report. https://stateofagile.com/#ufh-i-615706098-14th-annual-state-of-agile-report/702749. Accessed 27 Mar 2021
5. Zachman, J.A.: A framework for information systems architecture. IBM Syst. J. **26**(3), 276–292 (1987)

6. Kim, H., Oussena, S., Essien, J., Komisarczuk, P.: Towards event-driven enterprise architecture. In Perez-Castillo, R., Piattini, M. (eds.) Uncovering Essential Software Artifacts through Business Process Archeology, pp. 285–311, IGI Global (2014)
7. Gartner: Enterprise Architecture (EA). https://www.gartner.com/it-glossary/enterprise-architecture-ea/. Accessed 25 Mar 2021
8. Deming, W.E.: The New Economics For Industry Government & Education. MIT Press, Cambridge (1993)
9. Gudas, S., Valatavičius, A.: Extending model-driven development process with causal modeling approach. In: Dzemyda, G., Bernatavičienė, J., Kacprzyk, J. (eds.) Data Science: New Issues, Challenges and Applications. SCI, vol. 869, pp. 111–143. Springer, Cham (2020). https://doi.org/10.1007/978-3-030-39250-5_7
10. Agile Alliance: Manifesto for Agile Software Development. https://agilemanifesto.org/. Accessed 20 Mar 2021
11. Lucassen, G., Dalpiaz, F., van der Werf, E.M., Martijn, J., Brinkkemper, S.: The use and effectiveness of user stories in practice. In: Daneva, M., Pastor, O. (eds.) REFSQ 2016. LNCS, vol. 9619, pp. 205–222. Springer, Cham (2016). https://doi.org/10.1007/978-3-319-30282-9_14. ISBN 978-3-319-30281-2
12. Lucassen, G., Dalpiaz, F., E.M. van der Werf, Martijn, J., Brinkkemper, S.: Forging high-quality user stories: towards a discipline for agile requirements. In: IEEE International Conference on Requirements Engineering (RE), pp. 126–135. IEEE (2015). https://doi.org/10.1109/RE.2015.7320415
13. Leading Agile, Prior, D.: Agile Planning With Ties With Tom Churchwell. https://www.leadingagile.com/podcast/agile-planning-ties-tom-churchwell/. Accessed 20 Feb 2021
14. Menglong, L., Shuanghui, Y., Mengmeng, Z., Tao, C., Honghui, C., Xiaoxue, Z.: A coevolutionary framework of business-IT alignment via the lens of enterprise architecture. J. Syst. Eng. Electron. 31(5), 983–995 (2020). https://doi.org/10.23919/JSEE.2020.000073
15. DoD Architecture Framework Working Group. DoD Architecture Framework Version 2.0. Department of Defense, Washington DC (2009)
16. Weger, A., Haase, U.: How contradictions facilitate evolutionary transformation: an exploration into the dynamics of business-IT alignment from the perspective of activity theory. In: Proceedings of the European Conference on Information System, pp. 1–16, AIS Electronic Library (AISeL) (2016)
17. Vygotsky, L.S.V.: Mind and Society: The Development of Higher Psychological Processes. Harvard University Press, Cambridge (1978)
18. Gerow, J.E., Thatcher, J.B., Grover, V.: Six types of IT-business strategic alignment: an investigation of the constructs and their measurement. Eur. J. Inf. Syst. 24(5), 465–491 (2015). https://doi.org/10.1057/ejis.2014.6
19. Henderson, J.C., Venkatraman, H.: Strategic alignment: leveraging information technology for transforming organizations. IBM Syst. J. 38(2/3), 472–484 (1999)
20. Queiroz, M.: Mixed results in strategic IT alignment research: a synthesis and empirical study. Eur. J. Inf. Syst. 26(1), 21–36 (2017)
21. Noreika, K.: Business capabilities utilization enhancement using archimate for EAS projects delivery in an agile environment. In: Matulevičius, R., Robal, T., Haav, H-M., Maigre, R., Petlenkov, E. (eds.) Joint Proceedings of Baltic DB&IS 2020 Conference Forum and Doctoral Consortium co-located with the 14th International Baltic Conference on Databases and Information Systems (BalticDB&IS 2020) CEUR Workshop Proceedings, vol. 2620, pp. 49–56, Estonia (2020)

Software Engineering-Special Session on Intelligent Systems and Software Engineering Advances

An Analysis of ED Line Algorithm in Urban Street-View Dataset

Ciprian Orhei(✉)⬤, Muguras Mocofan⬤, Silviu Vert⬤, and Radu Vasiu⬤

Politehnica University of Timişoara, Timişoara, Romania
ciprian.orhei@cm.upt.ro, {muguras.mocofan,radu.vasiu}@upt.ro

Abstract. Building detection in urban street view scenarios is becoming an important aspect of Computer Vision applications. In this paper we present an analysis of EDLine and Edge Drawing algorithms in a street-view dataset scenario when changing the first order derivative operator used inside the algorithms. To do so, we focused firstly on the general use case, using a natural image dataset, and secondly we looked on the effects we obtain on the use case of building detection in street view urban scenarios. We observed from our experiments that the proposed change brings marginal improvements to the algorithm that we present in the paper, visually and statistically.

Keywords: Edge detection · Line detection · Edge drawing algorithm · EDLine algorithm · Building detection

1 Introduction

In Computer Vision, edge detection is a process which attempts to capture the significant properties of objects in the image. These properties include discontinuities in the photometrical, geometrical and physical characteristics of objects [1]. The importance of using edges is also confirmed by nature due to the gradient-based Gabor-like responses in which our visual system works [2].

Extracting edge features from images is a problem that was tackled in many different ways in the scientific literature. Solutions were proposed that vary from: unsupervised approaches like the classical Sobel [3], to complex algorithms like Canny [4]; semi-supervised algorithms like SemiContour [5]; supervised algorithms like DSCD [6].

Urban scenarios reconstruction and understanding is an area of research with several applications nowadays: entertainment industry, culture and tourism [7–9], computer gaming, movie making, digital mapping for mobile devices [10], digital mapping for car navigation, urban planning [11], education [12].

Edge detection is an important feature used in many algorithms that are employed in urban understanding scenarios. Classical edge detection algorithms are dependent on the kernels used in the processing steps. This dependence leads to one algorithm performing better with one kernel than with another, in a specific use case. In this paper we wish to analyze the effect of these two factors

© Springer Nature Switzerland AG 2021
A. Lopata et al. (Eds.): ICIST 2021, CCIS 1486, pp. 123–135, 2021.
https://doi.org/10.1007/978-3-030-88304-1_10

(kernel and use case) on a popular edge detection algorithm: Edge Drawing (ED).

We propose to modify the operators used for ED and EDLine algorithms and analyze the results we obtain. From our previous experiments, we concluded that changing the first order derivative kernel that we use, which seems like a small modification, can lead to important differences in the resulting features. The analysis we propose will be done using two different datasets: a natural images dataset [13] and a dataset containing images of buildings in urban scenario [14, 15].

The paper is organized as follows: in Sect. 2 we will present the used operators and other concepts important for this paper. In Sect. 3 the mentioned edge detection and line detection is briefly presented. The results of our simulation are presented in Sect. 4, using the dataset of natural images and using a dataset of human made structures (buildings) in urban street view images. In Sect. 5 we will present our conclusion and possible extensions of this work.

2   Preliminaries

In this section we will describe the necessary concepts and elements to better understand the experiments we present in this paper.

2.1   First Order Derivative Operators

The gradient is a measure of change in a function, and an image can be considered to be an array of samples of some continuous function of image intensity, typically two-dimensional equivalent of first derivative. Gradient magnitude is calculated using Formula 1, where $f(x,y)$ is the image and G_x, G_y are the components on x and y axis. The direction of the gradient is calculated using Eq. 2. [16]

$$G[f(x,y)] = \sqrt{G_x^2 + G_y^2} \approx |G_x| + |G_y| \tag{1}$$

$$\theta = \tan^{-1}\left[\frac{G_x}{G_y}\right] \tag{2}$$

For our experiments, we will use the first two of the most popular discrete differentiation operators: the **Sobel Operator** [3] and the **Prewitt Operator** [17] with an 3×3 kernel. The **Kirsch operator** [18] is a compass operator that is used as an gradient operator with kernel size of 3×3. The **Kitchen and Malin Operator** [19] or "two and three" kernel is a hybrid of the Prewitt and Sobel operators devised during studies. The **Kayalli Operator** [20] presents a kernel which is aligned to directions of south east - north west (S.E.N.W.) or north east - south west (N.E.S.W.). The kernels in this operator are designed to maximally ignore the response to edges running vertically and horizontally. The

Scharr Operator [21] is an optimized filter based on minimizing the weighted mean-squared angular error in the Fourier domain. The **Kroon Operator** [22] proposes an optimized kernel that is found minimizing the absolute angular errors of an image containing circular patterns with varying spatial frequencies. The **Orhei Operator** [23] presents an operator that considers giving a higher weight to the pixels on vertical and horizontal directions.

All the kernels we will use are presented in Fig. 1.

$$
\begin{bmatrix} -1 & 0 & 1 \\ -2 & 0 & 2 \\ -1 & 0 & 1 \end{bmatrix} \quad
\begin{bmatrix} -1 & 0 & 1 \\ -1 & 0 & 1 \\ -1 & 0 & 1 \end{bmatrix} \quad
\begin{bmatrix} -3 & -3 & 5 \\ -3 & 0 & 5 \\ -3 & -3 & 5 \end{bmatrix} \quad
\begin{bmatrix} -2 & 0 & 2 \\ -3 & 0 & 3 \\ -2 & 0 & 2 \end{bmatrix}
$$

Sobel   Prewitt   Kirsch   Kitchen

$$
\begin{bmatrix} -6 & 0 & 6 \\ 0 & 0 & 0 \\ 6 & 0 & -6 \end{bmatrix} \quad
\begin{bmatrix} -3 & 0 & 3 \\ -10 & 0 & 10 \\ -3 & 0 & 3 \end{bmatrix} \quad
\begin{bmatrix} -17 & 0 & 17 \\ -61 & 0 & 61 \\ -17 & 0 & 17 \end{bmatrix} \quad
\begin{bmatrix} -1 & 0 & 1 \\ -4 & 0 & 4 \\ -1 & 0 & 1 \end{bmatrix}
$$

Kayyali   Scharr   Kroon   Orhei

Fig. 1. First Order derivative edge operators kernels

2.2 Benchmarking the Edge and Line Results

For evaluating the obtained edge-maps we use the Pixel Corresponding Metric (PCM) algorithm [24]. This metric is reliable for correlating similarities because it searches for the optimal matching of the pixels between the edge images and then estimates the error produced by this matching. In Eq. 3 we present the definition of PCM between two images f and g, where $C(M_{opt}(f, g))$ is the cost of an optimal matching, η is the maximum localization error and $|f \cup g|$ is the total number of pixels that are not zero in both images. The optimal matching algorithm used is an approximation of the Weighted Matching Algorithm (more details in [24]), with a depth of 5 and localization error of 5 pixels.

$$
PCM_\eta(f, g) = 100(1 - \frac{C(M_{opt}(f, g))}{(|f \cup g|)}) \tag{3}
$$

For each image we calculated Precision (P) and Recall (R) [25]. Precision, presented in Formula 4, represents the probability that a resulting edge pixel is a true. Recall, presented in Formula 5, represents the probability that a true edge pixel is detected. Where TP (True Positive) represents the number of matched edge pixel, FP (False Positive) the number of edge pixels which are incorrectly highlighted and FN (False Negative) the number of pixel that have not been detected. Those two quantities are used to compute *F-measure* (F1-score) by applying the formula 6.

$$P = \frac{TP}{TP + FP}. \tag{4}$$

$$R = \frac{TP}{TP + FN}. \tag{5}$$

$$F - measure = \frac{2 * TP}{2 * TP + FP + FN}. \tag{6}$$

2.3   Datasets

Fig. 2. Example of images from the datasets, first three columns from the natural dataset [13] and the following columns from the urban dataset [14]

The **natural dataset** [13] we selected uses 500 test images which are split in three different sets, each having at least five human segmented boundary ground-truth images. The images contained in the dataset of natural images have been manually segmented. The human annotations serve as ground truth for the benchmark for comparing different segmentation and boundary detection algorithms. We can see examples of images and corresponding ground-truth images in Fig. 2.

The **urban dataset** [14,15] uses 160 test images, which are split in three different sets that were annotated using human subjects that were asked to label (draw) what they perceived as important edges of a building, like the boundaries of the building, as well as differences between facades of the building, different buildings, windows, doors and so on. The human subjects were asked not to fill edges or lines that are occluded by other structures even if it is natural that they are present. We can see examples of images and corresponding ground-truth images in Fig. 2.

As we can observe in Fig. 2, the two selected dataset differ essentially, beginning from the selection of images used and finishing with the methodology of annotation of labels. The first dataset focuses on boundaries of objects and structures that are found in the images while the second dataset focuses only on the buildings in the image and the edges/lines that are considered relevant on them.

2.4 Simulation Environment

All the simulation are done using EECVF - End-to-End Computer Vision Framework - [26,27] an open-source solution, Python based, that aims to support researchers in this field. We used this framework because it provides the necessary CV algorithms and evaluation algorithms. The experiments done in this paper can be reproduce by running *main_analysis_of_EDLine_urban_street_dataset* module. EECVF was executed on a PC AMD Ryzen 5 3600 6-Core Processor 3.95 GHz on both Windows and Linux operating system.

3 ED Line Algorithm

ED algorithm [28], described in Algorithm 1, can be summarized in the following steps: suppress the image with a Gaussian filter [29], calculate the gradient magnitude and orientation using Sobel filter [3], extract the anchor points, connect the anchor points using the smart routing concept.

The most crucial step of ED is connecting the anchors by drawing edges between them. To connect consecutive anchors, we simply go from one anchor to the next by proceeding over the cordillera peak of the gradient map mountain. This process is guided by the gradient magnitude and edge direction maps computed. Starting at an anchor, we look at the direction of the edge passing through the anchor. If an horizontal edge passes through the anchor, we start the connecting process by proceeding to the left and to the right. If a vertical edge passes through the anchor, we start the connection process by proceeding up and down. The process stops if we move out of the edge area or we encounter a previously detected edge [28].

Algorithm 1: ED Line Algorithm

Input: *image*
Parameters: *sigma, grad_thr, anchor_thr, scan_interval,*
        line_fit_err_thr, min_line_length
Output: *edge_segments, line_segments*
`/* ED Algorithm start` */
if *image is RGB* **then**

> `/* Edge Drawing algorithm works only on grey-scale images` */
> *image* ← Convert image to grey-scale

`/* Suppression using Gaussian filtering with` *sigma* `parameter` */
image ← Apply Gaussian filter smoothing
`/* Using Sobel kernels using` $\sqrt{G_x^2 + G_y^2} \approx |G_x| + |G_y|$ */
grad_map ← Calculate gradient map
`/* if` $|G_x| \geq |G_y|$ `vertical edge otherwise horizontal edge` */
orientation_map ← Calculate direction map
`/* Apply a global threshold scheme by` *grad_thr* `value` */
grad_map ← Threshold gradient map
`/* Anchor must be a local peak of the gradient map, using` *anchor_thr*
    `and` *scan_interval* */
anchor_list ← Extract anchors
`/* Three immediate neighbors are considered and the maximum gradient`
    `value is picked` */
edge_segments ← Smart routing
`/* ED Algorithm end` */
`/* Least Squares Line Fit of` *edge_segments*`, lineFitError > 1.0` */
line_segments_fitted ← Line Fit algorithm
`/* Validation is based on the length of the line segment and the`
    `number of aligned pixels using Helmholtz principle.` */
line_segments ← Line Validation algorithm

EDLines is comprised of three steps. Firstly, the image is processed using ED algorithm [28], which produces a set of clean, contiguous chains of pixels, called edge segments. Edge segments intuitively correspond to object boundaries. Secondly, the algorithm extracts line segments from the generated pixel chains by means of a straightness criterion, the Least Squares Line Fitting Method. Third step and final is a line validation step, done with Helmholtz principle [30], used to eliminate the false line segments detected [31].

4   Analysis Results

In this section, we propose to analyze to see the effects on the edge map and line segments we obtain when changing the first order operator used in the mentioned algorithms. For our simulation, we used the algorithm presented in Sect. 3 and the first order operator presented in Sect. 2.1. The experiments are done on the two datasets presented in Sect. 2.3 and evaluated with the algorithm presented in Sect. 2.2.

First, we would like to find the best suited parameters for ED algorithm using the original algorithm, presented in Algorithm 1, on natural image dataset. The results can be observed in Fig. 3. To find the optimal parameters for the best results, we vary the parameters as following: the Gaussian kernel size in the following range of $3 \rightarrow 9$ using a step of 2, the gradient threshold in range of $10 \rightarrow 150$ with a step of 10, the anchor threshold in the following range $10 \rightarrow 60$ with a step of 10 and the scan interval in the following range [1, 3, 5]. In the figures where we plot the F-1 measure score we use the following notations: TG = Gradient Threshold, TA = Anchor Threshold, SI = Scan interval, and GK = Gaussian Kernel size.

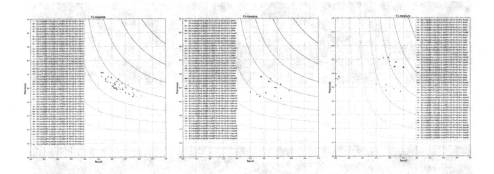

Fig. 3. ED parameter tuning on natural images

Fig. 4. ED results on natural image dataset

Fig. 5. EDLine results on natural image dataset

We observe that we obtain the best results using the following parameters: gradient threshold value of 50, anchor threshold value of 10, Gaussian kernel size of 9 and scan interval of 1. The difference is not substantial between the first F-1 we obtain, so, probably, in real life applications, this fine tuning step is not done so granular. We can see the resulting images in Fig. 6 column one.

Naturally, next we would like to see the effects of changing the edge operator used inside the ED algorithm, change that will affect the EDLine algorithm too. To do so, we used the algorithm parameters found in the tuning phase, see Fig. 3. To take in consideration the variation of the kernel calculation scheme we varied the parameters as following: Gaussian kernel taking values of 7 and 9; the gradient threshold in the following range $40 \rightarrow 60$ with a step of 10; the anchor threshold value of 10 and 20; and the scan interval of 1.

The best resulted cases for each operator are presented in Fig. 6, as visual results, and in Fig. 4, as $F1$ evaluation score. We can observe that not all the operators bring with them a visible improvement at first glance. But even if they have similar $F1$ scores, the P and R is different for each case. On one hand, a better percentage of P indicates a smaller FP rate in that case. On the other hand, a bigger value in R means a smaller number of FN that translates into more points being correctly marked as label pixel.

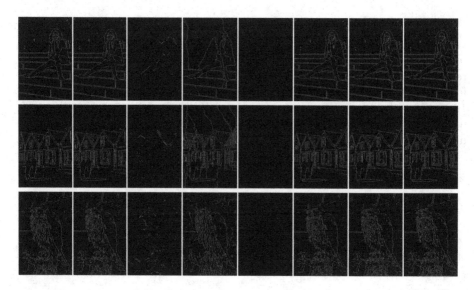

Fig. 6. ED results on natural image dataset. Columns: Sobel, Prewitt, Kirsch, Kitchen, Kayyali, Scharr, Kroon, Orhei

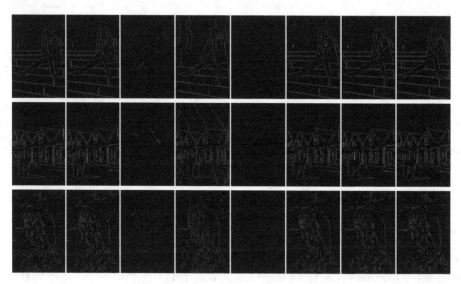

Fig. 7. ED Line results on natural image dataset. Columns: Sobel, Prewitt, Kirsch, Kitchen, Kayyali, Scharr, Kroon, Orhei

When looking on the results from ED Line algorithm using different operators, we can observe changes in the metrics we calculate, as presented in Fig. 5. As expected, the trend that we saw in the ED experiments is respected, being a natural result because the EDLine is strongly dependent on the ED algorithm.

We observe that changing the operator results in an improvement in the lines detected. The visual results are presented in Fig. 7.

Moving on to the street-view urban dataset, we would like to find the best suited parameters for ED algorithm using the original algorithm, presented in Algorithm 1. The results can be observed in Fig. 8. To find the optimal parameters for the best results, we vary the parameters as following: the Gaussian kernel size in the following range of $3 \rightarrow 9$ using a step of 2, the gradient threshold in range of $10 \rightarrow 150$ with a step of 10, the anchor threshold in the following range $10 \rightarrow 60$ with a step of 10 and the scan interval in the following range $[1, 3, 5]$. The best results we obtain using the following parameters: gradient threshold value of 40, anchor threshold value of 10, Gaussian kernel size of 9 and scan interval of 1.

In Fig. 9, we plotted the results when we use different first order operators and, of course, similar to the natural dataset, we vary the margins of the thresholds so we can obtain the best results.

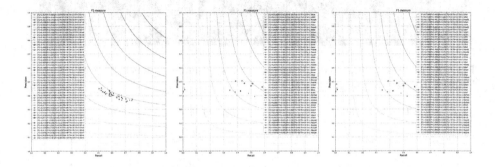

Fig. 8. ED parameter tuning on urban images   **Fig. 9.** ED results on urban image dataset   **Fig. 10.** EDLine results on urban image dataset

When looking over the results we see upon the ED Line algorithm (Fig. 10), we can observe that changing the operator actually brings small improvements to the results.

In Fig. 11 we are presented with the visual results for ED algorithm on the urban dataset. Similarly, we can see in Fig. 12 the ED Line results.

When we look over the results of Fig. 9 and Fig. 10, we see that changing the kernel from the original Sobel [3] kernel with kernels from Prewitt [17], Scharr [21] or Orhei [23] can bring small improvements to the results of the algorithms.

In Table 1 we have chosen the best results on ED algorithm and ED Line algorithm for each operator we simulated with. As we can see, changing the operator does not always bring better edges or lines results. For example, when using operators like Kayyali [20] or Kitchen [19] we obtain worse results.

After analysing the obtaining data (Fig. 3, 4, 5, 6, 7, 8, 9, 10, 11 and 12), we can conclude that changing the operator can bring small improvements to

Fig. 11. ED results on natural image dataset. Columns: Sobel, Prewitt, Kirsch, Kitchen, Kayyali, Scharr, Kroon, Orhei

Table 1. Best results of all operators on the selected dataset

Operator	Natural dataset						Urban dataset					
	ED			EDLine			ED			EDLine		
	R	P	F1	R	P	F1	R	P	F1	R	P	F1
Sobel	0.721	0.523	**0.606**	0.499	0.642	0.562	0.582	0.404	**0.504**	0.582	0.463	0.515
Prewitt	0.720	0.523	**0.606**	0.503	0.641	**0.564**	0.582	0.404	**0.504**	0.584	0.461	0.515
Kirsch	0.139	0.478	0.216	0.030	0.567	0.057	0.069	0.382	0.116	0.013	0.443	0.026
Kitchen	0.724	0.420	0.531	0.478	0.469	0.474	0.632	0.356	0.455	0.423	0.433	0.428
Kayyali	0.000	0.000	0.000	0.000	0.000	0.000	0.000	0.000	0.000	0.000	0.000	0.000
Scharr	0.723	0.522	**0.606**	0.501	0.643	0.563	0.672	0.403	**0.504**	0.582	0.462	0.515
Kroon	0.723	0.521	**0.606**	0.501	0.643	0.563	0.672	0.403	**0.504**	0.582	0.462	0.515
Orhei	0.721	0.522	**0.606**	0.499	0.643	0.562	0.671	0.403	0.503	0.582	0.463	**0.516**

the edge map and lines obtain by the presented algorithms. Another important aspect we can highlight is the fact that when changing the use case, in our case urban scenarios, the metrics obtained change. This is an expected outcome as some operators have better effect on a certain application than others.

In Table 1, we highlighted the main $F1$ evaluation metrics in order to better showcase the results of ED algorithm. In parallel, we added the ED Line results so we can observe the difference in trends and results. In case of ED algorithm, we see that the same operators (Sobel, Prewitt, Scharr, Kroon, Orhei) bring the best results in both cases, when evaluating on natural or urban datasets. In case

Fig. 12. ED Lines results on natural image dataset; Columns: Sobel, Prewitt, Kirsch, Kitchen, Kayyali, Scharr, Kroon, Orhei

of ED Line algorithm, when we evaluate the natural dataset, we observe that the Prewitt operator has the best results. But, when dealing with the urban dataset, we see that Orhei operator brings the best results.

5 Discussions and Conclusion

In this paper, we studied the effect that the changing of the first order operators, presented in Sect. 2, brings to the ED algorithm and EDLine algorithm output. As we highlighted in Sect. 4, we obtained small improvements to the overall results when doing the proposed changes with certain operators. The aim of our research was to show what effect this change has when dealing with an urban street-view dataset.

With the experiments presented in this paper we can conclude that changing the first order operator used in ED or ED Line results in different outcomes.

We wish to continue experimenting with EDLine algorithm in street-view urban scenarios when the images are preprocessed using a region of interest (ROI) selecting algorithm. The filtering of the image would cause the reduction of false edges that can be formed by the ED algorithm.

In our future work we would like to study the effect upon the lines detected by ED Lines when we dilate [32, 33] the kernel of the first order derivative operator.

References

1. Ziou, D., Tabbone, S.: Edge detection techniques: an overview. Int. J. Pattern Recognit. Image Anal. **4**, 537–559 (1998)
2. Daugman, J.G.: Uncertainty relation for resolution in space, spatial frequency, and orientation optimized by two-dimensional visual cortical filters. JOSA A **2**(7), 1160–1169 (1985)
3. Sobel, I., Feldman, G.: A 3×3 isotropic gradient operator for image processing. Pattern Classif. Scene Anal. 271–272 (1973)
4. Canny, J.: A computational approach to edge detection. IEEE Trans. Pattern Anal. Mach. Intell. **PAMI–8**, 679–698 (1986)
5. Zhang, Z., Xing, F., Shi, X., Yang, L.: Semicontour: a semi-supervised learning approach for contour detection. In: Proceedings of the IEEE Conference on Computer Vision and Pattern Recognition, pp. 251–259 (2016)
6. Deng, R., Liu, S.: Deep structural contour detection. In: Proceedings of the 28th ACM International Conference on Multimedia, pp. 304–312 (2020)
7. Vert, S., Vasiu, R.: Relevant aspects for the integration of linked data in mobile augmented reality applications for tourism. In: Dregvaite, G., Damasevicius, R. (eds.) ICIST 2014. CCIS, vol. 465, pp. 334–345. Springer, Cham (2014). https://doi.org/10.1007/978-3-319-11958-8_27
8. Vasiu, R.: Development of smart city applications based on open data. In: Contribution to the 13th NETTIES Conference (Network Entities) on "Open Data and Big Data-The Impact on Digital Society and Smart Cities", vol. 2. Humboldt Cosmos Multiversity, Tenerife (2015)
9. Vert, S., Andone, D., Vasiu, R.: Augmented and virtual reality for public space art. In: ITM Web of Conferences, vol. 29, p. 03006. EDP Sciences (2019)
10. Vert, S., Vasiu, R.: Integrating linked data in mobile augmented reality applications. In: Dregvaite, G., Damasevicius, R. (eds.) ICIST 2014. CCIS, vol. 465, pp. 324–333. Springer, Cham (2014). https://doi.org/10.1007/978-3-319-11958-8_26
11. Vert, S., Vasiu, R.: Augmented reality lenses for smart city data: the case of building permits. In: Rocha, Á., Correia, A.M., Adeli, H., Reis, L.P., Costanzo, S. (eds.) WorldCIST 2017. AISC, vol. 569, pp. 521–527. Springer, Cham (2017). https://doi.org/10.1007/978-3-319-56535-4_53
12. Vert, S., Vasiu, R.: School of the future: using augmented reality for contextual information and navigation in academic buildings. In: 2012 IEEE 12th International Conference on Advanced Learning Technologies, pp. 728–729. IEEE (2012)
13. Arbelaez, P., Maire, M., Fowlkes, C., Malik, J.: Contour detection and hierarchical image segmentation. IEEE Trans. Pattern Anal. Mach. Intell. **33**(5), 898–916 (2010)
14. CM Building Dataset Timisoara. https://github.com/CipiOrhei/TMBuD. Accessed 12 Mar 2021
15. Orhei, C., Vert, S., Mocofan, M., Vasiu, R.: TMBuD: a dataset for urban scene building detection. In: Lopata, A., Gudonienė, D., Butkienė, R. (eds.) ICIST 2021. CCIS, vol. 1486, pp. 251–262. Springer, Charm (2021). https://doi.org/10.1007/978-3-030-88304-1_20
16. Haralick, R.M., Shapiro, L.G.: Computer and Robot Vision, vol. 1. Addison-Wesley, Reading (1992)
17. Prewitt, J.M.: Object enhancement and extraction. In: Picture Processing and Psychopictorics, vol. 10, no. 1, pp. 15–19 (1970)

18. Kirsch, R.A.: Computer determination of the constituent structure of biological images. Comput. Biomed. Res. **4**(3), 315–328 (1971)
19. Kitchen, L., Malin, J.: The effect of spatial discretization on the magnitude and direction response of simple differential edge operators on a step edge. Comput. Vis. Graph. Image Process. **47**(2), 243–258 (1989)
20. Kawalec-Latała, E.: Edge detection on images of pseudoimpedance section supported by context and adaptive transformation model images. Studia Geotechnica et Mechanica **36**(1), 29–36 (2014)
21. Scharr, H.: Optimal operators in digital image processing. Ph.D. thesis (2000)
22. Kroon, D.: Numerical optimization of kernel based image derivatives, Short Paper University Twente (2009)
23. Orhei, C., Vert, S., Vasiu, R.: A novel edge detection operator for identifying buildings in augmented reality applications. In: Lopata, A., Butkienė, R., Gudonienė, D., Sukackė, V. (eds.) ICIST 2020. CCIS, vol. 1283, pp. 208–219. Springer, Cham (2020). https://doi.org/10.1007/978-3-030-59506-7_18
24. Prieto, M., Allen, A.: A similarity metric for edge images. IEEE Trans. Pattern Anal. Mach. Intell. **25**, 1265–1273 (2003)
25. Sasaki, Y.: The truth of the f-measure. Technical report, School of Computer Science, University of Manchester (2007)
26. Orhei, C., Mocofan, M., Vert, S., Vasiu, R.: End-to-end computer vision framework. In: 2020 International Symposium on Electronics and Telecommunications (ISETC), pp. 1–4. IEEE (2020)
27. Orhei, C., Vert, S., Mocofan, M., Vasiu, R.: End-to-end computer vision framework: an open-source platform for research and education. Sensors **21**(11), 3691 (2021)
28. Topal, C., Akinlar, C.: Edge drawing: a combined real-time edge and segment detector. J. Vis. Commun. Image Represent. **23**(6), 862–872 (2012)
29. Haralick, R.M.: Digital step edges from zero crossing of second directional derivatives. In: Readings in Computer Vision, pp. 216–226. Elsevier (1987)
30. Desolneux, A., Moisan, L., Morel, J.-M.: From Gestalt Theory to Image Analysis: A Probabilistic Approach, vol. 34. Springer, Heidelberg (2007). https://doi.org/10.1007/978-0-387-74378-3
31. Akinlar, C., Topal, C.: EDLines: a real-time line segment detector with a false detection control. Pattern Recogn. Lett. **32**(13), 1633–1642 (2011)
32. Bogdan, V., Bonchiş, C., Orhei, C.: Custom dilated edge detection filters (2020)
33. Orhei, C., Bogdan, V., Bonchiş, C.: Edge map response of dilated and reconstructed classical filters. In: 2020 22nd International Symposium on Symbolic and Numeric Algorithms for Scientific Computing (SYNASC), pp. 187–194. IEEE (2020)

Automated Nonlinked Two-Vehicle Towing System

Yaqin Wang[1(✉)], Matthew Viele[2], Anthony H. Smith[1], John A. Springer[1], and Eric T. Matson[1]

[1] Purdue University, West Lafayette, IN 47907, USA
{wang4070,ahsmith,jaspring,ematson}@purdue.edu
[2] Viele Technology, Woodland Park, CO 80863, USA
mviele@vieletech.com

Abstract. Towing capacity affects a vehicle's towing ability and it is usually costly to buy or even rent a vehicle that can tow certain amount of weight. A widely swaying towing trailer is one of the main causes for accidents that involves towing trailers. This study propose an affordable automated nonlinked towing system (ANTS) that does not require physical connection between the leading vehicle and the trailer vehicle by only using a computer vision system. The ANTS contains two main parts: a leading vehicle which can perform lane detection and a trailer vehicle which can automatically follow the leading vehicle by detecting the license plate of the leading vehicle. The trailer vehicle can adjust its speed according to the distance from the leading vehicle.

Keywords: Autonomous driving · Towing system · Computer vision · Lane detection · License plate detection

1 Introduction

Towing capacity determines the maximum weight that a vehicle can pull while towing any kind of cargo, such as a trailer, another vehicle or a boat. Even though we often refer towing for transportation, towing capacity also involves in water-based transportation. Table 1 shows the towing capacity of some popular vehicle models [1] in the market, as well as the manufacturer suggested retail price (MSRP).

From Table 1, we can see that it is very costly to buy or even rent a vehicle that can tow a certain amount of weight. According to Santander Consumer USA, the most popular vehicle model in USA in 2019 is Toyota Camry, which only has about 1000 pounds towing capacity. The other problem with towing is the high risk of vehicle accidents happening every year. According to NHTSA, there are over 50000 accidents every year that are related to towing, and over 400 people have died in those accidents [12]. There are more than half million trailers sold in the US annually [8], and not all of them are towed by a properly sized

© Springer Nature Switzerland AG 2021
A. Lopata et al. (Eds.): ICIST 2021, CCIS 1486, pp. 136–149, 2021.
https://doi.org/10.1007/978-3-030-88304-1_11

Table 1. Towing capacity for selected SUVs and pickup trucks in 2018.

Make	Model	Trim	Engine	Max tow capacity	MSRP
Jeep	Grand Cherokee	4WD	3.6L V-6	6200	$30895
Acura	MDX	AWD	3.5L V-6	3,500	$46200
Audi	Q7	Turbocharged	2.0L	4,400	$49900
BMW	X5	All	All	6,000	$57200
Ram	1500	Reg Std 4WD	3.6L V-6	7050	$46500
Ford	F-150	Reg Shortbed 4WD	3.3L V-6	7400	$37025
Chevrolet	Silverado	Reg Cab Bed 4WD	5.3L V-8	6500	$40230
Toyota	Tundra	Double Cab Bed 4WD	5.7L V-8	9900	$43635
Nissan	Titan	Reg Cab Bed 4WD	5.6L V-8	9560	$34000

tow vehicle because large tow vehicles may be impractical due to size, comfort, or the cost of a 3rd vehicle for a family that only tows occasionally.

There are several assumptions for the automated disconnected towing system to work correctly [17]. Firstly, the ANTS requires both leading and trailer vehicles having own individual their power systems. In addition, ANTS requires no other vehicles or objects appearing in between the leading vehicle and the trailer vehicle. Also, the leading vehicle can not conduct sudden braking because the trailer vehicle needs a certain time to process the distance information and adjust the speed accordingly.

The contribution of this study are: Firstly, for those who own small vehicles, such as a Volkswagen beetle, can tow a few thousands of pounds of cargo. People will not need to worry about the towing capacity of their vehicles when towing. Secondly, ANTS can help reducing vehicle accidents that are related to towing. Also, it is possible to adopt ANTS in any type of small vehicle, which is a not large truck or a semi bus, or a non-commercial vehicle. In that way, any vehicle can turn into a trailer.

2   Relative Works

2.1   Advanced Driver-Assistance System

ADAS (advanced driver-assistance system) assists human drivers when driving or parking. Current ADAS technology uses electronic systems, such as vehicle onboard computer system [13], electronic control units (ECU), and microcontroller units (MCU). The purpose of ADAS is to improve driver's safety and comfort, and more generally, to improve road safety and traffic flow [16].

According to ASIRT, there are about 1.25 million motor vehicle crash deaths each year, which is about 3287 per day [2]. Among those, most of the vehicle accidents are caused by human error. ADAS is developed to support, assist, automate, and improve safety and more comfortable driving for human drivers. ADAS has been proven to help minimize human errors to decrease fatal road accidents [9].

ADAS helps by reducing collisions and road accidents using its safety features. The technologies that ADAS provides can alert human drivers about potential risks and problems. Current ADAS technology can also detect objects and pedestrians, perform basic classification, and in some cases, take control of the vehicles when necessary. The conventional ADAS features in nowadays vehicles include automated lightning system, adaptive cruise control (ACC), lane keeping system, blind-spot monitoring, forward collision warning, surround-view cameras, lane departure warning, pedestrian detection system, road sign recognition, autonomous emergency braking, and parking assist.

2.2 Lane Detection

It seems that the issue of lane detection is not so difficult. Initially it seems that the vehicle only needs to identify the host lane, and detect a short distance ahead of itself. A commonly used, simple hue transform-based algorithm can solve the problem in about 90% of the high way scenarios [4]. However, there is no easy answer for lane detection. It takes a lot of effort, resource, and time to build an efficient lane detection system, because of the obvious gaps in research, diversity scenarios, and high liability requirement [11].

In fact, full automation is the most complicated task in the autonomous driving system because it needs to deal with all the subsystems and overall structure. Undoubtedly, people may believe that the current autonomous technologies have been fully explored by researchers on fully autonomous vehicles. However, this might not be true under certain circumstances, such as non-highway scenarios or severe weather conditions. The current autonomous technologies need to be combined with highly accurate map information and on-board the localization system to perform a relatively good road and lane perception.

Driver assistance system should fulfill the requirement of an extremely low error rate in order to serve the great public. In such alarming systems like LDW, a false alarm rate must have a lower limit because its high frequency would disturb the drivers and bring about the public to against it. The exact acceptable rate of the false alarm is still under discussion [5]. Some existing systems will have a few false alarms per hour, in which, one false alarm per hour equals with one error in 54000 frames [3]. For those features in closed-loop automatic driving, errors should be even lower[11]. This kind of lower error rate is very difficult to achieve in vision-oriented systems. For other kinds of complicated computer vision system, such as a web-based searching application or surveillance system, people tend to be more forgiven about the error rate in such systems [11].

2.3 Color Spaces

Definition of Noise. When employing a computer vision system in lane detection, interfering noise is one of the biggest challenges [14]. The noise usually refers to shadows caused by different lighting conditions. But when detecting the lane lines, the noise could be a lot of other things, such as skid marks caused by a sudden stop, pavement stains, heavy rains or snow, fog, and more. Figure 1 shows the noise created by the shadow and skid marks on the road that might interfere with the lane detection result. Image processing for lane detection is crucial in the autonomous/assistive driving system, and there are still problems remaining unsolved. Whenever there is interfering noise in the input image, the detection result will be compromised. To find a way to reduce the noise in image processing is a crucial step in lane detection using a computer vision system.

Fig. 1. Example of noises in the road and lane detection.

Color Spaces. One of the common tools used in image processing in lane detection is color filters [7]. Crisman and Thorpe developed a SCARF system which includes two-color cameras to process image segmentation by color. The different regions that are separated by color are classified. At the same time, they also use the hough-like transform to vote for various binary road models [7]. Turk developed the VITS system that also uses a two-color camera [15]. In VITS, the color red and blue is used to decrease the interfering noise caused by shadows. Another two-model algorithm developed by He can detect the right and left edges of the borderline of the road and can recognize and enhance the borderlines of the road [10]. Instead of a two-color camera, this two-model algorithm uses a full-color camera to process the input image. The other color-based method is approached by Chui and Lin, which can be applied in more challenging scenarios [6]. Their system can distinguish the borderlines of the lane by using color-based segmentation in image processing.

There have been many efforts made to reduce the interfering noise in image processing in lane detection. One of the common techniques used is color filters [17,18]. In this research, we have considered a few in the image processing, which are BGR, LAB, HSV, HSL, and LUV. By utilizing various color filters and setting different thresholds of each individual channel of the color filter, color filters could improve the accuracy of the computer vision system in the lane detection.

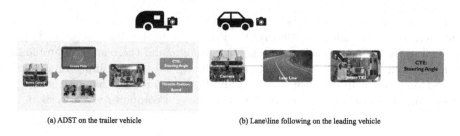

(a) ADST on the trailer vehicle   (b) Lane\line following on the leading vehicle

Fig. 2. ANTS overview.

3 Methodology

The goal of this study is to design an automated disconnected towing system (ANTS) that does not require a hard connection between the leading vehicle and trailer vehicle. ANTS contains two subsystems: a lane following system for the leading vehicle and license plate following system for the trailer vehicle, as showing in Fig. 2. The lane following system allows the leading vehicle to follow the lane line and drive by itself. And the automated disconnected towing system allows the trailer to detect the license plate that is attached to the back of the leading vehicle. The other important function of ANTS is to adjust the trailer car's current speed according to the distance from the leading vehicle. In the rest of this chapter, the requirements of the hardware and software will be discussed in the rest of this section.

3.1 Line Following System

The goal of the line following system is to design an image processing system that enables the leading vehicle to drive itself autonomously by following a lane line. Overall, this line following system takes video images as input and produces cross track error (CTE) as output. The CTE is used by Roboteq, which is a type of DC motor controller, to calculate the steering angle command. The overall structure is demonstrated in the Fig. 2b.

In order for the leading vehicle to follow the yellow lane line, it has to be able to recognize it first. A standard yellow tape is used to do indoor testing on the vision system and later, a pavement marking tape is used for outdoor testing. The camera will filter out the colors based on the RGB range, and it will only look for the color yellow. Then it will find the contour of the yellow area. If all the conditions are met and the lane line is found, the system will draw a blue cross in the middle of the yellow contour, as shown in Fig. 3.

All the computer programs, in this project, are written in Python. The Robotic Operating System (ROS) is used as the platform in this project to run all the computer programs. In order for the leading vehicle to follow the yellow lane line, it has to be able to recognize it first. To do so, firstly, the camera needs to find the region of interest in the input image. The region of interest (ROI) is set to be about lower one-third of the height of the original image, and

Fig. 3. The line following system detects the lane and draw a blue cross in the middle of the yellow contour. (Color figure online)

about center one-third of the image. And then, the program turns the ROI into an array of points. An image filled with zero intensities with the same dimensions of the trimmed image is created as a mask. Then, the program fills the mask with values of 1 when the area overlaps with the frame (RIO) and fills with values of zero outside of RIO. A bitwise operation is conducted between the mask and the frame to only keep the triangular area of the frame.

After getting the frame of interest, the camera needs to detect the contour of the yellow lane line. OpenCV is used here to do image processing. The program filters out the colors based on the settings of the RGB range and all non-yellow colors are filtered out from the image. Then the program converts the frame to grayscale because the computer vision only needs the luminance channel for detecting edges. Also, changing the image to grayscale helps to save some computational power. A 5×5 Gaussian blur is applied to make the process easier and simpler. Then canny edge detector is applied with a minimum value of 50 and a maximum value of 150 to get the contour of the image. At the last, the program draws a blue cross in the middle of the contour, which will be the center of the lane line.

Cross track error (CTE) is the key element to calculate the steering angle. The current CTE in Fig. 3 is the angle between the red line and the orange line. To calculate the current CTE, the program will calculate the absolute value between the center of the image and the center of the detected lane line. The red line is the shortest absolute value between the center of the license plate to the bottom of the image. And then the arctangent function in the math library can calculate the degree (CTE) of the angle between the red and the green line.

3.2 License Plate Following System

The goal of the automated disconnected towing system (ANTS) is to design a computer vision system that can detect the license plate of the leading vehicle and follow it by keeping a certain distance. There are two functions that the license plate following system has to fulfill: the first one is the plate detection function, which is to be able to detect the license plate by using similar technology that is used in the line following system; the second one is the speed control function, which is to control the speed according to the distance information from the stereo camera. The overview structure of the license plate following system is showing in Fig. 2a.

The license plate attached to the leading vehicle is made with two colors, red and yellow. The plate detection function allows the camera to detect the license plate by its colors and shapes. The input of the plate detection function is the image input, and the output is cross track error (CTE), which is used in calculating the steering angle. At the same time, the speed control takes the distance information from the stereo camera, and the program will adjust the speed of the trailer vehicle according to the distance. The input of the speed control system is the distance, and the output is the speed.

In order for the trailer vehicle to follow the leading vehicle, it has to be able to recognize the license plate attached to the leading vehicle first, which is the license detection function. To do so, firstly, the camera needs to find the region of interest in the input image. The region of interest (ROI) is set to be about lower one-third of the height of the original image, and about center of the one-third of the image. And then, the program turns the ROI into an array of points. An image filled with zero intensities with the same dimensions of the trimmed image is created as a mask. Then, the program fills the mask with values of 1 when the area overlaps with the frame (RIO) and fills with values of zero outside of RIO. A bitwise operation is conducted between the mas and the frame to only keep the triangular area of the frame.

After getting the frame of interest, the camera needs to detect the contour of the license plate, which includes shapes: a big rectangle and a relatively smaller circular. Again, OpenCV is used here to do image processing. The program filters out the colors based on the settings of the RGB range and all non-yellow and non-red colors are filtered out from the image. After the program finds the two combinations of colors, it will try to find a rectangle shape and a circular shape. The program converts the frame to grayscale by using it because we only need the luminance channel for detecting the edges of the shapes. Also, changing the image to grayscale helps to save some computational power. A 5×5 Gaussian blur is applied to make the process easier and simpler. Then Canny edge detector is applied with a minimum value of 50 and a maximum value of 150 to get the contour of the target shapes. After both shapes are located, the program draws a blue cross in the middle of the circular shape, which will be the center of the license plate.

In the speed control system, if the minimum distance between the leading vehicle and the trailer vehicle is less than 1.3 m, the trailer vehicle comes to a full stop to avoid collision. If the minimum distance is between 1.4 and 1.6 m, the trailer vehicle remains in a constant speed which is set to be 25 m per hour. If the minimum distance is between 1.6 and 2.2 m, the trailer vehicle increases its speed by 2 miles per hour to catch up with the leading vehicle. If the minimum distance is greater than 2.2 m, the trailer vehicle increases its speed by 4 m per hour to catch up with the leading vehicle.

Cross track error is also the key element to calculate the steering angle. The current CTE in Fig. 4 is the angle between the red line and the orange line. To calculate the current CTE, the program will calculate the absolute value between the center of the image and the center of the detected lane line, as shown in the red line in the Figure. The yellow line is the shortest absolute value between the center of the license plate to the bottom of the image. And then the arctangent function in the math library can calculate the degree of the angle (CTE) between the red and the orange lines.

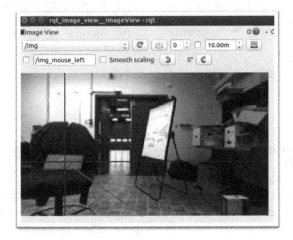

Fig. 4. CTE in license plate following system. (Color figure online)

4   Experiment Setup for ANTS

4.1   Experiment Setup for Vision System

The vision system for ANTS is divided into two parts: indoor testing and outdoor testing, for different lightning conditions. The camera used in lane following is Logitech Webcam C270, and the one used for license plate detection is a depth camera, ZED 1.

For the first stage of testing the vision system, the webcam and ZED camera is mounted to the robot cars. On one of the robot car, we have attached a real licence plate in the back, which functions as the leading vehicle.

4.2   Experiment Setup for ANTS

Experiments to test the system will be conducted in two parts: indoor and outdoor environments. The indoor experiment takes place in the company garage area with a concrete floor with a smooth finish on the ground, as shown in Fig. 5a. The outdoor experiments take place in the parking lot outside of the company building with uneven asphalt surface, as shown in Fig. 5b.

(a) Indoor experiment environment setup.

(b) Outdoor experiment environment setup

Fig. 5. Outdoor experiment environment setup.

Equipment Setup. First, the experiment will use two robot cars to experiment. Each of the robot car will use NVIDIA Jetson Nano as microprocessor and a webcam for the vision system. After testing the system on the robot cars, the next step is to test the system on two go-karts. The NVIDIA Jetson TX2 will be used on the leading vehicle, for its availability, and the Jetson Nano will be used in the trailer vehicle for the low-cost purpose. The experiments on the course tracks will only use the go-karts.

Course Tracks Design and Setup. There are three different course tracks to test the system, in different shapes, different lengths, and different floor surfaces. Course track I consists of 10-m straight lines in both indoor and outdoor environments, as shown in Fig. 6a. Course track II is a combination of straight lines and curves, about 20-m long and 8-m wide, as shown in Fig. 6b Course track III is an Fig. 8 course with about 10-m straight lines and 2.5-m radius curves Fig. 6c.

5   Evaluation and Results

5.1   Computer Vision System in ANTS

ANTS is an automated disconnected towing system that does not require a hard connection between the leading vehicle and the trailer vehicle. ANTS contains two computer vision subsystems: a line following system for the leading vehicle and an automated towing system for the trailer vehicle. The line following system allows the leading vehicle to follow the lane line and drive by itself. And the

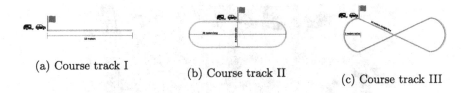

(a) Course track I

(b) Course track II

(c) Course track III

Fig. 6. Course tracks

automated disconnected towing system allows the trailer to detect the license plate that is attached to the back of the leading vehicle. The other important feature of ANTS is to adjust the trailer car's current speed according to the distance from the leading vehicle.

5.2   Line Following

The goal of the line following system is to design an image processing system that enables the leading vehicle to drive itself autonomously by following a lane line. Overall, this line following system takes video images as input and produces cross track error (CTE) as output. The CTE is used by Roboteq, which is a type of DC motor controller, to calculate the steering angle command.

During the experiments, we use different error types and error locations to measure the results when driving in the course, as shown in Table 2. For the error types, there are software error and hardware error; and for error locations, there are location I: at the beginning of the course; location II: at the middle part of the course; and location III: at the end of the course, as shown in Table 3.

In testing the single line following system, the biggest difference from indoor testing is the change in lighting conditions. The natural light changes along with the position of the sun. When driving towards the sun, which means the license plate is in the shadow, the camera was having a difficult time detecting. The vehicle drove on the course in both directions. Figure 7 shows course track III in the garage area.

When testing the lane following system in the outdoor environment, we apply the same error types and error locations as in the indoor environment, as shown in Table 2 and 3. The biggest difference for lane following from line following is implementing the Hough Transform algorithm to detect and calculate the slopes of the two lines in the frame. Overall, the system performance is more stable in the indoor environment.

Table 2. Error types

Type of errors	Error names	Example errors
Type I	Software error	Camera failure
Type II	Hardware error	Low battery

Fig. 7. Course Track III for indoor testing environment.

5.3 License Plate Following

The other computer vision system in ANTS is to detect the license plate of the leading vehicle and follow it by keeping a certain distance. There are two functions that the ANTS system has to fulfill: the first one is the plate detection function, which is to be able to detect the license plate by using just one camera; the second one is the speed control function, which is to control the speed according to the distance information from the stereo camera.

We have tested ANTS on both RC cars and go-karts. At first, a wagon was used and the license plate was attached on it as the leading vehicle. And then the wagon was pulled it manually to have the trailer vehicle follow the license plate on the cargo, as shown in Fig. 8. After successfully perform ANTS on the cargo and the trailer go-kart, we have two go-karts driving at the same time: the leading vehicle performs the line following system and the trailer vehicle performs the license plate following.

After successfully tested ANTS with a wagon and a go-kart, we used two go-karts and tested on course track I and II, in both indoor and outdoor environments. The results of the indoor tests again are better than the ones in the outdoor environment, because of the same reason for the line following tests: the change of the natural light according to the position of the sun. The shadow creates noises and interferes with the performance of the vision system.

Table 3. Error locations

Location of errors	Location names
Location I	At the beginning of the course
Location II	In the middle of the course
Location II	Towards the end of the course

Fig. 8. Using a cargo car as the leading vehicle to test ANTS.

5.4 Discussion

During the tests for line/lane following and the ANTS systems, there are some problems discovered which are not expected before the tests. The biggest issue with all the vision systems is the shadow interference that is caused by the sun. When the sunlight is not directly on the license plate, the camera sometimes cannot detect the plate because of the shadow. Often, with the impact of the shadow, the camera used is not able to recognize or detect anything, including lines or the license plates. This could also happen in cloudy days when there is not enough sunlight. But sunny days were chosen to do the tests on purpose because the clouds increase the possibilities of rains that might damage all the equipment used in the tests. Secondly, we were not able to test the ANTS on course track III, due to its availability and the weather conditions. However, we were able to build the track indoor in the garage area. Third, after the successful preformance of the license plate following by using the plate made with two colors, we implemented a small machine learning model, KNN, to recognize numbers and letters on the plate. The system is not accurate enough and is not stable during tests. It might be because the training set is not big enough, and the model needs longer training time. Lastly, we are only able to conduct tests on ANTS on go-karts on course track I and II, because of the weather conditions. We will conduct more tests for the next phase.

6 Conclusion

This study proposes an automated nonlinked towing system (ANTS) that does not require a physical connection between a leading vehicle and a trailer vehicle by only using a computer vision system. Each of the leading and trailer vehicle has a depth camera mounted in the front. The cameras on the leading vehicle can perform lane detection. And the one on the trailer vehicle is able to perform license detection and to detect the distance from the leading vehicle and adjust the speed accordingly.

The purpose of this study is to only use a camera, computer vision technology, to perform lane following and license plate following in the automated nonlinked towing system. By utilizing different tools, such as color filters and the Canny edge detector, the ANTS can perform the lane following and license plate following in the indoor environment with about 90% success rate. Once the tests were conducted in the outdoor environment, the shadow created by the sun is the main challenge for the vision system. For example, when the sunlight does not directly project on the license plate, the license plate will be covered by the shadow. The ANTS will have a difficult time capturing the outlines and the colors of the plate. Although the outdoor testing for ANTS is less than perfect, there are so many possibilities and potential in the vision system. To solve the shadow interference could be one of the future research topics.

During the experiments for ANTS, there are some problems discovered which are not expected before the tests. The biggest issue with all the vision systems is the shadow interference that is caused by the sun. When the sunlight is not directly on the license plate, the camera sometimes can't detect the plate because of the shadow. Some times, with the impact of the shadow, The camera we are using is not able to recognize or detect anything, including lines or the license plates. This could also happen in cloudy days when there is not enough sunlight. But we chose sunny days to do the tests on purpose because the clouds increase the possibilities of rains that might damage all the equipment used in the tests.

The problems mentioned above can be future studies. Using QR code, barcode, or PDF417 for license plate following is another possibility, instead of the plate we made with two colors. We can also look into other networks for license plate pattern recognition.

References

1. Advisor, A.: Complete towing capacity database 2018 (2019). https://axleadvisor.com/towing-capacity/. Accessed 7 Nov 2019
2. ASIRT: Annual Global Road Crash Statistics (2019). https://www.asirt.org/safe-travel/road-safety-facts/
3. Batavia, P.H.: Driver-adaptive lane departure warning systems. Carnegie Mellon University Pittsburgh, USA (1999)
4. Borkar, A., Hayes, M., Smith, M.T., Pankanti, S.: A layered approach to robust lane detection at night (2009)
5. Burzio, G., Guidotti, L., Perboli, G., Settanni, M., Tadei, R., Tesauri, F.: Investigating the impact of a lane departure warning system in real driving conditions: a subjectivefield operational test. In: European Conference on Human Centred Design for Intelligent Transport Systems (2010)
6. Chiu, K.Y., Lin, S.F.: Lane detection using color-based segmentation, pp. 706–711. IEEE (2005)
7. Crisman, J.D., Thorpe, C.E.: SCARF: a color vision system that tracks roads and intersections. IEEE Trans. Robot. Autom. 9(1), 49–58 (1993)
8. Ferries, C.: RV Statistics. https://www.condorferries.co.uk/rv-statistics. Accessed 8 Mar 2021

9. Hamid, U.Z.A., et al.: Autonomous emergency braking system with potential field risk assessment for frontal collision mitigation. In: 2017 IEEE Conference on Systems, Process and Control (ICSPC), pp. 71–76. IEEE (2017)

10. He, Y., Wang, H., Zhang, B.: Color-based road detection in urban traffic scenes. IEEE Trans. Intell. Transp. Syst. 5(4), 309–318 (2004)

11. Hillel, A.B., Lerner, R., Levi, D., Raz, G.: Recent progress in road and lane detection: a survey. Mach. Vis. Appl. 25(3), 727–745 (2014)

12. Koenigsberg, S.: Trailer Accident Statistics (2019). http://www.joshts.com/NationalTrailerAccidentStatistics.pdf. Accessed 7 Nov 2019

13. Meier, L., Tanskanen, P., Fraundorfer, F., Pollefeys, M.: PIXHAWK: a system for au- tonomous flight using onboard computer vision. In: 2011 IEEE International Conference on Robotics and Automation, pp. 2992–2997. IEEE (2011)

14. Srivastava, S., Singal, R., Lumba, M.: Efficient lane detection algorithm using different filtering techniques. Int. J. Comput. Appl. 88(3), 6–11 (2014)

15. Turk, M.A., Morgenthaler, D.G., Gremban, K.D., Marra, M.: VITS-a vision system for autonomous land vehicle navigation. IEEE Trans. Pattern Anal. Mach. Intell. 10(3), 342–361 (1988)

16. Van Arem, B., Van Driel, C.J., Visser, R.: The impact of cooperative adaptive cruise control on traffic-flow characteristics. IEEE Trans. Intell. Transp. Syst. 7(4), 429–436 (2006)

17. Wang, Y.: Automated disconnected towing system. Master thesis, Purdue University (2020)

18. Liu, D., Wang, Y., Chen, T., Matson, E.: Application of color filter adjustment andk-means clustering method in lane detection for self-driving cars. In: 2019 Third IEEE International Conference on Robotic Computing (IRC), pp. 153–158. IEEE (2019)

Automatic Programming Problem Difficulty Evaluation – First Results

Artūras Skarbalius and Mantas Lukoševičius[(✉)] [iD]

Faculty of Informatics, Kaunas University of Technology, Kaunas, Lithuania
{arturas.skarbalius,mantas.lukosevicius}@ktu.edu

Abstract. In this work, we address automatic evaluation of the difficulty of programming problems or exercises. Typically the problems consist of both text description and accompanying figures. We collect a suitable dataset, investigate the evaluation based on the text and the image data separately, as well as a combination of the two. The first results of this investigation are reported, together with the discussion and future work.

Keywords: Programming problem · Difficulty evaluation · Natural language processing · Convolutional neural network · Deep learning · Machine learning

1 Introduction

Programming problems of various kinds are regularly used to teach those interested in programming how to do so effectively in a practical way, and on occasion, they are also utilized to evaluate or demonstrate the ability of an individual regarding a particular field.

The issue with these sorts of problems, however, is that compared to other methods, these kinds of programming problems tend to be comparatively subjective - there is oftentimes very little objective way to evaluate exactly how difficult an exercise would be due to those writing them having a different perception of it compared to everyone else.

This project is an attempt to resolve part of this issue by utilizing machine learning to evaluate difficulty in regards to programming problems. Utilizing this system, it should be possible to have a more objective view of a problem and make it easier to perform the aforementioned teaching and evaluation of skills if successful.

The problem formulation usually includes both text and images, which makes this task more difficult, since typically different machine learning methods are used for the two types of data. Here we attempt to investigate the difficulty estimation based both on text, rendered image of the problem, and combination of both.

We review the previous related work in Sect. 2, explain the data that we use in Sect. 3, present our methods used and preliminary results in Sect. 4, and

© Springer Nature Switzerland AG 2021
A. Lopata et al. (Eds.): ICIST 2021, CCIS 1486, pp. 150–159, 2021.
https://doi.org/10.1007/978-3-030-88304-1_12

finally, a short discussion is given, alongside ways to improve it in the future, in Sect. 5.

2   Related Work

Here we review the basic approaches and algorithms used for this type of problem. Due to the unique nature of the task, exact methods for evaluation have not been fully considered. As such, a wider variety of methods is considered.

2.1   Approaches

There have not been many attempts to approach this problem in particular, but there have been attempts to achieve results in similar fields. One example in particular is an attempt at predicting the difficulty of various questions in reading problems [5] that utilized a particular framework called the Test-aware Attention-based Convolutional Neural Network (TACNN). According to the given results in the paper, the approach does improve on the result by some amount, and experts generally have lower accuracy on the evaluation than the resulting neural network.

Another notable approach has been the utilization of a hybrid AI [7] to evaluate exercise difficulty. To initialize the system, a teacher, as an expert, needs to input a rule set. After this is done, the feedback of any students that have taken the exercise is taken and used to adjust the results via a genetic algorithm. The results obtained from such indicates that a significant portion of exercises are initially evaluated incorrectly. However, this approach appears to be flawed - the method used indicates exactly one set of rules per difficulty level, which is fairly inaccurate to a realistic situation. In addition, if multiple rules for a single difficulty level are included in the starting rule set, the system cannot correctly determine which to use as the starting point to adjust from. According to the article, the rule to be used as a base for the genetic algorithm to adjust was chosen at random at the time of writing.

Beyond this, there do not appear to be many other methods utilized for tasks of this nature.

2.2   Algorithms

There are numerous algorithms that can be utilized. As the method we have been using (detailed in the Methods section) involves both text and images, there will be two subsections for algorithms associated with both, as well as another subsection indicating ways to combine multiple methods into one.

Text-Based Evaluation. Natural Language Processing (NLP) initially requires some amount of pre-processing for the text [10]. There are multiple parts of pre-processing that can be utilized, as well as many different methods, so only a small portion will be mentioned here:

1. **Tokenization** is a process during which large amounts of text are separated and occasionally classified into smaller sections that machine learning can utilize effectively. Commonly used methods involve separating text by sentences or separating text by words.
2. **Normalization** is a method utilized to improve a system by attempting to remove redundant words with similar meanings. **Stemming**, for instance, is a method used to reduce words to their root form, and **lemmatization** removes prefixes and suffixes from words.

As an example, the **bag-of-words** method gathers all of the tokens obtained from a text into a "bag" – a format that completely ignores word order and grammar, but retains the number of times each word has shown up in a text in a way that a computer can use in the future.

For text-based evaluation, various algorithms can be used. To simplify things, just some of the useful methods that have been evaluated will be described here.

1. **A decision tree** [8] is a simple method for classification. It makes use of multiple true/false statements to form a result. A decision tree classifier in machine learning forms this sort of tree through the use of training data to evaluate the exact values necessary. It is commonly used for relative simplicity and effectiveness, and there are several methods to improve the accuracy of these kinds of methods as well (detailed further under Model combination). A simple example of the way a decision tree works is shown in Fig. 1 – In this case, Y is a binary variable, while the other two variables, X1 and X2, are used in this case to determine what the result should be.

   Once a model is formed, pruning can be performed for the sake of lowering the redundant or otherwise excessive branches and simplify the resulting model. While unnecessary, it can help with speed on several occasions.

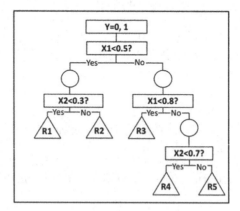

Fig. 1. Sample decision tree based on binary target variable Y. The image is used from [8] under the Creative Commons Attribution-NonCommercial-Share Alike 4.0 Unported License.

2. Light Gradient Boosting Machine (**LightGBM**) [6] is a gradient boosting decision tree (GBDT), designed by Microsoft. In particular, this implementation adds a couple of techniques: Gradient-based One-Side Sampling (GOSS), which allows for an accurate information gain with less data, and Exclusive Feature Bundling (EFB), which bundles mutually exclusive features together in a way that would allow for fewer variables that the model has to look into. Through this, the resulting method is approximately 20 times faster while providing roughly equivalent accuracy.

3. The Limited-memory Broyden–Fletcher–Goldfarb–Shanno algorithm (**L-BFGS**) [1], is a method to approximate the Broyden–Fletcher–Goldfarb–Shanno (BFGS) algorithm using a limited amount of available memory. Oftentimes this method is used for parameter estimation. The algorithm estimates an inverse Hessian matrix to help with determining the exact value.

Some classification methods are only created for the purposes of binary classification. To change these into multiclass classification, there are two methods to go about this, in particular [3]:

1. **One-vs-All** method creates n different versions of the same model, where n is the number of different classifications available, with each one having two different possible results - it is one of the available classifiers, or it is any of the others. When evaluating, the resulting model returns the classifier for which the model had the highest result. This method is generally faster and requires less memory to utilize.

2. **One-vs-One** method creates a different model for each possible combination of classifiers available, with each one having two of the possible multiple classifiers available. Once all of the different models finish, the correct answer is chosen by summing up or averaging all scores, and returning the highest result. This method is more complicated, slower, and requires more memory to utilize, but it may obtain more accuracy on occasion compared to One-vs-All.

Image-Based Evaluation. Computer vision is, to put it simply, an attempt to make a computer interpret vision in a similar way any other individual does [11]. Thus far, most cases of computer vision involve extremely specialized forms, such as **optical character recognition** (OCR) to interpret symbols from images. While more general-purpose methods do exist, they are not quite applicable to the task at hand presently, though there is a good chance that it will be more possible to use in the future.

For image-based evaluation, the main thing that is used is neural networks - a network made of several layers of interconnected artificial neurons that take in a value and return a result based on that value. The most common form of these neural networks that are utilized are **convolutional neural networks** [9]. Various sorts of variations and advancements have been made over the years, but as a general case, these sorts of neural networks rely on three forms of neuron layers:

1. **Fully-connected layers** are regularly used in all forms of artificial neural networks. The main characteristic of these layers is that they are completely connected to all adjacent layers, without being connected in any way to any other layers.
2. **Convolutional layers**, which are capable of learning various kernels that are then utilized to more efficiently evaluate a given image, are the primary layers the convolutional neural network utilizes. In most standard neural networks, reading an image would regularly result in a model that becomes too large to train in any effective manner. By using a convolutional layer, it is possible to reduce the complexity of a model significantly.
3. **Pooling layers**, which aim to pool together values in an attempt to gradually reduce the dimensions of the received image in such a way that it could be reliably used without making the system too complex.

Model Combination. Several different methods have been used to put together multiple models in a way that would make the end result more capable than any of the individual parts. Oftentimes, these models are mostly identical to the others it is being combined with, excluding the data it was trained with. This sort of model combination is referred to as ensemble learning. The most common examples of this are [12]:

1. **Bootstrap aggregating**, sometimes referred to as **bagging**, is by far one of the simplest methods of ensemble learning available. For this method, the data is randomized during learning for each of the base learners. The results are counted for each of the available results, then these results are taken and averaged. The value that has achieved the highest average is considered to be the correct result. One example of this is random forests - an ensemble model that makes use of many different decision trees to form a result, regularly more accurate than any of the individual decision trees. It is a particularly quick to create model, but it is significantly less accurate compared to the others.
2. **Bayesian model averaging** [4] is created in a fairly similar manner to bootstrap aggregating - the data is randomized during learning, then an overarching model puts together the result. The key difference, however, is that each of the individual models in this exact scenario has a set weight during the evaluation, influencing the end result in this way. The accuracy is significantly better compared to Bootstrap aggregating due to this.

Aside from this, there is another method to utilize multiple different models, however this one requires more specific methods - **two-branch neural networks** [2]. These networks utilize two different models - for example, one that takes in text and another that takes in images, obtains the partial results, then runs those results through another layer of neurons to get a final result. By making use of this, both text and images are evaluated together.

3   Datasets

The dataset has been created personally through web scraping from several free websites that can be utilized, such as hackerrank.com and codechef.com. The finalized dataset contains over 5000 different entries, each one containing difficulty (provided by the author), accuracy (a percentage of how many individuals successfully provided a suitable answer to the problem), the problem name, a description, and a variable number of images. At present, the model attempts to make use of the provided difficulty for the evaluation.

After this is finished, the data is recreated into multiple other methods to ensure simplicity for the actual evaluation. A CSV file is created from the text data (difficulty, problem name, description), and image data is combined with the description to create a set of images that contain the necessary text for evaluation.

4   Methods and Results

The methods we have utilized involve several different text classification methods to obtain different results - perceptrons, linear support vector machines, etc. A two-branch neural network is also used to improve the evaluation by adding deep-learning-based image recognition. A specially-made program is used to obtain results and return the possible accuracy.

4.1   Text-Based Evaluation

The results for text evaluation are fully detailed in Table 1. In this case, "MicroAccuracy" refers to an accuracy calculation from all available results, while "MacroAccuracy" takes the precision and recall in place of it instead.

The text preprocessing used for each of the models is as follows: Each of the possible end result labels is assigned a numerical key, then all of the text from the other two possible inputs is transformed into a vector of floats representing counts of n-grams (an identical continuous sequence of n items) for both words and characters. Through doing this, it can then evaluate what each word indicates for a problem's difficulty.

For the sake of a more comprehensible explanation, the basic way accuracy is calculated is

$$P_r = \frac{TP}{TP + FP}, \tag{1}$$

where TP refers to the number of true positives, and FP refers to the number of false positives.

Micro-average Accuracy, written here as MicroAccuracy, refers to adding all of the values together before calculations. So, as an example, if there were three classes to evaluate from, micro-average accuracy would be counted as

$$P_{r_{micro}} = \frac{TP1 + TP2 + TP3}{TP1 + TP2 + TP3 + FP1 + FP2 + FP3}. \tag{2}$$

Macro-average accuracy, written here as MacroAccuracy, refers to dividing each of the results before averaging them, thus ensuring that each class has an equal contribution to the result. Using the same example of three classes, this is how macro-average accuracy is calculated as

$$P_{r_{macro}} = \frac{\frac{TP1}{TP1+FP1} + \frac{TP2}{TP2+FP2} + \frac{TP3}{TP3+FP3}}{3}. \tag{3}$$

Micro-average accuracy is preferable when trying to calculate accuracy for a multi-class classification problem if it is believed that there may be some imbalance between the number of entries per class. In this case, macro-average accuracy is used to show that, while there is a small amount of imbalance in the data, it does not truly impact the result with most models.

Table 1. Text evaluation results

Model name	MicroAccuracy	MacroAccuracy
Random forest	0.718	0.725
Decision tree	0.711	0.712
LightGBM	0.701	0.708
Logistic regression (L-BFGS)	0.660	0.657
Maximum entropy (SDCA)	0.639	0.661
Stochastic gradient descent	0.620	0.623
Averaged perceptron	0.609	0.641
Linear support-vector machine	0.583	0.597
SymbolicSgdLogisticRegression	0.545	0.584
Maximum entropy (L-BFGS)	0.458	0.319

The algorithms mentioned use the same preprocessing methods, and no method of separating parts of the exercise are utilized. Regardless, limited manual testing shows that the results do not vary significantly if minor or irrelevant parts are changed.

4.2   Image-Based Evaluation

For image-based evaluation, a single image containing the whole problem description together with the illustrations was rendered for each problem. The size needed for the image is pre-calculated, the text and images are taken, then the text is rendered using a predefined style, with images being inserted in places where they were in the original problem. An example of the image formed from the text and images of an exercise is shown in Fig. 2.

Once that is finished, the result is used as data for a deep neural network, by which the data is evaluated. Several well known models were used – their names as well as the obtained results are shown in Table 2.

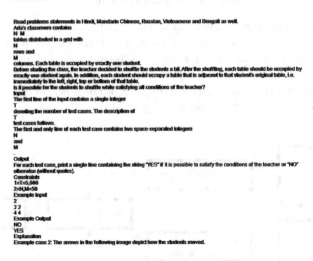

Ada School

Read problems statements in Hindi, Mandarin Chinese, Russian, Vietnamese and Bengali as well.
Ada's classroom contains
N M
tables distributed in a grid with
N
rows and
M
columns. Each table is occupied by exactly one student.
Before starting the class, the teacher decided to shuffle the students a bit. After the shuffling, each table should be occupied by exactly one student again. In addition, each student should occupy a table that is adjacent to that student's original table, i.e.
immediately to the left, right, top or bottom of that table.
Is it possible for the students to shuffle while satisfying all conditions of the teacher?
Input
The first line of the input contains a single integer
T
denoting the number of test cases. The description of
T
test cases follows.
The first and only line of each test case contains two space-separated integers
N
and
M
.
Output
For each test case, print a single line containing the string "YES" if it is possible to satisfy the conditions of the teacher or "NO"
otherwise (without quotes).
Constraints
1≤T≤5,000
2≤N,M≤50
Example Input
2
3 3
4 4
Example Output
NO
YES
Explanation
Example case 2: The arrows in the following image depict how the students moved.

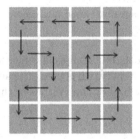

Fig. 2. Example of an image formed from a problem's text and images. The problem used is from codechef.com.

Table 2. Image evaluation results

Model name	MicroAccuracy	MacroAccuracy
ResNet50	0.403	0.343
ResNet101	0.436	0.385
MobileNet V2	0.297	0.239
Inception V3	0.339	0.258

Similarly to the text models, preprocessing is the same for each model – in this case, simply loading the image as raw bytes into the model. The rest is handled by the neural network for each model.

4.3   Combining Text and Image-Based Evaluation

In an attempt to improve the accuracy of the text-based and image-based methods, a two-branch neural network was used. The two separate models are used initially – one for text, the other for images. The outputs of the two models are then concatenated and re-evaluated to obtain the refined result. The two-branch neural network we are using is presented in Fig. 3. For now, we use a single layer neural network for the results refinement part.

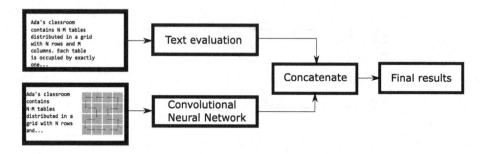

Fig. 3. Example of a two-branch neural network being used.

Before using the two-branch neural network, our image classification accuracy was about 40–50%. When a two-branch neural network is used, the accuracy goes up rapidly, up to about 80+% – significantly higher than either of the individual models (Table 3).

Table 3. Multiple variations for two-branch neural networks

Image model name	Text model name	MicroAccuracy	MacroAccuracy
ResNet50	Random forest	0.967	0.969
ResNet50	Logistic regression (L-BFGS)	0.925	0.937
ResNet50	Averaged perceptron	0.857	0.839
ResNet50	Stochastic gradient descent	0.804	0.793

5   Discussion and Future Work

At the time of writing, the things that have been attempted thus far are as follows:

1. Text-based processing
2. Image-based processing
3. Two-branch neural networks

With this, a varied set of initial results has been obtained, giving an opportunity to evaluate some of the given results and potentially improve on them.

Among text-based models, with a bag of n-grams preprocessing, the Random Forest ensemble model returned the best results.

Future work for text-based models may include the use of different text preprocessing methods – the completely different structure of the input may increase the accuracy of the models further.

More options for the image recognition network could be tested in the future.

When fully trained, the models can most likely accurately determine the difficulty of exercises correctly, so long as the data used for training is focused on the type of exercise being evaluated by the model. It is unclear whether or not these models can function for a wider variety of exercises simultaneously without additional adjustments, as no testing has been done in regards to this.

The two-branch neural network is particularly useful at the moment. The accuracy of the two-branch neural network is significantly greater (80%) than either the text-based (72%) or image-based (43%) models on their own.

More options for the combination of the two branches could be considered in the future, including a single fully trainable architecture with no intermediate interpretable results from the text and image-based models.

References

1. Bollapragada, R., Nocedal, J., Mudigere, D., Shi, H.J., Tang, P.T.P.: A progressive batching L-BFGS method for machine learning. In: International Conference on Machine Learning, pp. 620–629. PMLR (2018)
2. Chen, H., Lagadec, B., Bremond, F.: Partition and reunion: a two-branch neural network for vehicle re-identification. In: CVPR Workshops, pp. 184–192 (2019)
3. Galar, M., Fernández, A., Barrenechea, E., Bustince, H., Herrera, F.: An overview of ensemble methods for binary classifiers in multi-class problems: experimental study on one-vs-one and one-vs-all schemes. Pattern Recogn. **44**(8), 1761–1776 (2011)
4. Hoeting, J.A., Madigan, D., Raftery, A.E., Volinsky, C.T.: Bayesian model averaging: a tutorial. Stat. Sci. 382–401 (1999)
5. Huang, Z., et al.: Question difficulty prediction for reading problems in standard tests. In: Proceedings of the AAAI Conference on Artificial Intelligence, vol. 31 (2017)
6. Ke, G., et al.: LightGBM: a highly efficient gradient boosting decision tree. Adv. Neural. Inf. Process. Syst. **30**, 3146–3154 (2017)
7. Koutsojannis, C., Beligiannis, G., Hatzilygeroudis, I., Papavlasopoulos, C., Prentzas, J.: Using a hybrid AI approach for exercise difficulty level adaptation. Int. J. Continuing Eng. Educ. Life Long Learn. **17**(4–5), 256–272 (2007)
8. Myles, A.J., Feudale, R.N., Liu, Y., Woody, N.A., Brown, S.D.: An introduction to decision tree modeling. J. Chemometr.: J. Chemometr. Soc. **18**(6), 275–285 (2004)
9. O'Shea, K., Nash, R.: An introduction to convolutional neural networks. arXiv preprint arXiv:1511.08458 (2015)
10. Palmer, D.D.: Text preprocessing. Handb. Nat. Lang. Process. **2**, 9–30 (2010)
11. Szeliski, R.: Computer Vision: Algorithms and Applications. Springer, Heidelberg (2010). https://doi.org/10.1007/978-1-84882-935-0
12. Zhou, Z.H.: Ensemble learning. Encycl. Biometr. **1**, 270–273 (2009)

Blockchain Based Cryptocurrency Transaction Data and Balance Anonymity Improvement

Eligijus Sakalauskas[1(✉)] and Ausrys Kilciauskas[2]

[1] Department of Applied Mathematics, Kauno Kolegija/University of Applied Sciences,
K. Donelaicio St. 73, 44249 Kaunas, Lithuania
`eligijus.sakalauskas@ktu.lt`
[2] Department of Informatics, Kauno Kolegija/University of Applied Sciences,
Pramones pr. 20, 50468 Kaunas, Lithuania
`ausrys.kilciauskas@go.kauko.lt`

Abstract. In recent time many investigations in blockchain based cryptocurrencies are directed toward improving users anonymity, untraceability and transferred sums anonymity. The solution to improve transaction balance anonymity of blockchain cryptocurrencies based on Unspent Transaction Output (UTXO) paradigm is presented. Transferred money sums are hidden by discrete exponent function (DEF). Then due to isomorphism property of DEF, hidden UTXO balance is computed and this balance can be approved by the validators in this hidden form. The security is based on the discrete logarithm problem (DLP) complexity.

Cryptocurrencies are circulating in the peer-to-peer network and data can be represented by the vectors in certain linear space as it is in the general peer-to-peer network of nodes. To avoid pollution attacks and improve robustness of these general networks the signature based on idea to sign a linear subspace of transferred data for general content distribution among the nodes is created. The same idea is used in our proposed UTXO transactions anonymity improvement. Since transaction data composing a balance is represented by the vectors spanning certain linear subspace of some linear space, then this subspace is digitally signed by one-time (session) signature based on one-time (session) private and public keys generation. According to the original literature source the security of this signature relies on the DLP complexity.

Keywords: Blockchain · Cryptocurrency · Bitcoin · Transaction · Peer-to-peer network · Anonymity

1 Introduction

In this paper we propose a solution to improve anonymity of blockchain cryptocurrencies based on Unspent Transaction Output (UTXO) paradigm. We are using a method based on discrete exponent function (DEF) to hide amount of transferred money and their balance. Then the amount of money transferred and the balance are anonymous. The integrity and authenticity of a balance is provided by one-time signature scheme based on the idea to sign a linear subspace of transaction data used in [1] for peer-to-peer (P2P)

© Springer Nature Switzerland AG 2021
A. Lopata et al. (Eds.): ICIST 2021, CCIS 1486, pp. 160–168, 2021.
https://doi.org/10.1007/978-3-030-88304-1_13

networks [2]. Transaction composer must create different one-time signatures for every transaction.

Many peer-to-peer cryptocurrencies such as Bitcoin are using Unspent Transaction Output (UTXO) paradigm which defines the sum of spendable cryptocurrency [3]. Payments to be sent directly from one party to another without the presence of trusted third party.

Most cryptocurrencies based on UTXO have the heterogeneous nature of the system. There are two distinct types of participants in the system, those who issue transactions, and those who validate transactions [4]. Author promotes the idea that instead of two types of participants the same participant could issue and validate transactions. We agree with this idea but some restrictions should be added to avoid validation of transactions issued by the same person.

The data exchanged among the participants representing the nodes of the network consist of the following parts: money transfers data (Tr), transactions data (Tx), and blocks data (Bd) to be validated. Transfers data from different nodes are included in transactions data and some number of transactions issued by different nodes are included in block data. Hence we can assume that the atomic piece of information in cryptocurrency system is a money transfer data Tr consisting of several components, e.g. sender's address, receiver's address, transferred sum and etc. Therefore Tr in its nature is a vector represented by these components. The set of transfers with a destination to the same receiver address forms the input of corresponding receiver transaction vector Tx. These unspent sums of inputs are called Unspent Transaction Outputs (UTXO). So, UTXO is defined by the number and sums of money transfers from the sender nodes to the receiver node. They remain UTXO until the receiver redeems them to pay someone else at which time they are referred to as Spent Transaction Output (STXO). The data of UTXO and STXO consist of input and output transfers and compose transaction Tx. To avoid double spending the money balance between UTXO and STXO must be maintained, i.e. UTXO = STXO.

The input and output transfer data we denote by the vectors In and Out respectively. In general, transaction Tx contain the set of input and output vectors $\{In_i\}$ and $\{Out_j\}$, where $i = 1, 2, ..., I$ and $j = 1, 2, ..., J\}$.

Described system has some similarities with peer-to-peer (P2P) network for content distribution [2].

A nodes in P2P network are functioning as an encoders in the sense that they receives information from all the input links, encodes, and sends information to all the output links. It can be referred as a network coding.

To avoid so called pollution attacks and robustness of the system signatures for content distribution with network coding were introduced [1]. This signature scheme allows nodes to check the validity of a packet without decoding. The scheme makes use of the linearity property of the packets in a coded system. These packets spans the linear vector subspace of some space and the signature is formed on this subspace. This allows nodes to check the integrity of the packets received easily.

In the case of cryptocurrency P2P network the node receives inputs $\{In_i\}$ from the senders, checks their validity, creates transaction Tx by encoding transferred money sums as a set of outputs $\{Out_j\}$ and sends Tx to the network. In this case the sender's and receiver's coding is simple and is based on nodes addresses related to their public keys.

According to our proposal validators of blocks and transactions must check one-time signature and verify the anonymous balance with hidden transferred sums.

2 Transaction Data Structure

Let we have a transaction with a set of I inputs and J outputs denoted by vectors $\boldsymbol{In} = (In_1, In_2, ..., In_I)$ and $\boldsymbol{Out} = (Out_1, Out_2, ..., Out_J)$.

Let the amount of money in input In_i is m_i represented by 32 bits, i.e. $|m_i| = 32$ bits. Then to this amount 32 zero bits are concatenated as most significant bits from the left denoted by 0_{32}. In addition 64 bits of zero denoted by 0_{64} and 128 bits of nonce η_i, i.e. $|\eta_i| = 128$ are concatenated as a left significant bits from the right. As a result we obtain extended money format represented in Fig. 1 we name as a coin π_i and express by

$$\pi_i = 0_{32}||m_i||0_{64}||\eta_i. \tag{1}$$

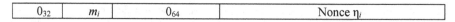

0_{32}	m_i	0_{64}	Nonce η_i

Fig. 1. Coin π_i representation.

The total length of coin π_i representation is equal to $|\pi_i|=256$ bits. The nonce η_i corresponding to every amount m_i is generated at random. Hence coin π_i has a nominal value m_i in the range $[1, 2^{32}-1]$ and nonce η_i being some kind of random serial number of the coin in the range $[1, 2^{128}-1]$. It is assumed that any nominal value of m_i exceeding $2^{32}-1$ and corresponding value of π_i exceeding $2^{224}-1$ are not valid and are rejected by the money recipient.

The amount of money m_i we interpret as a number of 224 bits length having 192 least significant bits equal to zero. Then π_i we can express as the following sum

$$\pi_i = m_i + \eta_i. \tag{2}$$

Now we define input and output data in some transaction $\boldsymbol{Tx}$. To be short we assume that the address of any user in this system corresponds to his public key.

Let the recipient of money in $\boldsymbol{Tx}$ is Bob and he receives a money from Alice$_1$, Alice$_2$, ... and Alice$_I$. So all Alices are the senders of money.

The set of inputs $\boldsymbol{In}$ in transaction $\boldsymbol{Tx}$ defines I senders named as Alices and having private-public key pairs defined in some public key cryptosystem, we denote by (x_i, a_i), where private key PrK $= x_i$ and public key PuK $= a_i$, and $i = 1, 2,..., I$. In the same way, Bob has a private-public key pair denoted by (y, b).

Let after receiving a money from Alices, Bob has the sum of unspent transaction output (UTXO) and this sum he is transferring to Ted$_1$, Ted$_2$, ..., Ted$_J$. All Teds have their private-public key pairs denoted by (z_j, t_j) respectively, $j = 1, 2,..., J$.

To satisfy the balance between received and spent amount of money in UTXO system we assume that Ted$_J$ is nobody else than Bob himself and he sends the money to himself to provide a change.

In general, Bob sends only a part of the received sum to other recipients, then change is an unspent sum sent to himself. So, after the transaction execution the senders are Alices and receivers are Teds while Bob is both a receiver and a sender.

To hide the amount of received-sent money in transaction we transform the value of coin π_i by the discrete exponent function (DEF) defined in certain algebraic systems.

Let p is cryptographically secure prime number of order 2^{2048}. Let q is a prime divisor of $p-1$, i.e. $q|(p-1)$ and q is of order 2^{256}. This setting is used in well known Digital Signature Algorithm (DSA) standard [5]. Prime number p defines multiplicative cyclic group of integers Z_p^* with operation modulo p (mod p) and prime number q defines the cyclic group G_q of order q, where all elements except 1 are generators. Let the generator in G_q is g. Since all elements in G_q are of prime order q then any exponent x of g is in the Galois field $F_q = \{0, 1, 2, ..., q-1\}$. We deal with the additive group of F_q, denoted by Z_q with addition operation mod q.

Then DEF is defined by two parameters g, p and is defined in the following way DEF: $Z_q \rightarrow Z_p^*$, i.e.

$$\text{DEF}_{g,p}(x) = g^x \bmod p = a; a \in Z_p * . \tag{3}$$

According to Lagrange and Fermat little theorem DEF is one-to-one mapping and is isomorphic. Then for any $x, z \in Z_q$ the following identity holds

$$\text{DEF}_{g,p}(x + z) = g^{(x+z)\bmod q} \bmod p = \text{DEF}_{g,p}(x)\text{DEF}_{g,p}(z) = (g^x \cdot g^z) \bmod p. \tag{4}$$

Together with Galois field F_q we introduce Galois field $F_p = \{0, 1, 2, ..., p\text{-}1\}$ with addition and multiplication operations mod p.

The inverse function to DEF is discrete logarithm function DLF which is defined by input g, p and $a \in Z_p^*$ and outputs the value of exponent x

$$\text{DLF}_{g,p}(a) = x; x \in Z_q. \tag{5}$$

The problem to find x in (2.5), when g, p and a are given is named as discrete logarithm problem (DLP).

The anonymity improvement of presented UTXO transactions relies on the following well known discrete logarithm assumption (DLA).

DLA assumption. For securely selected sufficiently large primes p, q solution of DLP in (5) is infeasible.

According DSA standard recommendations securely selected p and q are of 2048 and 256 bits length [5].

DEF we use to hide the value of π_i by computing value θ_i in the following way.

$$\theta_i = g^{\pi_i} \bmod p \tag{6}$$

We construct vector space of data for senders-receivers and validators over the field F_p.

To achieve coins validity and anonymity the standard asymmetric encryption and e-signature functions can be used, e.g. ElGamal for encryption and DSA for signature.

To provide message integrity we use any collision free H-function providing a mapping from any finite length bit string to 256 bit string H: $\{0, 1\}^* \rightarrow \{0, 1\}^{256}$. For example, if we have some transaction vector (data) Tx, formed by Bob then H-function of Tx is equal to the following h-value

$$h_{Tx} = H(Tx). \tag{7}$$

Let Alice$_i$ be a sender of coin π_i to the receiver Bob. Then Alice$_i$ encrypts π_i by Bob's PuK $= b$. Ciphertext vector c_i is composed of two components and symbolically is expressed in the following way

$$c_i = \text{Enc}(b, \pi_i) = (E_i, D_i). \tag{8}$$

Sender Alice$_i$ signs value θ_i in (6) using her PrK $= x_i$. The signature on θ_i we denote by two components vector σ_i and is expressed in the following way

$$\sigma_i = \text{DSA}(x_i, \theta_i) = (r_i, s_i). \tag{9}$$

In both cases E_i, D_i and r_i, s_i are in Z_p^*.

Decryption operation is performed by receiver's (Bob's) PrK $= y$ symbolically we denote by

$$\text{Dec}(y, c_i) = \pi_i. \tag{10}$$

Signature's σ_i verification, created e.g., by DSA with PrK $= x_i$ on the value θ_i is performed by the corresponding PuK $= a_i$ using the following function having True or False outcomes

$$\text{Ver}(a_i, \sigma_i, \theta_i) = \{\text{True, False}\}. \tag{11}$$

The input data received from Alice$_i$ to Bob we denote by in_i and express by the following vector with 8 components in the vector space F_p^8 for $i = 1, 2,..., I$

$$in_i = (a_i, b, E_i, D_i, \theta_i, r_i, s_i, h_{Txi}), \tag{12}$$

where $h_{Txi} = H(Tx_i)$ and Tx_i is a transaction formed by Alice$_i$.

Let 0_N be an N-dimensional zero vector $(0, ...,0)$ with components in Z_p^*. To represent data of the 1-st input vector In_1 we use a vector 0_N with zero components in Z_p^* of dimension $N = 8(I + J-1)$ in the following way

$$In_1 = (b, a_1, E_1, D_1, \theta_1, r_1, s_1, h_{Tx1}, 0_N). \tag{13}$$

Then the i-th vector representing data of i-th input will be

$$\mathbf{In_i} = (0_{8i}, b, a_i, E_i, D_i, \theta_i, r_i, s_i, h_{Txi}, 0_{N-8i}) \tag{14}$$

In the same way the I-th input data is represented by the vector

$$In_1 = (0_N, b, a_I, E_I, D_I, \theta_I, r_I, s_I, h_{TxI}). \tag{15}$$

All these vectors have $8(I + J-1)$ zero components and non-zero components are shifted by eight components right starting from In_2.

Vectors In_1, In_2, ..., In_1 are in the vector space $F_p^{8(I+J)}$.

For the output money amounts and nonces we use the notation m_{oi} and η_{oi} respectively in the same format as in the Table 1. Then using (5) we obtain corresponding θ_{oj}.

Let Bob received from all Alices the input sum $m_{In} = m_1 + m_2 + ... + m_I$. Then to prevent double spending he must spend the same sum $m_{Out} = m_{O1} + m_{O2} + ... + m_{OJ}$ to make a the following balance equation valid.

$$m_{In} = m_{Out}. \tag{16}$$

The same balance equation must be valid for the set of input nonces $\{\eta_i\}$ and output nonces $\{\eta_{oj}\}$.

$$\eta_1 + \eta_2 + ... + \eta_1 = \eta_{o1} + \eta_{o2} + ... + \eta_{oJ}. \tag{17}$$

But since nonces are generated at random then it is impossible to satisfy (17). One of the way to satisfy this equation is to express the last nonce η_{oJ} by the other nonces in (17)

$$\eta_{oJ} = \eta_1 + \eta_2 + ... + \eta_1 - \eta_{o1} - \eta_{o2} - ... - \eta_{o,J-1} \bmod q. \tag{18}$$

Then according to (2) the following extended balance equation holds.

$$\pi_1 + \pi_2 + ... + \pi_1 = \pi_{O1} + \pi_{O2} + ... + \pi_{OJ}. \tag{19}$$

Data sent from Bob to j-thTed is represented by the following vector out_j with 8 components in the vector space F_p^8 for all $j = 1, 2, ..., J$

$$out_j = (b, t_j, E_{Oj}, D_{Oj}, \theta_{Oj}, r_{Oj}, s_{Oj}, h_{Tx}), \tag{20}$$

where h_{Tx} is a H-value of transaction vector Tx created by Bob and will be defined below.

Analogously to the input case the vectors Out_1, Out_2, ..., Out_J are formed. They are in the vector space $F_p^{8(I+J)}$.

The special amount of money π_J must be realized for the last output Out_J when Bob sends a change to himself to satisfy (19).

Now we can construct a set of transaction vectors that spans vector subspace $F_p^{(I+J)}$ of vector space $F_p^{8(I+J)}$. Any transaction vector in this subspace we denote by Tx and express it in the following way.

$$Tx = \sum_{i=1}^{I} In_i + \sum_{j=1}^{J} Out_j \tag{21}$$

Transaction vector Tx we express by its vector components representing vectors In_1, In_2, ..., In_I and Out_1, Out_2, ..., Out_J in the following way.

$$Tx = (T_1, T_2, ..., T_{(I+J)}), \tag{22}$$

where $T_i = In_i$ if $i \leq I$ and $T_i = Out_i$ if $i > I$.

Vector Tx we represent by the scalar component set $\{\tau_k\}$, $k = 1, 2, \ldots, 8(I + J)$, i.e.
$Tx = (\tau_1, \tau_2, \ldots, \tau_{8(I+J)})$.

Vector Tx is distributed across the network and data included in it can be used for routing transactions. These transactions provides some kind of network coding and, in general, can be used in content distribution systems to improve the speed of downloads and the robustness of the systems.

For transaction authenticity we use some kind of one-time signature scheme for every transaction based on the method proposed in [1].

Proposed signature scheme is different for every transaction sent to the network and can be named as a session signature. It allows nodes to check the authenticity and integrity of transactions and is based on the linearity property of the packets of transactions.

3 Session Signature Creation and Transaction Validation

The signature creation is based upon the fact that transaction vector Tx is in the vector subspace $F_p^{(I+J)}$ of vector space $F_p^{8(I+J)}$ and upon an invariant signature for the linear span of $F_p^{(I+J)}$.

Transaction input data validation by the receiver. Let Bob receives from Alice$_i$ input vector In_i. Then using (10) he decrypts c_i and obtains π_i. According to format in Fig. 1 he extracts transferred money value m_i and checks if it corresponds to their contract obligations. Bob computes θ_i as in (5) and checks if it matches with received θ_i. Then Bob having received Alices$_i$ PuK$_i$ = a_i verifies signature $\sigma_i = \text{DSA}(x_i, \theta_i) = (r_i, s_i)$ according to (9), (11).

Session private key vector (SPrK) generation. Transaction creator Bob generates secret vector $v = (v_1, \ldots, v_{8(I+J)})$ at random being a SPrK.

Session public key vector (SPuK) generation. Having private key vector, vector $SPuK = (h_1, \ldots, h_{8(I+J)})$, where for every $k = 1, 2, \ldots, 8(I + J)$

$$h_k = g^{v_k} \bmod p \tag{23}$$

Session signature creation. Bob computes H-value of SPuK and signs SPuK by DSA using his PrK = y.

$$\sigma_{SPuK} = \text{DSA}(y, h_{SPuK}) = (r_{SPuK}, s_{SPuK}). \tag{24}$$

where $h_{SPuK} = H(SPuK)$.

Using vector Tx Bob finds vector $u = (u_1, \ldots, u_{8(I+J)})$ orthogonal to the space spanned by input and output vectors $In_1, In_2, \ldots, In_I$ and $Out_1, Out_2, \ldots, Out_J$ respectively. Then u must satisfy the following system of inner products we denote by $<, >$

$$<In_i, \mathbf{u}> = 0, i = 1, 2, \ldots, 8I, \tag{25}$$

$$<Out_j, \mathbf{u}> = 0, j = 1, 2, \ldots, 8J. \tag{26}$$

Using his session private key $SPrK$, Bob computes vector $d = (d_1, ..., d_{8(I+J)})$ in the following way

$$d_k = u_k/v_k \bmod p, k = 1, 2, \ldots, 8(I + J). \tag{27}$$

Bob signs vector d computing a signature on H-value $h_d = H(d)$.

$$\sigma_d = \text{DSA}(y, h_d), \tag{28}$$

Session signature verification. According to [1] signature is valid if verification variable $\vartheta = 1$. Variable ϑ is computed by the formula

$$\vartheta = \prod_{k=1}^{8(I+J)} h_k^{d_k \tau_k} \tag{29}$$

Security considerations. In [1] it is proved that compromising of this signature scheme is as hard as Discrete Logarithm Problem (DLP).

After all data are verified and computed, Bob can create his own transaction Tx according to (12)–(22) and (23)–(28).

Bob together with transaction vector Tx sends additional data to the network expressed by the vectors $SPuK$, σ_{SPuK}, d, σ_d and nonce η_{OJ}.

Transaction validation. To approve Bob's transaction Tx validator is verifying signature $\sigma_{SPuK} = \text{DSA}(y, h_{SPuK}) = (r_{SPuK}, s_{SPuK})$ in (24) formed on Bob's session public key $SPuK$ vector in (23) using Bob's $PuK = b$ received in Tx. If verification passes then using $SPuK$ validator checks the session signature on Tx using (25)–(29). If it passes then validator checks the balance of transaction between received and spent coins.

To do that validator collects input DEF values $(\theta_1, ..., \theta_I)$ and output DEF values $(\theta_{O1}, ..., \theta_{OJ})$ that are computed by Tx creator Bob using (6). If balance equation is valid then due to (4), (6) and (19) the following validation equation holds.

$$\prod_{i=1}^{I} \theta_i = \prod_{j=1}^{J} \theta_{Oj} \tag{30}$$

Validation equation holds if balance Eqs. (16)–(19) are valid due to isomorphic property of DEF in (4)

If (30) holds then validator includes current transaction Tx together with other non-validated transactions related with transaction Tx in the block according to the procedure defined in the existing blockchain system.

Validated blocks are included it in the blockchain and are published it in the network.

4   Discussion and conclusions

The solution to improve anonymity of blockchain cryptocurrencies based on Unspent Transaction Output (UTXO) paradigm is presented. It is based on proposed UTXO balance anonymity solution when transferred money sums are hidden by discrete exponent function (DEF). Then due to isomorphism property of DEF, anonymous UTXO balance is computed and this balance can be approved by the validators in the hidden form. The security of this anonymity is based on the discrete logarithm problem (DLP) complexity.

Cryptocurrencies are circulating in the peer-to-peer network and data can be represented by the vectors in certain linear space as it is in the general peer-to-peer network of nodes. Since transaction data composing a balance is represented by the vectors spanning certain linear subspace of some linear space, then this subspace is digitally signed by session signature based on generation session private and public keys generation. This signature is used in general peer-to-peer content distribution network and according to the original literature source the security relies on the DLP complexity.

References

1. Nakamoto, S.: Bitcoin: A peer-to-peer electronic cash system. Manubot (2019). https://www.klausnordby.com/bitcoin/Bitcoin_Whitepaper_Document_HD.pdf
2. Popov, S.: The tangle. White paper, 1, 3. https://assets.ctfassets.net/r1dr6vzfxhev/4i3OM9 JTleiE8M6Y04Ii28/d58bc5bb71cebe4adc18fadea1a79037/Tangle_White_Paper_v1.4.2.pdf. Accessed on 12 March 2021
3. Ahlswede, R., Cai, N., Li, S.Y., Yeung, R.W.: Network information flow. IEEE Trans. Inf. Theory **46**(4), 1204–1216 (2000). http://www.cs.cornell.edu/courses/cs783/2007fa/papers/acly.pdf
4. Zhao, F., Kalker, T., Médard, M., Han, K.J.: Signatures for content distribution with network coding. In: 2007 IEEE International Symposium on Information Theory, pp. 556–560. IEEE (2007). https://stuff.mit.edu/people/medard/papers08/security_for_NC_v3.pdf
5. Kerry, C.F., Gallagher, P.D.: Digital Signature Standard (DSS). FIPS PUB 186–4, Information Technology Laboratory National Institute of Standards and Technology Gaithersburg, MD 20899–8900 (2013). https://nvlpubs.nist.gov/nistpubs/FIPS/NIST.FIPS.186-4.pdf.

Cloud-Based Cyber Incidents Response System and Software Tools

Sergiy Gnatyuk[1,2](✉) (iD), Rat Berdibayev[3], Tetiana Smirnova[4] (iD),
Zhadyra Avkurova[5] (iD), and Maksim Iavich[6] (iD)

[1] National Aviation University, Kyiv, Ukraine
s.gnatyuk@nau.edu.ua
[2] Yessenov University, Aktau, Kazakhstan
[3] Almaty University of Power Engineering and Telecommunication, Almaty, Kazakhstan
[4] Central Ukrainian National Technical University, Kropyvnytskyi, Ukraine
[5] L.N. Gumilyov Eurasian National University, Nur-Sultan, Kazakhstan
[6] Caucasus University, Tbilisi, Georgia

Abstract. Cloud technologies and their applications are implementing in various ICT infrastructures. Today cyber threats mitigation in clouds is hot topic and it has scientific interest. Authors analyzed cyber threats detection methods and defined their disadvantages. Next, model of cloud service was proposed and it allows to ensure the cyber security of cloud services. An improved method for cyber threats detection has been developed, it allows to detect cyber threats in cloud services and classify them. The developed method was experimentally investigated using the NSL-KDD database as well as simulation tools RStudio and CloudSim. It was proved the correctness of its work and the possibility of application in cloud services as well as increase efficiency of cloud system security. Cyber Incidents Response System has been developed that can be used to build cloud services based on the various cloud computing architecture. It is significant because it can be the autonomous functional unit of cyber incident response system or other instrumental cybersecurity tools.

Keywords: Cyber security · Cloud · Cyber incident response · ICT · SIEM · CSIRT

1 Introduction

The usage of cloud computing has gained a significant advantage due to the reduced cost of ownership of information and communication technology (ICT) applications, extremely fast entry into the services market, as well as rapid increases in employee productivity [1]. Everything can be implemented in the cloud service: from data storage to data analysis, applications of any scale or size. Employees also implement their own cloud applications for work, contributing to the development of their own cloud culture. In addition, the use of cloud services is now available not only for large enterprises, but also for companies in medium and small businesses, which makes cloud technologies one of the main environments for the operation of their information systems [2]. However,

A. Lopata et al. (Eds.): ICIST 2021, CCIS 1486, pp. 169–184, 2021.
https://doi.org/10.1007/978-3-030-88304-1_14

such an increase in the efficiency of working with cloud technologies has led to increased attention to the problems of cyber threats, the growth of which is inseparably linked with the growth of ICT [3]. Information security (cybersecurity) ensuring in cloud is the responsibility of provider and it depends on requirements of international standards and national laws. For users the security of cloud is "invisible" and it is based only on the confidence [4–6]. There are many security risks related to intellectual resources losses, credentials and authentication compromising, system hacking and others [7–10]. The information is stored as well as processed and transmitted in cloud infrastructure. From this position, using cyber threats detection methods and systems is relevant and important for incident response centers and services. In cloud services cybersecurity ensuring is very actual and important challenge today. From this position, this research study is significant and proposed cyber threats detection method will be useful for cybersecurity monitoring in real cloud systems. Results can be used as an autonomous functional unit of Cyber Incident Response System or other instrumental cybersecurity tools.

This paper consists of the following sections: 1) Introduction; 2) Related papers review and problem statement; 3) Theoretical background of the system development; 4) Experimental study and discussion; 5) Conclusions.

2   Related Papers Review and Problem Statement

2.1   Scientific Literature Review

Modern cloud computing systems have a multi-level architecture including different services and management levels. Figure 1 depicts a classification of data security threats on each layer of the cloud system. The security of the SaaS platform can be divided into two categories: attacks on developed/smanagement tools [9, 10]. Security of the IaaS/PaaS platforms consist four issues: attacks on cloud services, attacks on virtualization, attacks on unified computing, and attacks on SLAs [11].

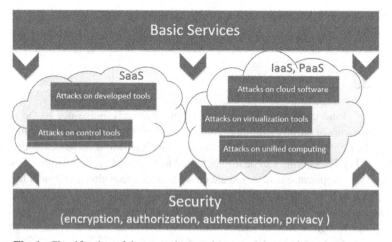

Fig. 1. Classification of data security attacks on each layer of the cloud system

Table 1 shows a multi-level classification of cyber threats for the three layers of clouds (forming first level). At the next level located cloud services, and at the third – the types of cyberattacks on these services [12, 13].

Table 1. Multilevel classification of the data security threats in cloud

Layer of cloud (service)	Cloud service	Security threat	Attack type	Risk value
SaaS	Web service	Data security	Confidentiality	Medium
		Interface attack	Signatures attack	Low
			Attacks on users credentials	Medium
	API	SSH attacks	Attacks on API keys	Medium
			Attacks on users credentials	Medium
IaaS and PaaS	Virtualization platform	Hardware level virtu-alization	ARP spoofing on virtual switching	High
			MAC spoofing on virtual switching	High
		Software level virtu-alization	Hacking on com-puting	Low
Development services	Cloud soft-ware	Harmful software	Scripts	High
	Computing services	Unified computing attacks	Attacks during data processing	Low
		SLA attacks	Hacking	High

The analysis of up-to-date approaches in this direction showed following results:

- *Method based on Deep Analytics* (Fig. 2) [14–16] is a combination of popular and effective methods (predictive analytics, descriptive analytics, graph analysis, analysis of unstructured information, optimization), which together allow to detect of cyber threats or anomalies (comparison in groups of the same class, clustering, trend analysis as well as developing prediction models like regressions, decision trees, neural networks, etc.).

- *System and Method of Data Collection, Processing, Analysis and Storage for Monitoring Cyber Threats and their Notification to Users* [17] were patented (Fig. 3). It collects intelligence data from multiple sources and then pre-processes the intelligence data for further analysis by the intelligence analyst. The analyst reviews the intelligence and determines if it is appropriate for the client to sign a cyber threat alert service. The system reforms and collects intelligence data and automatically transmits intelligence data through many delivery methods.

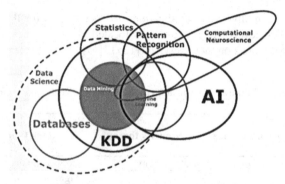

Fig. 2. Method based on deep analytics

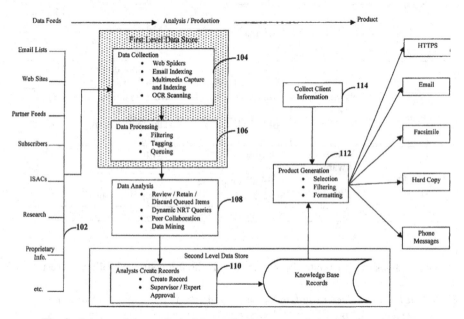

Fig. 3. Scheme of the method of data collection, processing, analysis and storage

- *Method for planning the structure of cyber threats and their application to reduce the impact of cyber threats* (Fig. 4) [18]. A security system consists of a computer, memory, data storage, containing a dictionary of the intellectual capacity of cyber-threats and a technological dictionary; and an application stored in memory. When executed by a computer, the program generates a report that identifies the intent of the cyber threat and identifies the cyber threat technology, in which the intent of the cyber threat is selected from several intentions for the cyber threat listed in the dictionary of cyber threat imposition and in which cyber threat technology is selected from the technology dictionary. The application also populates the values of the progression vector in cyber-threat, where the vector of visualization of the progression of cyber-threat contains elements, each of which corresponds to the action in the chain of actions related to cybercrime, when the values correspond to one present or absent. This vector is used to manage the cyber risks of an enterprise or organization.

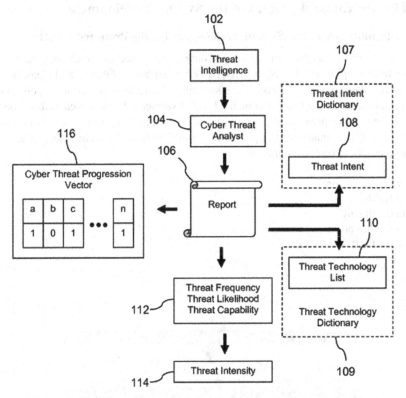

Fig. 4. Block scheme of the method for planning the structure of cyber threats

Other methods and systems [19–22] as well as mentioned were compared by following criteria: low demand for computing resources, simplicity of implementation, high degree of identification of known threats, real-time threat detection, logging of identified new threats and others.

2.2 Problem Statement

After the analysis of cyber threats detection methods from open sources [14–22] we can summarize that most them have high requirements for computing resources and are complicate to implement, as well as these methods are described only theoretically without practical application. Also not all algorithms have the ability to log new, not yet assigned to any category of cyber threats. This analysis shows the relevant problems of cyber threats detection methods in cloud environments. This paper is directed on one of this problem solving.

The main purpose of this work is to develop and investigate a cyber threats detection method appropriate for modern cloud services that can be used by cyber incident response system.

3   Theoretical Background of the System Development

3.1   Information Security System Architecture for the Protected Cloud

Figure 5 shows the structure of a protected data center based on cloud computing technology from the point of view of security, namely the models of threats and measures that need to be taken to minimize risks. The structure also reflects full control, compliance with requirements and agreements on the level of services. The key idea of this model is that information security should not be secondary or simply part of the overall security, it should be disseminated and implemented at all levels of the architecture. The threat profile consists of such elements as:

- service disruption;
- data leakage;
- data disclosure;
- data modification;
- identity theft and fraud;
- intrusion.

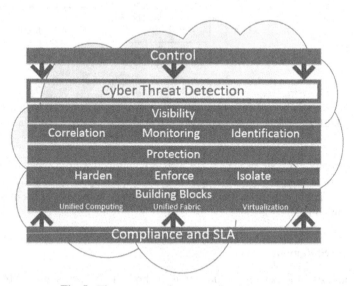

Fig. 5. The structure of a secure cloud data center

As can be seen from Fig. 5 cyber threats detection is one of the most important tasks in information security system of cloud. Two main security pillars are:

- *Control.* Aspects of security control of the "cloud" data center vary from management of systems support to management of access control systems. As a first step, we should review the basic level of security to more rigid conditions. Usually, the centralization of data leads to more frequent internal threats. Therefore, the compartmentalization strategy is the most key component of data control. Moreover, unencrypted data in the data center should be considered as part of risk management policy.
- *Compliance and Service Level Agreement (SLA).* Aspects of Compliance and SLA possess quite multifaceted features. It is necessary to clearly understand the features of the various components of the "cloud", which must be compatible. All service level agreements should be synchronized with key assurance mechanisms.

3.2 Secure Architecture of Cloud Data Center

Building a secure architecture of a cloud data center includes the implementation of six following levels of security:

- physical protection;
- server protection;
- protection of applications and platforms;
- network protection;
- data protection;
- secure encryption and key management system.

1. Physical Protection is an important component of security, which is closely related to all other types. The most balanced way to provide physical protection to a data center is to implement multi-level protection with multiple security perimeters. As with echeloned defense, a breakthrough of one level will not mean a breakthrough of the security system, while internal perimeters are no less important than external ones. Physical protection includes the following:

- inconspicuous appearance, especially in populated areas. Avoid any signs that refer to the data center and preserve the appearance of the building as close as possible to other buildings in the area;
- minimizing the usage of windows, but there should be no windows where data is processed or stored;
- boundary entry points;
- constant control of access to the building;
- prohibition of re-passage and usage of "man-traps";
- hinges on the inside: a common mistake when converting an old building to a new one involves upgrading the locks on the doors and windows, leaving the hinges on the outside of the building;
- many cameras: surveillance cameras serve as a good deterrent factor and cover one of the basic principles of security - identification;
- fire doors only on the way out (and install an alarm on them): Fire doors are a necessary condition for health and safety, but you need to make sure that they only open to the outside and have active alarms at all times;

- door control and;
- continuous testing and testing of external security systems. No matter how simple or complex the security system is, it will be useless not to check it on a regular basis to make sure everything is working as expected;
- two-factor authentication to access the data center;
- basic requirement for physical protection: multilevel. Security systems must be multilevel for each other. The main idea is that when someone passes one test, it does not mean that at the next level he will succeed.

2. Servers are an environment for the operation of processes and their computing, so the operating systems deployed on them must be protected and to the extent that they offer the least area for attack. The technical basis for reliable and secure provision and use of cloud computing should be provided by broadband connection, standardized and widely used transmission protocols, service-oriented architecture and, above all, virtualization. Means of protection of cloud data centers servers include the following:

- technical means of host protection (firewalls, integrity checks, intrusion detection systems);
- protected basic server configuration (deployment of protected OS, disabling unnecessary services, etc.);
- the ability of users to use their own images of virtual machines or use high-quality and secure images provided by the provider;
- use of certified hypervisors (at least Common Criteria EAL).

3. Network. Improper system setup is often the reason for a successful attack. Since the network for "cloud" computing consists of many different components, the overall configuration is complex and important. Changing the settings for one component can cause security vulnerabilities when interacting with other components. It is important to isolate the provider's management network from the data network. In addition, it must be ensured that the networks are adequately segmented, preventing any errors from spreading freely. In this case, it is necessary to establish security zones within the network, namely:

- secured network control area "cloud";
- secured network area for migration provided the virtualization server is used;
- secured network area for data storage system;
- secured network zone for virtual machines, provided IaaS is used.

To implement network security, we use the following means of protection:

- means of protection against malicious software;
- means of protection against network attacks (built-in system for responding to abnormal traffic, which only detects its fact, but does not classify the threat, does not determine which element it is aimed at; as a result, only determines the percentage of "wrong" traffic);
- minimization of DDoS attacks;

- segmentation of the management network from the data network;
- secure configuration of all components of cloud architecture;
- remote administration via secure communication channels (SSH, TLS/SSL, IPSec);
- encrypted communication between the SS provider and the SS user;
- "redundancy" of the "cloud" data center network.

4. Platform and Applications. Deploying a variety of applications on cloud computing platforms involves pre-testing them to identify vulnerabilities and errors. The security of the platform and applications is ensured by the following means:

- security throughout the life cycle (review, automated testing, vulnerability detection tests);
- securely isolated applications;
- automatic scanning of user applications for vulnerabilities before they run on the platform;
- manage patches and changes;
- ensuring the compatibility of patches on test systems before launch.

5. Data. The data life cycle includes its creation, storage, use, distribution and destruction. The data center must support all these phases with appropriate security mechanisms. Common to all storage technologies (SAN, NAS, etc.) is that many users share storage systems. In this case, secure sharing of user data is extremely important and must be guaranteed. Data protection can be achieved through the use of the following means of protection:

- isolation of user data (virtual storage areas, tagging);
- regular backup, the parameters of which (volume, time intervals between storage, storage duration) are changed by the user;
- data must be completely and securely deleted at the request of the user.

6. Encryption and Key Management. Cryptographic methods and software products must be used to securely store, process, and transport critical data. Managing cryptographic keys in cloud computing environments is complex, and there are currently no appropriate tools for key management. Therefore, more than six providers do not encrypt data classified in the so-called "at rest" category. For clients of IaaS service providers, there is a possibility to manually encrypt the data before storing it in the provider's system – that is, they retain full control over the cryptographic keys, as well as deal with their management. Key management for a secure data center model based on Cloud Computing technology includes:

- keys are generated in a secure environment using certified generators;
- encryption keys should not be stored in the system in the open, it is necessary to provide excessive backup and recovery;
- ensuring reliable distribution of keys;
- the administrator of cloud services should not have access to the user's keys;
- if the key is no longer needed, it must be destroyed immediately.

3.3   Categories of Cyber Threats and Cyberattacks

Today one of the most complete dataset with descriptions of all cyber threats and attacks that can be implemented is the NSL-KDD database [23]. It consists of the following categories and sub-categories of cyberattacks (Fig. 6):

Class	Attacks in the training data
DOS	Back, Land, Smurf, Pod, Neptune, and Teardrop
Probe	IPsweep, Portsweep, Nmapr, and Satan
U2R	Load module, Rootkit, Perl, and Buffer_overflow
R2L	Guess_passwd, Multihop, Ftp_write, Spy, Phf, Imap, Warezclient, and Warezmaster

Fig. 6. NSL-KDD dataset contents

The data is compared by certain attributes, namely:

- [1] "duration" "protocol_type"
- [3] "service" "flag"
- [5] "src_bytes" "dst_bytes"
- [7] "land" "wrong_fragment"
- [9] "urgent" "hot"
- [11] "num_failed_logins" "logged_in"
- [13] "num_compromised" "root_shell"
- [15] "su_attempted" "num_root"
- [17] "num_file_creations" "num_shells"
- [19] "num_access_files" "num_outbound_cmds"
- [21] "is_host_login" "is_guest_login"
- [23] "count" "srv_count"
- [25] "serror_rate" "srv_serror_rate"
- [27] "rerror_rate" "srv_rerror_rate"
- [29] "same_srv_rate" "diff_srv_rate"
- [31] "srv_diff_host_rate" "dst_host_count"
- [33] "dst_host_srv_count" "dst_host_same_srv_rate"
- [35] "dst_host_diff_srv_rate" "dst_host_same_src_port_rate"
- [37] "dst_host_srv_diff_host_rate" "dst_host_serror_rate"
- [39] "dst_host_srv_serror_rate" "dst_host_rerror_rate"
- [41] "dst_host_srv_rerror_rate" "label"

Figure 7 shows a block diagram of cyber threats detection in the cloud.

When the host is connected to the cloud, network traffic begins to be generated. Next is the data processing unit, where the network traffic arrives at the behavior analyzer, which contains the records of the NSL-KDD database. The analyzer compares the data captured from the network traffic with the database and begins to use classifiers to determine.

The next block is the identification and analysis, where the pre-classified threat is analyzed in detail, and it is determined to which resources the threat was directed.

After that, the system issues a warning message that part of the traffic is abnormal, and at the same time begins to check the identified threat with previously found or recorded immediately in the database. If such a match is found, a notification with further actions can be issued (in case of their previous successful application). The last two modules are actually a record of detailed data about the threat (date, group, whether it was previously identified, etc.) and the formation of a mini-report for review, which shows the overall result.

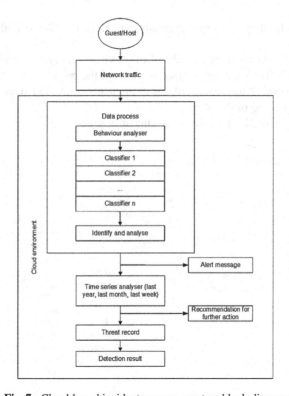

Fig. 7. Cloud-based incident response system block diagram

Next Section of the work consists the experiments of the proposed cloud-based incident response system and software tools.

4   Experimental Study and Discussion

4.1   Experiments Using RStudio

Input/output of the experiment: the input data is 20% of the NSL-KDD dataset, the output data are classified data (normal or abnormal – threat). Experimental environment: open-source development environment for R (programming statistics and RStudio data visualization). RStudio includes a console, a syntax highlighting editor that supports direct code execution, and tools for scheduling, logging, debugging, and desktop management.

The window is divided into four following parts (Fig. 8):

- working part – for direct writing and running code, there is also a standard toolbar for all programs;
- after viewing the data – there are tabs of the environment (you can view the loaded data sets and libraries) and history (see versions of the project);
- console – to display the results of the written program, and data related to the environment (loading of the library);
- field of view of visualized results (diagrams, histograms, etc.).

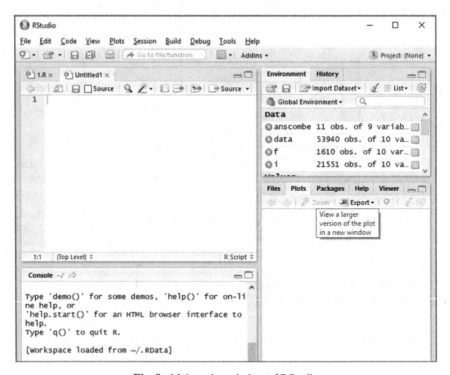

Fig. 8. Main active window of RStudio

Stages of research study

Stage 1: Connection of all necessary libraries, loading of a training data set of NSL-KDD database.

Stage 2: Analysis of the test data set. Only 20% of the training data of the NSL-KDD database have 25,191 elements that have 43 features.

Stage 3: Direct testing of the method. Next, we test our method using built-in functions and data set. Initially, residual data and duplicates were separated, and separate small data sets were identified. After that, the traffic is analyzed and the normal and anomalous data are determined, as well as the accuracy of the result.

Stage 4: The result of the experiment. During the experiment, the following results were obtained: the total percentage of threats detected – 96.356%, correctly classified – 95.89%, incorrectly classified – 4.11%.

Next subsection contains study using CloudSim tool and NSL-KDD data set.

4.2 Experiments Using CloudSim

Input/output of the experiment: the input data is a set of NSL-KDD data and captured network traffic, the output – classified data (normal or abnormal – threat) and the value of the efficiency of the methods of cyber threat detection. Experimental environment: CloudSim simulation system. CloudSim platform is a generalized and scalable simulation tool that allows full-fledged modeling and simulation of cloud computing systems and infrastructure, including the construction of data centers using the "cloud". It is an extension of the basic functionality of the GridSim platform, providing the ability to model data storages, web services, resource allocation between virtual machines. The logs study in RStudio was done to visualize the results: distribution of identified threats and attacks; diagram of the dependence of the percentage of detection on the type of threat. The most detected attacks are related to DoS [24] (Fig. 9). Comparison of the results of simulations on the CloudSim platform is shown in Table 2.

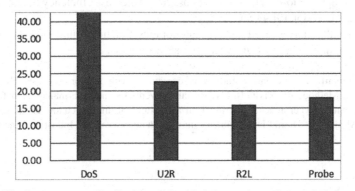

Fig. 9. Percentage distribution of identified threats depending on their type

The displayed results indicate that when simulating the data center model without methods of cyber threat detection, but provided that there is a built-in threat level security network detector, the level of detected threats is at 45.87%, which indicates insufficient security of the cloud service, because it means that if only the built-in anti-attack module is present, less than half of the attacks will be detected.

Table 2. Simulation results for proposed system

Experiment	With/without proposed method	Detected threats
1	–	45.8%
2	+	93.8%

After the simulations with the built-in cyber threat detection method, we can declare that the level of detected cyber threats is 93.89%, which indicates the effectiveness of proposed method for cyber incidents response system.

5 Conclusions

In this paper up-to-date systems and cyber threats detection method were analyzed, it was defined that their disadvantages are lack of data on experimental research, the impossibility of its use in cloud services and others.

A cloud service model has been developed, and it uses technological architecture, high-speed communication and unified structures. These allow to ensure the cyber security of cloud service based as well as conduct simulations of its functioning.

Proposed cyber threats detection method and cloud-based response system have been developed. These use dynamic resources, autonomous self-adaptation and scalability and deterministic calculations. By the way, this allows to detect cyber threats in cloud services and classify them by NSL-KDD dataset (for example). This system was experimentally investigated using mentioned data base. It has proved the correctness of its work and the possibility of application in cloud services as well as increase efficiency of cloud system cyber threats detection till 93.8%.

Given results can be used for the autonomous functional unit of cyber incident response system or other instrumental cybersecurity tools.

Acknowledgment. This research study was conducted with support of research grant № AP06851243 "Methods, models and tools for security events and incidents management for detecting and preventing cyber attacks on critical infrastructures of digital economics" (2020–2022), funded by Ministry of Digital Development, Innovation and Aerospace Industry of the Republic of Kazakhstan.

References

1. Abidar, R., Moummadi, K., Moutaouakkil, F., Medromi, H.: Intelligent and pervasive supervising platform for information system security based on multi-agent systems. Int. Rev. Comput. Softw. **10**(1), 44–51 (2015)

2. Ivanov, A.: Security as main pain of the cloud computing, Online access mode. http://www.cnews.ru/reviews/free/saas/articles/articles12.shtml
3. Active security for advanced threats counteraction, Online access mode. http://www.itsec.ru/articles2/target/aktivnaya-zaschita-kak-metod-protivodeystviya-prodvinutym-kiberugrozam
4. The 6 Major Cyber Security Risks to Cloud Computing, Online access mode. http://www.adotas.com/2017/08/the-6-major-cyber-security-risks-to-cloud-computing/
5. Google Security Whitepaper for Google Cloud Platform, Online access mode. https://habrahabr.ru/post/183168/
6. Dokas, P., Ertoz, L., Kumar, V.: Data mining for network intrusion detection. Recent Adv. Intrusion Detect. **15**(78), 21–30 (2014)
7. Ahmed, P.: An intrusion detection and prevention system in cloud computing: a systematic review. J. Netw. Comput. Appl. **11**, 1–18 (2016)
8. Iavich, M., Gnatyuk, S., Odarchenko, R., Bocu, R., Simonov, S.: The novel system of attacks detection in 5G. In: Barolli, L., Woungang, I., Enokido, T. (eds.) AINA 2021. LNNS, vol. 226, pp. 580–591. Springer, Cham (2021). https://doi.org/10.1007/978-3-030-75075-6_47
9. Carl, G., Kesidis, G., Brooks, R.R., Rai, S.: Denial-of-service attack-detection techniques. Internet Comput. IEEE **10**, 82–89 (2006)
10. Hu, Z., et al.: Statistical techniques for detecting cyberattacks on computer networks based on an analysis of abnormal traffic behavior. Int. J. Comput. Netw. Inf. Secur. **12**(6), 1–13 (2020)
11. Chatzigiannakis, V., Androulidakis, G., Maglaris, B.: A Distributed Intrusion Detection Prototype Using Security Agents, HP OpenView University Association, pp. 14–25 (2004)
12. Berdibayev, R., Gnatyuk, S., Yevchenko, Y., Kishchenko, V.: A concept of the architecture and creation for SIEM system in critical infrastructure. In: Zaporozhets, A., Artemchuk, V. (eds.) Systems, Decision and Control in Energy II. SSDC, vol. 346, pp. 221–242. Springer, Cham (2021). https://doi.org/10.1007/978-3-030-69189-9_13
13. Zaliskyi, M., Odarchenko, R., Gnatyuk, S., Petrova, Y., Chaplits, A.: Method of traffic monitoring for DDoS attacks detection in e-health systems and networks. CEUR Workshop Proceedings, 20186, vol. 2255, pp. 193–204
14. Dilek, S., Çakır, H., Aydın, M.: Applications of artificial intelligence techniques to combating cyber crimes: a review. Int. J. Artif. Intell. Appl. **6**(1), 21–39 (2015)
15. How Big Data Can Improve Cyber Security, Online access mode. https://csce.ucmss.com/cr/books/2017/LFS/CSREA2017/ABD3239.pdf
16. Kirichenko, L.: Cyber threats detection using social networks analysis. Int. J. Inf. Technol. Knowl. **11**, 23–32 (2017)
17. Charles, E., Samuel, M., Roger, N., et al.: Pat. № US20020038430 A1. System and method of data collection, processing, analysis, and annotation for monitoring cyber-threats and the notification thereof to subscribers (2012)
18. John, P., Frederick, D., Henry, P., et al.: Pat. № US9749343B2. System and method of cyber threat structure mapping and application to cyber threat mitigation (2013)
19. Chouhan, M.: Adaptive detection technique for cache-based side channel attack using Bloom Filter for secure cloud. Conf. Comput. Inf. Sci. **1**, 293–297 (2016)
20. Sakr, M.M., Tawfeeq, M.A., El-Sisi, A.B.: An Efficiency optimization for network intrusion detection system. Int. J. Comput. Netw. Inf. Secur. **11**(10), 1–11 (2019). https://doi.org/10.5815/ijcnis.2019.10.01
21. Byrski, A., Carvalho, M.: Agent-based immunological intrusion detection system for mobile ad-hoc networks. In: Bubak, M., van Albada, G.D., Dongarra, J., Sloot, P.M.A. (eds.) ICCS 2008. LNCS, vol. 5103, pp. 584–593. Springer, Heidelberg (2008). https://doi.org/10.1007/978-3-540-69389-5_66
22. Zhang, Z.: Hide: a hierarchical network intrusion detection system using statistical preprocessing and neural network classification. IEEE Workshop Inf. Assur. Secur. **16**, 85–90 (2001)

23. Arora, I.S., Bhatia, G.K., Singh, A.P.: Comparative analysis of classification algorithms on KDD'99 data set. Int. J. Comput. Netw. Inf. Secur. **8**(9), 34–40 (2016). https://doi.org/10.5815/ijcnis.2016.09.05
24. Hassan, Z., Odarchenko, R., Gnatyuk, S. et al.: Detection of distributed denial of service attacks using snort rules in cloud computing & remote control systems. In: Proceedings of the 2018 IEEE 5th International Conference on Methods and Systems of Navigation and Motion Control, October 16–18, pp. 283–288. Kyiv, Ukraine (2018)

Efficient and Secure Digital Signature Scheme for Post Quantum Epoch

Maksim Iavich[1]($\boxtimes$), Giorgi Iashvili[1], Sergiy Gnatyuk[2], Andrii Tolbatov[3], and Lela Mirtskhulava[4]

[1] Caucasus University, Paata Saakadze 1, 0102 Tbilisi, Georgia
miavich@cu.edu.ge
[2] National Aviation University, Liubomyra Huzara Ave, 1, Kyiv, Ukraine
[3] Sumy National Agrarian University, Herasima Kondratieva St, 160, Sumy, Ukraine
[4] Iv. Javakhishvili Tbilisi State university, Ilia Chavchavadze Avenue 1, 0179 Tbilisi, Georgia

Abstract. It is expected the massive release of quantum computers in the near future. Quantum computers can easily break the crypto schemes, which are used in practice. Therefore, classical encryption systems have become vulnerable to quantum computer-based attacks. This involves the research efforts that look for encryption schemes that are immune to quantum computer-based attacks. This paper describes the digital signature schemes, which are safe against quantum computer attacks, but these schemes have different efficiency problems. The signature size of the scheme is very large and one-way function are used many time during the signature process. The paper offers the ways of reducing the signature size and acceleration the process of using one-way functions. It is offered to integrate the quantum key distribution algorithms into the scheme. It is also offered to use Blake family hash function as the one-way function.

Keywords: Digital signature · Secure digital signature · Post quantum · Digital signature scheme

1 Introduction

The world's leading scientists and experts are actively working on the creation of quantum computers. An article was recently published claiming that Google, NASA, and the Universities Space Research Association (USRA) have signed a partnership with a manufacturer of quantum D-Wave processors.

A quantum computer will be able to crack most or all of the traditional cryptosystems that are widely used in practice and specifically based on the task of factorization of integers (e.g. RSA). Some cryptographic systems, such as the RSA - four thousand-bit key, are considered safe from the attacks of large classical computers but are powerless against the attacks of large quantum computers. The RSA cryptosystem is used in different products, on different platforms in many industries. Today, the RSA cryptosystem is being introduced in many commercial products, the number of which is constantly growing. It is also used in the operating systems of Microsoft, Apple, Sun, and Novell.

A. Lopata et al. (Eds.): ICIST 2021, CCIS 1486, pp. 185–193, 2021.
https://doi.org/10.1007/978-3-030-88304-1_15

In hardware performance, the RSA algorithm is used in secure phones, Ethernet network cards, smart cards, and is widely used in cryptographic hardware. In addition, the algorithm is part of the core protocols of Internet-protected communications, including S/MIME, SSL, and S/WAN, and is also used in many institutions, such as government agencies, banks, most corporations, state laboratories, and universities [1].

Various "quantum attack-resistant" alternatives to RSA have been developed. There are a number of effective attacks on these systems today.

The importance of the efficiency aspect is noteworthy. Nowadays, experts have achieved quite good results in the speed of execution of crypto algorithms. Research shows that the proposed post-quantum cryptosystems are relatively less efficient because their implementation algorithms require much more time to execute and verify.

The research problem of the scientists is to improve the efficiency and security of the existing post-quantum alternatives.

2 Digital Signatures

As Digital signature has become an important technology in the security of the Internet and other IT infrastructures. The digital signature ensures authenticity, integrity, and data identification. Digital signatures are widely used in identification and authentication protocols. Thus, the existing secure digital signature algorithm is crucial for supporting IT security.

Digital signature algorithms that are used in practice today are RSA, DSA, ECDSA. However, they are not quantumly stable because their safety is based on complex factorization, large composite integers, and the calculation of discrete logarithms.

The hash-based digital signature schemes we present offer very interesting alternatives. Like any other digital signature scheme, a hash-based digital signature scheme uses a cryptographic hash function.

2.1 Lamport–Diffie One-Time Signature Scheme

Hash based one-time signature scheme offered by Lamport–Diffie is considered as alternative digital signature scheme for the post-quantum era [2].

Key Generation
In this system the signature key X

$$X = (x_{n-1}[0], \ x_{n-1}[1], \ \ldots, \ x_0[0], \ x_0[1]) \in \{0, 1\}^{n, 2n} \tag{1}$$

Verification key Y consists of randomly selected 2n lines of length n.

$$Y = (y_{n-1}[0], \ y_{n-1}[1], \ \ldots, \ y_0[0], \ y_0[1]) \in \{0, 1\}^{n, 2n} \tag{2}$$

We use one-way function f to calculate the key:

$$f : \{0, 1\}^n \to \{0, 1\}^n \tag{3}$$

$$y_i[j] = f(x_i[j]), \ 0 <= i <= n - 1, \ j = 0, 1 \tag{4}$$

Document Signature
By means of the hash function arbitrary size message m, is transformed into size n:

$$h(m) = hash = (hash_{n-1}, \ \dots, \ hash_0) \tag{5}$$

h function is used as the cryptographic hash function:

$$h : \{0, 1\} * \rightarrow \{0, 1\}^n \tag{6}$$

The signature can be got as following:

$$sig = (x_{n-1}[hash_{n-1}], \dots, \ x_0[hash_0]) \in \{0, 1\}^{n, \ n} \tag{7}$$

If the i-th bit in the message is equal to 0, i-th string in this signature is assigned to $x_i[0]$.

If the i-th bit in the message is equal to 1, i-th string in this signature is assigned to $x_i[1]$.

The length of the signature is n^2.

Signature Verification
For sig = $(sig_{n-1}, \dots, sig_0)$ signature verification, the hash is calculated.
    hash = $(hash_{n-1}, \dots, hash_0)$ and we have to verify following equality:

$$(f(sig_{n-1}), \ \dots, \ f(sig_0)) = (y_{n-1}[hash_{n-1}], \ \dots, \ y_0[hash_0]) \tag{8}$$

Signature will be verified in case this equation is correct.

2.2 Winternitz One Time Signature Scheme

We can tell, that key and signature generation is effective in Lamport–Diffie one-time signature scheme, but signature size equals to n2, that is pretty large. One-time signature scheme offered by Winternitz significantly reduces the signature size as in this scheme we can use one string of the key to sign several bits of the hashed message [3].

Key Generation
In this scheme signature key X consists of randomly selected sn lines of length n.

To be signed simultaneously Winternitz parameter w >= 2 must be equal to the number of bits. This way we get s1 and s2.

$$s1 = n/w \tag{9}$$

$$s2 = (log2s1 + 1 + w)/w \tag{10}$$

$$s = s_1 + s_2 \tag{11}$$

$$X = (x_{s-1}[0], \ldots, x_0) \in \{0, 1\}^{n,s} \tag{12}$$

We get the next verification key:

$$Y = \left(y_{s-1}[0], \ldots, y_0\right) \in \{0, 1\}^{n,s}, \text{ where} \tag{13}$$

$$y_i = f^{2^{\wedge}w-1}(xi), 0 <= i <= s - 1 \tag{14}$$

The signature and verification key is equal to ns bits.

Document Signature
If the hash length is not divisible by w, the minimum number of zeros is added to the hash, and it is divided into s1 parts of length w.

$$hash = k_{s-1}, \ldots, k_{s-s1} \tag{15}$$

So we get c checksum:

$$c = \sum_{i=s-s1}^{s-1} (2^w - k_i) \tag{16}$$

as $c <= s_1 2^w$, we have it's binary length : $\log_2 s_1 2^w + 1 \tag{17}$

If the binary length can't be divided by w, the minimum number of zeros are added to it and is divided into s2 parts of length w.

$$c = k_{s2-1}, \ldots, k_0 \tag{18}$$

We have the signature of m in result:

$$sig = (f^{\wedge}k_{s-1}(x_{s-1}), \ldots, f^{\wedge}k_0(x_0)) \tag{19}$$

The signature size is sn.

Signature Verification
$k_{s-1}, \ldots, k_0$ bit strings are calculated to verify the signature: $sig = (sig_{n-1}, \ldots, sig_0)$ (Table 1)
If the following equation matches:

$$(f^{\wedge}(2^w - 1 - k_{s-1})(Sig_{n-1}), \ldots, (f^{\wedge}(2^w - 1 - k_0)(Sig_0) = y_{n-1}, \ldots y_0 \tag{20}$$

Then: $sig_i = f^{\wedge}k_i(x_i)$.

$$(f^{\wedge}(2^w - 1 - k_i)(Sig_i), \ldots, (f^{\wedge}(2^w - 1)(x_i) = y_i; i = s - 1 \ldots, 0 \tag{21}$$

Table 1. Lamport and Winternitz.

	Lamport	Winternitz
Key size	$2n^2$	ns
Using f for key generation	$2n$	$k(2^w-1)$
Signature length	n^2	ns
Using f for signature generation	Not used	$k(2^w-1)$
Using f for signature verification	n	$k(2^w-1)$

2.3 Merkle Crypto-System

We face the problem when use one time signature scheme to exchange big number of the keys as it uses different key pairs for every message. To solve this problem Merkle digital signature scheme uses a binary tree to avoid using large number of verification keys with one public key [4]. The verification key here is the root of this tree [5, 6]. In Merkle crypto-system are used one-time signature scheme and a cryptographic hash function:

$$h : \{0, 1\}* \to \{0, 1\}^n \tag{22}$$

The document's signature in the case of Merkle is the concatenation of one-time signature, one-time verification key, corresponding index and all fraternal nodes in relation to verification key. As we can see the signature size is much bigger, then in one time signature schemes.

3 The BLAKE Hash Function

The BLAKE Hash Function - is a cryptographic hash function based on Dan Bernstein's ChaCha stream cipher, where XOR of permuted copy of the input block with round constants is added before each ChaCha round [7, 8]. There are two variants, differentiated by the scale of words. The first category uses 32-bit words and includes BLAKE-256 and BLAKE-224, with result of 256 bits and 224 bits appropriately and second category, which uses 64-bit words - BLAKE-512 and BLAKE-384 and produce digest sizes of 512 bits and 384 bits appropriately.

BLAKE-256 and BLAKE-224 use 32-bit words and produce digest sizes of 256 bits and 224 bits, respectively, while BLAKE-512 and BLAKE-384 use 64-bit words and produce digest sizes of 512 bits and 384 bits, respectively.

The BLAKE2 hash function, based on BLAKE, was announced in 2012. The BLAKE3 hash function, based on BLAKE2, was announced in 2020.

The BLAKE2 Hash Function
In 2012, the BLAKE2 cryptographic hash function was developed based on BLAKE by Jean-Philippe Aumasson, Samuel Neves, Christian Winnerlein and Zooko Wilcox-O'Hearn.

BLAKE2 provides security superior to SHA-2 and similar to that of SHA-3: immunity to length extension, undifferentiability from a random oracle, etc. BLAKE2 provides higher security level than SHA-2 and same security level that gives SHA-3: as it has immunity to length extension, undifferentiability from a random oracle, etc..The BLAKE2 set incorporates two main functions: BLAKE2b and BLAKE2s. therefore, BLAKE2s is well optimized for 8-bit and 32-bit platforms, and it outputs between 1 and 32 bytes long hash values. Moreover, BLAKE2b is well optimized for 64-bit × 86–64 and ARM architectures. It outputs between 1 and 64 bytes long hash values. It is notable that both BLAKE2b and BLAKE2s work on any CPU, and if they are optimized, they can produce up to 100% speed up. The BLAKE2b makes 12 cicles, and BLAKE2s makes 10 cicles, while in the original version of BLAKE 16 and 14 cicles were made. In this paper we prove that reduction of cicles does not have any impact on the security. Shortening the cycles gives us 25% and 29% optimizations for large inputs, respectively. Moreover, BLAKE-512 interleaves four 64-bit words of 32, 25, 16 and 11 bits, while BLAKE2b replaces 25 with 24, and 11 with 63. Therefore, using 24-bit rotation, it allows processors with SSSE3 support, perform 2 rotations with only one SIMD instruction through an in-place byte shift operation called packed bytes in random order (pshufb). New processors low the arithmetic cost of the processing 12%. Besides, 63-bit rotations can also be transformed using addition and shift operations followed by logical OR operations. This approach speeds up platforms where add and shift operations can be performed in parallel. We offer to use blake2b as the one way function in the scheme.

4 Quantum Key Distribution

The concept of quantum key distribution (QKD) was first proposed in the 1970s. In 1980s it already seemed to be realistic. In 1990s the physicists began to work seriously on QKD, because the connection was transferred to entanglement. QKD technology became commercially available for the last 15 years [9, 10].

QKD offers a way of distributing and sharing the secret keys which are obligatory for the different cryptographic protocols. During QKD the information is encoded on the single photons. Alice can encode the conversation using one of two states, using vertical or horizontal ways of polarization. Alice chooses to encode the message in two different states; these states are labeled as $+45°$ and $-45°$. Afterwards Bob choses to measure in one of the two, so he measures in $+45°$, $-45°$. If Bob makes a measurement in a base that is different from the one Alice used, then his reply will be considered as random and it will be canceled, but if both of the chose the same one, then both of them will receive the correlated results. Alice can send one of the states and Bob detects it, and the states are saved. During the last stage Alice and Bob communicate about which of the bases was used but this process does not reveal the information about the final result, and the result is the secret key. This is the basic way of implementing of QKD, but there exist many different variations [11–15].

Like this, we can generate the secret key. If an eavesdropper tries to get the key he will fail, because he will introduce the mistake and will reveal himself. We offer to use quantum key distribution to transfer the key Winternitz one time signature scheme.

5 The Novel Scheme

Key generation - in key generation phase w is the number of bits, which must be signed simultaneously. s_1 and s_2 are calculated:

$$s1 = n/w \tag{23}$$

$$s2 = (\log 2 s1 + 1 + w)/w \tag{24}$$

$$s = s_1 + s_2 \tag{25}$$

$$X = (x_{s-1}[0], \ldots, x_0) \in \{0, 1\}^{n,s} \tag{26}$$

The verification key is:
$Y = (y_{s-1}[0], \ldots, y_0) \in \{0,1\}^{n,s}$, where

$$y_i = f^{2^{\wedge}w-1}(x_i), 0 <= i <= s - 1 \tag{27}$$

The signature and verification key is equal to ns bits. As the one-way function blake2b is used.

Document Signature

Before signing the message, we hash it: $H = h(m)$. If length of hash is not devisable by w the needed number of zeros must be prepended to H and it is must be divided into the s1 parts of the length w each.

$$H = k_{s-1}, \ldots, k_{s-s1} \tag{28}$$

The checksum is received as:

$$c = \sum_{i=s-s1}^{s-1} (2^w - k_i) \tag{29}$$

$c < = s_1 2^w$, so the length of the binary representation is equal to $\log_2 s_1 2^w + 1$.

If the length of representation can not be divided by w, the concrete number of 0-s must be prepended to it and must it be divided into s2 parts of the length w each.

$$c = k_{s2-1}, \ldots, k_0 \tag{30}$$

The signature is:

$$signature = (f^{\wedge}ks - 1(xs - 1), \ldots, f^{\wedge}k0(x0)) \tag{31}$$

The final signature size is sn. As the hahs function blake2b is used.

Signature Verification

$k_{s-1}, \ldots, k_0$ bit strings must be calculated in order to verify the signature:

$$signature = (sig_{n-1}, \ldots, sig_0) \tag{32}$$

The following equality must be checked:

$$(f^\wedge(2w - 1 - ks - 1))(sign - 1), \ldots, (f(2w - 1 - k0))(sig0) = yn - 1, \ldots y0 \tag{33}$$

Therefore: $sig_i = f^\wedge k_i(x_i)$

$$(f^\wedge(2w - 1 - ki))(sig_i) = (f^\wedge(2w - 1))(x_i) = x_i; i = s - 1, \ldots, 0 \tag{34}$$

In order to sign multiple messages we can transfer the key using quantum key distribution protocol, so the final signature size will be sn, which is much smaller the in the case of Merkle.

6 Security and Results

In the offered scheme is the classical Winternitz one time signature scheme is used, which is secure. The classical Quantum Key Distribution algorithm is integrated into the scheme, which is also secure. As one-way function and as the hash function blake2b function is used, which is also secure.

To break the scheme we must break Winternitz one time signature scheme, blake2b hash function or Quantum Key Distribution protocol, which is impossible because of the assumption. Therefore, the scheme is secure. As the result we have received the efficient and secure hash based digital signature. The size of the signature is significantly reduced comparing it to classical Merkle signature scheme.

Acknowledgement. The work was conducted as a part of PHDF-19–519 financed by Shota Rustaveli National Science Foundation of Georgia.

References

1. Paquin, C., Stebila, D., Tamvada, G.: Benchmarking post-quantum cryptography in TLS. In: Ding, J., Tillich, J.-P. (eds.) PQCrypto 2020. LNCS, vol. 12100, pp. 72–91. Springer, Cham (2020). https://doi.org/10.1007/978-3-030-44223-1_5
2. Ajtai, M.: Generating hard instances of lattice problems. In Complexity of computations and proofs, volume 13 of Quad. Mat., pp. 1–32. Dept. Math., Seconda Univ. Napoli, Caserta (2004). Preliminary version in STOC 1996. 8. Babai, L.: On Lovász lattice reduction and the nearest lattice point problem. Combinatorica, 6:1*13 (1986)
3. Buchmann, J., Dahmen, E., Klintsevich, E., Okeya, K., Vuillaume, C.: Merkle signatures with virtually unlimited signature capacity. In: Katz, J., Yung ,M. (eds.) Ap-plied Cryptography and Network Security. ACNS 2007. Lecture Notes in Computer Science, vol 4521. Springer, Berlin, Heidelberg (2007). https://doi.org/10.1007/978-3-540-72738-5_3
4. Katz, J., Yung, M. (eds.): ACNS 2007. LNCS, vol. 4521. Springer, Heidelberg (2007). https://doi.org/10.1007/978-3-540-72738-5
5. Lee, D., Park, N.: Blockchain based privacy preserving multimedia intelligent video surveillance using secure Merkle tree. Multimedia Tools Appl. 1–18 (2020). https://doi.org/10.1007/s11042-020-08776-y

6. Gagnidze, A., Iavich, M., Iashvili, G.: Novel version of merkle cryptosystem. Bulletin of the Georgian National Academy of Sciences (2017)
7. Sklavos, N., Kitsos, P.: BLAKE HASH Function Family on FPGA: From the Fastest to the Smallest. In: 2010 IEEE Computer Society Annual Symposium on VLSI, pp. 139–142. Lixouri, Greece (2010). https://doi.org/10.1109/ISVLSI.2010.115
8. Wang, H., Zhang, H.: A fast pseudorandom number generator with BLAKE hash function. Wuhan Univ. J. Nat. Sci. **15**, 393–397 (2010). https://doi.org/10.1007/s11859-010-0672-0
9. Gottesman, D., Lo, D., Lutkenhaus, N., Preskill, J.: Security of quantum key distribution with imperfect devices. In: International Symposium onInformation Theory, 2004. ISIT 2004. Proceedings, Chicago, IL, USA (2004). https://doi.org/10.1109/ISIT.2004.1365172
10. Liao, S.K., Cai, W.Q., Liu, W.Y.: Satellite-to-ground quantum key distribution. Nature **549**, 43–47 (2017). https://doi.org/10.1038/nature23655
11. Hu, Z., Gnatyuk, S., Okhrimenko, T., Kinzeryavyy, V., Iavich, M., Yubuzova, K.: High-speed privacy amplification method for deterministic quantum cryptography protocols using pairs of entangled Qutrits. CEUR Workshop Proc. **2393**, 810–821 (2019)
12. Gnatyuk, S., Okhrimenko, T., Iavich, M., Berdibayev, R.: Intruder control mode simulation of deterministic quantum cryptography protocol for depolarized quantum channel. In: Proceedings of 2019 International Scientific-Practical Conference on the Problems of Infocommunications. Science and Technology (PIC S&T 2019), pp. 825–828. Kyiv, Ukraine, October 08–11 (2019)
13. Lucamarini, M., Yuan, Z.L., Dynes, J.F.: Overcoming the rate–distance limit of quantum key distribution without quantum repeaters. Nature **557**, 400–403 (2018). https://doi.org/10.1038/s41586-018-0066-6
14. Lucamarini, M., Yuan, Z. L., Dynes, J. F., Shields, A. J.: Overcoming the rate–distance limit of quantum key distribution without quantum repeaters. Nature (London) **557**, 400 (2018)
15. Cui, C.-H., et al.: Twin-field quantum key distribution without phase postselection. Phys. Rev. Appl. **11**, 034053 (2019)

Investigation of Recurrent Neural Network Architectures for Prediction of Vessel Trajectory

Robertas Jurkus[1,2(✉)] [ID], Povilas Treigys[1] [ID], and Julius Venskus[1,2] [ID]

[1] Institute of Data Science and Digital Technologies, Vilnius University,
Vilnius, Lithuania
robertas.jurkus@mif.stud.vu.lt
[2] Faculty of Marine Technology and Natural Sciences, Department of Informatics
and Statistics, Klaipėda University, Klaipėda, Lithuania

Abstract. Modern deep learning algorithms are able to handle large amounts of data and therefore are particularly important in automating vessel movement prediction in intensive shipping. This could be one of the support tools for monitoring, managing the increasing maritime traffic and its participants.

Applying deep learning algorithm, a recurrent networks is created that is able to predict the further vessel movement. The developed architectural model is based on sequences when data change over time, therefore the article investigates the most optimal recurrent network structure and network hyper-parameters, which aim to obtain the most accurate prediction results. Different recurrent network architectures were used to compare the results those are: fully-connected (simple) recurrent neural network, basic (vanilla), bidirectional, stacked Long Short-Term Memory network, autoencoder, and gated recurrent unit. The accuracy of the predictions for each architecture is monitored by varying the number of cells size in the hidden layer. The research was performed on a specific sample of data from the Netherlands (North Sea) coastal region and the proposed algorithm can be applied as one of the ways to improve maritime safety. The research showed that the most accurate prediction of the vessel trajectory prediction is achieved with the bidirectional Long Short-Term Memory network architecture in which the variance is less shifting even with the smallest cell selection, and autoenoder network architecture which depends on the choice of the appropriate cell size, because distribution range increasing in 100 and 150 cells.

Keywords: Marine traffic monitoring · Recurrent neural networks for trajectory prediction · Multivariate multi steps · Cell of network hyper-parameters · Autoencoder

1 Introduction

There is intense traffic at sea, with many ships being loaded and unloaded in ports, so information on the whereabouts of shipping vessels, their trajectories

A. Lopata et al. (Eds.): ICIST 2021, CCIS 1486, pp. 194–208, 2021.
https://doi.org/10.1007/978-3-030-88304-1_16

and final destinations is crucial for maritime safety, the marine environment and the economy. The International Union of Marine Insurance (IUMI) in 2019 publication announces that about 10% suffered losses due to collisions. Losses are also caused by other factors (poorly trained crew, equipment failures, weather conditions) [1]. For example, one incident in Norway occurred at the end of 2018 when the Royal Norwegian Navy frigate *Helge Ingstad* collided with a tanker because it was upheld by shore-based constructions. By forecasting and predicting the trajectory of a particular vessel, it would be possible to assess the risk of a collision or to detect abnormal behavior in ongoing traffic. Although increasingly complex constructions of deep neural networks are emerging, LSTM networks are still being analyzed and applied to solve the problem of maritime traffic forecasting [2–4]. The purpose of this work is to research deep recurrent neural networks for prediction of vessel movement using different architectures and their dependence on cell size combinations. This article is reviewed as follow: in Sect. 2 is presented the sea traffic data and explained how data are processed, and structured into sequences. In Sect. 3 is created and provided recurrent network architectures. Section 4 shows the progress of the experiment and performed an analysis of the research results.

2   Vessel Traffic Data

An important part that identifies big data is variety, which means that there may be heterogeneous sources where the data is not structured, so in order to use the collected information, firstly, it is necessary to process it.

At the United Nations conference was presented the largest global terminal operators, throughput and capacity in 2019. Based on the statistics of the publication [5], the research region with the highest traffic flow in Europe were selected - the Netherlands and its embankment. Traffic data for this region was collected and extracted from the *Shipfinder* automatic identification system (known as AIS). *Shipfinder* is a provider of vessel tracking and maritime intelligence services which is based on coastal AIS network stations (historical traffic data can be downloaded at MarineCadastre[1] or can be purchased from MarineTraffic[2]). Big data of sea traffic allows to forecast ship trading activity, flows or intensity. In order to visualize the available data, a graphical image was generated (see Fig. 1a). Densely spaced data indicate that traffic flow is significantly more intense.

Cargo ships are one of the most popular and most commonly found types of industrial ship in traffic, transporting cargo, goods and materials in containers from one port to another. Due to the abundance of data, it specializes in forecasting the progress of this type of vessel. Collected 5 months data between September 2018 and February 2019 (nearly 21 million records), distributed in the territory of North sea.

---

[1] https://marinecadastre.gov/ais.

[2] https://www.marinetraffic.com/en/p/ais-historical-data.

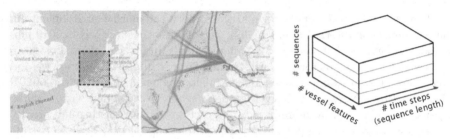

(a) Visualization of AIS traffic data in the research region.

(b) Three-dimensional view of the vessel data structure.

Fig. 1. Collected data views.

Raw vessel records are stored and break down into multiple csv files by date-time period. Data processing steps begin with records structural formation and centralization into data warehouses. Also, vessel tracking information system data have plenty of messy records: repetitive duplicates of records, incomplete information (missing vessel characteristics), undefined data types. For the following reasons were used ETL (extract-transform-load) processes. ETL processes consist of three database functions combined into one tool, during which data is extracted from data sources, transformed and transferred to a central/host computer (data warehouse). It was the ETL processes that performed the primary AIS data source filtering and data consolidation. The big data set consists of the main vessel features which represent traffic flow in the particular region:

- VesselId (MMSI): maritime mobile service identity (Id used only for sequence generation);
- Latitude: geographic latitude coordinate;
- Longitude: geographic longitude coordinate;
- SpeedKnt: vessel speed measured in knots;
- HeadingDeg: vessel sailing direction;
- DateDiff: difference between two time steps in the trajectory (minutes);
- Δ Latitude: latitude difference of two time steps in time (1);
- Δ Longitude: longitude difference of two time steps in time (2).

Coordinate changes in time between two points can be calculated by deriving functions (extra features) [6]. These values shows how fast the vessel moved in time between the current and the previous time step. It is a fine-tune data by combination of the existing parameters (conjunction of time and coordinate features).

$$X_{\Delta t} = t_s - t_{s-1}$$

$$X_{\delta Lat} = \frac{X_{Lat,s} - X_{Lat,s-1}}{X_{\Delta t}} \quad (1) \qquad X_{\delta Lon} = \frac{X_{Lon,s} - X_{Lon,s-1}}{X_{\Delta t}} \quad (2)$$

where:

- s - is the time in different measurement intervals,
- $X_{\Delta t}$ - is the time difference value of the previous step,
- $X_{\delta Lat}$ - is the latitude coordinate (variation),
- $X_{\delta Lon}$ - is the longitude coordinate (variation).

2.1 Data Sequence Generation

As the article is being based on the principles of supervised training, where input variables X and output variables Y are available, and deep learning architectures would learn the inter-dependencies of these variables, so that further vessel trajectory could be reconstructed from the new data. The trajectory forecasting by time steps can be divided into two ways: one time step prediction and multiple time steps prediction. The problem of forecasting is being analysed by Xu Liu and his colleagues in their work to create a bike sharing opportunity and predict their availability [7]. The authors argued that multi-time step output Long Short-Term Memory (LSTM) is much better than the standard uni-time step output. Based on their research and the gathered AIS data, this research developed a data structure called multivariate multi steps.

The data processed by the ETL must be analyzed, structured and prepared for use in the recurrent networks. The main data set is three-dimensional (see Fig. 1b), the dimensions of which can be viewed by axis: sequences, vessel features, time steps. Analyzing the data, it was noticed that in the studied period only about 1/4 vessels are in movement progress. Standing or floating vessel is considered when the speed attribute value is equal to 0. After several experiment results showed, that data set with stationary vessels data is noise that can offset net weights for forecasting progress. Therefore, these records were eliminated, leaving only vessels in motion (more than 5 million records). The generation of the vessel sequences was performed at the SQL level, the decomposition process is shown in the illustration below (see Fig. 2).

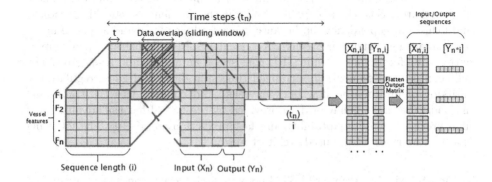

Fig. 2. Vessel data sequencing.

Vessel feature (F_n) are broken down into sequences of equal length (i), which overlap by the so-called lag or sliding window method and are sorted in synchronous order (by time t_n). The overlap method is a fixed number of time-lapse and memorized time steps where the time series of one observation set overlap with the series of the next sequence, because in the context of time series forecasting, it is important to present past values so that recurrent networks could learn to predict the future. Sequence overlap is performed by dividing the sequence in half. Each sequence are divided into equal-sized input (X_n, F_n) and output (Y_n, F_n) matrices (or otherwise features and labels) because this regression task is assigned to supervised learning where input features are fed to the network, and the network provides predicted output features. All deep recurrent architectures in this article as final output layer uses a two-dimensional structure, so output must be flattened before training the network.

Specific criteria for sequence generation were applied: Each sequence are classified as cargo type; Single sequence cannot consist of two different MMSI; A 150-min filter was applied to the smoothness and integrity of the time steps. The filter ensures that there is no step size gap greater than 150 min in the sequence. A large time step interval is detected in the data because the AIS observations were not performed consistently, so the intervals between the time steps (t_n) and $(t_n - 1)$ are not the same. To maintain a strong and accurate relationship between time steps, large gaps in the sequence need to be eliminated. The filter parameter was selected based on the calculated time step difference frequency (in minutes), as the maximum data concentration is distributed over 150 min.

3 Recurrent Network Architectures

The characteristics of recurrent networks have at least one cyclic pathway from the synaptic connections. All activities in neural networks are repeated [8]. Unlike standard feed-forward neural networks a typical RNN network transmits information repeatedly from one block to another. The paper investigates not only simple RNN, but also improved deep learning recurrent networks - LSTM and gated recurrent unit (GRU) with different architectural combinations. These improved architectures are capable of solving the problems of vanishing gradient and long-term dependency [9], because it has feedback links and a special memory management structure (cells). A typical LSTM cell consists of: an input, output, and forget gates, while GRU consists of: an update and reset gates. The cells can process sequentially arranged time step data, and gates regulate the variation of information flow between cells. And compared to the traditional methods, the ship's behavior data provided by the LSTM has the advantages of high precision, good adaptability and fast prediction speed [10]. The following is a brief overview of the used architectures.

Basic LSTM. The standard LSTM network architecture consists of one hidden LSTM cell layer. General network design: input layer, LSTM and dropout hidden layers and dense output layer (see Fig. 3 without note). The hidden layer consists of blocks of LSTM cells connected (uni-directional) in a circuit. They are all connected by a main status signal, which is changed by a cell gate.

Bidirectional LSTM. Bi-directional LSTMs are able to process the sequence data in two directions including forward and backward ways with two separate hidden layers and then feed forward to the same output layer [11]. In this case forward and backward ways are constructed in the same single LSTM hidden layer (see Fig. 3 with note). The other parts are similar to the structure of basic LSTM, main difference that signal goes in both directions. The regularization technique is applied to the hidden layer as the dropout layer, which randomly sets input units to 0 with a frequency of rate at each step during training time. Based on the literature, better LSTM results can be obtained using bidirectional constructions [12].

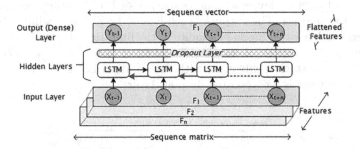

Fig. 3. Basic uni-directional and bidirectional LSTM architectures. Note: bidirectional marked with red line. (Color figure online)

Simple Recurrent Neural Network simple RNN layer uses a loop to iterate over the time steps of a sequence, while maintaining an internal state that encodes information about the time steps it has seen so far. This means, that the current time steps hidden state is only calculated using information of the previous time step's hidden state and the current input. RNN being able to model short term dependencies, because it does not have a specialized gates. Simple RNN architecture is constructed the same as all other architectures the main difference - cell structure (see Fig. 4 with RNN cells).

Gated Recurrent Unit. GRU network uses update gate and reset gate for information flow control and which decide what information should be passed to the output. Full architecture can be visualize the same as basic LSTM or RNN, but instead with dissimilar cell structure in the hidden layer (see Fig. 4 with GRU cells).

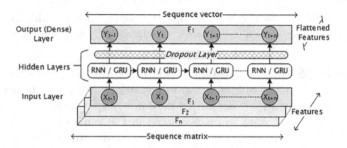

Fig. 4. Simple RNN and GRU architectures.

Stacked LSTM. The standard LSTM architecture extension is the LSTM stack. The main difference from the basic LSTM architecture is that the structure consists of more than one hidden LSMT layer [13]. In this architecture (see Fig. 5), LSTM network layers are additionally added so that they are connected in parallel to the stack. The output of each hidden LSTM layer will be the input of the next hidden layer. Based on studies in the literature [15] where comparing the accuracy of networks by varying the number of layers, it was decided to create the LSTM stack architecture with three hidden LSTM layers. After each LSTM hidden layer is incorporated dropout layer.

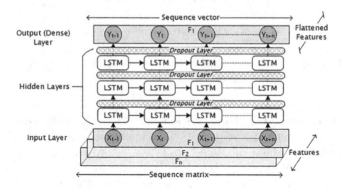

Fig. 5. Stacked LSTM architecture.

LSTM Autoencoder. This is a special type of neural network in which the input is compressed into a smaller dimension code and the compressed code at the output is reconstructed [14]. The architecture consists of three components (see Fig. 6): encoder, latent space vector, and decoder. Typically, data is encoded by dividing the layer in half and decoded by doubling the layer. In this case a LSTM encoder turn input sequences into a single vector that contains information about the entire sequence, then repeat this vector n times (where n is the number of time steps in the output sequence), and in the decoder part try to turn this constant sequence into the target sequence. Dimensional reduction was applied by changing the number of LSTM cells.

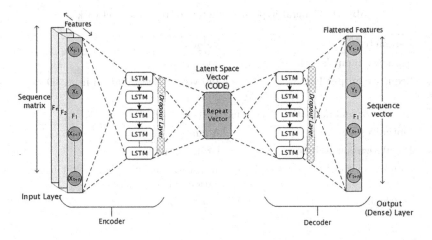

Fig. 6. LSTM autoencoder architecture.

The learning process of deep neural networks has sets of parameters to choose from before beginning any learning. These parameters are called hyperparameters. Some of them describe the architecture of a neural network, such as the number of layers and their size. Others define the learning process, such as the speed of learning and its adjustment. If the network configuration is selected incorrectly, the network may learn slowly or may not learn at all. An attempt is made to investigate which recurrent network architecture and with what number of cells most accurately reproduces the further course of time steps in the sequence.

4   Experiment and Results

4.1   Instructions for Network

The experiments were performed by changing the architectures and changing the number of cells/units. In order to keep the same conditions for all architectures, the same data order for training, the same network parameters (see Table 1) and cells size interval are used. It has been observed that quite often in the literature the number of cells can vary from tens to hundreds, so was decided to follow these numbers and analyse cells in range from 25 to 300, each size incremented by 25. To ensure the reliability of the models, each architecture with a different cell combination was trained 10 times (models = 6 architectures × 12 cell sizes × 10 times).

Various hyperparameter modifications were tested during the experiment. Changed activation functions RELU/TANH. As prevention for regression models overfitting was tested L2 and dropout regularization techniques. However, after practical testing, the most suitable parameters were obtained with the components listed in the table below.

Table 1. General hyper-parameters of recurrent networks.

Parameter	Value
Sequence input length	30 steps
Sequence output length	140 vector elem. (flatten from 3D - 20 steps)
Loss/error and activation functions	MSE and RELU
Optimizer algorithm	Adam (0.001)
Regularization technique	Dropout (0.01)
Number of epochs	400 (with EarlyStopping event by patience 15)
Batch size	256

According to the population in the region the selected cargo vessels were cut into more than 123 thousands sequences. The scale of the vessels feature data is relatively small, making it difficult to train models with such accuracy. For example, the area of the research region latitude range variate from 51.635 to 52.12 while longitude value range between 3.1 and 4.5, so normalization (3) is applied to the whole data set. During normalization, the values in the numeric columns of the data set are changed to an overall scale without distorting the ranges of values. In this way, the scales of the independent vectors are scaled and all numerical values take on a common scale from 0 to 1. In many cases, this transformation speeds up the network learning process by simplifying calculations by reducing high input and increasing minimum values.

$$X_{norm} = \frac{X - X_{min}}{X_{max} - X_{min}} \quad (3) \qquad MSE = \frac{1}{n}\sum_{i=1}^{n}(y_i - \hat{y_i})^2 \quad (4)$$

where (3):

- X - is the feature of the vessel,
- X_{norm} - is the normalized value,
- X_{max} and X_{min} - is the maximum and the minimum value of the feature.

where (4):

- n - is the number of samples,
- y_i - is the true value,
- $\hat{y_i}$ - is the predicted value.

It was decided to create the sequence from 50 time steps, of which 30 constitute input and 20 constitute output. This means that 30 time steps will be fed into the network, and the developed model will predict the next 20 (140 elements in flatten structure - $features_{number} * output_{steps}$). Estimated that one sequence of vessel can predict on average about hour and a half further course of the trajectory, when the average sequence length consists of 4 h duration.

The generated and normalized sequence matrices are shuffled before presenting the data to the network architectures. Mixing the matrices ensures that each new sequence in the model will be independent of the previous sequence, reducing the variance, making the gradient more changeable. The data set was split into samples with ratio 70:15:15 (70% training data, 15% test data, and 15% validation data). The training sample is used to create models. The validation sample is used to monitor and verify the modeling process. The test sample is used to evaluate the accuracy of the final model.

4.2   Models Evaluation

The accuracy of the networks is calculated by the root mean square error (MSE), which estimates the predicted and actual values (4). Since the architectures have been trained with all the features of the vessel, this means that the model tries to predict not only the course (coordinates) of the vessel, but also the remaining features (speed, direction, etc.). However, our goal and attention is on trajectory, and thats why slight change in true and predicted data is made before evaluations. All feature vector values (except latitude and longitude) are ignored and only geographical coordinates are used for evaluation (see Fig. 7). Almost 16 thousand sequences are estimated for single model (whole test data set).

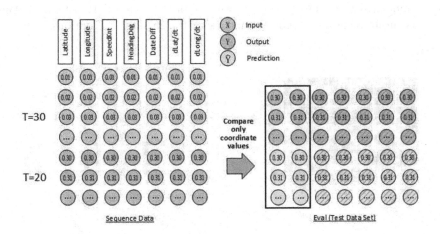

Fig. 7. Model evaluation strategy.

After we created and trained all these six different kinds of deep recurrent neural networks, we evaluated 720 models on our data set from test samples. The MSE loss value is calculated as the average of the total number of experiments (devided by 10 times). Table 2 showing results. Systematized data shows

Table 2. MSE loss results with different cell hyper-parameter sets.

Cells	Simple RNN, ×10⁻⁴	Basic LSTM, ×10⁻⁴	LSTM Stack, ×10⁻⁴	GRU, ×10⁻⁴	AE, ×10⁻⁴	Bidirectional, ×10⁻⁴
25	6.910	5.181	4.434	5.563	4.581	6.582
50	5.334	4.381	4.361	4.620	3.944	3.939
75	4.904	4.211	4.146	4.290	4.010	4.177
100	4.819	3.947	4.150	4.021	4.031	3.697
125	4.702	4.039	4.075	3.914	3.688	3.721
150	4.739	3.875	4.240	3.916	3.996	3.683
175	4.635	3.920	4.067	3.914	3.789	3.822
200	4.628	3.999	4.564	3.826	3.706	3.900
225	4.679	4.024	4.482	3.819	3.987	3.636
250	4.630	4.085	4.133	3.742	3.946	3.736
275	4.660	3.998	4.099	3.827	3.724	3.645
300	4.681	4.086	3.956	3.710	3.782	3.618

which architecture more accurately predicts vessel movement. In regression, the prediction is considered accurate when the error value is closest to zero.

The table below indicates the smallest errors (marked with color) in a given architecture with the appropriate cell size. It can be seen that the smallest error in the test data sample was obtained by Bidirectional LSTM, a slight difference between the following AE and GRU. All architectures rating by loss with the best fitting cell size can be found in Fig. 8b. Also, Fig. 8a depicts with which cell combinations the smallest errors were obtained after all 10 attempts. The most accurate results were not obtained with the smallest cell options.

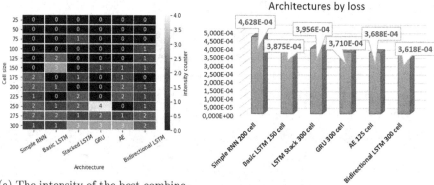

(a) The intensity of the best combination set during the experiments.

(b) Architectures by lowest loss with combination of specific cell size.

Fig. 8. Accuracy of recurrent network architectures.

Table 3. A more detailed comparison of the three best architectures.

Attribute	GRU	AE	Bidirectional
Best with cell size	300	125	300
Random trajectory loss (from Fig. 10)	0.634×10^{-6}	4.831×10^{-6}	0.303×10^{-6}
Mean value of all tests	3.710×10^{-4}	3.688×10^{-4}	3.618×10^{-4}
Variance	1.204×10^{-10}	2.714×10^{-10}	1.059×10^{-10}
Standard deviation of the observations	1.098×10^{-5}	1.647×10^{-5}	3.255×10^{-5}
The Minimum loss achieved in the tests	3.526×10^{-4}	3.416×10^{-4}	3.218×10^{-4}
The Maximum loss achieved in the tests	3.903×10^{-4}	4.002×10^{-4}	4.234×10^{-4}

The three best architectures are analyzed deeper by attributes of cell, parameters and loss. More details of the comparison can be found in Table 3. The data in the table shows that although the error in the bidirectional architecture is smaller, the number of trainable parameters is quite large compared to GRU and AE. As a result, the model development time is also longer.

These three architectures are reviewed statistically below (see Fig. 9). Box plots visually show the distribution of numerical data and skewness through displaying the data quartiles (or percentiles) and averages.

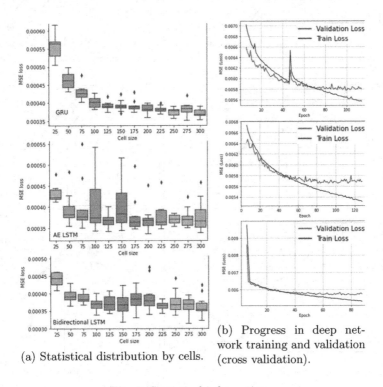

(a) Statistical distribution by cells.

(b) Progress in deep network training and validation (cross validation).

Fig. 9. Statistical information.

According to Fig. 9a, it can be argued that the AE depends on the choice of the appropriate cell size, because distribution range increasing in 100 and 150 cells. The smallest distribution is obtained in the bidirectional network even with a smaller number of cells, meanwhile in GRU increases the deviation at the beginning due to a simpler cell structure. Figure 9b shows network learning progress. Somewhere since the 50–60 epoch, the networks is being trained.

A random sequence was chosen for the final testing of the networks. The results are visible in the Fig. 10. The results are visualized with the best cell sizes fit. The green line indicates the input sequence (30 time steps), the original vessel output trajectory is marked in yellow (20 time steps), the blue line visualizes the prediction of vessel movement in the trained network (20 time steps), and the gray line indicates the traffic intensity from the other sequances. Visually noticeable that Bidirectional and AE networks trajectory prediction most accurate (this is also shown by the calculated mse loss. The turn is navigated closest to the actual line.

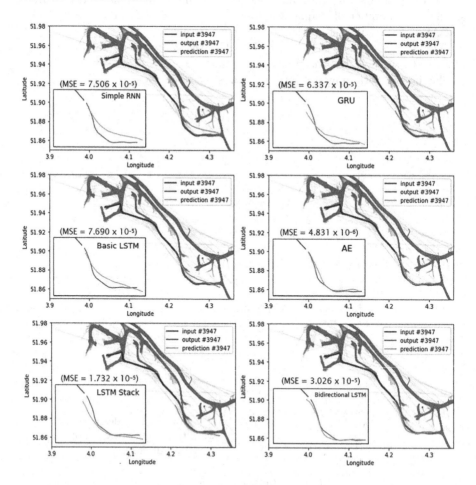

Fig. 10. Vessel movement forecast in random trajectory.

5   Conclusions

For prediction of vessel movement were analysed and developed recurrent networks which are based on time sequences where information is managed by specific cell structures. The research found that different choices of their size have a direct relationship to the results, depending on the type of architecture. The six different architectures were tested in the study: simple RNN, basic LSTM, LSTM stack, GRU, AE and basic bidirectional LSTM. It was determined that the most accurate prediction and least MSE loss is achieved with the bidirectional 3.218×10^{-4} (with 300 cells) and autoencoder 3.416×10^{-4} (with 125 cells) architectures. The AE is dependent on the right choice of the appropriate cell size, because the dispersion waves from the selected size. The obtained network accuracy was obtained specifically in the data sample examined in this research. A study of this work could be developed in the future for improving forecasting accuracy. For example, better harmonize the interdependencies between vessel data and their impact on accuracy or try the more sophisticated type of neural network which is more and more popular in these days with a attention mechanism (transformers).

References

1. Seltmann, A.: Marine insurance - casualty trends. CEFOR publications 2019 Nordic marine insurance statistics. The Nordic Association of Marine Insurers, Oslo, Norway (2019)
2. Chen, C.W., Harrison, C., Huang, H.H.: The unsupervised method of vessel movement trajectory prediction. ArXiv, volume abs/2007.13712 (2020)
3. Forti, N., Millefiori, L.M., Braca, P., Willett, P.: Prediction of vessel trajectories from AIS data via sequence-to-sequence recurrent neural networks. Research Department, NATO STO Centre for Maritime Research and Experimentation (CMRE) Department of Electrical and Computer Engineering, Barcelona, Spain, pp. 8931–8935 (2020). ISBN 978-1-5090-6631-5. https://doi.org/10.1109/ICASSP40776.2020.9054421
4. Gao, D., Zhu, Y., Zhang, J., He, Y., Yan, K., Yan, B.: A novel MP-LSTM method for ship trajectory prediction based on AIS data. Ocean Eng. **228**, 108956 (2021). https://doi.org/10.1016/j.oceaneng.2021.108956
5. United Nations Conference on Trade and Development.: Review of Maritime Transport 2020. United Nations Publications, Geneva (2020). ISSN 0566-7682
6. Venskus, J., Treigys, P., Markevičiūtė, J.: Detecting maritime traffic anomalies with long-short term memory recurrent neural network. In: Nonlinear Analysis: Modelling and Control, Vilnius (2020). ISSN 1392-5113
7. Liu, X., Gherbi, A., Li, W., Cheriet, M.: Multi features and multi-time steps LSTM based methodology for bike sharing availability prediction. Proc. Comput. Sci. **155**, 394–401 (2019). The 14th International Conference on Future Networks and Communications (FNC), Halifax, Canada
8. Rizal, A.A., Soraya, S., Tajuddin, M.: Sequence to sequence analysis with long short term memory for tourist arrivals prediction. In: Journal of Physics: Conference Series, Indonesia, pp. 1–8 (2018). https://doi.org/10.1088/1742-6596/1211/1/012024

9. Vinayakumar, R., Soman, K.P., Prabaharan, P.: Applying deep learning approaches for network traffic prediction. In: 2017 International Conference on Advances in Computing, Communications and Informatics (ICACCI), pp. 2353–2358. Amrita Vishwa Vidyapeetham, India (2017). ISBN 978-1-5090-6367-3

10. Yang, S., Xinya, P., Zexuan, D., Jiansen, Z.: An approach to ship behavior prediction based on AIS and RNN optimization model. SciencePG: Int. J. Transp. Eng. Technol. 16–21 (2020). ISSN 2575-1743. https://doi.org/10.11648/j.ijtet.20200601.13

11. Cheng, Y., Zhang, W.: Concise deep reinforcement learning obstacle avoidance for under actuated unmanned marine vessels. Neurocomputing **272**, 63–73 (2018)

12. Liu, C., Li, Y., Jiang, R., Lu, Q., Guo, Z.: Trajectory-based data delivery algorithm in maritime vessel networks based on Bi-LSTM. In: Yu, D., Dressler, F., Yu, J. (eds.) WASA 2020. LNCS, vol. 12384, pp. 298–308. Springer, Cham (2020). https://doi.org/10.1007/978-3-030-59016-1_25

13. Li, Y., Cao, H.: Prediction for tourism flow based on LSTM neural network. Proc. Comput. Sci. **129**, 277–283 (2018). 2017 International Conference on Identification, Information and Knowledge in the Internet of Things, China

14. Murray, B., Prasad, L.P.: A dual linear autoencoder approach for vessel trajectory prediction using historical AIS data. Ocean Eng. **209**, 107478 (2020). https://doi.org/10.1016/j.oceaneng.2020.107478

15. Venskus, J., Treigys, P.: Preparation of training data by filling in missing vessel type data using deep multi-stacked LSTM neural network for abnormal marine traffic evaluation. In: ITISE 2019: International Conference on Time Series and Forecasting: Proceedings of Abstracts, Granada, Spain, p. 38 (2019). ISBN 9788417970796

RTCAnalysis: Practical Modular Performance Analysis of Automotive Systems with RTC

Mahmoud Bazzal[✉], Lukas Krawczyk, and Carsten Wolff

Dortmund University of Applied Sciences and Arts, Otto-Hahn-Str. 23,
44227 Dortmund, Germany
{mahmoud.bazzal,lukas.krawczyk,carsten.wolff}@fh-dortmund.de

Abstract. With the inherent complexity of heterogeneous embedded systems in the automotive domain, it becomes necessary to consider the modularity of components in such systems. Modular Performance Analysis (MPA) is a framework that attempts to analyse timing properties of these systems using the techniques of Real-Time Calculus (RTC). In this paper, we present the RTCAnalysis tool that performs practical MPA analysis on automotive systems during early design phases to identify metrics required to determine whether the system under analysis satisfies safety requirements.

Keywords: Real-Time Calculus · Automotive embedded systems · Amalthea · APP4MC

1 Introduction

The emergence of Advanced Driver Assistance Systems (ADAS) applications has led to a significant increase in the amount of computational loads that are required to be performed by automotive embedded hardware. The safety-critical nature of these applications imposes an additional constraint on automotive systems. To address this, system designers usually use different commercial off-the-shelf hardware components which do not necessarily have a similar architecture. This increasing heterogeneity and complexity of automotive embedded systems has increased the difficulty with which the safety of these systems could be determined. Many automotive embedded systems are at least Weakly-Hard Real-Time Systems (WHRTs), meaning that they have to satisfy a set of timing constraints where a system is only allowed to miss a limited number of subsequent deadlines while maintaining its functional correctness [4]. Satisfying these timing constraints is one of the most important aspects in the design process of these systems.

The research leading to these results has been partially funded by the Federal Ministry for Education and Research (BMBF) under grant agreement 01IS18057D in the context of the ITEA3 EU-Project PANORAMA.

RTC was extended to use the same notion of arrival and service to model and analyse real-time systems [22]. A combination of basic RTC modelling elements allows for conducting Modular Performance Analysis (MPA). The flexibility of RTC elements helps with the analysis of heterogeneous systems since they consist of multiple hardware and software components that do not follow the same computational model or scheduling strategy. Examples of this are systems consisting of multiple hardware accelerators.

Modular Performance Analysis [23] is a timing analysis framework based on RTC that can statically derive timing properties of real-time systems.

In this paper, we present RTCAnalysis, an MPA tool that is tailored towards automotive real-time systems. It allows for converting models of those systems to networks of RTC components and analyses these systems such that broad timing properties will be derived during early design phases.

The tool presented in this paper aims to unify the notions of RTC with the unique characteristics and semantics of Amalthea models and therefore will enable the use of RTC as a static analysis step in system design.

The remainder of this paper is structures as follows: Sect. 2 discusses related analysis frameworks and tools that exist to perform RTC analysis as well as analysis of automotive systems. Section 3 provides an introduction to RTC, MPA and the mathematical approach used to analyse RTC components. Section 4 describes the transformation of Amalthea model elements to an intermediate RTC system model representation that serves as the basis for performing RTC analysis. Section 5 describes the steps to analyse an RTC system model. Section 6 discusses the analysis runtime of the RTCAnalysis tool and the factors that affect it. Finally, Sect. 7 concludes this work and briefly describes possible future extensions of the tool.

2   Related Work

This section explores existing open source tools that can perform timing analysis on various aspects of automotive embedded systems. With RTC being an extension of Network Calculus (NC) [6], we take a look at existing open source tools aiming to perform NC analysis on switched networks. The DiscoDNC tool [5] is an open-source NC analysis tool that models packets going through network elements as flows passing through server nodes. This is used to conduct different analyses to determine the service available to a given flow and thus aiding with the design process of the system, as well as provide delay and buffer bounds for flows going through a pre-defined system. While it is possible to use this tool to perform crude analysis of a scheduled system, this tool only supports the notion of tokens being processed by FIFO servers, which makes the modelling of complex scheduling policies more difficult.

In terms of modular and interface-based analysis, the Compositional Performance Analysis (CPA) [16,20] framework analyses systems components by abstracting the occurrence of events in one of standard event models, and using a sliding window approach to derive the timing properties of each component.

This approach is implemented in tools such as the open-source framework pyCPA [9], or Symtavision's commercial scheduling analysis tool suite SymTA/S [1]. Furthermore, Wandeler et al. [23] developed a Matlab toolbox to perform MPA analysis. The back-end used in this toolbox to operate on curves in the $(max, +)$ and $(min, +)$ algebra domains is also used by the tool presented in this paper as for curve representation and transformation as explained in Sect. 5.

Holistic timing analysis tools that use a sliding-window-based approach such as MAST [11] are purposely built to support specific scheduling situations. They perform significantly better in terms of analysis run time, but are less flexible than MPA or CPA-based tools, given the reduced ability to describe system component that are not natively supported.

The importance of Model Based Systems Engineering in the design of automotive systems has led to many methods, processes, and tools tailored towards the needs of the automotive industry. One of the most recent standards for artefact exchange and modelling these systems is the *Amalthea* data model [24]. It allows describing various facets important to e.g., performance simulation, such as a system's software, hardware, timing constraints, and mappings from software to hardware. A reference implementation of the Amalthea System Model along with various tools for e.g., timing analysis as well as optimization [17–19] are available in the open-source tool platform *Eclipse APP4MC* [2].

For the purposes of the tool presented in this paper, the Amalthea model needs to provide a minimum amount of information that allows conducting timing analysis of a given system. In particular, this consists of:

- *Software Model:* It includes the tasks into which the software is partitioned. Each task has more granular software elements associated with it, that are further annotated with computational resource specific execution times.
- *Hardware Model:* This includes both computational resources such as processing units and hardware accelerators, in addition to communication and storage resources such as communication buses and memory elements.
- *Mapping Model:* A mapping that describes the allocation of modelled software elements to the corresponding computational resources from the system's hardware.
- *Stimulus Model:* It includes the stimulus elements of the system. A stimulus element models the activation pattern of a corresponding software element.
- *OS Model:* The schedulers that model the resource sharing policies implemented in the modelled system are contained in the OS model. Each scheduler element has a defined scheduling algorithm and manages a set of software elements and is assigned to a set of computational elements modelled in the hardware model.

3   Background

The RTCAnalysis tool extends the notions defined in our previous work [3]. For the sake of completeness, we include the introduction to RTC that was presented in [3].

3.1   Real-Time Calculus

RTC can derive various metrics of real-time systems—such as upper and lower bounds on a component's response time—by modelling the computational demands in the system as events propagating through shared resources. These events propagate along a path that depends on the given scheduling/arbitration strategy [22]. Analysis of the event propagation is enabled by modelling the rates of events incoming to a component and the rate of events being served by a resource assigned to that component, with *arrival curves* and *service curves* respectively.

Arrival and service curves are defined over the $\Delta = s - t$ domain; Where s and t are absolute time instants chosen such that Δ represents a time window of width $s - t$. A bound on the number of occurring events inside a time window of an arbitrary width Δ can be represented by a by an arrival curve or service curve depending on the type of events in a given event stream.

Definition 1 (Arrival Curve [3,22]). *Let f be an event flow, and $R(t)$ a function representing the accumulated number of events in f at time t. The accumulated number of events in f within a time interval Δ is defined as the arrival curve $\alpha_f(\Delta)$ of flow f.*
An upper arrival curves α_f^u and a lower arrival curve α_f^l represent the upper and lower bounds on the accumulated number of events in f within Δ such that $\alpha_f^l(t - s) \leq R[s,t] \leq \alpha_f^u(t - s), \forall s < t$.
The set of upper and lower arrival curves of flow f is denoted as an arrival curve pair, $\alpha_f^{l,u} = \{\alpha_f^l, \alpha_f^u\}$.

Definition 2 (Service Curve [3,22]). *Let r be a system resource, and $c(t)$ a function denoting the accumulated number of events services by r at time t. The upper service curve β_c^u and the lower service curve β_c^l are defined as the respective upper and lower bounds on the accumulated number of serviced events within a time interval Δ such that $\beta_R^l(t - s) \leq C[s,t] \leq \beta_R^u(t - s), \forall s < t$.*
The set of upper and lower service curves of resource r is denoted as a service curve pair, $\beta_r^{l,u} = \{\beta_r^l, \beta_r^u\}$.

3.2   Greedy Processing Component

In addition to the ability of modelling computational demands in terms of arrival curves, as well as modelling resource capacity in terms of service curves, it is important to model the processing of these demands with by the underlying computational resource. This modelling is performed in RTC by defining the *Greedy Processing Component* (GPC).

Definition 3 (Greedy Processing Component [7]). *Let an event flow f be processed by a resource r, the Greedy Processing Component (GPC) represents the transformation of arrival curves and service curves of f and r respectively as illustrated in Fig. 2. The set of output service curves $\beta_r^{l\prime}, \beta_r^{u\prime}$ denote the remaining service provided by r after processing the events in f. Similarly, the set of*

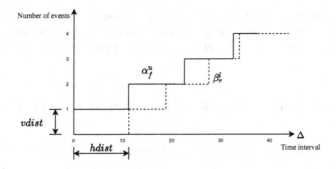

Fig. 1. The maximum horizontal *hdist* and vertical *vdist* distances between upper arrival curve α_f^u and (adjusted) lower service curve β_r^l [3].

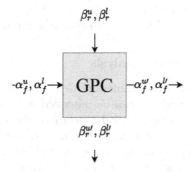

Fig. 2. A Greedy Processing Component (GPC) element transforms the input pairs of arrival and service curves ($[\alpha_f^u, \alpha_f^l]$ and $[\beta_r^u, \beta_r^l]$ respectively) into output pairs representing the changed arrival curve pair ($[\alpha_f^{u'}, \alpha_f^{l'}]$) of f when it is processed by r. The remaining available service of r is represented by $[\beta_r^{u'}, \beta_r^{l'}]$ [3].

output arrival curves $\alpha f^{l'}, \alpha f^{u'}$ *denote the pattern with which events from f are processed by r.*

The output arrival and service curves of a GPC can be computed as follows [7]:

$$\alpha^{u'}(\Delta) = min\{(\alpha^u \otimes \beta^u) \oslash \beta^l, \beta^u\} \tag{1}$$

$$\alpha^{l'}(\Delta) = min\{(\alpha^l \oslash \beta^u) \otimes \beta^l, \beta^l\} \tag{2}$$

$$\beta^{u'}(\Delta) = max\{(\beta^u - \alpha^l) \,\bar{\oslash}\, 0, 0\} \tag{3}$$

$$\beta^{l'}(\Delta) = (\beta^l - \alpha^u) \,\bar{\otimes}\, 0 \tag{4}$$

Where $\otimes, \oslash, \bar{\otimes}, \bar{\oslash}$ are min-plus convolution/deconvolution and max-plus convolution/deconvolution operations respectively. For the definition of these operations, the reader is invited to refer to [12]. Note that the GPC models the behaviour where arrival events from f are being processed by r on a FIFO basis [6]. In addition to deriving the transformed service and arrival curves of a GPC, it is possible to derive an upper bound on the delay D experienced by an event and the backlog of events B of flow f being processed by a resource r as follows [7]:

$$D_{f,r} \leq hdist(\alpha_f^u, \beta_r^l) = sup_{0 \leq \lambda}\{inf\{\tau \in [0, \lambda] : \alpha^u(\lambda - \tau) \leq \beta^l(\lambda)\}\} \quad (5)$$

$$B_{f,r} \leq vdist(\alpha_f^u, \beta_r^l) = sup_{0 \leq \lambda}\{\alpha^u(\lambda) - \beta^l(\lambda)\} \quad (6)$$

Where $vdist$, $hdist$ represent the maximum vertical and horizontal distance between α_f^u, β_f^l respectively. Figure 1 illustrates the graphical equivalent of these operations.

The transformation of arrival and service curves allows for chaining of GPCs to model various resource sharing/arbitration policies usually used in real-time systems such as fixed priority and round-robin scheduling.

3.3   Modular Performance Analysis

In order to use the mathematical framework defined in the previous section, various aspects of real-time systems can be modelled with a combination of RTC components. This combination is called a *scheduling network*, and the analysis conducted on it is known as *Modular Performance Analysis* (MPA). Scheduling networks can be used to model timing as well as functional aspects of a system [13]. MPA can exploit the fact that the analysis of RTC components are modular. Due to the use of Variability Characterization Curves (VCCs) as inputs and outputs of RTC components, the curves representing the upper and lower bound on events produced by a component are valid as long as the input events to that components are within their upper and lower bound. This enables analysing systems based on *Assumptions and Guarantees* [8]. Figure 3 shows an example scheduling network modelling tasks sharing a processing unit and being scheduled using a Fixed Priority Pre-emptive Scheduler (FPPS).

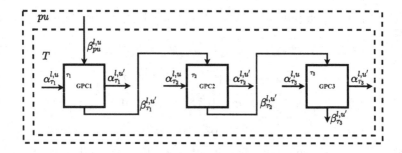

Fig. 3. Scheduling network of a task set T under FPPS scheduling.

4   RTCAnalysis System Model

In order to perform MPA analysis on Amalthea models, the RTCAnalysis tool maps the Amalthea model elements to an *RTC system model*. This system model abstracts the complexity of the full Amalthea model by only addressing the aspects required for RTC analysis. To conduct the concrete analysis, the RTC system model is converted to a scheduling network. The analysis results of the scheduling network are then correlated to the corresponding Amalthea elements.

The Amalthea model consists of sub-models representing various aspects of the modelled system in detail. The RTCAnalysis tool addresses a subset of them that is relevant for conducting MPA analysis. Figure 4 illustrates the subset of Amalthea model elements used in this mapping, and their inter-dependencies.

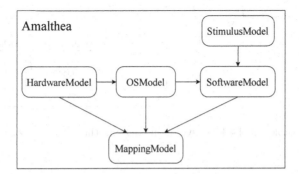

Fig. 4. A subset of Amalthea model elements used for the mapping to the RTC system model.

The stimulus model represents the occurrence of events in the system. This can represent task release events, interrupt releases, and clocks available in the system. The RTCAnalysis tool converts stimuli in the Amalthea model to arrival curves. Standard event models which are frequently used to model task occurrence in real-time systems are translated to upper and lower arrival curves that follow the η^+, η^- notation introduced in [20] respectively.

We denote the arrival curve pair derived from a stimulus element s as $\alpha_s = \{\alpha_s^l, \alpha_s^u\}$.

The software model represents software elements in the modelled system. This mainly includes processes, which represent tasks and Interrupt Service Routines (ISRs) in the system. Processes consist of a set of runnables which represent the most granular software components. Processes can also include labels which represent memory accesses. Stimulus elements are used to define the release of processes. This is reflected with the dependency of the software model on the stimulus model. A UML diagram representing processes is shown in Fig. 4.

We denote an Amalthea process as the tuple $\tau = \{s, P, cp\}$, with s being the stimulus element triggering the process, $P = \{\rho_1, \cdots, \rho_n\}$ being a set of

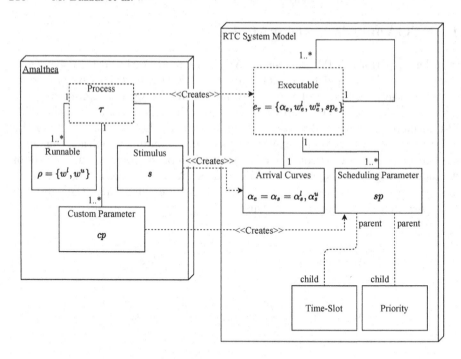

Fig. 5. Executables in the RTC system model and their equivalent in Amalthea

called n runnables, and cp a set of custom parameters associated with τ. A runnable is defined as a tuple $\rho = \{w_\rho^l, w_\rho^u\}$ where w_ρ^l, w_ρ^u are the scalar upper and lower bounds on the computational demand for a computational resource ρ respectively. Custom parameters can be used to describe scheduler, or scenario specific aspects of the process that are not a part of the software model. An example of custom properties is scheduling parameters such as a process priority that can be used when modelling systems with priority-based scheduling.

We define executables as the equivalent of Amalthea processes in the RTC system model. Figure 5 illustrates the structure of executables in the RTC system model.

Definition 4 (Executable). *Let τ be an Amalthea process. An executable $e_\tau = \{\alpha_e, w_e^l, w_e^u, sp_e, E\}$ is an equivalent of τ where (i) $\alpha_e = \alpha_s$ (ii) $w_e^l = \sum_n w_{\rho_i}^l$ and $w_e^u = \sum_n w_{\rho_i}^u$ (iii) $E = \{e_1, \cdots, e_n\}$ is the set of internal executables comprising e_τ.*

In order to represent Amalthea software components on the same level of granularity with the RTC system model, each executable can include a list of children executables that represent the immediate software component levels. While it is theoretically possible to nest executables infinitely with this model, the conversion from Amalthea models only addresses software components down to the runnable level.

In addition to defining executables that are independent in terms of their arrival curves, we define *event streams* in the RTC system model such that they model the chain of executables where each executable is released by its predecessor. This is the equivalent of processes in the Amalthea model that have an *inter process stimulus*.

Definition 5 (Event Stream). *A set* $es = \{e_1, \cdots, e_n\}$ *of executables such that* $\alpha_{e_{i+1}} = \alpha'_{e_i}$ *is defined as an event stream. Where* α'_{e_i} *is the arrival curve resulting from executable e being executed on its assigned processing unit.*

The Amalthea hardware model represents the system's hardware with hierarchical hardware structure elements. Each bottom level hardware structure element contains a set of modules. These modules can represent processing units, memory elements, and bus elements. The attributes describing each hardware element are also described. Since RTCAnalysis focuses on high-level schedulability analysis, the Amalthea hardware model is simplified by only addressing *computational resources* which are the equivalent of processing unit elements in Amalthea, in addition to *communication elements* which are the equivalent of bus and memory element in Amalthea. We denote an Amalthea processing unit as pu, and its frequency as F. The computational resource corresponding to pu is denoted as cr_{pu}.

Definition 6 (Computational Resource). *Let pu be an Amalthea processing unit element. A computational resource cr_{pu} is defined in the RTC system model. We define* $\beta^l_{cr} = \beta^u_{cr} = F.\Delta$ *as the unloaded service curve pair associated with* cr_{pu}.

The unloaded service curve pair associated with a computational resource cr is used as an input to scheduling networks representing a combination of hardware and software. We similarly denote the communication elements as ce where the unloaded service curve pair depends on the bandwidth of the corresponding hardware element modelled in Amalthea. In addition to the ability to model hardware and software elements separately in the RTC system model, the sharing policies of the system related to scheduling of available resources have to be modelled in order to fully describe the system modelled in Amalthea. These scheduling policies are defined in terms of task scheduler. We define the corresponding scheduler elements in the RTC system model as $sched_E$. Furthermore, the scheduler description in the RTC system model uses the software elements to scheduler mapping and the hardware to scheduler mapping described in the Amalthea mapping model. Figure 6 illustrates the transformation of schedulers from the Amalthea scheduler representation to the corresponding RTC system model representation. We formally define the scheduler element in the RTC system model as follows:

Definition 7 (Scheduler). *Let $T = \{\tau_1, \cdots, \tau_n\}$ be a set of Amalthea processes that are modelled by the executable set $E = \{e_1, \cdots, e_n\}$. Let processes in T be mapped to an Amalthea Processing unit pu which is modelled in Amalthea* by a computational resource cr. A scheduler sched = {E, cr, SCHED} is the equivalent of the Amalthea task scheduler that schedules tasks in T and manages pu, where SCHED = {sched₁, ⋯, schedₙ} is the set of child schedulers being managed by sched.

In the system model, we differentiate between *unit schedulers* that directly schedule executables, and *hierarchical schedulers* that do not directly manage the allocation of computational capacity from computational resources to executables, but manages the allocation of that capacity to its sub-schedulers.

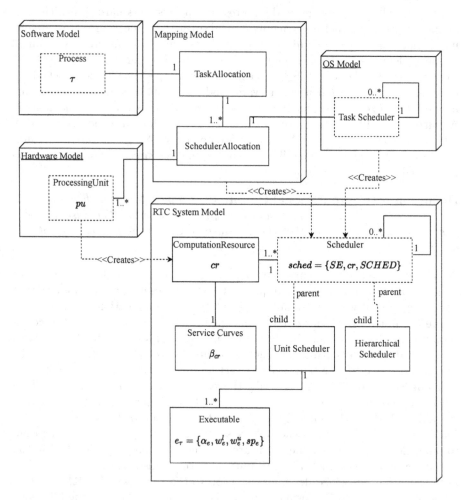

Fig. 6. Schedulers in the RTC system model and their equivalent in Amalthea

5 Model Analysis

To enable RTC analysis on the system model described in the previous chapter, the system model is converted to an MPA scheduling network. Nodes in the resulting scheduling network are GPCs corresponding to executables in the system model. The service curve inter-dependencies between GPCs in this scheduling network are determined by the scheduler element that contain the executables corresponding to GPCs under consideration. Arrival curve dependencies are determined through event stream elements in the system model.

To maintain the practicability of the RTCAnalysis tool, we conduct finitary RTC analysis on the scheduling network [12]. Finitary analysis provides the same upper and lower bounds on the delay and buffering of events in a GPC while requiring a shorter runtime for the analysis compared to directly computing the outputs of that GPC as shown in Sect. 3.1.

After deriving the delay and buffering bounds on each GPC in the scheduling network, the results if these GPCs are correlated to their corresponding system model elements. This can be illustrated by the example of correlating the delay upper and lower bounds of a GPC to the worst and best case response times of the executable corresponding to that GPC respectively.

6 Evaluation

To evaluate the applicability of the RTCAnalysis to automotive embedded systems, we use the tool to derive timing metrics of three industrial case studies related to the automotive domain. Each of these case studies differs in terms of size, complexity, and area of application.

The first case study is based on the Democar model [10] and represents a single core real-time system consisting on three periodic tasks related to braking, engine control, and adaptive cruise control. All processes are assigned to a single-core processing unit that employs a fixed-priority preemptive scheduler. Being the smallest example in our evaluation, the resulting scheduling network consisting of merely three GPC elements similar to the configuration shown in Fig. 3.

The second case study represents a complex engine management system that was released in 2017 by the *Robert Bosch GmbH* as part of the WATERS2017 industrial challenge [14]. It consists of four processing units and a set of 1250 software elements (runnables) that are partitioned into 21 tasks and ISRs, and communicate via 10000 variables (labels). All processes have different types of activation patterns with non-homogeneous periods. Furthermore, each process is assigned to one of the processing units of the systems, and is managed by a corresponding fixed-priority preemptive scheduler.

Finally, the third case study denotes an ADAS application that is based on the WATERS2019 industrial challenge [15]. The underlying hardware platform of this application is represented by a heterogeneous NVIDIA Jetson TX2 Module, which consists of two different processor islands with a dual-core NVIDIA Denver

CPU as well as an ARM Cortex-A57 quad-core respectively, and a 256-core dGPU accelerator. The application's temporal behaviour is represented by a set of 16 communicating processes that implement the overall data and event flow realizing the ADAS functionality. In terms of analysis complexity, the main challenge of this application lies in addressing the heterogeneous nature of the underlying hardware as well as the usage of accelerators that are invoked by self-suspending processes.

We start by comparing the number of GPC elements in the scheduling networks generated by the tool for these models. The number of GPCs in a scheduling network partially corresponds to the analysis complexity as well as the analysis runtime required by the tool to produce the analysis results. The results of this evaluation provide insights into not only the modelling of systems with the RTCAnalysis tool, but also the effects of the model size and complexity on the analysis runtime, in addition to the role played by the analysis method used.

Table 1. Overview of the evaluation results for analysing various automotive systems along with the systems major characteristics. Runtime is measured in milliseconds

Model	GPC elements	Scheduler types	Flows	Finitary runtime	Direct analysis runtime
Democar [10]	3	1	0	132	88
WATERS2017 [14]	21	1	0	548	413
WATERS2019 [15]	16	2	2	393	40720

The number of elements in a scheduling network generated out of a model has a proportional effect on runtime, as shown in Table 1. The larger the scheduling network the more time it takes to perform the analysis. Furthermore, the increased complexity of a system leads to more complicated analysis, this can be seen by the very sharp increase in runtime when analysing the WATERS2019 model using direct analysis, in comparison to analysing it with finitary analysis. This complexity is attributed to the existence of flows in the model that causes arrival curves to GPCs in these flows to have a high number of segments. This also can be seen in the fact the system uses multiple scheduler types for different components. The WATERS2019 model represents a system where some tasks run under FPPS scheduling and other tasks run on a hardware accelerator that uses a Weighted Round Robin scheduler. We see that this complexity is compensated by using finitary RTC since it prepares the scheduling network such that RTC computations described in Sect. 3.1 are performed only within the busy period of each component, i.e., only when each component is experiencing the maximum amount of interference possible. The amount of speed-up occurring in this example is in line with experiments performed on finitary RTC in [12].

The fact that finitary RTC has a longer runtime in the case of the other examples demonstrates the existence of an overhead for performing finitary RTC that is proportional to the size of the model. This demonstrates that the tool presented in this work is can be scaled for larger, more complicated systems as long as finitary RTC analysis is applied.

7 Conclusion and Outlook

In this paper we presented the RTCAnalysis tool that aims to provide a framework for conducting practical RTC timing analysis on automotive embedded systems. We formalized the required transformation steps in order to compile an arbitrary Amalthea system model into an RTC network by creating an intermediate model that abstracts the complexity of Amalthea. This RTC system model is then used to create an MPA scheduling network which we analysed using finitary and direct RTC analysis. These steps are then integrated into the RTCAnalysis tool. Our evaluation shows the applicability of the RTCAnalysis tool to determine the timing properties of embedded systems during early design phases, in addition to highlighting the benefits of using the techniques of finitary RTC to efficiently analyse complex systems.

Our next steps lie in deriving timing metrics relevant to the automotive domain other than bounds on response time and deadline misses which are currently derived by the tool. This includes the quantification of bounds on the number of preemption events experienced by a process as well as delays of global functions (event chains). Finally, we plan to extend the tooling in order to perform probabilistic analysis using the techniques presented in e.g. [21].

References

1. Automotive—Luxoft. https://www.luxoft.com/automotive/
2. Eclipse APP4MC—The Eclipse Foundation. https://www.eclipse.org/app4mc/. Accessed 30 July 2020
3. Bazzal, M., Krawczyk, L., Govindarajan, R.P., Wolff, C.: Timing analysis of car-to-car communication systems using real-time calculus: a case study. In: 2020 IEEE 5th International Symposium on Smart and Wireless Systems within the Conferences on Intelligent Data Acquisition and Advanced Computing Systems (IDAACS-SWS), pp. 1–8 (2020). https://doi.org/10.1109/IDAACS-SWS50031. 2020.9297100
4. Bernat, G., Burns, A., Llamosí, A.: Weakly hard real-time systems. IEEE Trans. Comput. 50, 308–321 (1999)
5. Bondorf, S., Schmitt, J.B.: The DiscoDNC v2 - a comprehensive tool for deterministic network calculus. In: Proceedings of the International Conference on Performance Evaluation Methodologies and Tools, ValueTools 2014, pp. 44–49, December 2014. https://dl.acm.org/citation.cfm?id=2747659
6. Boudec, J., Thiran, P.: Network Calculus: A Theory of Deterministic Queuing Systems for the Internet. LNCS. Springer, Heidelberg (2003). https://books.google. de/books?id=LcpuCQAAQBAJ
7. Chakraborty, S., Künzli, S., Thiele, L.: A general framework for analysing system properties in platform-based embedded system designs. In: Proceedings of the 6th Design, Automation and Test in Europe (DATE), Munich, Germany, pp. 190–195, March 2003
8. Chakraborty, S., Liu, Y., Stoimenov, N., Thiele, L., Wandeler, E.: Interface-based rate analysis of embedded systems. In: Proceedings - Real-Time Systems Symposium, pp. 25–34 (2006). https://doi.org/10.1109/RTSS.2006.26

9. Diemer, J., Axer, P., Ernst, R.: Compositional performance analysis in python with pyCPA (2012)

10. Frey, P.: A timing model for real-time control-systems and its application on simulation and monitoring of AUTOSAR systems. Ph.D. thesis, Universität Ulm (2011). https://doi.org/10.18725/OPARU-1743. https://oparu.uni-ulm.de/xmlui/handle/123456789/1770

11. Gonzalez Harbour, M., Gutierrez Garcia, J.J., Palencia Gutierrez, J.C., Drake Moyano, J.M.: Mast: modeling and analysis suite for real time applications. In: Proceedings 13th Euromicro Conference on Real-Time Systems, pp. 125–134 (2001). https://doi.org/10.1109/EMRTS.2001.934015

12. Guan, N., Yi, W.: Finitary real-time calculus: efficient performance analysis of distributed embedded systems. In: Proceedings - Real-Time Systems Symposium, pp. 330–339 (2013). https://doi.org/10.1109/RTSS.2013.40

13. Haid, W., Thiele, L.: Complex task activation schemes in system level performance analysis. In: Proceedings of the 5th IEEE/ACM International Conference on Hardware/Software Codesign and System Synthesis - CODES+ISSS 2007, p. 173. ACM Press, New York (2007). https://doi.org/10.1145/1289816.1289860. http://portal.acm.org/citation.cfm?doid=1289816.1289860

14. Hamann, A., Dasari, D., Kramer, I., Pressler, M., Wurst, F., Ziegenbein, D.: WATERS industrial challenge 2017. In: 8th International Workshop on Analysis Tools and Methodologies for Embedded and Real-time Systems (WATERS) (2017)

15. Hamann, A., et al.: WATERS industrial challenge 2019. In: 10th International Workshop on Analysis Tools and Methodologies for Embedded and Real-time Systems (WATERS) (2019)

16. Hofmann, R., Ahrendts, L., Ernst, R.: CPA: compositional performance analysis. In: Ha, S., Teich, J. (eds.) Handbook of Hardware/Software Codesign, pp. 721–751. Springer, Dordrecht (2017). https://doi.org/10.1007/978-94-017-7267-9_24

17. Krawczyk, L., Bazzal, M., Govindarajan, R.P., Wolff, C.: An analytical approach for calculating end-to-end response times in autonomous driving applications. In: 10th International Workshop on Analysis Tools and Methodologies for Embedded and Real-time Systems (WATERS 2019) (2019)

18. Krawczyk, L., Bazzal, M., Govindarajan, R.P., Wolff, C.: Model-based timing analysis and deployment optimization for heterogeneous multi-core systems using eclipse APP4MC. In: 2019 ACM/IEEE 22nd International Conference on Model Driven Engineering Languages and Systems Companion (MODELS-C). IEEE, September 2019. https://doi.org/10.1109/models-c.2019.00013

19. Krawczyk, L., Wolff, C., Fruhner, D.: Automated distribution of software to multi-core hardware in model based embedded systems development. In: Dregvaite, G., Damasevicius, R. (eds.) ICIST 2015. CCIS, vol. 538, pp. 320–329. Springer, Cham (2015). https://doi.org/10.1007/978-3-319-24770-0_28

20. Richter, K.: Compositional scheduling analysis using standard event models. Ph.D. thesis, December 2004

21. Santinelli, L., Cucu-Grosjean, L.: A probabilistic calculus for probabilistic real-time systems. ACM Trans. Embed. Comput. Syst. **14**(3) (2015). https://doi.org/10.1145/2717113

22. Thiele, L., Chakraborty, S., Naedele, M.: Real-time calculus for scheduling hard real-time systems. In: Proceedings of IEEE International Symposium on Circuits and Systems, ISCAS 2000, Emerging Technologies for the 21st Century, Geneva, Switzerland, 28–31 May 2000, pp. 101–104. IEEE (2000). https://doi.org/10.1109/ISCAS.2000.858698

23. Wandeler, E.: Modular Performance Analysis and Interface-based Design for Embedded Real-time Systems. TIK-Schriftenreihe, Shaker (2006). https://books. google.de/books?id=SPnSAwAACAAJ
24. Wolff, C., et al.: AMALTHEA: tailoring tools to projects in automotive software development. In: 2015 IEEE 8th International Conference on Intelligent Data Acquisition and Advanced Computing Systems: Technology and Applications (IDAACS). IEEE, September 2015. https://doi.org/10.1109/idaacs.2015.7341359

Run-Time Class Generation: Algorithms for Difference of Homogeneous and Inhomogeneous Classes

Dmytro O. Terletskyi$^{(\boxtimes)}$ [ID]

V. M. Glushkov Institute of Cybernetics of NAS of Ukraine, Kyiv, Ukraine
dmytro.terletskyi@nas.gov.ua

Abstract. The integration of new extracted or acquired knowledge into the knowledge base is a crucial task for modern knowledge-based systems, which requires dynamic analysis of the relevance, similarity, and difference of new knowledge. It can be done using special operations defined over the representation structures provided by chosen knowledge model. Within an object-oriented approach, such operations can be implemented in a form of universal exploiters of classes, which adapt and implement for classes the idea of corresponding set-theoretical operations, such as intersection, union, difference, and decomposition into subsets. Therefore corresponding algorithms for implementation of a few forms of universal difference exploiter of classes within such a knowledge representation model as object-oriented dynamic networks are presented in the paper. Developed algorithms can dynamically create new classes of objects via computing the difference of homogeneous and heterogeneous classes as well as the difference of two heterogeneous classes of objects if such a difference exists. The proposed approach provides an opportunity to generate new knowledge structures in a form of classes of objects based on the previously obtained ones. It allows evaluation of the relevance and novelty level of extracted or acquired pieces of knowledge compared with previously obtained ones by computing the difference between them, which can be used for efficient integration of the new knowledge into the knowledge base.

Keywords: Run-time code generation (RTCG) · Run-time class generation (RTClG) · Universal difference exploiter of classes · Difference of classes

1 Introduction

Knowledge integration is one of the most important tasks among a variety of knowledge management tasks which modern knowledge-based systems (KBSs) designed to solve. First of all, it requires the dynamic generation of suitable representation structures for performing the representation of pieces of knowledge and their analysis. Within the object-oriented approach to knowledge representation, *objects*, *classes*, *metaclasses*, and *relations* among them, are the main

© Springer Nature Switzerland AG 2021
A. Lopata et al. (Eds.): ICIST 2021, CCIS 1486, pp. 224–240, 2021.
https://doi.org/10.1007/978-3-030-88304-1_18

representation structures within many models. Therefore, the dynamic generation of presentation structures is reduced to the generation of one of these structures. However, the representation of new knowledge can require the dynamic generation of new instances of such structures in the system run-time, which can be achieved via the *run-time code generation (RTCG)* approach.

According to the RTCG [4–6,19,20], a system should produce new program structures, execute them, as well as manipulate them at the run-time. In this case, the program metastructure is available at the run-time, therefore a program can analyze, modify and extend its own source codes or codes of other available programs. After that, generated code can be integrated within existed source codes of the program and used in the future. Corresponding metaprogramming tools are implemented in some modern object-oriented programming languages with dynamic typing such as Python, Ruby, and JavaScript. They provide dynamic generation and manipulation of objects and classes at the program run-time. As it was noted in [5,6,19], very often RTCG is reduced to template-based code generation, which provides faster compilation. However, such an approach requires that corresponding templates are developed before then code generation will be started, and it is an important restriction of this approach.

The next important stage is the integration of extracted or acquired knowledge into the system knowledge base. According to the definition of knowledge integration proposed by Murray and Porter in [2,8–11], it is defined as a task of incorporating new information into a knowledge base, which requires elaborating new information and resolving inconsistencies with existing knowledge. This concept was implemented within a corresponding computational model, which consists of three prominent activities:

1. *Recognition*: Detection of previously obtained knowledge, which is relevant to newly obtained knowledge.
2. *Elaboration*: Determination of how the newly obtained knowledge interacts with previously obtained knowledge, and how it can affect them.
3. *Adaptation*: Elimination of all anomalies in the knowledge base, discovered in the previous stage.

The proposed computation model was implemented within the knowledge acquisition tool called KI [9,10], which was developed to help knowledge engineers to manage and to extend the Botany Knowledge Base, which incorporates large knowledge about plant anatomy, physiology, and development. The proposed concept of knowledge integration as well as the corresponding computational model can be adapted and embedded for object-oriented knowledge representation models. Some suggestions on how such embedding can be done within object-oriented knowledge representation models were noted in [26].

To perform the recognition and elaboration stages a KBS should verify some relations between newly extracted and previously obtained knowledge, such as *equivalence, inclusion, generalization, specification, similarity, difference,* etc. Some of these relations can be verified via the application of special operations, defined over the representation structures typical for chosen knowledge representation model. Within such knowledge representation model as object-oriented dynamic networks (OODNs), which was proposed in [28,29] and then extended in [24], main representation structures are objects, classes, and relations among them. However, in contrast to other object-oriented knowledge representation models, OODNs use a distinctive model of classes, which defines *homogeneous* and *inhomogeneous (heterogeneous) classes of objects*. The model also provides special operations defined over the classes, which allow the dynamic creation of new classes based on previously defined ones. As it was shown in [25–27], some of them can be used for the analysis of new pieces of knowledge and their future integration into the knowledge base. Let us consider the corresponding class model and operations over the classes in more detail.

2   Classes of Objects

Most known object-oriented knowledge representation models, such as frames, object-oriented entity-relationship model, as well as class-based object-oriented programming use model of homogeneous classes. It means that class is considered as a template, which provides a particular structure and behavior for all its instances, usually called objects. In other words, a class defines a collection of objects of the same type, where all objects have the same structure and behavior, which defined by this type. Therefore such a model of classes defines homogeneous classes, and the notion of a class and a type can be considered as equivalent ones.

Similar to other models, OODNs provide the concept of homogeneous classes of objects, which allows the definition of homogeneous collections of objects.

Definition 1. *Homogeneous class of objects T is a tuple $T = (P(T), F(T))$, where $P(T) = (p_1(T), \ldots, p_n(T))$ is a collection of properties of the class T, and $F(T) = (f_1(T), \ldots, f_m(T))$ is a collection of its methods.*

However, all classes in OODNs consist of two kinds of properties – *quantitative* and *qualitative* ones, and it is the main difference compared with other models of homogeneous classes [22,28,29]. Despite all advantages of homogeneous classes they have such restriction as an ability to define only a single type of objects, and consequently a homogeneous collection of objects. Therefore OODNs provide a concept of an inhomogeneous class of objects, which simultaneously can define a collection of types. As it was noted in [22,28,29], the main idea of such a model of classes is to organize all types of objects defined within the class in the form of a *core* and *projections of types*. A core of the class consists of properties and (or) methods, which are common for all its types of objects. Each projection consists of properties and (or) methods, which are typical only for the corresponding type of objects. Such features of inhomogeneous classes allow avoiding redundant representation of types defined by the class, which was demonstrated in [22,24]. If a heterogeneous class of objects has only one core, it is called a *single-core inhomogeneous class of objects (SCIC)*.

Definition 2. *Single-core inhomogeneous class of objects T is a tuple*

$$T = (Core(T), pr_1(t_1), \ldots, pr_n(t_n)),$$

where $Core(T) = (P(T), F(T))$ is a core of the class T, which contains properties and (or) methods that are common for types of objects $t_1, \ldots, t_n$ defined by the class T, and $pr_i(t_i) = (P(t_i), F(t_i))$, $i = \overline{1, n}$, is a projection of the type t_i, $i = \overline{1, n}$ which contains properties and methods that are typical only for this type of objects.

However, there are situations when there is a collection of properties and (or) methods, which are common only for m types of objects among n types of objects defined by the same inhomogeneous class, where $m < n$. For such cases, the concept of the *core of level m* and the concept of *multi-core inhomogeneous classes of objects (MCIC)* were introduced in [22].

Definition 3. *The core of level m of inhomogeneous class $T_{1,\ldots,n}$ is a tuple*

$$Core^m \left(T_{1,\ldots,n}\right) = \left(P\left(T_{i_1,\ldots,i_m}\right), F\left(T_{i_1,\ldots,i_m}\right)\right),$$

where $1 \leq m \leq n$, $1 \leq i_1 \leq \cdots \leq i_m \leq n$, and $P\left(T_{i_1,\ldots,i_m}\right)$, $F\left(T_{i_1,\ldots,i_m}\right)$ are specification and signature of the core of inhomogeneous class $T_{i_1,\ldots,i_m}$, which contain properties and methods, which are common for types of objects $t_{i_1}, \ldots, t_{i_m}$.

The idea of cores of level m provides an opportunity to define a collection of cores for different levels of similarity among the types of objects, defined by the class, and to increase their representation efficiency. Therefore in [22], it was used to extend the concept of a single-core inhomogeneous class of objects to a multi-core case.

Definition 4. *Multi-core inhomogeneous class of objects $T_{1,\ldots,n}$ is a tuple*

$$T_{1,\ldots,n} = \left(Core_1^n \left(T_{1,\ldots,n}\right), Core_1^{n-1} \left(T_{1,\ldots,n}\right), \ldots, Core_{k_{n-1}}^{n-1} \left(T_{1,\ldots,n}\right), \ldots,\right.$$
$$\left. Core_1^1 \left(T_{1,\ldots,n}\right), \ldots, Core_{k_1}^1 \left(T_{1,\ldots,n}\right), pr_1(t_1), \ldots, pr_n(t_n)\right),$$

where $Core_1^n \left(T_{1,\ldots,n}\right)$ is a core of level n of the class $T_{1,\ldots,n}$, $Core_{i_{n-1}}^{n-1} \left(T_{1,\ldots,n}\right)$ is an i_{n-1}-th core of level $n-1$ of the class $T_{1,\ldots,n}$, where $i_{n-1} = \overline{1, k_{n-1}}$ and $k_{n-2} \leq C_n^{n-1}$, $Core_{i_1}^1 \left(T_{1,\ldots,n}\right)$ is an i_1-th core of level 1 of the class $T_{1,\ldots,n}$, where $i_1 = \overline{1, k_1}$ and $k_1 \leq C_n^1$, $pr_i(t_i)$ is a projection of the type t_i, $i = \overline{1, n}$, which contains properties and methods, which are typical only for this type of objects.

Inhomogeneous classes of objects provide an opportunity to define heterogeneous collections of objects, which belong to different types defined by a particular class.

Besides the homogeneous and inhomogeneous classes of objects, OODNs provide special operations defined over them, called *universal exploiters* [24, 28, 29].

Such operations use the classes of objects as the unchangeable input parameters for the creation of new classes of objects. Generally, there are two kinds of exploiters – *specific* and *universal* ones. Specific exploiters create new classes of objects based on some features of the input parameters, and their applications are restricted by these classes. Universal exploiters can be applied to any classes of objects for the creation of new classes of objects, despite the features of the input parameters. They can be implemented via adaptation of the idea of set-theoretical operations, such as intersection, union, difference, and decomposition on the subsets, for homogeneous and inhomogeneous classes of objects. The result of the application of a particular universal exploiter is a new class of objects created base on other classes of objects used as parameters. It allows us to reformulate a task of run-time code generation (RTCG) to *run-time class generation (RTClG)*. Let us consider a run-time class generation using universal difference exploiter of classes of objects in more detail and develop corresponding algorithms for its implementation.

3   Difference of Classes

The idea to use basic set-theoretical operations, such as intersection, union, and difference, for computations over objects, was used in different query algebras for object-oriented databases [1,3,7,16–18,21], and in algebra for extensible object model [30,31]. However, such applications of set-theoretical operations were mainly focused on manipulations with collections of objects stored within the object-oriented databases or manipulations with collections of XML objects. Another approach to the application of basic set-theoretical operations was introduced in [12–15], where intersection, union, difference, and symmetric difference were defined for the classes in object-oriented databases. The proposed interpretation of basic set-theoretical operations allows the creation of new classes based on the previously defined.

A difference is a basic set-theoretic operation, however, Rundensteiner and Bic defined two forms of difference operation, where the first form means the full difference between classes, while the second one means the partial difference, which can be determined by particular properties of the classes. Both proposed forms of difference operation allow comparison of newly extracted or acquired pieces of knowledge with previously obtained ones and computing of their level of novelty. It is important information for the future integration of new knowledge into the knowledge base. Therefore an adaptation of such operation for homogeneous and inhomogeneous classes, within OODNs, and the development of corresponding algorithms for its implementation are topical issues.

The idea of operations on sets was used to develop corresponding universal exploiters of classes for OODNs. As the result, such exploiters of classes as intersection, union, and difference were introduced in [28,29] and then generalized in [24]. Later, the corresponding algorithms for the implementation of these exploiters of classes were proposed in [23,25,26]. In addition, the concept of decomposition exploiter, as well as algorithm for its implementation were proposed in [27]. Let us consider the concept of universal difference exploiter of classes in more detail.

Definition 5. *Difference $T_1 \setminus T_2$ of classes of objects T_1 and T_2, which define types of objects $t_1^1, \ldots, t_n^1$ and $t_1^2, \ldots, t_m^2$, correspondingly, where $n, m \geq 1$, is a class of objects $T_{1 \setminus 2}$, which defines types $t_1^{1 \setminus 2}, \ldots, t_k^{1 \setminus 2}$, such that $k \leq n + m$ and*

$$\forall t_i^{1 \setminus 2}, t_w^2, \exists t_j^1 \mid \left(t_i^{1 \setminus 2} \subset t_j^1 \right) \wedge \not\exists \left(t_i^{1 \setminus 2} \cap t_w^2 \right) \wedge$$

$$\wedge \left(\not\exists t^{1 \setminus 2} \mid \left(t_i^{1 \setminus 2} \subset t^{1 \setminus 2} \right) \wedge \left(t^{1 \setminus 2} \subseteq t_j^1 \right) \wedge \not\exists \left(t^{1 \setminus 2} \cap t_w^2 \right) \right),$$

where $i = \overline{1, k}$, $j = \overline{1, n}$, $w = \overline{1, m}$. The class $T_{1 \setminus 2}$ exists if and only if

$$\exists p_{i_1} \left(t_j^1 \right), \exists p_{i_2} \left(t_w^2 \right) \mid Eq \left(p_{i_1} \left(t_j^1 \right), p_{i_2} \left(t_w^2 \right) \right) = 0,$$

where $p_{i_1} \left(t_j^1 \right)$ is i_1-th property of the type t_j^1, $i_1 = \overline{1, \left| P \left(t_j^1 \right) \right|}$, and $p_{i_2} \left(t_w^2 \right)$ is i_2-th property of the type t_w^2, $i_2 = \overline{1, \left| P \left(t_w^2 \right) \right|}$.

As we can see, the exploiter provides an opportunity to compute the difference between two classes of objects, via creating a new class $T_{1 \setminus 2} = T_1 \setminus T_2$, which can be homogeneous or heterogeneous, depending on equivalence and level of heterogeneity of classes T_1 and T_2. Since homogeneous and heterogeneous classes have different structures, thus it is necessary to consider three possible interpretations of the difference of classes, as for the cases of intersection and union of classes, described in [25] and [26]. However, the difference is not symmetric operation, i.e. $A \setminus B \neq B \setminus A$ for any sets A and B, such that $A \neq B$, therefore we need to consider four possible situations:

$$(T_1 \setminus T_2), \ (T_1 \setminus T_{1,\ldots,n}^1), \ (T_{1,\ldots,n}^1 \setminus T_1), \ (T_{1,\ldots,n}^1 \setminus T_{1,\ldots,m}^2),$$

where T_1 and T_2 are arbitrary homogeneous classes of objects, which define types t_1 and t_2 respectively, and $T_{1,\ldots,n}^1$, $T_{1,\ldots,m}^2$ are arbitrary heterogeneous classes of objects, which define collections of types $t_1^1, \ldots, t_n^1$ and $t_1^2, \ldots, t_m^2$ correspondingly. The algorithm, which implements a difference exploiter for homogeneous classes of objects (case $T_1 \setminus T_2$), was proposed in [23]. It requires two homogeneous classes of objects as the input data, and if they have unique properties and (or) methods, the algorithm dynamically creates a new homogeneous class of objects. Let us develop the appropriate algorithms for the rest cases.

According to the idea of difference exploiter of classes of objects, an appropriate algorithm for its implementation should analyze specifications and signatures of types, defined by classes of objects T_1 and T_2, and create a new class of objects $T_{1 \setminus 2}$, which defines a collection of types, which contain properties and (or) methods that are typical only for the class T_1. Depending on the heterogeneity level of classes T_1 and T_2 class $T_{1 \setminus 2}$ can be homogeneous as well as heterogeneous.

Let us consider a situation when the class T_1 is a homogeneous and defines a single type of objects t_1, while the class T_2 is a multi-core inhomogeneous

---

Algorithm 1. Difference of Homogeneous and Inhomogeneous Classes.

Require: T_1 – homogeneous class of objects

   $T_{1,\ldots,n}^2$ – multi-core inhomogeneous class of objects

Ensure: $T = T_1 \setminus T_{1,\ldots,n}^2$

 1: $T := \{\}$;

 2: $P :=$ h_inh_difference$(P(T_1), (P(Core_1^n(T_{1,\ldots,n}^2)), \ldots, P(Core_{i_1}^1(T_{1,\ldots,n}^2)),$
   $P(pr_1(t_1)), \ldots, P(pr_n(t_n))))$;

 3: **if** $|P| > 0$ **then**

 4:    T.add(P);

 5: $F :=$ h_inh_difference$(F(T_1), (F(Core_1^n(T_{1,\ldots,n}^2)), \ldots, F(Core_{i_1}^1(T_{1,\ldots,n}^2)),$
   $F(pr_1(t_1)), \ldots, F(pr_n(t_n))))$;

 6: **if** $|F| > 0$ **then**

 7:    T.add(F);

 8: **return** T.

---

and defines a collection of types $t_1^2, \ldots, t_n^2$. In this case, the algorithm should find the set of properties and (or) methods of the class T_1, which are typical only for it, and at the same time not common for the class T_2, if they exist. This idea was implemented in Algorithm 1, which uses homogeneous classes of objects T_1, which defines the type of objects t_1, and an inhomogeneous class of objects $T_{1,\ldots,n}^2$, which defines a collection of types of objects $t_1^2, \ldots, t_n^2$, as the input data. If the class T_1 has properties and (or) methods, which are typical only for it, then the algorithm creates a new homogeneous class of objects $T = T_1 \setminus T_{1,\ldots,n}^2$, such that $T \subseteq T_1$. The main part of the algorithm, which computes the difference between specification/signatures of the class T_1 and specifications/signatures of all cores and projections defined within a class $T_{1,\ldots,n}^2$ is implemented in Procedure 1. If the specification/signature of the class T_1 has a difference from the specification/signature of the class $T_{1,\ldots,n}^2$, Procedure 1 computes it in the form of the specification/signature of the class T and returns it as the result.

The polymorphic function `is_equivalent` checks the equivalence of properties p_i, p_j or methods f_i, f_j and returns $true$ if they are equivalent ones, or $false$ in the opposite case. It can be implemented using [25, Algorithm 1] for checking of the equivalence of quantitative properties, [25, Algorithm 2] – for checking of the equivalence of qualitative properties, and [25, Algorithm 3] – for checking of the equivalence of methods.

Let us consider the opposite situation when the class T_1 is multi-core inhomogeneous and defines a collection of types $t_1^1, \ldots, t_n^1$, while class T_2 is homogeneous and defines a single type of objects t_2. In this case, the algorithm should analyze all types of the class T_1 and find for each of them corresponding properties and (or) methods, which are typical only for that type or other types of the class T_1 compared to type of the class T_2. This idea was implemented in Algorithm 2, which uses an inhomogeneous class of objects $T_{1,\ldots,n}^1$, which defines a collection of types of objects $t_1^1, \ldots, t_n^1$, and homogeneous classes of objects T_2, which defines the type of objects t_2, as the input data.

Procedure 1. h_inh_difference $\left(X(T_1), X^*\left(T^2_{1,...,n}\right)\right)$

Input: $X(T_1)$ – specification/signature of homogeneous class of objects T_1
$\qquad X^*\left(T^2_{1,...,n}\right)$ – specifications/signatures of cores and projections of multi-core
$\qquad\qquad$ inhomogeneous class of objects $T^2_{1,...,n}$

Output: $X(T) = X(T_1) \setminus X^*\left(T^2_{1,...,n}\right)$

1: $X(T) := \{\}$;
2: unique := **true**;
3: **for all** $x_i \in X(T_1)$ **do**
4: $\quad$ **for all** $X\left(Core\left(t^2_1,...,t^2_n\right)\right)$ **and** $X\left(pr_k\left(t^2_k\right)\right) \in X^*\left(T^2_{1,...,n}\right)$ **do**
5: $\quad\quad$ **for all** $x_j \in X(Core(t_1,...,t_n))$ **or** $X(pr_k(t_k))$ **do**
6: $\quad\quad\quad$ **if** is_equivalent(x_i, x_j) **then**
7: $\quad\quad\quad\quad$ unique := **false**;
8: $\quad\quad\quad\quad$ **break**;
9: $\quad\quad$ **if** unique **then**
10: $\quad\quad\quad$ $X(T)$.add(x_i);
11: $\quad\quad$ **else**
12: $\quad\quad\quad$ unique := **true**;
13: **return** $X(T)$.

Algorithm 2. Difference of Inhomogeneous and Homogeneous Classes.

Require: $T^1_{1,...,n}$ – multi-core inhomogeneous class of objects
$\qquad T_2$ – homogeneous class of objects

Ensure: $T = T^1_{1,...,n} \setminus T_2$

1: $T := \{\}$;
2: $P := $ inh_h_difference$((P(Core^n_1(T^1_{1,...,n})),...,P(Core^1_{i_1}(T^1_{1,...,n})),$
$\qquad\qquad P(pr_1(t_1)),...,P(pr_n(t_n))), P(T_2))$;
3: **if** $|P| > 0$ **then**
4: $\quad T$.add(P);
5: $F := $ inh_h_difference$((F(Core^n_1(T^1_{1,...,n})),...,F(Core^1_{i_1}(T^1_{1,...,n})),$
$\qquad\qquad F(pr_1(t_1)),...,F(pr_n(t_n))), F(T_2))$;
6: **if** $|F| > 0$ **then**
7: $\quad T$.add(F);
8: **return** T.

If the class $T^1_{1,...,n}$ has properties and (or) methods, which are typical only for it, then the algorithm creates a new homogeneous or inhomogeneous class of objects $T = T^1_{1,...,n} \setminus T_2$, such that $T \subseteq T^1_{1,...,n}$. If the specification/signature of the class $T^1_{1,...,n}$ has a difference from the specification/signature of the class T_1, Procedure 2 computes it in the form of the specification/signature of the class T and returns it as the result. The polymorphic function is_equivalent has the same meaning and can be implemented in the same way as in Procedure 1.

Now let us consider the one more situation when both classes T_1 and T_2 are multi-core inhomogeneous ones and define corresponding collections of types of objects $t^1_1,...,t^1_n$ and $t^2_1,...,t^2_m$. In this case, the algorithm should analyze all types of objects, which are defined by the class T_1 and find for each of them corresponding properties and (or) methods, which are typical only for that type or other types of the class T_1 compared to types of objects, which are defined

---

Procedure 2. inh_h_difference $\left(X^*\left(T_{1,\ldots,n}^1\right), X(T_2)\right)$

Input: $X^*\left(T_{1,\ldots,n}^1\right)$ – specifications/signatures of cores and projections of multi-core inhomogeneous class of objects $T_{1,\ldots,n}^1$

$X\left(T_2\right)$ – specification/signature of homogeneous class of objects T_2

Output: $X(T) = X^*\left(T_{1,\ldots,n}^1\right) \setminus X\left(T_2\right)$

1: $X(T) := \{\}$;
2: unique := **true**;
3: eq_elements := $\{\}$;
4: **for all** $X\left(Core\left(t_1^1,\ldots,t_n^1\right)\right)$ **and** $X\left(pr_k\left(t_k^1\right)\right) \in X^*\left(T_{1,\ldots,n}^1\right)$ **do**
5:     **for all** $x_i \in \left(X\left(Core\left(t_1^1,\ldots,t_n^1\right)\right) \text{ or } X\left(pr_k\left(t_k^1\right)\right)\right)$ **do**
6:         **for all** $x_j \in X(T_1)$ **do**
7:             **if** is_equivalent(x_i, x_j) **then**
8:                 eq_elements.add(x_i);
9:                 unique := **false**;
10:     **if** unique **then**
11:         T.add $\left(X\left(Core\left(t_1^1,\ldots,t_n^1\right)\right) \text{ or } X\left(pr_k\left(t_k^1\right)\right)\right)$;
12:     **else**
13:         **if** $|$eq_elements$| < |X\left(Core\left(t_1^1,\ldots,t_n^1\right)\right) \text{ or } X\left(pr_k\left(t_k^1\right)\right)| > 1$ **then**
14:         $X\left(Core\left(t_1^3,\ldots,t_n^3\right)\right) \text{ or } X\left(pr_k\left(t_k^3\right)\right) := \{\}$;
15:         **for all** $x_i \in \left(X\left(Core\left(t_1^1,\ldots,t_n^1\right)\right) \text{ or } X\left(pr_k\left(t_k^1\right)\right)\right)$ **do**
16:             **if** $x_i \notin$ eq_elements **then**
17:                 $\left(X\left(Core\left(t_1^3,\ldots,t_n^3\right)\right) \text{ or } X\left(pr_k\left(t_k^3\right)\right)\right)$.add$(p_i)$;
18:         T.add $\left(X\left(Core\left(t_1^3,\ldots,t_n^3\right)\right) \text{ or } X\left(pr_k\left(t_k^3\right)\right)\right)$;
19:         eq_elements := $\{\}$;
20:         unique := **true**;
21: **return** $X(T)$.

Algorithm 3. Difference of Inhomogeneous Classes.

Require: $T_{1,\ldots,n}^1$, $T_{1,\ldots,m}^2$ – multi-core inhomogeneous classes of objects
Ensure: $T = T_{1,\ldots,n}^1 \setminus T_{1,\ldots,m}^2$

1: $T := \{\}$;
2: $P := $ inh_inh_difference $\left(\left(P\left(Core_1^n\left(T_{1,\ldots,n}^1\right)\right), \ldots, P\left(Core_{i_1}^1\left(T_{1,\ldots,n}^1\right)\right),\right.\right.$
        $P\left(pr_1\left(t_1^1\right)\right), \ldots, P\left(pr_n\left(t_n^1\right)\right)\right), \left(P\left(Core_1^n\left(T_{1,\ldots,m}^2\right)\right), \ldots,$
        $P\left(Core_{i_1}^1\left(T_{1,\ldots,m}^2\right)\right), P\left(pr_1\left(t_1^2\right)\right), \ldots, P\left(pr_m\left(t_m^2\right)\right)\right)\right)$;
3: **if** $|P| > 0$ **then**
4:     T.add(P);
5: $F := $ inh_inh_difference $\left(\left(F\left(Core_1^n\left(T_{1,\ldots,n}^1\right)\right), \ldots, F\left(Core_{i_1}^1\left(T_{1,\ldots,n}^1\right)\right),\right.\right.$
        $F\left(pr_1\left(t_1^1\right)\right), \ldots, F\left(pr_n\left(t_n^1\right)\right)\right), \left(F\left(Core_1^n\left(T_{1,\ldots,m}^2\right)\right), \ldots,$
        $F\left(Core_{i_1}^1\left(T_{1,\ldots,m}^2\right)\right), F\left(pr_1\left(t_1^2\right)\right), \ldots, F\left(pr_m\left(t_m^2\right)\right)\right)\right)$;
6: **if** $|F| > 0$ **then**
7:     T.add(F);
8: **return** T.

---

by the class T_2. This idea was implemented in Algorithm 3, which uses inhomogeneous classes of objects $T_{1,\ldots,n}^1$ and $T_{1,\ldots,m}^2$, which define collections of types of objects $t_1^1,\ldots,t_n^1$ and $t_1^2,\ldots,t_m^2$ respectively, as the input data.

Procedure 3. inh_inh_difference $\left(X^*\left(T^1_{1,\ldots,n}\right), X^*\left(T^2_{1,\ldots,m}\right)\right)$

Input: $X^*\left(T^1_{1,\ldots,n}\right)$ – specifications/signatures of cores and projections of multi-core
inhomogeneous class of objects $T^1_{1,\ldots,n}$

$X^*\left(T^2_{1,\ldots,m}\right)$ – specifications/signatures of cores and projections of multi-core
inhomogeneous class of objects $T^2_{1,\ldots,m}$

Output: $X(T) = X^*\left(T^1_{1,\ldots,n}\right) \setminus X^*\left(T^2_{1,\ldots,m}\right)$

1: $X(T) := \{\}$;
2: unique := **true**;
3: eq_elements := $\{\}$;
4: **for all** $X\left(Core\left(t^1_1,\ldots,t^1_n\right)\right)$ and $X\left(pr_k\left(t^1_k\right)\right) \in X^*\left(T^1_{1,\ldots,n}\right)$ **do**
5:    **for all** $x_i \in X\left(Core\left(t^1_1,\ldots,t^1_n\right)\right)$ or $X\left(pr_k\left(t^1_k\right)\right)$ **do**
6:       **for all** $X\left(Core\left(t^2_1,\ldots,t^2_m\right)\right)$ and $X\left(pr_w\left(t^2_w\right)\right) \in X^*\left(T^2_{1,\ldots,m}\right)$ **do**
7:          **for all** $x_j \in X\left(Core\left(t^2_1,\ldots,t^2_m\right)\right)$ or $X\left(pr_w\left(t^2_w\right)\right)$ **do**
8:            **if** is_equivalent(x_i, x_j) **then**
9:               eq_elements.add(x_i);
10:               unique := **false**;
11:               **break**;
12:    **if** unique **then**
13:       T.add$\left(X\left(Core\left(t^1_1,\ldots,t^1_n\right)\right)$ or $X\left(pr_k\left(t^1_k\right)\right)\right)$;
14:    **else**
15:       **if** $|$eq_elements$| < |X\left(Core\left(t^1_1,\ldots,t^1_n\right)\right)$ or $X\left(pr_k\left(t^1_k\right)\right)| > 1$ **then**
16:          $X\left(Core\left(t^3_1,\ldots,t^3_n\right)\right)$ or $X\left(pr_k\left(t^3_k\right)\right) := \{\}$;
17:          **for all** $x_i \in X\left(Core\left(t^1_1,\ldots,t^1_n\right)\right)$ or $X\left(pr_k\left(t^1_k\right)\right)$ **do**
18:            **if** $x_i \notin$ eq_elements **then**
19:               $\left(X\left(Core\left(t^3_1,\ldots,t^3_n\right)\right)$ or $X\left(pr_k\left(t^3_k\right)\right)\right)$.add$(x_i)$;
20:          T.add$\left(X\left(Core\left(t^3_1,\ldots,t^3_n\right)\right)$ or $X\left(pr_k\left(t^3_k\right)\right)\right)$;
21:       eq_elements := $\{\}$;
22:       unique := **true**;
23: **return** $X(T)$.

If the specification/signature of the class $T^1_{1,\ldots,n}$ has a difference from the specification/signature of the class $T^2_{1,\ldots,m}$, Procedure 3 computes it in the form of the specification/signature of the class T and returns it as the result, where T is inhomogeneous class of objects $T = T^1_{1,\ldots,n} \setminus T^2_{1,\ldots,m}$, such that $T \subseteq T^1_{1,\ldots,n}$. The polymorphic function is_equivalent has the same meaning and can be implemented in the same way as in Procedure 1 and Procedure 2.

All algorithms, which implement different versions of the universal difference exploiter compute the difference of one class of objects from another one via the creation of new classes of objects. However, sometimes such difference does not exist, therefore in such cases, developed algorithms return the empty set T.

4 Application Example

To illustrate one of the possible scenarios of applications for developed algorithms let us consider some examples of homogeneous and inhomogeneous classes of objects in terms of object-oriented dynamic networks, which define particular kinds of convex quadrangles. Suppose we have homogeneous class of objects Rb, which describes rhombuses and has the following structure

$$Rb(p_1 = ((v_1, cm), (v_2, cm), (v_3, cm), (v_4, cm)),$$
$$p_2 = ((v_1,°), (v_2,°), (v_3,°), (v_4,°)),$$
$$p_3 = (p_1.v_1 == p_1.v_2 == p_1.v_3 == p_1.v_4),$$
$$p_4 = (p_2.v_1 + p_2.v_2 + p_2.v_3 + p_2.v_4 = 360,°),$$
$$p_5 = ((p_2.v_1 == p_2.v_3) \wedge (p_2.v_2 == p_2.v_4)),$$
$$f_1 = p_1.v_1 \cdot 4,$$
$$f_2 = (p_1.v_1)^2 \cdot \sin(p_2.v_1))$$

where quantitative property p_1 means sizes of figure sides measured in cm; quantitative property p_2 means degree measures of figure angles; qualitative property p_3 means the equality for all figure sides; qualitative property p_4 means that sum of all degree measures of figure angles is equal to 360°; qualitative property p_5 means that degree measures of opposite angles of the figure are equal; method f_1 means the procedure for computing the perimeter of the figure; method f_2 means the procedure for computing the area of the figure.

Suppose we have a multi-core inhomogeneous class of objects $RtSqPr$ which defines types Rt, Sq, and Pr, which describe rectangles, squares, and parallelograms respectively. Let us assume that the class $RtSqPr$ has the following structure

$$RsSqPr(Core_1^3(RtSqPr)(p_3 = (p_2.v_1 + p_2.v_2 + p_2.v_3 + p_2.v_4 = 360,°),$$
$$p_4 = ((p_1.v_1 == p_1.v_3) \wedge (p_1.v_2 == p_1.v_4)),$$
$$p_5 = ((p_2.v_1 == p_2.v_3) \wedge (p_2.v_2 == p_2.v_4))),$$
$$Core_1^2(RtSq)(p_2 = ((v_1,°), (v_2,°), (v_3,°), (v_4,°)),$$
$$p_6 = (p_2.v_1 == p_2.v_2 == p_2.v_3 == p_2.v_4 == 90,°)),$$
$$Core_2^2(RtPr)(f_1 = (p_1.v_1 + p_1.v_2) \cdot 2),$$
$$Core_1^1(Rt)(f_2 = p_1.v_1 \cdot p_1.v_2),$$
$$Core_2^1(Sq)(p_7 = (p_1.v_1 == p_1.v_2 == p_1.v_3 == p_1.v_4),$$
$$f_1 = p_1.v_1 \cdot 4,$$
$$f_2 = (p_1.v_1)^2),$$
$$Core_3^1(Pr)(f_2 = p_1.v_1 \cdot p_1.v_3 \cdot \sin(p_2.v_2))),$$
$$pr_1(Rt)(p_1 = ((v_1, cm), (v_2, cm), (v_3, cm), (v_4, cm))),$$
$$pr_2(Sq)(p_1 = ((v_1, cm), (v_2, cm), (v_3, cm), (v_4, cm))),$$
$$pr_3(Pr)(p_1 = ((v_1, cm), (v_2, cm), (v_3, cm), (v_4, cm)),$$
$$p_2 = ((v_1,°), (v_2,°), (v_3,°), (v_4,°))))$$

where $Core_1^3(RtSqPr)$ contains properties, which are common for types Rt, Sq, and Pr; $Core_1^2(RtSq)$ contains properties and method, which are common for types Rt and Sq; $Core_2^2(RtPr)$ contains method, which is common for types Rt and Pr; $Core_1^1(Rt)$ contains method, which is common for all objects of the type Rt; $Core_2^1(Sq)$ contains property, which is common for all objects of the type Sq; $Core_3^1(Pr)$ contains property, which is common for all objects of the type Pr; $pr_1(Rt)$ and $pr_2(Sq)$ contains properties, which are typical only for types of objects Rt and Sq; $pr_3(Pr)$ contains property and methods, which are typical only for type of objects Pr.

Quantitative property p_1 in projections $pr_1(Rt)$, $pr_2(Sq)$, and $pr_3(Pr)$ means sizes of figure sides measured in cm; quantitative property p_2 in $Core_1^2(RtSq)$ and $pr_3(Pr)$ means degree measures of figure angles; qualitative property p_3 in $Core_1^3(RtSqPr)$ means that sum of all degree measures of figure angles is equal to $360°$; qualitative property p_4 in $Core_1^2(RtSq)$ means the quality of opposite sides of figure; qualitative property p_5 in $Core_1^2(RtSq)$ means that degree measures of opposite angles of the figure are equal; qualitative property p_6 in $Core_1^2(RtSq)$ means that all degree measures of figure angles are equal to $90°$; qualitative property p_7 in $Core_2^1(Sq)$ means the equality for all figure sides; method f_1 in $Core_2^2(RtPr)$ and $Core_2^1(Sq)$ means the procedure for computing the perimeter of the figure; method f_2 in $Core_1^1(Rt)$, $Core_2^1(Sq)$, and $Core_3^1(Pr)$ means the procedure for computing the area of the figure.

Let us compute the differences $Rb \setminus RsSqPr$ and $RsSqPr \setminus Rb$ using for this Algorithm 1 and Algorithm 2 correspondingly. As we can see, for both cases the polymorphic function `is_equivalent` detected the following equivalences

$$p_3(Rb) \equiv p_7(Core_1^2(Sq)(RsSqPr)),$$
$$p_4(Rb) \equiv p_3(Core_1^3(RsSqPr)(RsSqPr)),$$
$$p_5(Rb) \equiv p_5(Core_1^3(RsSqPr)(RsSqPr)),$$
$$f_1(Rb) \equiv f_1(Core_2^1(Sq)(RsSqPr)),$$

therefore using these facts Algorithm 1 created a new homogeneous class of objects $Rb \setminus RsSqPr \subseteq Rb$ with the following structure

$$Rb \setminus RsSqPr(p_1 = ((v_1, cm), (v_2, cm), (v_3, cm), (v_4, cm)),$$
$$p_2 = ((v_1,°), (v_2,°), (v_3,°), (v_4,°)),$$
$$f_2 = (p_1.v_1)^2 \cdot \sin(p_2.v_1)),$$

which represents the difference of the class Rb from the class $RsSqPr$ and all types of objects, which it defines. The existence of the class $Rb \setminus RsSqPr$ means that pieces of knowledge represented by classes Rb and $RsSqPr$ have some distinct features. Moreover, fact $Rb \setminus RsSqPr \subseteq Rb$ means that these pieces of knowledge have some intersection, i.e. they are relevant.

Using equivalences mentioned above, Algorithm 2 created a new multi-core inhomogeneous class of objects $RsSqPr \setminus Rb \subseteq RsSqPr$ with the following structure

$$RsSqPr \setminus Rb(Core_1^3(RtSqPr)(p_4 = ((p_1.v_1 == p_1.v_3) \wedge (p_1.v_2 == p_1.v_4))),$$
$$Core_1^2(RtSq)(p_2 = ((v_1,^\circ), (v_2,^\circ), (v_3,^\circ), (v_4,^\circ)),$$
$$p_6 = (p_2.v_1 == p_2.v_2 == p_2.v_3 ==$$
$$== p_2.v_4 == 90,^\circ)),$$
$$Core_2^2(RtPr)(f_1 = (p_1.v_1 + p_1.v_2) \cdot 2),$$
$$Core_1^1(Rt)(f_2 = p_1.v_1 \cdot p_1.v_2),$$
$$Core_2^1(Sq)(f_2 = (p_1.v_1)^2),$$
$$Core_3^1(Pr)(f_2 = p_1.v_1 \cdot p_1.v_3 \cdot \sin(p_2.v_2)),$$
$$pr_1(Rt)(p_1 = ((v_1, cm), (v_2, cm), (v_3, cm), (v_4, cm))),$$
$$pr_2(Sq)(p_1 = ((v_1, cm), (v_2, cm), (v_3, cm), (v_4, cm))),$$
$$pr_3(Pr)(p_1 = ((v_1, cm), (v_2, cm), (v_3, cm), (v_4, cm)),$$
$$p_2 = ((v_1,^\circ), (v_2,^\circ), (v_3,^\circ), (v_4,^\circ))))$$

which represents the difference of the class $RsSqPr$ from the class Rb and the type of objects, which it defines. Similar to previous case, the existence of the class $RsSqPr \setminus Rb$ means that pieces of knowledge represented by classes $RsSqPr$ and Rb have some distinct features.

Now let us consider single-core inhomogeneous class of objects $PrRb$, which defines parallelograms and rhombuses and have the following structure

$$PrRb(Core_1^2(PrRb)(p_3 = (p_2.v_1 + p_2.v_2 + p_2.v_3 + p_2.v_4 = 360,^\circ),$$
$$p_4 = ((p_1.v_1 == p_1.v_3) \wedge (p_1.v_2 == p_1.v_4)),$$
$$p_5 = ((p_2.v_1 == p_2.v_3) \wedge (p_2.v_2 == p_2.v_4))),$$
$$Core_1^1(Pr)(f_1 = (p_1.v_1 + p_1.v_2) \cdot 2,$$
$$f_2 = p_1.v_1 \cdot p_1.v_3 \cdot \sin(p_2.v_2)),$$
$$Core_2^1(Rb)(p_6 = (p_1.v_1 == p_1.v_2 == p_1.v_3 == p_1.v_4),$$
$$f_1 = p_1.v_1 \cdot 4,$$
$$f_2 = (p_1.v_1)^2 \cdot \sin(p_2.v_1)),$$
$$pr_1(Pr)(p_1 = ((v_1, cm), (v_2, cm), (v_3, cm), (v_4, cm)),$$
$$p_2 = ((v_1,^\circ), (v_2,^\circ), (v_3,^\circ), (v_4,^\circ))),$$
$$pr_2(Rb)(p_1 = ((v_1, cm), (v_2, cm), (v_3, cm), (v_4, cm)),$$
$$p_2 = ((v_1,^\circ), (v_2,^\circ), (v_3,^\circ), (v_4,^\circ))))$$

where $Core_1^2(PrRb)$ contains properties, which are common for types Pr and Rb; $Core_1^1(Pr)$ contains methods, which are common for all objects of the type Pr; $Core_2^1(Rb)$ contains property and methods, which are common for all objects of the type Rb; $pr_1(Pr)$ and $pr_2(Rb)$ contains properties which are typical only for types of objects Pr and Rb respectively.

Quantitative property p_1 in projections $pr_1(Pr)$ and $pr_2(Rb)$ means sizes of figure sides measured in cm; quantitative property p_2 in projections $pr_1(Pr)$ and $pr_2(Rb)$ means degree measures of figure angles; qualitative property p_3 in $Core_1^2(PrRb)$ means that sum of all degree measures of figure angles is equal to $360°$; qualitative property p_4 in $Core_1^2(PrRb)$ means the quality of opposite sides of figure; qualitative property p_5 in $Core_1^2(PrRb)$ means that degree measures of opposite angles of the figure are equal; qualitative property p_6 in $Core_2^1(Rb)$ means the equality for all figure sides; method f_1 in $Core_1^1(Pr)$ and $Core_2^1(Rb)$ means the procedure for computing the perimeter of the figure; method f_2 in $Core_1^1(Pr)$ and $Core_2^1(Rb)$ means the procedure for computing the area of the figure.

Let us compute the differences $RsSqPr \setminus PrRb$ using for this Algorithm 3. As we can see, the polymorphic function is_equivalent detected the following equivalences

$$p_3(Core_1^3(RtSqPr)(RtSqPr)) \equiv p_3(Core_1^2(PrRb)(PrRb)),$$
$$p_4(Core_1^3(RtSqPr)(RtSqPr)) \equiv p_4(Core_1^2(PrRb)(PrRb)),$$
$$p_5(Core_1^3(RtSqPr)(RtSqPr)) \equiv p_5(Core_1^2(PrRb)(PrRb)),$$
$$p_7(Core_2^1(Sq)(RtSqPr)) \equiv p_6(Core_2^1(Pr)(PrRb)),$$
$$f_1(Core_2^2(RtPr)(RtSqPr)) \equiv f_1(Core_1^1(Pr)(PrRb)),$$
$$f_2(Core_3^1(Pr)(RtSqPr)) \equiv f_2(Core_1^1(Pr)(PrRb)),$$

therefore using these facts Algorithm 3 created a new multi-core inhomogeneous class of objects $RsSqPr \setminus PrRb \subseteq RsSqPr$ with the following structure

$$RsSqPr \setminus PrRb(Core_1^2(RtSq)(p_2 = ((v_1, °), (v_2, °), (v_3, °), (v_4, °)),$$
$$p_6 = (p_2.v_1 == p_2.v_2 == p_2.v_3 ==$$
$$== p_2.v_4 == 90, °)),$$
$$Core_1^1(Rt)(f_2 = p_1.v_1 \cdot p_1.v_2),$$
$$Core_2^1(Sq)(f_1 = p_1.v_1 \cdot 4,$$
$$f_2 = (p_1.v_1)^2),$$
$$pr_1(Rt)(p_1 = ((v_1, cm), (v_2, cm), (v_3, cm), (v_4, cm))),$$
$$pr_2(Sq)(p_1 = ((v_1, cm), (v_2, cm), (v_3, cm), (v_4, cm))),$$
$$pr_3(Pr)(p_1 = ((v_1, cm), (v_2, cm), (v_3, cm), (v_4, cm)),$$
$$p_2 = ((v_1, °), (v_2, °), (v_3, °), (v_4, °)))))$$

which represents the difference of the class $RsSqPr$ from the class $PrRb$ and the type of objects, which it defines. Similar to previous cases, the existence of the class $RsSqPr \setminus PrRb$ means that pieces of knowledge represented by classes $RsSqPr$ and $PrRb$ have some distinct features.

Application of proposed algorithms, which implements different variants of the universal difference exploiter can be considered as a method for computing the relevance between new pieces of knowledge and those ones, which were obtained previously. It allows us to perform the recognition stage according to the knowledge integration model proposed by Murray and Porter.

5   Conclusions

Knowledge integration is one of the important tasks for modern knowledge-based systems, to perform which a system should be able dynamically to analyze the relevance, similarity, and difference between newly extracted or acquired knowledge and previously obtained ones. Therefore, algorithms for the implementation of universal difference exploiter of classes of objects were presented in the paper. Each of the developed algorithms implements a particular version of universal difference exploiter, that allows application of the exploiter to different combinations of homogeneous and inhomogeneous classes of objects. Algorithms compute the difference of one class of objects from another one in a form of subclasses if such a difference exists, i.e. it dynamically creates new classes of objects if it is possible. The proposed approach provides an opportunity to perform verification of difference relation between newly extracted or acquired pieces of knowledge with previously obtained ones, by computing the difference between them. It allows partially to implement the recognition and elaboration stages of knowledge integration, according to the computational model proposed in [2,8–11]. Using Algorithm 1, Algorithm 2, and Algorithm 3 the concept of universal difference exploiter, as well as concepts of intersection, union, and decomposition exploiters, which were introduced in [25–27], can be integrated into a particular object-oriented knowledge representation model or programming languages. However, despite all advantages, constructed algorithms require further analysis and optimization.

References

1. Andonoff, E., Hubert, G., Le Parc, A., Zurfluh, G.: A query algebra for object-oriented databases integrating versions. In: Proceedings of of the Third Basque International Workshop on Information Technology - BIWIT 1997 - Data Management Systems, Biarritz, France, pp. 62–72, July 1997. https://doi.org/10.1109/BIWIT.1997.614052
2. Bareiss, R., Porter, B.W., Murray, K.S.: Supporting start-to-finish development of knowledge bases. Mach. Learn. 4(3–4), 259–283 (1989). https://doi.org/10.1007/BF00130714
3. Bhalla, N., Balasundaram, S.: Operations and queries in object-oriented databases supporting complex objects. Inf. Softw. Technol. 35(1), 54–62 (1993). https://doi.org/10.1016/0950-5849(93)90029-3
4. Kamin, S.: Routine run-time code generation. ACM SIGPLAN Not. 38(12), 208–220 (2003). https://doi.org/10.1145/966051.966059
5. Keppel, D., Eggers, S.J., Henry, R.R.: A case for runtime code generation. Technical report, 91–11-04, University of Washington, Department of Computer Science and Engineering, January 1991

6. Leone, M., Lee, P.: Lightweight run-time code generation. In: Proceedings of ACM SIGPLAN Workshop on Partial Evaluation and Semantics-Based Program Manipulation, Orlando, FL, USA, pp. 97–106, June 1994

7. Leung, T.W., Subramanian, B., Vandenberg, S.L., Mitchell, G., Vance, B., Zdonik, S.B.: The AQUA data model and algebra. In: Beeri, C., Ohori, A., Shasha, D.E. (eds.) Database Programming Languages (DBPL-4). Workshops in Computing, pp. 157–175. Springer, London (1994). https://doi.org/10.1007/978-1-4471-3564-7_10

8. Murray, K.S.: Learning as knowledge integration. Ph.D. thesis, Faculty of the Graduate School, University of Texas at Austin, Austin, Texas, USA, May 1995

9. Murray, K.S.: KI: a tool for knowledge integration. In: Proceedings of the 13th National Conference on Artificial Intelligence, AAAI 1996, Portland, Oregon, USA, pp. 835–842, August 1996

10. Murray, K.S., Porter, B.W.: Controlling search for the consequences of new information during knowledge integration. In: Proceedings of the 6th International Workshop on Machine Learning, New York, USA, pp. 290–295, June 1989

11. Murray, K.S., Porter, B.W.: Developing a tool for knowledge integration: initial results. Int. J. Man-Mach. Stud. **33**(4), 373–383 (1990)

12. Rundensteiner, E.A.: Object-oriented views: a novel approach for tool integration in design environments (dissertation). Technical report, 92–83, Department of Information and Computer Science, University of California, Irvine, California, USA, August 1992

13. Rundensteiner, E.A., Bic, L.: Set operations in semantic data models. Technical report, 89–22, Department of Information and Computer Science, University of California, Irvine, California, USA, June 1989

14. Rundensteiner, E.A., Bic, L.: Set operations in a data model supporting complex objects. In: Bancilhon, F., Thanos, C., Tsichritzis, D. (eds.) EDBT 1990. LNCS, vol. 416, pp. 286–300. Springer, Heidelberg (1990). https://doi.org/10.1007/BFb0022177

15. Rundensteiner, E.A., Bic, L.: Set operations in object-based data models. IEEE Trans. Knowl. Data Eng. **4**(3), 382–398 (1992). https://doi.org/10.1109/69.149933

16. Savnik, I., Tari, Z., Mohorič, T.: QAL: a query algebra of complex objects. Data Knowl. Eng. **30**(1), 57–94 (1999). https://doi.org/10.1016/S0169-023X(98)00049-4

17. Shaw, G.M., Zdonik, S.B.: A query algebra for object-oriented databases. Technical report, CS-89-19, Department of Computer Science, Brown University, Providence, Rhode Island, USA, March 1989

18. Shaw, G.M., Zdonik, S.B.: A query algebra for object-oriented databases. In: Proceedings of the 6th International Conference on Data Engineering, Los Angeles, CA, USA, pp. 154–162, February 1990. https://doi.org/10.1109/ICDE.1990.113465

19. Smith, F., Grossman, D., Morrisett, G., Hornof, L., Jim, T.: Compiling for run-time code generation (extended version). Technical report, TR2000-1824, Cornell University, Ithaca, NY, USA, October 2000

20. Smith, F.M.: Certified run-time code generation. Ph.D. thesis, Faculty of the Graduate School of Cornell University, Ithaca, NY, USA, January 2002

21. Straube, D.D., Özsu, M.T.: Queries and query processing in object-oriented database systems. ACM Trans. Inf. Syst. **8**(4), 387–430 (1990). https://doi.org/10.1145/102675.102678

22. Terletskyi, D.: Object-oriented knowledge representation and data storage using inhomogeneous classes. In: Damaševičius, R., Mikašytė, V. (eds.) ICIST 2017.

CCIS, vol. 756, pp. 48–61. Springer, Cham (2017). https://doi.org/10.1007/978-3-319-67642-5_5

23. Terletskyi, D.O.: Algorithms for runtime generation of homogeneous classes of objects. In: Proceedings of the International Conference on Cyber Security and Computer Science, ICONCS 2018, Safranbolu, Turkey, pp. 160–164, October 2018

24. Terletskyi, D.O.: Object-oriented dynamic model of knowledge representation within intelligent software systems. Ph.D. thesis, Faculty of Computer Science and Cybernetics, Taras Shevchenko National University of Kyiv, Kyiv, Ukraine, April 2018

25. Terletskyi, D.O.: Run-time class generation: algorithms for intersection of homogeneous and inhomogeneous classes. In: Proceedings of IEEE 2019 14th International Scientific and Technical Conference on Computer Sciences and Information Technologies (CSIT), Lviv, Ukraine, vol. 3, pp. 272–277, September 2019. https://doi.org/10.1109/STC-CSIT.2019.8929736

26. Terletskyi, D.O.: Run-time class generation: algorithms for union of homogeneous and inhomogeneous classes. In: Damaševičius, R., Vasiljevienė, G. (eds.) ICIST 2019. CCIS, vol. 1078, pp. 148–160. Springer, Cham (2019). https://doi.org/10.1007/978-3-030-30275-7_12

27. Terletskyi, D.O.: Run-time class generation: algorithm for decomposition of homogeneous classes. In: Lopata, A., Butkienė, R., Gudonienė, D., Sukackė, V. (eds.) ICIST 2020. CCIS, vol. 1283, pp. 243–254. Springer, Cham (2020). https://doi.org/10.1007/978-3-030-59506-7_20

28. Terletskyi, D.O., Provotar, O.I.: Mathematical foundations for designing and development of intelligent systems of information analysis. Probl. Program. 16(2–3), 233–241 (2014)

29. Terletskyi, D.O., Provotar, O.I.: Object-oriented dynamic networks. In: Setlak, G., Markov, K. (eds.) Computational Models for Business and Engineering Domains, IBS IS&C, vol. 30, pp. 123–136, 1st edn. ITHEA (2014)

30. Zhang, D., Dong, Y.: A data model and algebra for the web. In: Proceedings of the 10th International Workshop Database Expert System Applications, DEXA 1999, Florence, Italy, pp. 711–714, September 1999. https://doi.org/10.1109/DEXA.1999.795271

31. Zhang, D., Dong, Y.: An object oriented data model for web and its algebra. In: Proceedings of the Technology of Object-Oriented Languages and Syst. (Cat. No.PR00393), Nanjing, China, pp. 83–88, September 1999. https://doi.org/10.1109/TOOLS.1999.796470

The Applications of Z-numbers in the Delphi Method

Marcin Lawnik[ID] and Arkadiusz Banasik[✉][ID]

Department of Mathematics Applications and Methods for Artificial Intelligence,
Silesian University of Technology, Kaszubska 23, 44-100 Gliwice, Poland
{marcin.lawnik,arkadiusz.banasik}@polsl.pl

Abstract. In many areas of life, we are dealing with predicting the value
of certain phenomena and processes. One of the methods that allow for
long-term prediction is the Delphi method. It uses aggregated expert
knowledge, which is available future for experts in subsequent rounds.
One of the Delphi method variations is the method that uses Z-numbers,
that is, ordered pairs of fuzzy numbers as prediction values. Such a variant of the Delphi method proposed in the literature does not directly use
Z-numbers' calculus. Still, it reduces them in an appropriate way to fuzzy
numbers, significantly simplifying the calculations but, at the same time,
losing a certain amount of information. This article proposes a different
approach to the Z-number-based Delphi method. This modification uses
simple Z-number calculations. Only in the last step of the experts' round,
it is converted to a fuzzy number so that finally, after going through all
the rounds, the prediction value is crisp. The analysis of this aspect is
critical in the case of complex decision-making processes in which the
loss of information may result in a wrong decision. The Delphi method's
proposed variant is illustrated by the example of determining the price
of a product and combined with previous work of authors presents the
new approach.

Keywords: Z-number · Delphi method · Fuzzy sets · Decision-making

1   Introduction

Decisions are an essential part of humans' life. It is evident for every people
to decide his or her life from the early beginning. The decisions are present in
our private and business part of life [40]. Most decisions are connected with the
managerial aspect of our lives [8,13,25]. It is also apparent that decisions are
made in a natural environment [26]. The choices are also made to psychological
attitude towards problems, and that aspect is also visible in the decision making
process [20,38].

Making decisions is also an essential aspect of business activity. The decisions are a part of the responsibility, and the consequences are often connected
with finances. So it is vital to make the proper one. That provides a helpful

© Springer Nature Switzerland AG 2021
A. Lopata et al. (Eds.): ICIST 2021, CCIS 1486, pp. 241–250, 2021.
https://doi.org/10.1007/978-3-030-88304-1_19

solution – a decision support system, which is usually based on business intelligence [4,10,35,45]. According to that aspect, it is necessary to cope with many problems and find a solution using experts' knowledge and skills. A way to cope with that problems is a Delphi method [7,18,27,29]. The Delphi method, which modification is discussed in the article, is one of the ways to make decisions based on the knowledge of experts, which corresponds to the basic assumption of this article – modification of the decision-making process.

In the modern world, it is often necessary to make decisions based on incomplete or expressed in natural language data. Mathematically to cope with this issue, fuzzy numbers are used [14,24,33]. The modification of fuzzy numbers are the Z-numbers, which perfectly fit into the methods of making decisions under uncertainty [31], in decision models [11,39], and also in expert systems [43]. Z-numbers are now a highly exploited scientific deliberation topic initiated by Lotfi A. Zadeh [47] and then developed by many scientists. Currently popular are approaches to discrete Z-numbers [34] or proposals for a different approach to Z-numbers such as Mixed-discrete Z-numbers [36] and ZE-numbers [44].

The article presents a modified Delphi method approach using Z-numbers to cope with experts' recommendations and their reviews. The mathematical apparatus with the use of Z-numbers is associated with the loss of some information related to the issue in question, its minimization is crucial when assessing the usefulness of the method, which has been shown. This article's subject is therefore topical and fits in with the trends in the use of the mathematical apparatus in the decision-making process, which, as indicated above, is an essential part of today's professional and business life.

The article contains the Introduction part, which shows the importance of the decision-making process's presented aspect. Then is the Related Work exposing other approaches or other fields of implementation of the presented method. Another part contains mathematical Preliminaries showing basic mathematical foundations and the Method section, which shows the proposed modification of Z-number based Delphi method. Next is the Discussion part following by the numerical Example of the presented approach and Conclusions containing a summary of the studies.

1.1   Related Work

The proposed approach is based on reliability and representation of uncertain information. That approach is also shown in the field of quality function deployment [42]. It is also implemented in FUCOM and MABAC models [11].

The article presents the use of Z-numbers, which are a widely used methodology in the fuzzy environment and decision making, especially in multiple criteria decision making (MCDM) involving the relations among various alternatives [28]. It is also a part of assessment and ranking methods, which are a part of the Fuzzy AHP-Z Number Model [9]. The topic of decision-making is an essential aspect of different areas of application, e.g., health-care waste management (HCW). The process of multi-criteria decision making is also present in the field of safety and occupational health [48]. The Z-numbers are also implemented in

Demspert-Shafer theory [23]. The Z-numbers are often used with other AI methods such as neural networks [19], AQM [32]. That approach is also connected with group decision-making, and the opinions of experts [5,6,12].

The ground for the presented approach was the article [30]. The authors explain in this work the Delphi method, which uses the Z-numbers. The basis of this approach was an iterative approach to the proposed value determination. The mathematical background was transforming Z-numbers into fuzzy numbers using the center of gravity method. Then the fuzzy average value was calculated and sent back to the experts. The considerations were based on triangular membership functions, which are the simplest with their characteristics, but they cause changes in the obtained values when converted to crisp. Therefore, it was necessary to modify the presented approach. However the main aspect of modification was based on information loss, which is the consequence of the implementation of algorithm from the article [30].

As shown above, Z-numbers' principles in decision-making, especially the Delphi Method, are important. The importance is shown by the number of publications in recent years and their contribution to the research topic. Our approach contains another vision of the use of Z-numbers in the field of the Delphi method.

2 Preliminaries

This part of the article contains basic definitions and mathematical formulas necessary to define the discussed method.

The fuzzy set A defined in space X is set of pairs [46]

$$A = \{(x, \mu_A(x)) : x \in X\}. \tag{1}$$

Function $\mu_A : X \to [0,1]$ is named the membership function and it defines the element's degree of belonging x to A.

The membership function can be defined in many ways. One of them is the trapezoidal membership function:

$$(a, b, c, d) = \begin{cases} 0, & x \leqslant a \\ \frac{x-a}{b-a}, & a < x \leqslant b \\ 1, & b < x \leqslant c \\ \frac{d-x}{d-c}, & c < x \leqslant d \\ 0, & x > d \end{cases} \tag{2}$$

Fuzzy number is a fuzzy set A (where $A \subseteq \mathbb{R}$), which membership function fulfill listed conditions [17]:

1. $\sup_{x \in \mathbb{R}} \mu_A(x) = 1$ (fuzzy set A is normal),
2. $\mu_A(\lambda x_1 + (1 - \lambda)x_2) \geq \min\{\mu_A(x_1), \mu_A(x_2)\}$ (set A is convex),
3. $\mu_A(x)$ is intervally continuous function.

The fuzzy number A can be converted to crisp value in a process called defuzzification. One of such methods is the center of gravity method defined by the formula [37]

$$\alpha_A = \frac{\int x\mu_A(x)dx}{\int \mu_A(x)dx}. \tag{3}$$

Fuzzy sets can also be defined in the interval form with the help of their bandwidth. Bandwidth A^b of fuzzy number A is the value [41]

$$A^b = |x_1 - x_2|, \tag{4}$$

where $\mu_A(x_1) = \mu_A(x_2) = 0.5$. Using the bandwidth of fuzzy set A, its interval form $[A^{b1}, A^{b2}]$ can be defined as [15]:

$$\mu_{[A^{b1}, A^{b2}]}(x) = \begin{cases} \frac{1}{2}, & A^{b1} \leq x \leq A^{b2} \\ 0, & \text{otherwise} \end{cases}. \tag{5}$$

Z-number [47] is an ordered pair of fuzzy numbers (A, R), where number A is a fuzzy bound of real variable x, and R is a measure of reliability of the first component.

Simple form of arithmetic operations on Z-numbers can be found in [2,47]. For two Z-numbers $Z_1 = (A_1, R_1)$ and $Z_2 = (A_2, R_2)$ basic arithmetic operations $\{+, -, \cdot, /\}$ are defined as follow:

$$Z_1 * Z_2 = (A_1^b * A_2^b, R_1 \times R_2), \tag{6}$$

where A_1^b, A_2^b means bandwidth of number A_1 and A_2; $R_1 \times R_2$ is the product of the fuzzy numbers R_1 and R_2.

The Z-number $Z = (A, R)$ with trapezoidal components can be converted into a fuzzy number according to the formula [21]:

$$Z' = (\sqrt{\alpha_R}a, \sqrt{\alpha_R}b, \sqrt{\alpha_R}c, \sqrt{\alpha_R}d), \tag{7}$$

where α is obtained by the formula (3) for a fuzzy number R, i.e.

$$\alpha_R = \frac{\int x\mu_R(x)dx}{\int \mu_R(x)dx}. \tag{8}$$

3   Method

The general outline of the Delphi method with the use of Z-numbers is presented in the points:

1. Experts give feedback in the form of Z-numbers.
2. The information expressed in the opinions is aggregated and sent to the experts.

3. The next round of expert opinions starts, taking into account their aggregated information from the previous round.
4. Steps 1–3 are repeated until a satisfactory opinion is reached.

The above steps are very general, and it is necessary to detail them. An important step is that the Delphi method uses aggregated expert knowledge to work out a typical prediction value. For this article, the aggregate value will be the arithmetic mean of $\overline{Z}$ of consecutive Z-numbers Z_i. To find its value, the authors propose to use the formula (6) with an appropriate modification. The suggested value of the arithmetic mean might look like this

$$\overline{Z} = \frac{1}{k} \sum_{i=1}^{k} Z_i \tag{9}$$

$$= \left(\left[\frac{1}{k} \sum_{i=1}^{k} A_i^{b1}, \frac{1}{k} \sum_{i=1}^{k} A_i^{b2} \right], \left(\sqrt[k]{\prod_{i=1}^{k} a_i}, \sqrt[k]{\prod_{i=1}^{k} b_i}, \sqrt[k]{\prod_{i=1}^{k} c_i}, \sqrt[k]{\prod_{i=1}^{k} d_i} \right) \right).$$

Using the given formulas, Delphi method with Z-numbers can be described by steps expressed below:

1. Experts E_i ($i = 1, 2, \ldots, n$) declare their opinions giving trapezoidal Z-numbers

$$A_i = (a_i, b_i, c_i, d_i; \text{reliability}), \tag{10}$$

where the component *reliability* is a trapezoidal fuzzy number defined on the range $[0, 1]$.
2. The $\overline{Z}$ fuzzy average of the expert ratings is calculated according to the formula (9).
3. The $\overline{Z}$ value is converted to fuzzy number with formulas (7) and (8). The obtained value is sent to the experts for inclusion in the next evaluation process. This step opens another evaluation round.
4. Steps 1–3 are repeated for a specified number of turns or until the value of $\overline{Z}$ is stable.
5. The last value of $\overline{Z}$ converted to a crisp using the formulas (7) and (8) and finally the value obtained by (3) is the predicted value throughout the evaluation process.

4   Discussion

The proposed variant of the Delphi method differs significantly from that given in [30]. The variant of the method discussed in [30] converted Z-numbers into fuzzy numbers using the algorithm given in [21], and then the fuzzy Delphi method was used. Each time you replace a Z-number with its corresponding fuzzy number, some information is lost. This loss impacts the results, including the aggregate value that the experts use in the next round. This situation is undesirable, and a better solution is to perform the calculations directly on the Z-numbers and return the experts a value that is a fuzzy number. This approach is presented in this paper.

One problem that an expert may encounter is how he or she has to express his expert knowledge in a Z-number form. It should be noted here that such an opinion may depend on many factors, and it will not necessarily be easy for an expert to model such knowledge in the form of Z-numbers. Therefore, in the literature, one can find works that relate to this issue, e.g. [16,22].

Another important issue discussed in the article is the computation of Z-numbers. There are many approaches to this issue in the literature. Most of them require complex mathematical operations, such as [1,3]. This article uses the simplest, according to the authors, way to perform arithmetic operations on Z-numbers. Zadeh proposed it in the first Z-number paper [47] and then it was expanded in [2]. This approach is related to the fact that the necessary mathematical apparatus and programming skills needed to carry out the discussed Delphi method may be much smaller than other approaches to this issue.

5   Example

Table 1. Experts' opinions on the proposed price of the product expressed in linguistic form.

Expert	Z-number
1	(*about 11, vh*)
2	(*about 10, vh*)
3	(*about 10, h*)
4	(*about 9.75, vh*)

The Delphi method can be used, among others, to make decisions. As an example illustrating the method's operation with the use of Z-numbers, we chose to determine the price of a new product that is just about to enter the sales market. The manufacturer, taking into account the production costs and an adequate margin, is interested in a price of about USD 10. To confirm whether such a price is appropriate to the competition, he asks four experts to determine the best price in their opinion. The quoted forecasts of 4 experts in the form of Z-numbers are presented in the Table 1.

In turn, the Table 2 contains the reliability values used by experts.

Converting linguistic values into numerical values, the opinions of experts can be found in the Table 3.

The arithmetic mean of Z-numbers expressed as (9) is

$$((8.659375, 11.715625), (0.8872, 0.9172, 0.9573, 0.9873)). \tag{11}$$

Table 2. Reliability levels in the form of fuzzy trapezoidal numbers.

Variable	Value
vh	(0.9, 0.93, 0.97, 1)
h	(0.85, 0.88, 0.92, 0.95)
m	(0.8, 0.83, 0.87, 0.9)
c	(1, 1, 1, 1)

Table 3. Opinions of experts on the proposed price of the product expressed in numerical form.

Expert	Z-number
1	((8.8, 9.9, 12.1, 13.2), (0.9, 0.93, 0.97, 1))
2	((8.0, 9.0, 11.0, 12.0), (0.9, 0.93, 0.97, 1))
3	((8.0, 9.0, 11.0, 12.0), (0.85, 0.88, 0.92, 0.95))
4	((7.8, 8.775, 10.725, 11.7), (0.9, 0.93, 0.97, 1))

The value of (11) after conversion to a fuzzy value using the formulas (7) and (8) is *approximately 9.8627*. This value is sent to the experts, starting the second reviewing round. Opinions from the second round of experts are presented in the Table 4.

Table 4. Experts' opinions on the proposed price of the product expressed in a linguistic form from the second round of opinions.

Expert	Z-number
1	(*about 10.5, vh*)
2	(*about 10, c*)
3	(*about 10, vh*)
4	(*about 9.75, c*)

Conversion of linguistic values into numerical values, the opinions of experts from the second round can be found in the Table 5.

The arithmetic mean of Z numbers expressed as (9) is

$$((8.5531, 11.5719), (0.9487, 0.9644, 0.9849, 1.0)). \tag{12}$$

The value of (12) after conversion to a fuzzy value using the formulas (7) and (8) is *approximately 9.9331*. This value becomes the final opinion of experts about the reviewed product. Converted to crisp by (3), the product price should be 9.93 USD.

Table 5. Experts' opinions on the proposed price of the product expressed in numerical form from the second round of evaluation.

Expert	Z-number
1	$((8.4, 9.45, 11.55, 12.6), (0.9, 0.93, 0.97, 1))$
2	$((8.0, 9.0, 11.0, 12.0), (1, 1, 1, 1))$
3	$((8.0, 9.0, 11.0, 12.0), (0.9, 0.93, 0.97, 1))$
4	$((7.8, 8.775, 10.725, 11.7), (1, 1, 1, 1))$

6 Conclusions

This article discusses modifications to the Delphi method. A general variant of such a method has been proposed when experts' opinions are expressed in the form of Z-numbers. The presented modifications assume the direct use of Z-number arithmetic. This approach means that some information is not lost during the calculations, as was the case in this method's first variant. Also, it was proposed, among others, a formula for the arithmetic mean of Z-numbers. The operation of the process is illustrated by the example of determining the price of the product.

Further work on this subject will concern specific areas of application of the Delphi method's proposed variant. A decision support system can use the obtained knowledge to forecast or make decisions in the analyzed issue.

References

1. Aliev, R., Alizadeh, A., Huseynov, O.: The arithmetic of discrete Z-numbers. Inf. Sci. **290**, 134–155 (2015). https://doi.org/10.1016/j.ins.2014.08.024
2. Aliev, R., Huseynov, O., Aliyev, R.: A sum of a large number of Z-numbers. Procedia Comput. Sci. **120**, 16–22 (2017). https://doi.org/10.1016/j.procs.2017.11.205. 9th International Conference on Theory and Application of Soft Computing, Computing with Words and Perception, ICSCCW 2017, Budapest, Hungary, 22–23 August 2017
3. Aliev, R., Huseynov, O., Zeinalova, L.: The arithmetic of continuous Z-numbers. Inf. Sci. **373**, 441–460 (2016). https://doi.org/10.1016/j.ins.2016.08.078
4. Arnott, D., Pervan, G.: A critical analysis of decision support systems research. J. Inf. Technol. **20**(2), 67–87 (2005)
5. Banasik, A., Lawnik, M.: Fuzzy method with Z-numbers for choosing target group of users for UX applications, vol. 2, pp. 878–881 (2019)
6. Banasik, A., Lawnik, M.: Decisions ranking based on Z-numbers, pp. 12271–12280 (2020)
7. Barwood, M., et al.: Menthol as an ergogenic aid for the Tokyo 2021 Olympic games: an expert-led consensus statement using the modified Delphi method. Sports Med. **50**(10), 1709–1727 (2020)
8. Bazerman, M.H., Moore, D.A.: Judgment in Managerial Decision Making. Wiley, Hoboken (2012)

9. Bobar, Z., Božanić, D., Djurić, K., Pamučar, D.: Ranking and assessment of the efficiency of social media using the fuzzy AHP-Z number model-fuzzy MABAC. Acta Polytech Hungarica **17**, 43–70 (2020)

10. Bonczek, R.H., Holsapple, C.W., Whinston, A.B.: Foundations of Decision Support Systems. Academic Press, Cambridge (2014)

11. Bozanic, D., Tešić, D., Milić, A.: Multicriteria decision making model with Z-numbers based on FUCOM and MABAC model. Decis. Making Appl. Manag. Eng. **3**(2), 19–36 (2020)

12. Chen, X., Lin, J., Li, X., Ma, Z.: A novel framework for selecting sustainable healthcare waste treatment technologies under Z-number environment. J. Oper. Res. Soc. 1–14 (2020)

13. Eisenhardt, K.M., Zbaracki, M.J.: Strategic decision making. Strateg. Manag. J. **13**(S2), 17–37 (1992)

14. Faizi, S., Sałabun, W., Ullah, S., Rashid, T., Wieckowski, J.: A new method to support decision-making in an uncertain environment based on normalized interval-valued triangular fuzzy numbers and comet technique. Symmetry **12**(4), 516 (2020)

15. Fuh, C.F., Jea, R., Su, J.S.: Fuzzy system reliability analysis based on level $(\lambda,1)$ interval-valued fuzzy numbers. Inf. Sci. **272**, 185–197 (2014). https://doi.org/10.1016/j.ins.2014.02.106

16. Glukhoded, E.A., Smetanin, S.: The method of converting an expert opinion to Z-number. Trudy ISP RAN/Proc. ISP RAS **1**, 7–20 (2016)

17. Hanss, M.: Applied Fuzzy Arithmetic. Springer, Heidelberg (2005)

18. Hsu, I., Shih, Y.J., Pai, F.Y., et al.: Applying the modified Delphi method and DANP to determine the critical selection criteria for local middle and top management in multinational enterprises. Mathematics **8**(9), 1396 (2020)

19. Jafari, R., Razvarz, S., Gegov, A.: Applications of Z-numbers and neural networks in engineering. In: Arai, K., Kapoor, S., Bhatia, R. (eds.) SAI 2020. AISC, vol. 1230, pp. 12–25. Springer, Cham (2020). https://doi.org/10.1007/978-3-030-52243-8_2

20. Janis, I.L., Mann, L.: Decision Making: A Psychological Analysis of Conflict, Choice, and Commitment. Free Press (1977)

21. Kang, B., Wei, D., Li, Y., Deng, Y.: A method of converting Z-number to classical fuzzy number. J. Inf. Comput. Sci. **9**(3), 703–709 (2012)

22. Kang, B., Deng, Y., Hewage, K., Sadiq, R.: Generating z-number based on OWA weights using maximum entropy. Int. J. Intell. Syst. **33**(8), 1745–1755 (2018). https://doi.org/10.1002/int.21995

23. Kang, B., Zhang, P., Gao, Z., Chhipi-Shrestha, G., Hewage, K., Sadiq, R.: Environmental assessment under uncertainty using Dempster-Shafer theory and Z-numbers. J. Ambient. Intell. Humaniz. Comput. **11**(5), 2041–2060 (2020)

24. Karimi, H., Sadeghi-Dastaki, M., Javan, M.: A fully fuzzy best-worst multi attribute decision making method with triangular fuzzy number: a case study of maintenance assessment in the hospitals. Appl. Soft Comput. **86**, 105882 (2020)

25. Kirkwood, C.W.: Strategic Decision Making, vol. 149. Duxbury Press (1997)

26. Klein, G.: Naturalistic decision making. Hum. Factors **50**(3), 456–460 (2008)

27. Kroshus, E., et al.: What do parents need to know about concussion? Developing consensus using the Delphi method. Clin. J. Sport Med. (2020)

28. Lai, H., Liao, H., Šaparauskas, J., Banaitis, A., Ferreira, F.A., Al-Barakati, A.: Sustainable cloud service provider development by a Z-number-based DNMA method with Gini-coefficient-based weight determination. Sustainability **12**(8), 3410 (2020)

29. Lawnik, M., Banasik, A.: Delphi method supported by forecasting software. Inf. (Switzerland) **11**(2) (2020)

30. Lawnik, M., Krakowczyk, J., Banasik, A.: Fuzzy Delphi method with Z-Numbers. In: Damaševičius, R., Vasiljevienė, G. (eds.) ICIST 2019. CCIS, vol. 1078, pp. 24–32. Springer, Cham (2019). https://doi.org/10.1007/978-3-030-30275-7_3

31. Li, Y., Garg, H., Deng, Y.: A new uncertainty measure of discrete Z-numbers. Int. J. Fuzzy Syst. 1–17 (2020)

32. Liu, H.-C., You, X.-Y.: GSSOA using linguistic Z-numbers and AQM. In: Liu, H.-C., You, X.-Y. (eds.) Green Supplier Evaluation and Selection: Models, Methods and Applications, pp. 297–320. Springer, Singapore (2021). https://doi.org/10.1007/978-981-16-0382-2_13

33. Liu, P., Wang, Y., Jia, F., Fujita, H.: A multiple attribute decision making three-way model for intuitionistic fuzzy numbers. Int. J. Approximate Reasoning **119**, 177–203 (2020)

34. Liu, Q., Cui, H., Tian, Y., Kang, B.: On the negation of discrete Z-numbers. Inf. Sci. **537**, 18–29 (2020)

35. Marakas, G.M.: Decision Support Systems in the 21st Century, vol. 134. Prentice Hall, Upper Saddle River (2003)

36. Massanet, S., Riera, J.V., Torrens, J.: A new approach to Zadeh's z-numbers: mixed-discrete Z-numbers. Inf. Fusion **53**, 35–42 (2020)

37. Patel, A., Mohan, B.: Some numerical aspects of center of area defuzzification method. Fuzzy Sets Syst. **132**(3), 401–409 (2002). https://doi.org/10.1016/S0165-0114(02)00107-0

38. Plous, S.: The Psychology of Judgment and Decision Making. Mcgraw-Hill Book Company (1993)

39. Ren, Z., Liao, H., Liu, Y.: Generalized Z-numbers with hesitant fuzzy linguistic information and its application to medicine selection for the patients with mild symptoms of the Covid-19. Comput. Ind. Eng. **145**, 106517 (2020)

40. Saaty, T.L.: Decision Making with Dependence and Feedback: The Analytic Network Process, vol. 4922. RWS Publication (1996)

41. Singh, H., Lone, Y.A.: Deep Neuro-Fuzzy Systems with Python. Apress (2020)

42. Song, C., Wang, J.Q., Li, J.B.: New framework for quality function deployment using linguistic Z-numbers. Mathematics **8**(2), 224 (2020)

43. Tian, Y., Liu, L., Mi, X., Kang, B.: ZSLF: a new soft likelihood function based on Z-numbers and its application in expert decision system. IEEE Trans. Fuzzy Syst. (2020)

44. Tian, Y., Mi, X., Ji, Y., Kang, B.: ZE-numbers: a new extended Z-numbers and its application on multiple attribute group decision making. Eng. Appl. Artif. Intell. **101**, 104225 (2021)

45. Turban, E., Sharda, R., Delen, D.: Decision support and business intelligence systems (required) (2010)

46. Zadeh, L.A.: Fuzzy sets. Inf. Control **8**(3), 338–358 (1965)

47. Zadeh, L.A.: A note on Z-numbers. Inf. Sci. **181**(14), 2923–2932 (2011). https://doi.org/10.1016/j.ins.2011.02.022

48. Zhang, X., Mohandes, S.R.: Occupational health and safety in green building construction projects: a holistic Z-numbers-based risk management framework. J. Clean. Prod. **275**, 122788 (2020)

TMBuD: A Dataset for Urban Scene Building Detection

Ciprian Orhei$^{(\boxtimes)}$ ⓘ, Silviu Vert ⓘ, Muguras Mocofan ⓘ, and Radu Vasiu ⓘ

Politehnica University of Timişoara, Timişoara, Romania
ciprian.orhei@cm.upt.ro, {silviu.vert,muguras.mocofan,radu.vasiu}@upt.ro

Abstract. Building recognition and 3D reconstruction of human made structures in urban scenarios has become an interesting and actual topic in the image processing domain. For this research topic the Computer Vision and Augmented Reality areas intersect for creating a better understanding of the urban scenario for various topics. In this paper we aim to introduce a dataset solution, the TMBuD, that is better fitted for image processing on human made structures for urban scene scenarios. The proposed dataset will allow proper evaluation of salient edges and semantic segmentation of images focusing on the street view perspective of buildings. The images that form our dataset offer various street view perspectives of buildings from urban scenarios, which allows for evaluating complex algorithms. The dataset features 160 images of buildings from Timişoara, Romania, with a resolution of 768 × 1024 pixels each.

Keywords: Building dataset · Facade detection · Edge detection · Semantic segmentation · Edge detection ground-truth · Semantic segmentation ground-truth

1 Introduction

Computer Vision (CV) aims to create computational models that can mimic the human visual system. From an engineering point of view, CV aims to build autonomous systems which could perform some of the tasks that the human visual system is able to accomplish [1].

Urban scenarios reconstruction and understanding of it is an area of research with several applications nowadays: entertainment industry, computer gaming, movie making, digital mapping for mobile devices, digital mapping for car navigation, urban planning, driving. Understanding urban scenarios has become much more important with the evolution of Augmented Reality (AR). AR is successfully exploited in many domains nowadays, one of them being culture and tourism, an area in which the authors of this paper carried multiple research projects [2–4].

Automatic urban scene object recognition describes the process of segmentation and classification of buildings, trees, cars and so on. This job is done using a fixed number of categories on which a model is trained for classifying

© Springer Nature Switzerland AG 2021
A. Lopata et al. (Eds.): ICIST 2021, CCIS 1486, pp. 251–262, 2021.
https://doi.org/10.1007/978-3-030-88304-1_20

scene components [5]. Object detection, recognition and estimation in 3D images have gained momentum due to the availability of more complex sensors and an increase in large scale 3D data. Visual recognition of buildings can be a problematic task due to image distortions, image saturation or obstacles that are blocking the line of sight. The assumption that local shape structures are sufficient to recognise objects and scenes is largely invalid in practice since objects may have a similar shape [6].

In the last decades research in this domain has increased; annually, multiple new approaches and algorithms are presented in literature regarding urban building detection. The variety of solutions used to reach the detection goal can be a combination of any of the following: edge detection algorithms [7,8], line detection [9,10], line matching features [11,12], semantic segmentation and so on. In Fig. 1 we present snapshots of steps of a building detection algorithm. All proposed algorithms bring to the table a novel approach to solve corner cases of an existing problem.

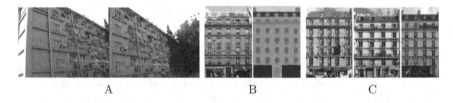

A   B   C

Fig. 1. A: Example of line matching algorithm [12]; B: Example of semantic segmentation algorithm [13]; C: Example of window detection algorithm [13]

We believe that this dataset will help enhance the novel algorithms in this domain because of the gap of edges and structural details on buildings images used in other benchmarks. This need occurred when trying to develop algorithms that focus not only on boundaries or contours but on details present in the facade of buildings. For example, in Fig. 5 we present an image from the popular BSDS500 [14] dataset, alongside the ground-truth for that image offered by them. In parallel we labeled the same image in our proposed concept of ground-truth. We can observe that the focus of the annotated edges is different: they focus more on boundaries and not on facade details and in our case the other way around. This difference can be an impediment to evaluate correctly the results of an algorithm depending on the scope of it: a general edge detection algorithm will not perform properly if tuned on a building-oriented dataset and of course the other way around.

The Timişoara Building Dataset - TMBuD - [15] is composed of 160 images with the resolution of 768 × 1024 pixels. Our motivation for this is the belief that this resolution is a good balance between the processing resources needed for manipulating the image and the actual resolution of pictures made with smart devices. Moreover, this is the actual video resolution for filming using a smartphone, the main sensor for building detection systems.

The paper is organized as following: in Sect. 2 we will present popular existing edge detection datasets with ground-truth and in Sect. 3 we will present similar semantic annotated datasets. In the end, in Sect. 4 we will describe our proposed dataset and the issues that we observed that resulted in the need of this new dataset.

2 Edge Detection Annotated Datasets

In this section we present the existing datasets for evaluating edge detection algorithms. Even if edges do not serve as stand alone features in the new CV universe, they still represent a fundamental block for line feature detection.

Fig. 2. Examples of images and equivalent ground-truth. Rows: original image, ground-truth; Coloumns: BSDS500 [14,16], NYUDV2 [17], MCUE [18], StructED [19]

The Berkeley Segmentation Data Set [14,16] is one of the most cited paper benchmarks. This benchmark is often used to compare algorithm generated contours or segmentations to human ground-truth data. For the Berkeley database, 1000 representative images of 481×321 RGB images from the Corel image database were chosen. The main criterion for selecting images was that it contains at least one distinctive object [16].

NYU Depth Dataset V2 [17] consists of 1449 RGBD images comprising of commercial and residential buildings in three different cities from US. The image dataset contains 464 different indoor scenes across 26 scene classes. Each image has a dense per-pixel depth labeling using Microsoft Kinect. If a scene contained multiple instances of an object class, each instance received a unique instance label.

The multi-cue boundary detection dataset [18] concerns to study the interaction of several early visual cues (luminance, color, stereo, motion) during boundary detection in challenging natural scenes. They considered a variety of places (from university campuses to street scenes and parks) and seasons to minimize possible biases. The dataset contains 100 scenes, each consisting of a left and right view short (10-frame) color sequence. Each sequence was sampled at a rate of 30 frames per second. Each frame has a resolution of 1280 by 720 pixels.

The Structural Edge dataset [19] propose a new concept of structural edge. Structural edges include occluding contours of objects as well as orientation discontinuities in surfaces are important for understanding the 3D structure of objects and environments. The validity of structural edges was tested using an eye tracking test. The structural edge dataset contains 600 images in natural indoor and outdoor scenes. The structural edges are labeled manually and validated by eye-tracking data from 10 participants with overall 20 trials.

In Fig. 2 we present images with the ground-truth from the dataset presented in this section. The mentioned datasets don't focus on certain domain of images of future specific scope to be used. This is a positive point when concerning with a wide range scope algorithm evaluation but is a negative aspect when focusing on a single use case, as we concern ourselves.

3   Semantic Segmentation Annotated Datasets

In this section we will present existing semantic segmentation datasets that focus on urban scenarios and that would be a good candidate to be used in constructing a building detection algorithm in the end.

The datasets which are selected and used by system designers play a very important role in the quality of the trained model and thereby system performance. So, selecting an appropriate dataset for a task can be one of the most challenging steps at the beginning of the research process [20].

eTRIMS Image Database [21] is comprised of 60 annotated images and offers two distinct labels: the 4-Class eTRIMS Dataset with 4 annotated object classes and the 8-Class eTRIMS Dataset with 8 annotated object classes. In the 8-class dataset are the following eight object classes: sky, building, window, door, vegetation, car, road, pavement.

LabelMeFacade Database [22,23] contains 945 images with labeled polygons that describe the different classes. The classes provided are: buildings, windows, sky, and a limited number of unlabeled regions (maximum 20% of the image). The pixelwise labeled images are created by utilizing the eTRIMS categories and a simple depth order heuristic.

Ecole Centrale Paris Facades Database [24,25] contains 109 images of Paris facades with annotations that have been manually rectified. Classes used for annotation are: window, wall, door, roof, sky, shop.

ICG Graz50 Facade Database [26] is a dataset of rectified facade images and semantic labels that was created with the goal of studying facades. It is comprised of 50 images of various architectural styles (Classicism, Biedermeier, Historicism, Modern and so on).

The Paris Art Deco Facades dataset [27] consists of 80 images of rectified facades of the Art Deco style. The dataset offers 79 RGB images with 6 annotated labels. Occlusions of the facade are ignored but the occlusion reasoning is offered by the dataset.

Fig. 3. Data sets class correlations. Rows: Original image, Original labels, transition to TMBuD labels; Columns: eTRIMS, LabelMeFacade, ECP, ICG Graz5, INRIA, CPM, VarCity

The CMP Facade Database [28] consists of facade images assembled at the Center for Machine Perception. The dataset includes 606 rectified images of facades from various cities of the world, which have been manually annotated. Annotation is defined as a set of rectangles scope with assigned class labels that can overlap if needed.

VarCity 3D Dataset [29, 30] consists of 700 images along a street annotated with pixel-level labels for facade details. Classes provided are: windows, doors, balconies, roof, etc. The dataset provides images, labels and indexes to the 3D surface together with evaluation source code for comparing different tasks.

In Fig. 3 we can observe examples of images and the associated labels that are offered in the dataset presented in this section. As we can see the perspective of each dataset is different. ECP, ICG Graz5, CMP focus more on facade details offering several classes to better understand the facade features. In the VarCity dataset we see that the focus is on the main building discarding the rest of the buildings in the image.

4   Our Proposed TMBuD Dataset

We intend with our dataset, TMBuD, to unify several ground truth evaluation in the same framework. Of course doing so in a global fashion is close to impossible so we wish to limit the use case to detection, feature extraction and localization of buildings in urban scenarios, based on image understanding.

Building detection is the process of obtaining the approximate position and shape of a building, while building extraction can be defined as the problem of precisely determining the building outlines, which is one of the critical problems in digital photogrammetry [31].

TMBuD is created from images of buildings in Timisoara. Each building is presented from several perspectives, so this dataset can be used for evaluating a building detection algorithm too. The dataset contains ground-truth images for salient edges, for semantic segmentation and the GPS coordinates of the buildings. The dataset contains 160 images grouped in the following sets: 100 consist of the training dataset, 25 consist of the validation data and 35 consist of the test data. We can see examples of images from the dataset in Fig. 4.

As we can observe in Fig. 4, the database focuses on a view that will be available if the input sensor device is a mobile phone. We consider this to be a very important aspect because the main domain where the building detection algorithm is used is the AR domain. Even if the edge features are focused only in the building area we desire to offer a full understanding of the environment via the semantic segmentation label.

The data was annotated using human subjects that were asked to label (draw) what they perceived as important edges of a building, like the boundaries of the building and differences between facades of the building, different buildings, windows, doors and so on. We asked them not to fill edges or lines that are occluded by other structures even if it's natural that they are present. Secondly they were asked to semantically label the image they created according to the label specification. After this step was finished, we proceeded to unify and correct the edges and labels created by the human subjects into one single ground-truth image. The correction was mainly to eliminate as much as possible the false salient edges that can occur when the data is labeled by a human subject unaware by the inner works of line detection or line matching algorithm.

We believe that a dataset is useful for evaluating algorithms for facade detection or building if it is focused on the building itself present in the image. Firstly, the images should be selected having in mind the street view perspective and uniqueness of features available on them. Secondly, the ground truth images should offer a basis for evaluating boundaries - an important aspect indeed -, but to offer a solution for evaluating facade edges and boundaries.

Boundary detection and edge detection are similar but not identical. Edges represent discontinuities of brightness which are usually found using low-level CV processes. The process of feature extraction of edges works under the assumption of ideal edge models. Boundary detection is viewed as a mid-level process of finding margins of objects in scenes. This task has close ties both with grouping/segmentation and object shape detection [32].

If we analyse the available datasets and benchmarks for edge detection, as we did in Sect. 2, we can observe that they focus on edges or boundaries generated from all structures from the image. Of course as we can see in Fig. 2 they clearly focus on evaluating and training edge algorithm for natural scenes and do not consider a certain use case of the resulting features.

Fig. 4. Images from proposed dataset. Rows: original image, edge ground-truth, label ground-truth

BSDS500 image   BSDS500 gt image   Our gt image

Fig. 5. Images and ground truth

Modern urban building detection techniques like [33,34] use line segment matching for performing this task. In parallel, the domain of line feature matching [11,35] for finding relevant features is growing, bringing to the table new solutions for this complex problem. In this scope we consider that our proposed approach for annotating the edges for a dataset becomes more relevant.

As we can observe in Fig. 5, we concern ourselves with salient edges produced by the details or shape of the building and ignore the edges produced by adjacent structures in the image, such as persons, cars, sky, ground and so on. We consider that this will help better fine tune the line features extraction algorithms that concern with building detection.

Semantic segmentation is an important aspect in the field of computer vision. The importance of scene understanding is highlighted by the fact that an increasing number of applications emerge from inferring knowledge from imagery. This step in the pipeline has become more popular in object detection applications, even if we talk about building detection.

The proposed dataset focuses more on the scene understanding of the environment rather than on semantically understanding the structures of the building. As we can see in Fig. 4, the existing datasets offer solid grounds for training and evaluating semantic segmentation solutions but lack a certain capability to be used to fine tune a semantic segmentation for urban building scenario (as we can see from the last column where we made a transition from there label scheme to ours).

In Table 1 we can observe the existing classes offered by TMBuD, by value and RGB code, and the corresponding classes from the datasets presented in Sect. 3. Most of the classes are self explanatory but by correlating the classes from TMBuD with other dataset we aim to explain our view for segmenting the environment. We consider it essential to differentiate between BACKGROUND, that we consider unclassified data, and NOISE that we consider elements or objects that appear temporary in the field of view, such as cars, people, terraces, human made temporary structure and so on.

Table 1. Dataset's corelations

TMBuD	Label	RGB	eTRIMS	LabelMeFacade	ECP	ICG Graz5	INRIA	CPM	VarCity
Background	0	(0, 0, 0)	Not labeled	Various	Outlier	–	Various	BAckground	Background
Building	1	(125, 125, 0)	Building	Building	Wall Balcony Roof Chimney Shop	Wall	Wall Balcony Roof Shop	Facade Cornice Sill Balcony Molding Deco Pillar Shop	Wall Balcony Roof Shop
Door	2	(0, 125, 125)	Door	Door	Door	Door	Door	Door	Door
Window	3	(0, 255, 255)	Window	Window	Window	Window Blind	Window	Window	Window
Sky	4	(255, 0, 0)	Sky	Sky	Sky	Sky	Sky	Background	Sky
Vegetation	5	(0, 255, 0)	Vegetation	Vegetation	–	–	–	–	–
Ground	6	(125, 125, 125)	Pavement Road	Pavement Road	–	–	–	–	–
Noise	7	(0, 0, 255)	Car	Car	–	–	–	–	–

The TMBuD does not offer a build-in benchmarking capability of edge detection or semantic segmentation but it is part of EECVF [36,37], our Python-based End-To-End CV Framework, where a user can evaluate capabilities of algorithms. The dataset offers the possibility of extending or reorganizing the image in the train - validate - test groups by using a Python module that exists in the repository.

5 Conclusion

In this paper we presented a review o existing boundaries and edges dataset and a review of existing semantic segmentation dataset with the scope of highlighting current evaluation solutions. Afterwards we proposed a dataset that is better fitted to serve the tuning and evaluation of urban scenario building detection algorithms.

We believe that the proposed TMBuD dataset can facilitate research in image processing when focusing on urban scenarios. TMBuD has two main benefits: the unified evaluating system for several linked problems from this area and the targeted dataset on human made structures in urban scenarios. Both aspects mentioned can become relevant aspects for future development and research work.

TMBuD has proven to be a useful dataset for evaluation when trying to determine the best fitted edge detection variant or the best fitted semantic segmentation model for urban scenarios [37,38]. From the experience of our work we consider that the proposed dataset as an useful component in constructing a content based image retrieval urban building systems.

We want to expand in the near future the quantity of the dataset images and ground truth images respecting the same principles that we exposed in the paper: important human made structures in urban areas, from a street perspective and different angles.

Regarding the expansion of the dataset we are thinking of including a series of metadata information to be available for each landmark so we can serve algorithms focused on classifying buildings according to facts like: age of the building, architecture style.

Appendix A

(See Fig. 6).

Fig. 6. Images from proposed dataset. Rows: original image, edge ground-truth, label ground-truth

References

1. Huang, T.: Computer vision: evolution and promise (1996)
2. Vert, S., Vasiu, R.: Relevant aspects for the integration of linked data in mobile augmented reality applications for tourism. In: Dregvaite, G., Damasevicius, R. (eds.) ICIST 2014. CCIS, vol. 465, pp. 334–345. Springer, Cham (2014). https://doi.org/10.1007/978-3-319-11958-8_27
3. Vert, S., Vasiu, R.: Augmented reality lenses for smart city data: the case of building permits. In: Rocha, Á., Correia, A.M., Adeli, H., Reis, L.P., Costanzo, S. (eds.) WorldCIST 2017. AISC, vol. 569, pp. 521–527. Springer, Cham (2017). https://doi.org/10.1007/978-3-319-56535-4_53

4. Vert, S., Andone, D., Vasiu, R.: Augmented and virtual reality for public space art. In: ITM Web of Conferences, vol. 29, p. 03006. EDP Sciences (2019)
5. Babahajiani, P., Fan, L., Gabbouj, M.: Object recognition in 3D point cloud of urban street scene. In: Jawahar, C.V., Shan, S. (eds.) ACCV 2014. LNCS, vol. 9008, pp. 177–190. Springer, Cham (2015). https://doi.org/10.1007/978-3-319-16628-5_13
6. Fu, J., Kämäräinen, J.-K., Buch, A.G., Krüger, N.: Indoor objects and outdoor urban scenes recognition by 3D visual primitives. In: Jawahar, C.V., Shan, S. (eds.) ACCV 2014. LNCS, vol. 9008, pp. 270–285. Springer, Cham (2015). https://doi.org/10.1007/978-3-319-16628-5_20
7. Orhei, C., Vert, S., Vasiu, R.: A novel edge detection operator for identifying buildings in augmented reality applications. In: Lopata, A., Butkienė, R., Gudonienė, D., Sukackė, V. (eds.) ICIST 2020. CCIS, vol. 1283, pp. 208–219. Springer, Cham (2020). https://doi.org/10.1007/978-3-030-59506-7_18
8. Topal, C., Akinlar, C.: Edge drawing: a combined real-time edge and segment detector. J. Vis. Commun. Image Represent. **23**(6), 862–872 (2012)
9. Von Gioi, R.G., Jakubowicz, J., Morel, J.-M., Randall, G.: LSD: a fast line segment detector with a false detection control. IEEE Trans. Pattern Anal. Mach. Intell. **32**(4), 722–732 (2008)
10. Akinlar, C., Topal, C.: Edlines: real-time line segment detection by Edge Drawing (ED). In: 2011 18th IEEE International Conference on Image Processing, pp. 2837–2840. IEEE (2011)
11. Zhang, L., Koch, R.: An efficient and robust line segment matching approach based on LBD descriptor and pairwise geometric consistency. J. Vis. Commun. Image Represent. **24**(7), 794–805 (2013)
12. Fan, B., Wu, F., Hu, Z.: Robust line matching through line-point invariants. Pattern Recogn. **45**(2), 794–805 (2012)
13. Liu, H., Zhang, J., Zhu, J., Hoi, S.C.: DeepFacade: a deep learning approach to facade parsing (2017)
14. Arbelaez, P., Maire, M., Fowlkes, C., Malik, J.: Contour detection and hierarchical image segmentation. IEEE Trans. Pattern Anal. Mach. Intell. **33**(5), 898–916 (2010)
15. CM Building Dataset Timisoara. https://github.com/CipiOrhei/TMBuD. Accessed 12 Mar 2021
16. Martin, D., Fowlkes, C., Tal, D., Malik, J.: A database of human segmented natural images and its application to evaluating segmentation algorithms and measuring ecological statistics. In: Proceedings Eighth IEEE International Conference on Computer Vision, ICCV 2001, vol. 2, pp. 416–423. IEEE (2001)
17. Silberman, N., Hoiem, D., Kohli, P., Fergus, R.: Indoor segmentation and support inference from RGBD images. In: Fitzgibbon, A., Lazebnik, S., Perona, P., Sato, Y., Schmid, C. (eds.) ECCV 2012. LNCS, vol. 7576, pp. 746–760. Springer, Heidelberg (2012). https://doi.org/10.1007/978-3-642-33715-4_54
18. Mély, D.A., Kim, J., McGill, M., Guo, Y., Serre, T.: A systematic comparison between visual cues for boundary detection. Vision. Res. **120**, 93–107 (2016)
19. Sun, W., You, S., Walker, J., Li, K., Barnes, N.: Structural edge detection: a dataset and benchmark. In: 2018 Digital Image Computing: Techniques and Applications (DICTA), pp. 1–8 (2018)
20. Zlateski, A., Jaroensri, R., Sharma, P., Durand, F.: On the importance of label quality for semantic segmentation. In: 2018 IEEE/CVF Conference on Computer Vision and Pattern Recognition, pp. 1479–1487 (2018)

21. Korc, F., Förstner, W.: eTRIMS image database for interpreting images of man-made scenes. Department of Photogrammetry, University of Bonn, Technical report TR-IGG-P-2009-01 (2009)
22. Fröhlich, B., Rodner, E., Denzler, J.: A fast approach for pixelwise labeling of facade images. In: Proceedings of the International Conference on Pattern Recognition (ICPR 2010) (2010)
23. Brust, C.-A., Sickert, S., Simon, M., Rodner, E., Denzler, J.: Efficient convolutional patch networks for scene understanding. In: CVPR Workshop on Scene Understanding (CVPR-WS) (2015)
24. Teboul, O., Simon, L., Koutsourakis, P., Paragios, N.: Segmentation of building facades using procedural shape priors. In: 2010 IEEE Computer Society Conference on Computer Vision and Pattern Recognition, pp. 3105–3112 (2010)
25. Teboul, O., Kokkinos, I., Simon, L., Koutsourakis, P., Paragios, N.: Shape grammar parsing via reinforcement learning. In: CVPR 2011, pp. 2273–2280 (2011)
26. Riemenschneider, H., et al.: Irregular lattices for complex shape grammar facade parsing. In: 2012 IEEE Conference on Computer Vision and Pattern Recognition, pp. 1640–1647. IEEE (2012)
27. Gadde, R., Marlet, R., Paragios, N.: Learning grammars for architecture-specific facade parsing. Int. J. Comput. Vis. **117**(3), 290–316 (2016)
28. Tyleček, R., Šára, R.: Spatial pattern templates for recognition of objects with regular structure. In: Proceedings of the GCPR, (Saarbrucken, Germany) (2013)
29. Riemenschneider, H., Bódis-Szomorú, A., Weissenberg, J., Van Gool, L.: Learning where to classify in multi-view semantic segmentation. In: Fleet, D., Pajdla, T., Schiele, B., Tuytelaars, T. (eds.) ECCV 2014. LNCS, vol. 8693, pp. 516–532. Springer, Cham (2014). https://doi.org/10.1007/978-3-319-10602-1_34
30. Martinovic, A., Knopp, J., Riemenschneider, H., Gool, L.: 3D all the way: semantic segmentation of urban scenes from start to end in 3D. In: 2015 IEEE Conference on Computer Vision and Pattern Recognition (CVPR), pp. 4456–4465 (2015)
31. Elshehaby, A.R., Taha, L.G.E.-D.: A new expert system module for building detection in urban areas using spectral information and lidar data. Appl. Geomatics **1**(4), 97–110 (2009)
32. Ren, X.: Multi-scale improves boundary detection in natural images. In: Forsyth, D., Torr, P., Zisserman, A. (eds.) ECCV 2008. LNCS, vol. 5304, pp. 533–545. Springer, Heidelberg (2008). https://doi.org/10.1007/978-3-540-88690-7_40
33. Yi, Y., Zhang, Z., Zhang, W., Zhang, C., Li, W., Zhao, T.: Semantic segmentation of urban buildings from VHR remote sensing imagery using a deep convolutional neural network. Remote Sens. **11**(15), 1774 (2019)
34. Wang, W., Gao, W., Cui, H., Hu, Z.: Reconstruction of lines and planes of urban buildings with angle regularization. ISPRS J. Photogramm. Remote. Sens. **165**, 54–66 (2020)
35. Li, K., Yao, J., Xia, M., Li, L.: Joint point and line segment matching on wide-baseline stereo images. In: 2016 IEEE Winter Conference on Applications of Computer Vision (WACV), pp. 1–9. IEEE (2016)
36. Orhei, C., Mocofan, M., Vert, S., Vasiu, R.: End-to-end computer vision framework. In: 2020 International Symposium on Electronics and Telecommunications (ISETC), pp. 1–4. IEEE (2020)
37. Orhei, C., Vert, S., Mocofan, M., Vasiu, R.: End-to-end computer vision framework: an open-source platform for research and education. Sensors **21**(11), 3691 (2021)
38. Orhei, C., Mocofan, M., Vert, S., Vasiu, R.: An analysis of ED line algorithm in urban street-view dataset. In: Lopata, A., et al. (eds.) International Conference on Information and Software Technologies, ICIST 2021. CCIS, vol. 1486, pp. 123–135. Springer, Cham (2021)

Information Technology Applications-Special Session on Smart e-Learning Technologies and Applications

A Complex Model of Blended Learning: Using a Project Approach to Organize the Educational Process

Anna Marchenko$^{(\boxtimes)}$ ⓘ, Viktoriia Antypenko ⓘ, Svitlana Vashchenko ⓘ, Nataliia Fedotova ⓘ, Yana Chybiriak ⓘ, and Alla Krasulia ⓘ

Sumy State University, Sumy, Ukraine

{a.marchenko,v.antypenko,s.vashchenko,n.fedotova, y.chibiryak}@cs.sumdu.edu.ua, a.krasulia@gf.sumdu.edu.ua

Abstract. This article presents the experience of using blended learning methods and digital technologies to organize the educational process at Sumy State University. Based on the experience of using a combination of classical models of blended learning and interactive digital technologies in the educational process, a unified complex model has been proposed. The classic model of a flipped classroom is integrated with project approach to provide the collaborative problem-solving methods in the proposed model. The group-project approach for solving collective tasks is described step by step. The purpose of the research is to elaborate the complex structure of the blended learning model, including the educational load distribution, which will meet the requirements for teaching multiple subjects and different disciplines.

Keywords: Blended learning · Complex model · Active learning methods · Project approach · Independent work · Digital education

1 Introduction

Nowadays the world society is at the stage of active informatization of almost all spheres of life accompanied by the active use of information technologies to support the main business processes of society and business. Digital technologies are becoming increasingly important today. One of the keys to success in any field of human activity is the mastering of digital competences [1, 2]. According to the strategic approach to the development of digital skills and competences [3], today it is impossible to support the development of human personality without the digital transformation of education. It should be considered that, on average, the ratio of hours for the processing of course material in and outside the classroom in the academic curriculum of higher education institutions is 40:60%. Such distribution is typical of European higher education institutions of both private and public types. A similar approach to time distribution is also found in Ukrainian higher education institutions in accordance with the strategy of Europeanization of the education system adopted by the Ministry of Education and Science of Ukraine and the strategies for developing the individual higher education institutions

A. Lopata et al. (Eds.): ICIST 2021, CCIS 1486, pp. 265–278, 2021.
https://doi.org/10.1007/978-3-030-88304-1_21

[4–6]. Therefore, the emphasis should be on involving students in active independent work.

Furthermore, it should be noted that the informatization of education has become even more vital within the coronavirus COVID-19 pandemic. This has led to the disruption of the classical approach to the full-time educational process and to the forced transition of educational institutions to distance learning. Heads of institutions and teaching staff have faced the problem of building the educational process, using all available means, to provide quality training through remote interaction. To accomplish this, the following digital educational resources and services are being actively used:

- mass open online courses (Prometheus, Coursera, etc.);
- mobile-based training applications;
- tools for collaboration (Skype, Zoom, Google Meet);
- programs for creating the digital educational content.

Despite the wide range of Internet technologies, most higher education institutions are experiencing some difficulties in designing a new format for teaching and learning. Sumy State University started a blended learning experiment in 2016 to find the optimal model for the educational process. The organizational platform mix.sumdu.edu.ua, developed to implement the program and support the experiment, is actively used by university teaching staff both inside and outside the experiment.

The authors aim to offer a template for the methodological and organizational aspects of the digital educational process, and to describe their personal experience of using modern online developments to integrate the organization and support of informational and analytical activity of higher education within the mode of remote work.

2   Context and Review of Literature

2.1   Previous Investigation

Blended learning, which combines face-to-face classroom work with interactive online elements using digital technologies, has replaced the classic approach of organizing the educational process. Its main feature is the use of information and communication technologies to identify new didactic opportunities [7–11].

Application of the blended learning principles in pedagogical practice supports the following goals:

- provide enhanced educational opportunities by increasing the accessibility of training materials and flexibility of the educational process, taking into account the individual needs and physical abilities of the participants;
- use mechanisms for increasing students' motivation, independence and activity in learning the training material, and consequently, to increase the effectiveness of educational process in general;
- encourage the teacher to optimize the presentation of learning materials and use of digital technologies with the aim of increasing student interaction in the learning process;

- individualize and personalize the educational process, allowing students to define learning goals, as well as the ways they might be achieved, through their ongoing communication with the teacher who acts as a mentor and advisor.

Additionally, there is a need to streamline the models of blended learning. A great amount of research and articles have been devoted to this issue. In particular, the classifications of digital educational technologies and methodological and technological approaches presented in the works [12–15] can be considered as the most interesting ones. Digital educational technologies can be developed or used in formal and informal educational contexts for educational purposes.

The most well-balanced combination brings digital and educational technologies together. This is the essence of blended learning technologies. Today, universities attract and invest in blended learning. This contributes to the growth of technology and its potential to improve learning, improves didactics and offers increased access to knowledge anytime and anywhere. It also brings positive aspects to cost-effectiveness and ease of revision [16].

Among all blended learning models, the flipped classroom model is one of the simplest in relation to its organizational and technical aspects [17–20]. Essentially, the concept involves students learning a certain amount of theoretical material during the independent work outside the educational institution followed by classroom experiences where they actively discuss the material they have studied. Usually, these materials are prepared directly by the teacher. However, the presence of a large number of high quality open educational resources from leading educational institutions all over the world makes it possible to involve students of Sumy State University in their learning communities.

The choice of active learning methods used to organize students' work is determined by the specifics of the particular discipline or specialty, and usually is not wide enough. Preliminary analysis of imitation learning methods is advisable. One of the classifications of active learning methods described by Lapyhin [21] is presented in Fig. 1. In relation to obtaining practical skills, let's consider the imitation learning methods which are available to use during classroom meetings with students in more detail.

Case Study. The case study involves solving problems in real business situations. Students have to carry out a detailed analysis of the business situation, determine the content of the problem, offer a variety of solutions and choose the optimal one in terms of influential factors. Cases should be as close as possible to the real situation and can use the actual material.

Simulation Games. A business game and similar variations are simulation games. It is a method of simulating management decision making, at different levels in the business and in different business situations, in the presence of conflict or information uncertainty. In simulation games, the behavior of the players is determined by the simulation model of the business environment.

Project-Based Learning. The presence of an organizational stage for the project preparation, the selection of leaders from the project participants, the distribution of roles and the development of a separate project by each of the participants' groups are the key characteristics of the project form of training. The choice of this form of active learning

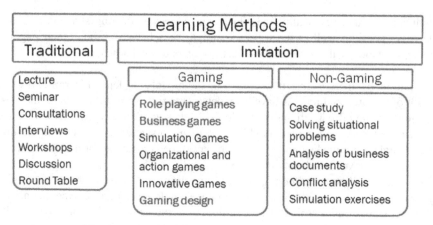

Fig. 1. General classification of active learning methods.

is determined by the specifics of working with real projects in accordance with the field in which the student's educational program belongs to. The expediency of choosing the project form of training is defined by the purpose of getting as close as possible to the real activity conditions of the future expert. Among the existing types of projects [22], the general classification of which is presented in Fig. 2, group projects (on the basis of the number of people involved in the project research tasks) and telecommunication projects (according to technologies used to achieve the aim of the project research) were selected.

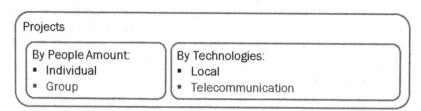

Fig. 2. General classification of projects as a training form.

The level of effort required from the student depends on both the different tasks they have to complete and the depth of the material they are learning. Students' independent cognitive activity should consist of purposeful, intensive and controlled independent work, supported by a teacher who possesses appropriate pedagogical technologies and teaching methods. From a student perspective, the challenge is to find an approach that motivates and sustains continuous training.

Therefore, the authors set the goal to form a universal complex model of blended learning that would allow students to master both professional and digital competences in the process of continuous digital learning. Moreover, a universal model includes the most effective teaching approaches and technologies and is adaptable for different specialties.

2.2 E-Learning Integrated Information System of Sumy State University

In the current circumstances, an integrated information system (IIS), which provides the effective interaction between the subjects of the educational and scientific process, plays a key role in the activities of Sumy State University (SSU). IIS includes the e-learning system, the efficiency of which is ensured by appropriate software and information modules (see Fig. 3):

- OCW SumDU is an open source of structured collections containing organizational, training and methodological materials of disciplines;
- Ekzamenarium is an open online resource of online courses;
- MIX is a platform for blended learning;
- Salamstein is a distance learning system;
- LecturED is an online tool to design the training materials;
- Library is an online catalog of the SSU library;
- eSSUIR is the university repository.

The presence of a joint database links the work of the software modules, ensures the unity of information processes and provides a common communication environment for the coordinated interaction between the participants of the educational process. Continuous content rotation in the information environment between the distance learning platform, the open educational resource, social networks and the design tool for training materials allows organizing diverse interaction with different user audiences, which ensures its constant evolution, improvement and evaluation by users.

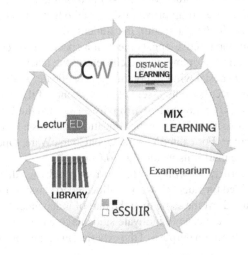

Fig. 3. The components of E-learning information system.

The main functions that the e-learning system provides to users are the following:

- creation of learning courses in different formats (textual, video, etc.);
- presentation of materials in the web space;
- flexible search of educational content according to different parameters;
- open access to training materials;
- organization of webcasts at a professional level;
- effective management of the training process.

These functions also allow carrying out career guidance activities and involving future applicants in the educational process. The transition from the model of studying in the classroom to the distance learning model involves some complications for a lot of higher education institutions. It should be noted that the success achieved by Sumy State University is based on the experience gained by scientific and pedagogical staff through working in the e-learning system environment. It was developed and implemented by their efforts and tested on the example of students enrolled in full time training. Currently, the educational platform provides the access to training materials, fully providing a high-level of distance learning.

3   Universal Complex Model of Blended Learning

Taking into account all the above, the flipped classroom model with some modification is accepted as a basic one to hold lessons within blended learning. One kind of study assignment is the independent study of a mass open online course (MOOC) with the gradual implementation of a group project using methods, technologies or approaches described in the course. In the classroom, the students demonstrate the results of independent study through their active engagement in a specific project task. Students are offered the choice to join the online-course chosen by the teacher. There also is a possibility to process the material without obtaining a certificate. According to this mode, the student usually has access to the essential components of the course, such as video lectures and tests. Recently Sumy State University has joined the Coursera for Campus program. Its courses are actively used in the educational process. However, this does not limit the teacher's choice. For example, MIT OpenCourseWare, Open EdX and others are used as basic online platforms in addition to Coursera.

As it was noted earlier, according to the current regulatory documents, the entire amount of hours provided for student's work is allocated to classroom work and independent study of the material. At the same time the part of independent work has increased. Therefore, the search for a means to motivate students to engage in active independent work is topical. This is the main purpose of the experiment of the introduction the blended learning.

As an option to solve this problem and involve students in more effective cooperation, work in project teams was used to organize the performance of independent work. Academic groups of at least 15 students allowed us to use the project approach. This solution also provided students with opportunity to gain necessary teamwork skills.

The proposed unified blended learning model combines a classical classroom approach and digital educational approaches, providing flexibility and continuous mastering of professional and digital competences. The model is presented in Fig. 4 [23].

The classroom work with the teacher covers the following:

- listening to classical lectures from the main theoretical blocks of the course in accordance with the syllabus of the discipline;
- implementation of practical/laboratory tasks that require access to the material base;
- discussion of problematic issues that have arisen during the video lectures of the MOOC during the lectures-seminars;
- analysis of smart maps developed in groups based on MOOC materials during lecture seminars (map analysis is performed in the mode of mutual evaluation of works on the basis of the keywords list defined by the teacher).

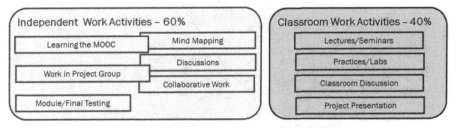

Fig. 4. Schematic representation of the tested blended learning model.

Independent work contains the following types of learning activities:

- learning the material from the MOOC and passing tests to define the level of learning using the platform environment (if available);
- performing the project work in groups;
- collaborative analysis of discussion issues with the results of the sources reviewed according to the declared problem case in the learning environment. To organize this type of work, it is possible to use the Google Classroom resource as well as LectureED. Later the material from this document is discussed in the classroom. Performing these tasks provides the formation of such important competences as the ability to analyze the available information in order to seek the solutions to the given tasks, and the ability to make informed decisions within changeable conditions of modern business;
- developing smart maps based on the material from the MOOC by means of cloud applications as a substitution for traditional note taking in order to learn the material more effectively [24].

The final control unit is organized in the form of testing the theoretical knowledge gained by students during the course.

Another important issue is the evaluation of students' work. A model of points distribution, which was tested during the pedagogical experiment and showing a satisfactory result, is presented in Fig. 5. This diagram clearly shows the evaluation of different learning activities in relative values (based on 100 percent of the points for the full tasks scope in the course). From the chart it is clear that the majority of points are assigned to the evaluation of students' independent and collective work. It should be emphasized that the proposed distribution of points is only recommended, and may be modified by the teacher in accordance with the particularities of the discipline within the educational program.

There is a possible scenario where among all learning activities are those that are compulsory to perform in order to get access to final test and optional ones that can be performed to get the higher points at the end of the course. However, it should be kept in mind that the student can get the required number of points to complete the course only if he/she performs all required tasks successfully.

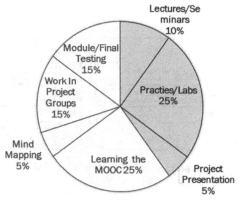

Fig. 5. Chart of percentage distribution between learning activities of the tested model of blended learning.

According to the proposed model, the first group of compulsory tasks included the learning in the MOOC (assessing the level of course learning was done through the testing of knowledge), the performance of individual home tasks in project teams and analysis of discussion issues presented by the teacher. The second group of optional tasks included the development of smart maps based on video lessons of the MOOC.

4 Findings

The research of existing imitative learning methods along with methods of active learning has allowed us to form a generalized algorithm for implementing the active method into the educational process. One of the features of this algorithm is using the project approach in academic disciplines (see Fig. 6).

The first stage concerns the analysis of existing models of roles distribution in project teams and the selection of the best one to form a successful balanced team. The easiest way to implement this is to use appropriate online resources.

According to the results of the experiment to organize the effective work in groups, the R. M. Belbin's model [24] was used by the majority of students. From the students' point of view, one of this model's advantages was the ability to combine several roles in one participant of the group (the number of students in groups was from 4 to 6 people, and the number of allocated roles by the author of the model was 9).

Then the role characteristics of the project team members are defined. According to [24] the roles of the project team are schematically divided into three main functional groups:

- the roles of a plant, a resource investigator and a monitor evaluator are focused on intellectual work;
- the roles of a team worker, a coordinator and a shaper are focused on working with people and creating a comfortable and friendly atmosphere in the project team;
- the roles of a completer finisher, an implementer and a specialist are focused on practical activity. Moreover, the specialist can actively participate in the intellectual work of the team.

Among the existing methods of determining roles, the most successful in this study was the questionnaire method for determining the main characteristics and qualities of candidates.

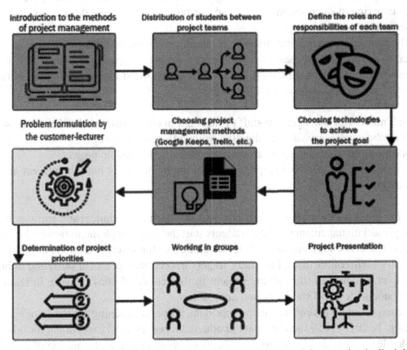

Fig. 6. Generalized algorithm for implementation the project approach into academic disciplines.

It is important to correlate the available qualities in the team for effective teamwork. Evaluating the balance of the role structure of within the project team is determined by the final assessment. This assessment determines the ability of each team member to fulfill their role. Key indicators enable assessors to determine the effectiveness of a team through balancing different roles within one group. The described selection of the team final assessment is based on the maximum ability of team members to perform these functions. Thus, the approach used to evaluate the role structure of the project team allows for distributing the role functions optimally from the point of view of managing the team work process within the project.

An important issue for successful completion of the project in terms of training is the choice of organizational structure of the project (matrix, functional and project). During the experiment, the choice of structure type was also assigned to the project team as part of joint work issues. Each organizational structure was evaluated according to such criteria as uncertainty of project implementation conditions, technology and complexity of the project, project cycle duration, project size, interdependence and interrelation between parts of the project, criticality of time and dependence of the project on higher level systems.

The choice of the certain structure that will be used to solve the project task may be determined by the specifics of the task and may be modified according to the specific requirements of the task. This process can be facilitated and/or supervised by the teacher. After analyzing the criteria for evaluating the structures, the students who participated in the experiment overwhelmingly chose the project structure. Additionally, it is the recommended one for use.

The project organizational structure is characterized by the solution of specific tasks related to the project and creating a temporary working group, which is dissolved when the project is completed. Among the main factors that the students highlighted in favor of the chosen structure were the following:

- small number of management staff of the team in comparison with other divisions;
- comprehensive approach to realization of the project objective;
- concentration of resources on solving one task of one specific project;
- strengthening the personal responsibility of the manager for both the project and its elements.

After the formation of project groups and selection the technical and software tools of the project management method, students start the direct implementation of the group project. The chosen method of flexible design allows for several iterations of designing in the short term of the discipline study, to get the necessary practical skills and to bring the implementation of the training project to the real conditions of work in teams in accordance with world standards and approaches.

An experiment was carried out to support the proposed teaching approach to organize learning. In 2018–2019 the university conducted a pedagogical experiment introducing blended learning technologies to the process of organizing the preparation of full-time students. Different directions of students' preparation were involved during the experiment. Up to 10 groups of students participated in the experiment during the academic year. The experimental groups included 24 students depending on the year of study they were undertaking. The disciplines of different components of the curriculum were taught using the blended form. These were professional subjects as well as humanitarian, social and economic ones.

According to the experiment results, we can confirm that the implementation of the project approach is appropriate through the flipped class. Each of the above-mentioned organisational stages was implemented by the chain of successive steps (Fig. 7). During the independent group work, the students studied the MOOC materials and analysed the Internet resources to find an array of possible solutions to the algorithm tasks. The results of the comparative analysis of the existing solutions were compiled in a jointly created document. During the classes, the students discussed the findings to make the best possible choice and the final decision regarding the optimal solution. Such redistribution of the learning activity types (LATs) between self-paced learning and classroom study aligns with Bloom's Modified Taxonomy [25].

The implementation phase in the classroom involved putting the MOOC independent self-paced learning results into a step-by-step action when the project team did the task according to the Scrum Agile methodology. Thus, students independently acquired the skills of Agile project design under the supervision of the instructor, who acted as a customer that had placed the order for the product and actively participated in the specification phase of the main functions of the product (i.e., backlog creation); and in the analysis phase of the product reviews (i.e., retrospective), helped the project manager to develop rapport and create a friendly, goal-oriented atmosphere in the project team.

The researchers used quantitative and qualitative indicators to analyze the success of implementing the presented blended learning model. The student participants completed the questionnaire anonymously. The questions covered the key peculiarities of the innovative approach to teaching the course and students' personal learning experiences. The survey participants were 20 out of 25 students (80%) of the experimental group. Based on the questionnaire responses about implementing the pedagogical experiment, we can highlight the positive results. They are the respondents' answers to the questions about the validity and efficacy of the innovative approaches to teaching, presented in Figs. 5, 6 and 7. The quality indicator of the group's success was 92%. The summary scores were broken down as follows: 72% of students received an 'excellent' grade, 20% received a 'good' one. The outcomes prove the students' positive attitude to using active teaching methods and justify implementing a wide range of learning activities.

On the other hand, one-half of the students (52% or 13 out of 25 persons) are actively involved in the study process based on a more conventional teaching style. The experimental results are in perfect agreement with the level of success determined by the meaningful use of the project approach and team members' responsibility for the quality of the project results. The latter allowed the students to raise their final grades since the project team members gained the same level of individual success. The identical learning outcomes were noted in another experimental group of master students in a different major course based on a similar teaching model (the experimental results and the model description are not discussed in the present paper).

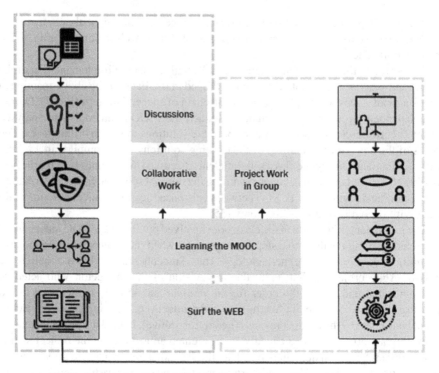

Fig. 7. Implementation the flipped class model into the project approach.

5 Conclusions

The proposed unified complex learning model has been created as a result of experimental testing the different blended learning models in SSU. The key feature of the proposed model is that it combines the classic approach in the classroom and digital educational approaches. It is effective in supporting and facilitating students' independent work with the material. The model is easily adapted to the teaching of different disciplines, of both professional and general orientation, taking into account their specific needs and characteristics. It is achieved due to the structural complexity of the unified learning model and to the distribution of educational load.

The combination of different types of learning activities to practice a curriculum component in one model creates a comfortable learning environment for mastering the material. The combination of classical and interactive learning methods personalizes education and provides opportunities of gaining knowledge to all categories of students without exception.

The model tested in this research focuses on enhancing students' independent work and increasing the level of responsibility of each student for successful completion of a collective task. Applying a project approach to performing collective tasks supports the development of digital and communication skills, which are essential for the success of the individual and the society, as well as the economy in general. Formation of the project team brings the project conditions as close as possible to the conditions of modern business functioning, preparing the adapted specialists who are capable to start solving professional tasks in the shortest possible time.

Integrating the debate-oriented group approach of a flipped class model with the project approach enhances traditional pedagogical technologies in developing more flexible, personalized self-paced learning. Lastly, a teacher can help students develop more complex analysis, evaluation, and synthesis skills in discussions and debates in the classroom.

The search for the optimal combination of learning technologies, of course, requires considerable time costs for the formation of methodological support and can take several iterations with a continuous process of implementing and evaluating new components. Consistent deep analysis of the discipline purpose and tasks for identifying all the learning components of the course, which is better to represent online, is required as well as a detailed analysis of available educational advanced technologies for selecting those that best meet students' needs.

Advance to the next level of the presented blended learning model usage is based on deepening the mechanisms for implementing digital educational technologies and searching for new teaching methods.

References

1. Kluzer, S., Priego, L. P., Gomez, S C.: DigComp into Action - Get inspired, make it happen. Publications Office of the European Union. https://publications.jrc.ec.europa.eu/repository/bitstream/JRC110624/dc_guide_may18.pdf. Accessed 15 Mar 2020
2. Cabinet of Ministers of Ukraine: Regulation No. 386-p, Strategy for the Development of the Information Society in Ukraine. https://zakon.rada.gov.ua/laws/show/386-2013-%D1%80. Accessed 17 Apr 2020
3. Brolpito, A.: Digital Skills and Competence, and Digital and Online Learning. ETF European Training Foundation, Turin (2018)
4. Law of Ukraine: No. 1556-VII, On Higher Education. https://zakon.rada.gov.ua/laws/show/1556-18. Accessed 21 Mar 2020
5. Gorbunova, L., Debych, M., Zinchenko, V.: Higher Education Internationalization in Ukraine: Guidelines. IHE NAESU of Ukraine, Kyiv (2016)
6. Ministry of Education and Science of Ukraine: Higher Education Reform Strategy. https://osvita.ua/doc/files/news/438/43883/HE_Reforms_Strategy_11_11_2014.pdf. Accessed 19 Jan 2020
7. Smith, B., Brame, C.: Blended and Online Learning. https://cft.vanderbilt.edu/guides-sub-pages/blended-and-online-learning/#research. Accessed 03 Jan 2020
8. Korotun, O.: Methodological bases of blended learning in the higher education. Inf. Technol. Educ. 3(28), 117–129 (2016)
9. Krasulia, A.: The convergence of technology, pedagogy, and language learning. In: Shudlo, S., Zabolotna, L. (eds.) IV International Scientific Conference "Implementation of European Standards into Ukrainian Educational Research" 2020, pp. 80–83. Trek-LTD, Drogobych (2020)
10. Krasulia, A., Saks, K.: Students' perceptions towards mobile learning in an English as a foreign language class. In: IEEE 20th International Conference on Advanced Learning Technologies Proceedings. https://ieeexplore.ieee.org/abstract/document/9155750. Accessed 18 Sep 2020

11. Romanovskyi, O.: Development Factors and Directions for Improving Distance Learning in Higher Education System of Ukraine. https://journal.iitta.gov.ua/index.php/itlt/issue/view/103. Accessed 20 Jan 2020
12. Castro, R.: Blended learning in higher education: trends and capabilities. Educ. Inf. Technol. **24**, 2523–2546 (2019)
13. Alammary, A., Sheard, J., Carbone, A.: Blended learning in higher education: three different design approaches. Australas. J. Educ. Technol. **30**(4), 440–454 (2014)
14. Mozelius, P., Hettiarachchi, E.: Critical factors for implementing blended learning in higher education. ICTE J. **6**(1), 4–18 (2017)
15. Teach Though staff: 12 of The Most Common Types of Blended Learning. https://www.teachthought.com/learning/12-types-of-blended-learning. Accessed 15 Nov 2019
16. Bonk, C., Graham, C., Cross, J., Moore, M.: The Handbook of Blended Learning: Global Perspectives, Local Designs. https://www.researchgate.net/publication/26872610_The_Handbook_of_Blended_Learning_Global_Perspectives_Local_Designs. Accessed 4 Mar 2020
17. Sagenmüller, I.: 6 types of flipped classroom to innovate in higher education. https://www.u-planner.com/en-us/blog/flipped-classroom-six-types. Accessed 16 Mar 2019
18. O'Flaherty, J., Phillips, C.: The use of flipped classrooms in higher education: a scoping review. https://www.sciencedirect.com/science/article/abs/pii/S1096751615000056. Accessed 15 Mar 2020
19. Wang, K., Zhu, C.: MOOC-based flipped learning in higher education: students' participation, experience and learning performance, https://educationaltechnologyjournal.springeropen.com/articles/10.1186/s41239-019-0163-0#citeas. Accessed 15 Mar 2020
20. Al Zahrani, A.M.: From passive to active: the impact of the flipped classroom through social learning platforms on higher education students' creative thinking. Br. J. Educ. Technol. **6**(46), 1133–1148 (2015)
21. Lapyhin, Y.: Active Learning Methods. Textbook and Workshop, Urait, Moscow (2015)
22. Buzan, T., Buzan, B.: Superthinking. Popurri, Minsk (2014)
23. Marchenko, A., Antypenko, V., Vashchenko, S., Fedotova, N., Chybiriak, Y.: Aspects of implementation the digital technologies into the educational process. In: IX International Scientific and Practical Conference "Information Control Systems and Technologies", pp. 73–75. Ekologiya, Odessa (2020)
24. Belbin, R.: Team Roles at Work. Elsevier, Oxford (2010)
25. Lopes, A.P., Soares, F.: Flipping a mathematics course, a blended learning approach. In: Proceedings of INTED2018 Conference 2018, pp. 3844–3853. Valencia, Spain (2018)

An Engineering Solution for a Correlation Between a Competences Framework and Learning Units in an Educational Platform

Rita Butkiene, Daina Gudoniene, and Evelina Staneviciene(⊠)

Kaunas University of Technology, Kaunas, Lithuania
{rita.butkiene,daina.gudoniene,evelina.staneviciene}@ktu.lt

Abstract. The paper presents research on the engineering solutions on how to connect the competences frameworks and the learning units (LU) in open courses, i.e. how the competences correlate with LU. The existing literature shows that there is a big challenge for educators on how to construct their courses in a logical way. The aim of the paper is to present the architecture of a logic matrix of the correlation between the LU and the competences framework and learning outcomes. The objectives are to present (1) a methodology of the research design, (2) the architecture of the engineering solution, and (3) the evaluation results.

Keywords: MOOCs · Online learning · Competences · Learning units

1 Introduction

We use a lot of different technologies and applications that change day after day. In nowadays education, educators need new skills and competences in the technological and pedagogical aspects, especially when it comes to the delivery processes of Massive open online courses (MOOCs). It is also important to know how to integrate existing open resources and open courses into the existing study programs. This means that the competences of teachers and trainers have to be constantly monitored and improved. This paper presents a conception of an innovative instructional approach for curriculum design, which is based on self-assessment. Adopting the approach will help teachers and trainers of higher education institutions (HEIs) to take responsibility for their professional growth. The approach proposes that the latter can be achieved by identifying the current state of their pedagogical skills related to the re-design and delivery of the MOOCs-based curricula at any stage.

Moreover, it suggests areas for improving certain pedagogical and technological skills. Both less and highly experienced educators can apply the proposed self-evaluation tool. Using the tool, educators with limited experience in MOOCs will get a first impression of the MOOCs instructional design techniques when answering predefined questions, whereas advanced educators will be enabled to determine specific areas for improving their skills. The paper discusses and proposes a conception that is based on

A. Lopata et al. (Eds.): ICIST 2021, CCIS 1486, pp. 279–290, 2021.
https://doi.org/10.1007/978-3-030-88304-1_22

an innovative instructional approach. Moreover, the paper explains how the aforementioned tool is connected to one specific training program and can be applied by different users. The innovativeness of the developed tool also lies in its interlinking with specific recommendations for improving educators' skills.

2   A Literature Review of the Existing Practices

Many authors (e.g., Teixeira et al. [12], Ramirez-Montoya et al. [10], Stracke [11], Oh et al. [9], Gordilio et al. [3]) identify that the quality of the massive open online courses design depends on the successful implementation of technology enhanced learning (TEL) which is directly related to the design of MOOCs and competences of the academic staff. Even though several studies identified a large set of criteria for the successful design of TEL systems in general, not all of them can be used in the MOOC context due to some unique features of MOOCs. Yousef et al. [6] suggested specific criteria to assure the design quality of MOOCs from both learners' and teachers' perspectives. In this case, the authors identified 74 criteria classified into the dimensions of pedagogy and technology. These dimensions are allocated into different categories, such as instructional design, assessment, user interface, video content, social tools, and learning analytics. From the pedagogical view, MOOCs allow teachers to explore new ways of teaching and learning with technology in blended ways (Tømte [13]).

Huang et al. [4] discuss that the course's difficulty negatively affects the relationship between course content and students' course attendance and positively affects the relationship between teacher subject knowledge and students' course attendance. Moreover, course difficulty mainly does not have an important effect on the interactivity between technology and the students' course attendance. Fidalgo-Blanco et al. [2] acknowledge that the highest dropout rate occurs after the first module and stabilizes to the end of the course and this is related to cooperation level increase. Xing [14] considers three different models of MOOC features and the extent to which they correlate with the dropout rate.

Kerr et al. [7] present a MOOC design mapping framework (MDMF). The authors discuss the importance of selecting and sequencing different learning activities that allow the users to create a learner-centered approach to online learning. Conole [1] presents a specific quality approach called the 7Cs of Learning Design framework, enabling the teachers to prepare more pedagogically informed design courses by effective use of new technologies. The framework contains the following actions performed by the learner: conceptualize, capture, communicate, collaborate, consider, combine, and consolidate.

In search of an effective design solution for developing MOOC courses, Ichimura & Suzuki [5], in their study, synthesized previous research and mapped the elements of MOOC design. Many different types of MOOCs have been discovered to reflect the unique intentions of course providers. The authors classified these types and identified a total of ten key features of the MOOC design.

Liyanagunawardena et al. [8] discuss that students who participate are usually highly educated and employed when it comes to massive open online courses. The authors also state that a greater interest can be seen in courses offered for people interested in social sciences and business.

Academic staff competences are very widely discussed in the European Framework for the Digital Competence of Educators (DigCompEdu), which is a scientifically sound framework describing what it means for educators to be digitally competent. It provides a general reference frame to support the development of educator-specific digital competences in Europe. DigCompEdu is directed towards educators at all levels of education (Fig. 1).

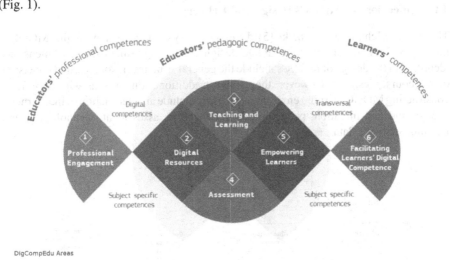

Fig. 1. DigCompEdu details 22 competences organised in six areas.

The European Framework for Digitally Competent Educational Organisations (DigCompOrg) is focused on promoting effective digital-age learning. The impact of digital technologies, content, and processes can be seen in all educational sectors (e.g. formal education and also informal and non-formal learning), affecting all aspects of the educational value chain (e.g. curricular reform, teaching and learning practices, assessment, as well as initial and continuing teacher professional development) and encompassing all educational actors (teachers, learners, and school leaders).

3 Methodology

The aim of the current research is to explore the factors that affect the effective MOOC design, competences necessary for the academic staff and the designers, and develop an engineering solution for implementing an educational platform. This study's target group consisted of respondents from higher education academic staff (professors, lecturers, etc.) and instructional designers (support staff). Thirteen respondents participated in the study.

The most important task for the focus groups invited is to allow us to collect information about the existing situation in their countries regarding the development of academic staff competences needed to work effectively on the design of open online courses. With a special emphasis on training that is available online as a massive open online course.

4   Results and Discussion

This section presents an engineering solution for the competences framework and course learning units correlation and the survey results.

4.1   Dimensions of MOOCs Design and Delivery

The authors Ichimura & Suzuki [5] developed a systematic review of the MOOCs, identifying ten key features of the MOOC design. According to them, the key dimensions identified in the design of MOOCs include the general structure, resources, and the vision of the course designer. However, they suggest additional dimensions with regards to constructing MOOC learning environments. They include an interrelation of the learner's background and intention, pedagogy, communication, assessment, technologies, and learning analytics data.

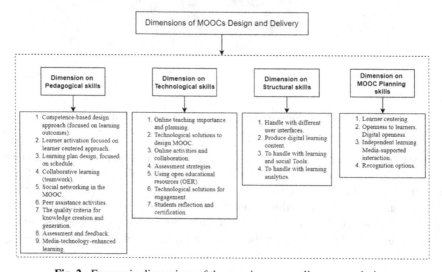

Fig. 2. Four main dimensions of the massive open online course design.

The model proposed here includes four main dimensions of MOOCs design, as exemplified in Fig. 2. The figure also shows the identified skills to be integrated into the assessment tool for teachers' competencies evaluation. Engineering solutions on how the competences framework will be integrated into the educational platform are shown in the section below.

4.2 An Engineering Solution for the Competences Framework and Course Learning Units Correlation

Competences framework in educational platform is directly related to learning results. However, learning units and learning outcomes also have direct relations in an educational platform. The authors of the present research suggest the competences framework that could also be designed not only on competences but also on the challenges as well if we are planning to use challenge-based learning methods in the study process (see Fig. 3).

Competences framework integration into educational platform assures a direct link between competences, learning units, and learning outcomes when we plan and develop an open online course.

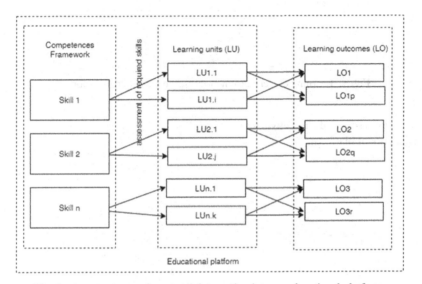

Fig. 3. A competences framework integration into an educational platform.

Also, the identification of skills in different competence areas is very important. A review of the existing literature shows that it is a big challenge for teachers to establish relations between competences, learning units, and learning outcomes. The assessment questions' data basis is also related to the units identified in the educational platform. The lifecycle of the learning objects in educational platforms is shown in Fig. 4. Objectives design should be directly related to the identified competences framework.

It is very important to assure the interoperability strategy of embedding the pre-existing tools into component assemblies, which requires a carefully thought-out interoperability strategy. Our approach needs to address these key challenges related to the coordination of different components of the educational platform (see Fig. 5):

1. competences design environment;
2. learning objects design environment;

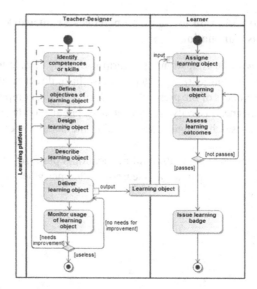

Fig. 4. Learning objects design processes in educational platforms.

3. learning passport design environment;
4. educational platform.

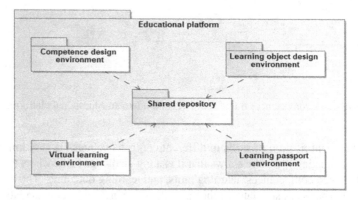

Fig. 5. The components of an unified modeling language (UML) diagram.

The UML diagram shows the relations between all the components of the educational platform, which helps assure the quality not only of the design process but of the delivery process as well.

5 Evaluation

The research was implemented with the aim to identify necessary focus group competences to work in the platform recommended by authors to develop a high quality online learning course based on technologies enhanced method.

In total, 13 respondents having the only background in courses design were invited to express their opinion. The respondents were asked to answer questions regarding which skills and knowledge are needed to design and deliver a massive open online course in the educational platform based on the Likert scale statements.

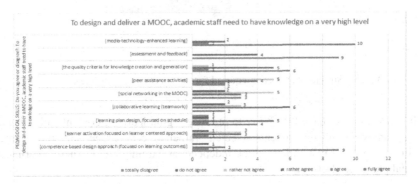

Fig. 6. Pedagogical skills needed for massive open online course design.

As shown in Fig. 6, 77% of respondents thought that a teacher-designer needs to have media-technology-enhanced learning knowledge on a very high level to design and deliver a MOOC. Knowledge of assessment, feedback, and competence-based design approach is also very important (69% of the respondents).

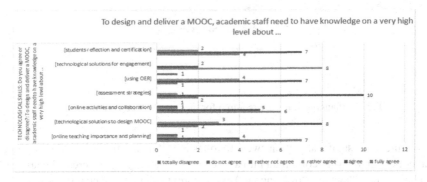

Fig. 7. Technological skills are required for the massive open online course.

According to the respondents, academic staff needs to have all technological skills (see Fig. 7). Only 15% of the respondents think that "online activities and collaboration" and "online teaching importance and planning" are not necessary to design the course.

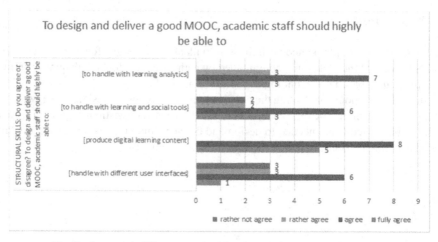

Fig. 8. Structural skills are required for the massive open online course.

It is necessary to have the ability to produce digital learning content and to handle learning analytics (all respondents selected "rather agree," "agree," or "fully agree") (see Fig. 8). 54% of respondents think independent learning and learner centering are essential planning skills (see Fig. 9).

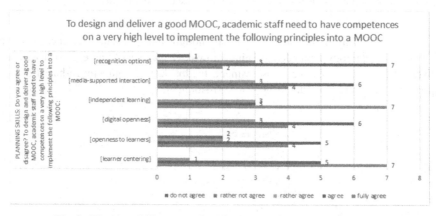

Fig. 9. Planning skills are required for the massive open online course.

For the purpose of analysis, answers for questions "totally disagree," "do not agree," "rather not agree" were combined into a category "do not agree," whereas the last three ("rather agree," "agree," "fully agree") were combined into a category "agree" (see Tables 1, 2).

78% of all respondents thought that teachers-designers pedagogical skills have to be on a high level. Out of the responses, respectively 93% thought that the technological, 90% - structural, and 96% - planning skills are necessary to design and deliver massive open online courses. (see Tables 1, 2).

Table 1. The need for pedagogical and technological skills.

PEDAGOGICAL SKILLS: Do you agree or disagree?:To design and deliver a MOOC, academic staff need to have knowledge on a very high level	Answers		TECHNOLOGICAL SKILLS: Do you agree or disagree?:To design and deliver a MOOC, academic staff need to have knowledge on a very high level about …	Answers	
	Agree	Do not agree		Agree	Do not agree
Competence-based design approach (focused on learning outcomes)	92%	8%	Online teaching importance and planning	92%	8%
Learner activation focused on learner centered approach	69%	31%	Technological solutions to design MOOC	100%	-
Learning plan design, focused on schedule	77%	23%	Online activities and collaboration	92%	8%
Collaborative learning (teamwork)	62%	38%	Assessment strategies	100%	-
Social networking in the MOOC	46%	54%	Using OER	92%	8%
Peer assistance activities	62%	38%	Technological solutions for engagement	77%	
The quality criteria for knowledge creation and generation	92%	8%	Students reflection and certification	100%	-
Assessment and feedback	100%	-			
Media-technology-enhanced learning	100%	-			

Table 2. The need for structural and planning skills.

STRUCTURAL SKILLS: Do you agree or disagree? To design and deliver a good MOOC, academic staff should highly be able to:	Answers		PLANNING SKILLS: Do you agree or disagree? To design and deliver a good MOOC, academic staff need to have competences on a very high level to implement the following principles into a MOOC:	Answers	
	Agree	Do not agree		Agree	Do not agree
Handle with different user interfaces	77%	23%	Learner centering	100%	-
Produce digital learning content	100%	-	Openness to learners	85%	15%
To handle with learning and social tools	85%	15%	Digital openness	100%	-
To handle with learning analytics	100%	-	Independent learning	100%	-
			Media-supported interaction	100%	-
			Recognition options	92%	8%

All of the respondents totally 100% stated that course design is directly related to the identified structural skills, namely, the ability to produce digital learning content and handle learning analytics as well as the competences to implement principles, such as learner centering, digital openness, independent learning, and media-supported interaction.

6 Practical Implementation

The competences model was implemented in the MOOC course. Course participants were able to self-assess their level of skills and competences and receive advice from the assessment model on how to improve certain competences (see Fig. 10).

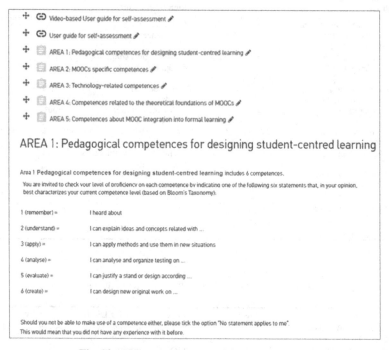

Fig. 10. The competences model implementation

Assessment procedures help to ensure the quality of the educational process and direct guidance on identified gaps related to the content of direct learning.

7 Conclusions

After conducting the study, the authors of the paper recommend the following:

(i)   to encourage the academic staff competences design in relation to technologies enhanced learning within educational organizations by progressively deepening their engagement with digital learning and pedagogy;

(ii) to enable academic staff to develop the integration technologies and effective use of digital learning technologies in education;

(iii) to assure the engineering solution on the educational platform by extending and relating with competences framework, by providing the users a full list of learning outcomes for completed massive open online courses.

Competencies framework should be integrated into the educational platform to get successful results of the academic staff competencies evaluation and direct suggestions for competences improvement.

Acknowledgement. The paper is developed in the frames of the Erasmus+ project "Curricular modernization by implementing MOOCs model" (MODE IT), project number 2019–1-DE01-KA203–005051.

References

1. Conole, G.: MOOCs as disruptive technologies: strategies for enhancing the learner experience and quality of MOOCs. RED, Revista de Educación a Distancia **39** (2013)
2. Fidalgo-Blanco, Á., Sein-Echaluce, M.L., García-Peñalvo, F.J.: From massive access to cooperation: lessons learned and proven results of a hybrid xMOOC/cMOOC pedagogical approach to MOOCs. Int. J. Educ. Technol. High. Educ. **13**(1), 1–13 (2016). https://doi.org/10.1186/s41239-016-0024-z
3. Gordillo, A., López-Pernas, S., Barra, E.: Effectiveness of MOOCs for teachers in safe ICT use training. Comunicar **27**(61), 98–107 (2019). https://doi.org/10.3916/C61-2019-09
4. Huang, L., Zhang, J., Liu, Y.: Antecedents of student MOOC revisit intention: moderation effect of course difficulty. Int. J. Inf. Manage. **37**(2), 84–91 (2017). https://doi.org/10.1016/j.ijinfomgt.2016.12.002
5. Ichimura, Y., Suzuki, K.: Dimensions of MOOCs for quality design: analysis and synthesis of literature. Int. J. **11**(1), 42–49 (2017)
6. Yousef, A.M.F., Chatti, M.A., Schroeder, U., Wosnitza, M.: What drives a successful MOOC? An empirical examination of criteria to assure design quality of MOOCs. In: 2014 IEEE 14th International Conference on Advanced Learning Technologies, pp. 44–48. IEEE (2014). https://doi.org/10.1109/ICALT.2014.23
7. Kerr, J.G., Dale, V.H.M., Gyurko, F.: Evaluation of a MOOC design mapping framework (MDMF): experiences of academics and learning technologists. Comput. Sci. **17**(1), 38–51 (2019)
8. Liyanagunawardena, T.R., Lundqvist, K.O., Williams, S.A.: Who are with Us: MOOC learners on a futurelearn course. Br. J. Edu. Technol. **46**(3), 557–569 (2015). https://doi.org/10.1111/bjet.12261
9. Oh, E.G., Chang, Y., Park, S.W.: Design review of MOOCs: application of e-learning design principles. J. Comput. High. Educ. **32**(3), 455–475 (2019). https://doi.org/10.1007/s12528-019-09243-w
10. Ramírez-Montoya, M.S., Mena, J., Rodríguez-Arroyo, J.A.: In-service teachers' self-perceptions of digital competence and OER use as determined by a xMOOC training course. Comput. Hum. Behav. **77**, 356–364 (2017). https://doi.org/10.1016/j.chb.2017.09.010
11. Stracke, C.M.: The quality of MOOCs: how to improve the design of open education and online courses for learners? In: Zaphiris, P., Ioannou, A. (eds.) LCT 2017. LNCS, vol. 10295, pp. 285–293. Springer, Cham (2017). https://doi.org/10.1007/978-3-319-58509-3_23
12. Teixeira, A., Garcia-Cabot, A., Garcia-Lopez, E., Mota, J., De-Marcos, L.: A new competence-based approach for personalizing MOOCs in a mobile collaborative and networked environment. RIED. Revista Iberoamericana de Educación a Distancia **19**(1), 143–160 (2015). https://doi.org/10.5944/ried.19.1.14578

13. Tømte, C.E.: MOOCs in teacher education: institutional and pedagogical change? Eur. J. Teach. Educ. **42**(1), 65–81 (2019). https://doi.org/10.1080/02619768.2018.1529752
14. Xing, W.: Exploring the influences of MOOC design features on student performance and persistence. Distance Educ. **40**(1), 98–113 (2018). https://doi.org/10.1080/01587919.2018.1553560

Ingame Design Framework

Daina Gudoniene[1][(✉)], Tomas Blazauskas[1], Vitalija Keršienė[1],
and Valentina Zangrando[2]

[1] Kaunas University of Technology, Kaunas, Lithuania
{daina.gudoniene,tomas.blazauskas,vitalija.kersiene}@ktu.lt
[2] University of Salamanca, Salamanca, Spain
vzangra@usal.es

Abstract. The paper presents the framework on the educational online game design for social inclusion. Authors are analysing the pedagogical approach and technological solutions for the game design and planning educational online games. The focus is placed on the social and civic skills development and values along with associated knowledge to be gained by the players during the gameplay. We are suggesting pedagogical aspects framework for the game planning in the INGAME project and technological framework for game design.

Keywords: Online game · Education · Technological framework · Social inclusion · Civic skills

1 Introduction

Nowadays learners have an opportunity to gain deeper skills by playing games in the educational process. Games have been recognized as a type of media that can engage students in experiential educational experiences [1].

Moreover, games are popular among younger generations and technology has always been part of their lives, therefore the use of gamification within education is ideal. Players are spending many hours developing their problem-solving skills in games. Gamification has a great potential to motivate students, consequently making school more attractive. However, it is important to note that although the use of gamification in education comes with many benefits, it is necessary to balance this alongside traditional teaching methods [2]. Many authors [3–5] declare that game thinking and motivational design have a positive influence on intrinsic motivation, by providing a meaningful and engaging experience, to promote an internal desire to play.

Digital Taxonomy [11] was created to help educators understand how to use technology and digital resources for improving learning experiences and outcomes. Its application suggested by Churches includes using digital tools in the educational process, in order to improve the process, in some cases, without even additional costs [11]. Further-

© Springer Nature Switzerland AG 2021
A. Lopata et al. (Eds.): ICIST 2021, CCIS 1486, pp. 291–300, 2021.
https://doi.org/10.1007/978-3-030-88304-1_23

more, ICT-enhanced activities can also be adapted to different learning styles and, as a set of digital activities, a didactic database for both teachers and students may be created [12].

In recent years, the implementation of gamification in the field of education proved to be a success. It has also been shown that gamification can be effective at all levels of education, from elementary school to university. Students' motivation, commitment, and academic achievement were all improved as a result of using gamified learning, according to the systematic analysis [13]. Gamification of the educational process has multiple uses, as it is commonly applied to improve achievements at school but may also be used with teaching methodologies such as project-based learning or in online learning environments [13].

As it was discussed by Parra-González et al., presently, as a result of technological advancements, games have undergone a digital transformation, allowing users to learn content ranging from conventional games to cutting-edge video games with large digital loads. Gamification may be used at various stages of education, showing its value at an early age, in adolescence, and even in university contexts. All of this leads to the conclusion that ICTs play an important role in gamification because they allow the development of various training scenarios through online games, and they can generate learning in any context, whether formal, non-formal, or informal, due to their ubiquity [14].

As it was identified by Spieler and Slany (2018) the game design elements can be broken into three subcategories: (1) gaming-world (e.g., level design, theme, genres, like adventure, action, puzzle, simulation, strategy); (2) game-structure (the rules of the game and the goal, MDAs); (3) game-play (e.g., the story, the player and their actions, strategies, and motives) [6].

Meanwhile, Zou et al. (2018) are focusing on the assessment dimension in the educational online game: (1) Performance (commonly used to judge the learning outcomes directly, including measures like task completion time, test scores, reaction time, interaction time, and accuracy of interaction); (2) Usability (the ease of use and learnability of a tool, device or an application); (3) Cognitive states (one of the crucial factors determining whether the learning is successful. Cognitive load, engagement, attention are widely used cognitive states in learning); (4) Affective states (In learning, affective processes are intertwined with cognitive processes); (5) Social interaction (Social interaction refers to the learner's interactions with peers and teachers) [7].

According to the literature review, we can identify 6 main areas of the game design and implementation in total, i.e. (1) Interface, (2) Challenges, (3) Time penalties, (4) Leader - board, (5) Music and (6) Feedback or reflection.

2   Methodology

The educational scope is one of the most important aspects if we are planning an educational online game. The authors focus is on the social and civic skills development , values along with associated knowledge to be gained by the players during gameplay. Required skills for players to interact with the game and the skills and knowledge will gain via interaction and gameplay, also see relevant learning outcomes – which of the game activities help to reach the learning outcomes.

The narrative and storyline - which relates to the background story of the game – the 'world' of the game, including the description of the characters and how they interact, the settings, the action fields, plot points, ethical dilemmas, the resolution of conflicts at the end of the game and also design the problems of the game. Design one or two scenarios and possible solutions.

The game genre - relates to the genre category of the game (puzzle/adventure/narrative game in our case) as well as to the single-player, the NPC and their interaction (dialogue, conflict, etc.). What are the motivations for action and types of actions that the player can take, for how long and what will the outcome be?

The experience of the players relates to the emotions that players develop during the gameplay. Moreover, it is important to consider the following aspects. How music or narration will be used? Can learners get any feedback at a different level? How maps or menus and score tables will be used? Is it planned that learning results to be provided?

All these educational aspects and technological solutions are identified in the paper.

3 Results and Discussion

This section presents a technological discussion on educational game implementation. The result authors are describing in the paper is based on the INGAME project results related to social inclusion (https://ingame.erasmus.site). The component of Visual and Audio Adequacy will refer to what the INGAME content under development actually looks like. Areas of concern include the interconnection of images, animations, text and music, and the type and format of content communicated to the user.

However, the technological aspect is not the only one when speaking about educational game design. The pedagogical implementation is also very important by possibly choosing a useful taxonomy [11] for the assessment assurance in the online game (see Fig. 1).

Technological advances, availability of digital tools, can help to improve student skills eventually leading to the emergence of taxonomy. However, pedagogical aspects are important in planning achieving learning outcomes.

The next step is choosing technologies and implementation. The specifications and guidelines for audiovisual content can be divided into the following parts: audio-related guidelines (background music, sound effects, audio dialogues), video-related guidelines (graphics, models), and general technical guidelines for game creation (execution environments, game engines, and development environments).

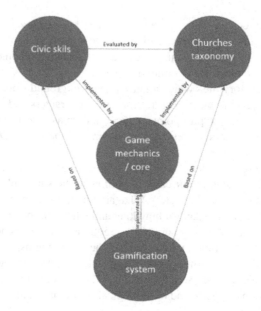

Fig. 1. The pedagogical aspects for the game of INGAME project.

All the above-mentioned specifications are connected to a single game mechanics model (Fig. 2).

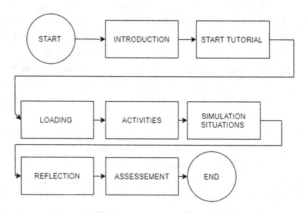

Fig. 2. Game mechanics.

INGAME ideas for civic engagement and social inclusion are focusing on the steps for game implementation (Fig. 3).

The technological framework includes a full learner journey from the beginning to the assessment by identifying the achieved learning outcomes.

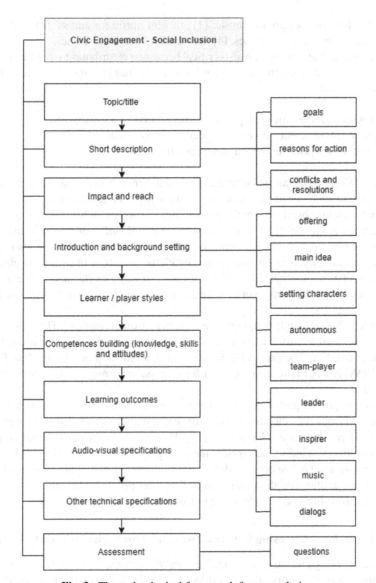

Fig. 3. The technological framework for game design.

3.1 Audiovisual and Other Technical Solutions for Educational Game Design

The following are audiovisual qualities that enhance the fulfilment of Action Fields. The right music is crucial in the game. We should define what the music will achieve. Music may perform several different functions. The genre and mood of the game have to be clearly defined. This is an important step, as it sets the tone and creates the ambience of the video game.

Possible type of background music: (1) ambient music for games, (2) battle music for games, (3) fast music for games, (4) instrumental music for games.

Moreover, in video games, music is critical because it contributes to the player's sense of immersion as one of its functions. Munday distinguishes [15] three main functions of video game music:

1. Environmental: how music supports the perception of a gameworld.
2. Immersion: how music supports the player's involvement in the game.
3. Diegetic: how music supports a game narrative.

Meanwhile, Peerdeman [16] identifies several different uses of sound effects, achieving preferred results, one of the main uses being to *attract attention*, for example, when interacting with an object, like picking up an item. Another audio feature that is often used in games is the ability of sound to *evoke an emotional response* by using certain sound effect when the player completes or fails a certain task. Audio can also be used to create a certain *ambience or suggestion* by choosing a type of music suitable for a particular scene or situation. The ability of audio to *enhance the structure* and *add a sense of location* in the game world is the final attribute on this list, helping the player with the orientation.

From a technical standpoint, there are a variety of sound formats. The music can be considered of good quality if it is encoded using a sampling frequency of 96 kHz (16bit) or 192 kHz at 24bit. The preferable formats for downloading are the lossless formats such as WAV, AIFF, FLAC. On the other hand, popular formats such as MP3 or AAC are sufficient.

Another important part of the game is the dialogue. Dialogues in video games should be carefully designed as they help to identify with characters and also written in a convincing style for the intended audience [18]. However, an emphasis should be put on the collaboration and individual work of the protagonist. Churches [11] even claims that 'Collaboration is not a 21st century skill, it is a 21st century essential'. UNESCO's publication [17] identifies collaboration as one of the four pillars of education: (1) learning to know; (2) learning to do; (3) learning to live together; (4) earning to be.

3.2 Video-Related Choosing Between Two- and Three-Dimensional Graphics

Two-dimensional games use flat graphics, called sprites. The sprites do not have three-dimensional geometry, although three-dimensional models might be used before converting them to sprites. These sprites are drawn to the screen as flat images.

Three-dimensional games are created by using objects with three-dimensional geometry. Besides geometry, the materials and textures are used to make geometry appear as solid environments, characters and objects that make up the game world.

Some two-dimensional games use three-dimensional geometry for the environment and characters but restrict the gameplay to two dimensions. Sometimes, the games that follow this approach are called the "2.5D games". In this case, the three-dimensional effect is used to enrich visual appearance.

When choosing what kind of a game should be created, it is necessary to consider the following criteria: (1) the team competencies, (2) the game development pipelines, (3) the animation, (4) the volume of data, (5) technical limitations, (6) the game performance, (7) the game level creation, (8) the game usability (9) the chosen devices, platforms, and execution environments will impose specific technical requirements (Fig. 4).

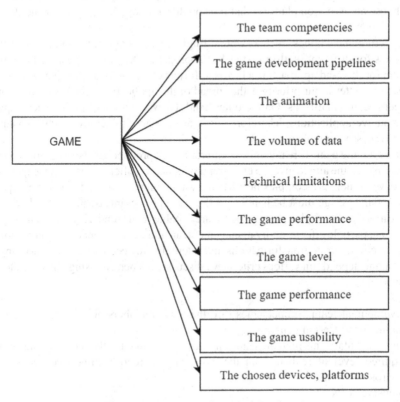

Fig. 4. Requirements for game planning.

The requirements for game implementation should be discussed in the online game planning process.

3.3 General Technical Requirements

Nowadays, a game can run on desktop computers, consoles, laptops, tablets, smartphones, TVs, smartwatches. Each group of these devices differs by a big margin in computing power. For example, smartphones have a hundred times less computing power in comparison to desktop computers. Because of the computer power, it is not possible to create such immersive environments for mobile devices. Therefore it is necessary to identify the target group and identify the preferences of the target group. Other factors also impact the choice. For example, if we wish that the game would be played during the breaks or travels - we would prefer to use mobile devices.

Moreover, the chosen devices influence the platforms. Some devices impose a specific platform (for example, Android, iOS, or Windows solutions), but there might be cross-platform solutions as well. There are two approaches that allow the creation of games for different platforms:

1. Choose an engine that is able to create native applications for different platforms.
2. Choose an execution platform that runs on different operating systems and devices.

Modern game engines, such as Unreal Engine, Unity engine, Godot, allow packaging games for different platforms (the 1-st approach). The most widespread execution platform for the 2-nd approach is a browser. It runs on virtually any device. The second approach is better if our priority is the spread of the application because we don't need to target specific platforms. On the other hand, browsers do not provide such capabilities as native applications. Therefore - it is not possible to achieve such realism and immersiveness using this approach.

However, the games are not only an entertainment product but also a complex technical system with the aim to give the end-user a satisfactory, often entertaining, experience, game development is a complex task where system engineering and creative competencies in art and design must be handled in the same project infrastructure [8–10]. Video Game Engines are complex pieces of software capable of 3D rendering, high-end physics processing, particle effects, entity management, artificial intelligence, UI, player control and interaction, terrain transformations and internal game economies [8]. Choosing the game engine depends on various criteria we discussed. When choosing one needs to take into account:

1. development team competencies (are the team members able to use the specific engine?) and learning curve;
2. supported platforms (can the game engine export game for the required platforms?);
3. required level of realism (can the game engine render immersive and realistic environments?);
4. licensing costs.

There might be many more factors considered when there is more information available about the game to be created. In this section, we will overview 3 popular choices.

Unreal Engine. This is a popular game engine created by the Epic company. This game engine is able to produce visuals and interactions required for AAA games. Such a popular game as Fortnite was created using this engine. The Unreal Engine supports many different platforms, but the support for browsers is discontinued; therefore, the development team should not choose this engine if the target platform is a browser. The licensing model is friendly – developers are free to use this engine until they earn a specified amount of money. The learning curve is steep as it is necessary to learn the internal structure of the game engine and the specific pipeline.

Unity Engine. This is also a popular game engine created by the Unity Technologies company. This game engine is able to produce quite good visuals and interactions, but there are limitations. The Unreal Engine is better in this regard. Such popular games as Tarkov, Hearthstone, Gwent, Wasteland were created using this engine. The Unity Engine supports many different platforms, as well as supports export for browsers. So, the development team could choose this engine if the target platform is a browser. The licensing model is friendly as well, developers are free to use this engine until they earn a specified amount of money. It is easier to learn this engine when compared to Unreal Engine.

Godot. Godot is an alternative to more sophisticated game engines such as Unreal and Unity engines. You can not achieve such good visuals and interactions as one can using mentioned engines, but it is easier to learn and to use, and it creates smaller execution files. It also supports export for browsers. Godot is a good choice if the priority is to create a simpler game dedicated to browser execution platforms.

4   Conclusions and Recommendations for Game Design

When choosing what kind of a game it is needed to create, it is necessary to consider the following criteria:

1. The team competencies. Creating two-dimensional games is easier because the math behind 3D games is far more complex. The programmers need to know effective 3D data structures. The game engines that support 3D games are more sophisticated and the learning curve is steep.
2. The game development pipelines. It's about - how the game assets are being created and integrated into the system. Three-dimensional games usually have more complex pipelines, and game engines require the use of specific pipelines.
3. The animation. Animation in two dimensions is just a compilation of flat graphics frames. When creating a three-dimensional animation one needs to deal with separate animation assets, bones, skinning, etc. On the other hand, sometimes it is easier to acquire required animations as the model contains all necessary information in contrast to 2D pictures.
4. The volume of data. If the amount of data might be a problem (for example - games for mobile), one needs to keep in mind that three-dimensional games usually contain a lot more resources.
5. Technical limitations. One needs to keep in mind various restrictions imposed by target devices, platforms, and game engines used.
6. The game performance. There are game performance requirements imposed by the market, device makers of publishing stores. Specific platforms and devices might severely limit the choice. If the game is dedicated to VR devices - strict performance requirements are imposed by publishing platforms.
7. The game usability. When creating 3D (or even - 2.5D) games, the game creators have to deal with camera tracking. It is a sophisticated task to implement intuitive control of a character in a three-dimensional world. Some users that didn't play 3D games before might struggle to learn the navigation.

The given list of criteria indicates that it is harder to create a 3D game. On the other hand, 3D games increase impressiveness, realism, versatility. Therefore the choice should be based on both - the aim of the game and the existing possibilities. The chosen devices, platforms, and execution environments impose specific technical requirements.

Acknowledgements. The paper is developed in the frames of project INGAME – Gaming for Social Inclusion and Civic Participation – A holistic approach for a cultural shift in education and policy Erasmus+ project number: 612166-EPP-1–2019-1-ES-EPPKA3-IPI-SOC-IN.

References

1. Castronovo, F., et al.: Design and development of a virtual reality educational game for architectural and construction reviews. In: ASEE Annual Conference and Exposition, June 2019
2. Bryan, S.J., Campbell, A., Mangina, E.: Scenic spheres-an AR/VR educational game. In: 2018 IEEE Games, Entertainment, Media Conference (GEM), pp. 1–9. IEEE, August 2018
3. Groh, F.: Gamification: state of the art definition and utilization. In: Proceedings of the 4th Seminar on Research Trends in Media Informatics, pp. 39–46 (2012)
4. Nicholson, S.: A user-centered theoretical framework for meaningful gamification. In: Games+Learning+Society 8.0, Madison, WI, June 2012
5. Ryan, R.M., Deci, E.L.: Intrinsic and extrinsic motivations: classic definitions and new directions. Contemp. Educ. Psychol. **25**(1), 54–67 (2000). https://doi.org/10.1006/ceps.1999.1020
6. Spieler, B., Slany, W.: Game development-based learning experience: Gender differences in game design (2018). arXiv preprint: arXiv:1805.04457
7. Zhou, Y., Tao, X., Zhu, Z., Wang, Z.: Learning in doing: a model of design and assessment for using new interaction in educational game. In: Zaphiris, P., Ioannou, A. (eds.) Learning and Collaboration Technologies. Learning and Teaching, pp. 225–236. Springer International Publishing, Cham (2018). https://doi.org/10.1007/978-3-319-91152-6_18
8. Toftedahl, M., Engström, H.: A taxonomy of game engines and the tools that drive the industry. In: DiGRA 2019, The 12th Digital Games Research Association Conference, Kyoto, Japan, August, 6–10, 2019. Digital Games Research Association (DiGRA) (2019)
9. Geisler, B.J., Kavage, S.L.: Aspect weaving for multiple video game engines using composition specifications. In: ENASE, pp. 454–462 (2020)
10. Maskeliūnas, R., Kulikajevas, A., Blažauskas, T., Damaševičius, R., Swacha, J.: An interactive serious mobile game for supporting the learning of programming in javascript in the context of eco-friendly city management. Computers **9**(4), 102 (2020)
11. Churches, A.: Bloom's digital taxonomy, pp. 1–44 (2008). http://burtonslifelearning.pbworks.com/f/BloomDigitalTaxonomy2001.pdf
12. Netolicka, J., Simonova, I.: SAMR model and bloom's digital taxonomy applied in blended learning/teaching of general English and ESP. In: 2017 International Symposium on Educational Technology (ISET), pp. 277–281. IEEE, June 2017
13. Manzano-León, A., et al.: Between level up and game over: a systematic literature review of gamification in education. Sustainability **13**(4), 2247 (2021)
14. Parra-González, M.E., López Belmonte, J., Segura-Robles, A., Fuentes Cabrera, A.: Active and emerging methodologies for ubiquitous education: potentials of flipped learning and gamification. Sustainability **12**(2), 602 (2020)
15. Munday, R.: Music in video games. In: Sexton, J. (ed.) Music, Sound and Multimedia: From the Live To The Virtual, pp. 51–67. Edinburgh University Press (2007). https://doi.org/10.3366/edinburgh/9780748625338.003.0004
16. Peerdeman, P.: Sound and Music in Games. VrijeUniversiteit, Amsterdam (2010)
17. Tawil, S., Cougoureux, M.: Revisiting Learning: The Treasure Within–N 4–Assessing the impact of the 1996 'Delors Report'. UNESCO (2013)
18. Igartua, J.J., Vega Casanova, J.: Identification with characters, elaboration, and counterarguing in entertainment-education interventions through audiovisual fiction. J. Health Commun. **21**(3), 293–300 (2016)

Initial Usability Evaluation of the DigiCulture Courses on UniCampus

Silviu Vert[✉] , Oana Rotaru , Daniela Stoica , and Diana Andone

Politehnica University of Timisoara, Timisoara, Romania
{silviu.vert,diana.andone}@upt.ro, {oana.rotaru,
daniela.stoica}@student.upt.ro

Abstract. We live in a fast-changing world, where we often have the feeling that we must keep ourselves studying repeatedly. A helpful solution to this human need can be the existence of MOOCs (Massive Open Online Courses), which offer a large variety of courses that are designed to be accessible by anyone, from any location. Such courses are offered through the Erasmus + Digital Culture (DigiCulture) project, which aims to create a sustainable and efficient educational program dedicated to adult learners with low digital skills and low-qualified adults involved in the creative industries sector from Romania, Italy, Austria, Denmark, Lithuania, UK, and Ireland. The multilingual online courses are hosted on the UniCampus platform, which is the first MOOC platform in Romania open to all universities. In this paper, we present the initial usability evaluation of the DigiCulture courses, realized as a capstone project within the Multimedia Technologies master's degree program at the Politehnica University of Timişoara (Romania). We report on its main findings and formulate some recommendations for improving the usability of the platform.

Keywords: Human computer interaction · Usability evaluation · User experience · User testing · MOOC

1 Introduction

We live in a fast-changing world in which we need to keep ourselves updated in many knowledge domains. One of the advantageous ways of expanding our knowledge is through Massive Open Online Courses (MOOCs).

A MOOC is defined as being an online course, addressed to an unlimited number of participants, sustaining an open education.

According to [1], an extended definition of a MOOC includes the following aspects: an online course that doesn't need physical presence; an available and accessible course for everyone, from anywhere; the course is self-directed, self-paced or time limited, having a start and an end date; it consists of video lectures and/or readings, examinations in the form of assignments, exams, experiments; it supports interactivity between the participants and the tutors through online forums or other social media platforms; its content meets high academic standards; and it supports the creation of educational communities.

© Springer Nature Switzerland AG 2021
A. Lopata et al. (Eds.): ICIST 2021, CCIS 1486, pp. 301–311, 2021.
https://doi.org/10.1007/978-3-030-88304-1_24

An important requirement when it comes to MOOCs is the level of usability offered to the people attending the courses. A high level of usability can be accomplished after several usability evaluations on the product, in this case, on the MOOC. According to [2], the usability evaluation methods are procedures composed of well-defined series of activities, meant to collect the information regarding the interaction between the final user and the digital product, in order to identify if the final aim of the product is reached by the end users.

The term usability is defined in the context of Human Computer Interaction as a "quality attribute that assesses how easy user interfaces are to use" [3]. In the context of MOOCs and LMSs (Learning Management Systems), usability defines the measure in which students can do the proposed tasks with efficiency, effectiveness, and satisfaction [4].

When it comes to usability evaluation methods, an important aspect is also the classification of them. One of the most accepted classification represents the classification of Nielsen [5] and Holzinger [6]. This classification splits the evaluation methods in two categories: usability inspection methods and usability testing methods. The main difference between these two consists of the fact that the usability inspection methods involve expert's opinion in the evaluation and the usability testing methods involve possible users of the evaluated product.

According to [7], the most famous usability inspection methods are the heuristic evaluation and the cognitive evaluation. On the other hand, usability testing methods are the ones that involve future users and some of the most used methods are the focus group and the survey.

In this paper, we will present the usability evaluation of the DigiCulture online courses and describe the main findings of the research.

The Erasmus+ DigiCulture project aims to create a sustainable and efficient educational program dedicated to adult learners with low digital skills and low-qualified adults involved in the creative industries sector from Romania, Italy, Austria, Denmark, Lithuania, UK, and Ireland. The project is developed by a partnership between Politehnica University of Timisoara, Aalborg University, Graz University, Dublin City University, Roma Tre University, Interart TRIADE Foundation, and National Association of Distance Education [8].

The evaluated courses are hosted on the UniCampus platform, a project developed by the e-Learning Center of the Politehnica University of Timisoara. It is the first Romanian MOOC, open, available, and accessible to anyone. UniCampus is also open for other Romanian universities wishing to sustain an open online education [9].

Due to COVID-19 restrictions, the usability evaluation of the DigiCulture courses was organized entirely remotely. Research shows no differences between (a) synchronous remote testing and lab-based usability testing under favorable operational conditions, which was the case for the UniCampus platform [10].

The usability evaluation methods, performed both on the website and the mobile application of the UniCampus platform, consist of: the observation session method, the focus group, the error testing, and the questionnaire method.

2   Related Work

Despite MOOCs being in the mainstream for several years now – New York Times declared 2012 "The Year of the MOOC" [11] – the depth of knowledge in the areas of user experience and usability of MOOCs is still shallow.

In [1], the authors develop a list of usability guidelines in the form of an adaptable usability checklist for evaluating the user interface of MOOCs. Their research showed that such a checklist should be personalized for each context of use of a MOOC (of which there are many).

In [12], the authors propose a methodology for assessing user satisfaction of MOOCs on the basis of questionnaires UMUX Lite, SUS, Testbirds Company's approach, and the ISO standards. They test the methodology on two MOOC platforms, namely Coursera and Open Education (Russia).

Another research with a focus on the comparative side of the usability evaluation of MOOCs is described in [13]. The paper's methodology combined user testing and questionnaires and involved 31 participants who evaluated edX, Coursera and Udacity.

In [14], the authors of this paper have done a similar usability evaluation, this time on the Open Virtual Mobility Learning Hub, an innovative multilingual ICT-based environment with a focus on virtual mobility MOOCs. The usability evaluation was spread over 8 months, involved 139 participants, and used a mix of 5 usability testing methods.

3   Evaluation of the Digiculture Courses

3.1   Methodology

For this paper, we identified 2 main research questions:

Q1. How is the integration of the DigiCulture courses on the UniCampus platform?
Q2. What is the students' experience of the first implementation of the DigiCulture MOOCs?

To be able to answer these questions, we performed a usability evaluation of the DigiCulture MOOCs as part of the Interactivity and Usability class of the Multimedia Technologies master's degree program at the Politehnica University of Timisoara (Romania). 26 students of this class were involved in the evaluation, some as facilitators and observers, others as participants, all under the supervision of their tutors (the authors of this paper). The students, 23–25 years old, have good IT skills and use the Internet and mobile applications in extensive ways.

The DigiCulture aims to create MOOCs on 13 domains relevant for IT skills in creative industries, namely 1. The Internet, World Wide Web, and introduction to the digital world, 2. Digital Content & Publishing, 3. Data Protection and Open Licenses, 4. Digital Curation - Digital Libraries and Museums 5. Digital Safety, Security and Ethics, 6. Digital Storytelling, 7. Digital Audiences, Digital Analytics, 8. Social Media for Culture, 9. Augmented and Virtual Reality, 10. Mobile Apps and Mobile User Experience, 11. Digital Management in Culture, 12. Digital Communication & Presentations and 13. Online and Mobile Digital Media Tools.

Only 8 MOOCs out of these 13 have been evaluated, since the other 5 had insufficient content at the time the research was conducted, to be a valid target for usability testing.

During a class at the end of May, the students were divided in 3 groups in Zoom Breakout Rooms: the first group evaluated MOOC no 5 on the web platform using the user observation method, the second group evaluated MOOC no 9 in the mobile app also using the user observation method, while the third group evaluated MOOCs no 4, 6, 8, 10, 11 and 13 using the error testing method on both platforms (web and mobile). After all the groups were finished, the whole class participated in a focus group session. Some smaller usability tests were left for the following days.

In the following sections, we describe each of the usability testing methods, separately for web and mobile, for the reader to understand the methodology more easily. The outcomes, i.e., usability issues, are described in greater detail in Sect. 4.

3.2   Evaluation of the DigiCulture Courses on the Web Platform

The evaluation of the DigiCulture web courses was done on the UniCampus[1] platform (Fig. 1).

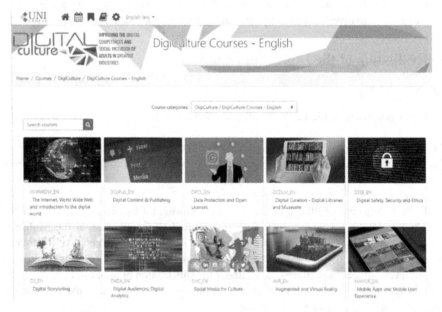

Fig. 1. Homepage of the Digiculture platform on Unicampus

The User Observation Session. For this evaluation method, a group of 7 students were organized on different roles, 1 student being the moderator, 2 the observers and 4 the actual participants in the study.

---

[1] http://unicampus.ro/digiculture.

The user testing began with the briefing of the participants and with a prequestionnaire, which included some context related questions about the users.

The tested MOOC was no 5, titled "Digital Safety, Security and Ethics", and the participants had to carry out 9 tasks. The participants were required to perform tasks such as: creating a user account on the platform; finding some specific topic in the course; identifying the learner's progress; sending a question to the tutor of the course; or answering a questionnaire in the course.

6 out of 9 tasks were successfully completed by all the participants. In general, they encountered issues while trying to find out what the courses are about and what their current progress was inside a course.

The Questionnaire Method. For this usability evaluation method, the students used a standardized questionnaire, SUS (System Usability Scale), a well-known questionnaire for its replicability and ease of use [15]. Also, according to [16], the students opted for this type of questionnaire for the fact that it's a short questionnaire and it's easier to be filled by the participants, rather than a longer questionnaire which can be overwhelming for them. Also, they chose SUS for its balance between the positive and negative questions, which brings more objectiveness to the results.

The survey was filled online by 15 participants, after casually navigating on the DigiCulture courses on the UniCampus website. Using the SUS methodology, we derived the total score of the platform, which is 73. In adjective rating scale (*Worst Imaginable – Awful – Poor – OK – Good – Excellent – Best Imaginable*), a SUS score of 73 equals to *Good* [17].

In addition to SUS, the participants were able to leave written remarks, which were mainly related to issues in website navigation and information finding.

Error Testing Method. For this usability evaluation method, several students received the task to enroll in and finish a course in order to observe if there are any problems or errors by the time of their progress. They wrote down all the issues that they encountered in a structured manner, so we were able to properly analyze the results.

Two courses were evaluated in this manner: "digital Curation – Digital Library and Museums" and "Digital Storytelling in Creative Industries". This time, because of the nature of this evaluation, the participants' remarks were related to issues with the learning content itself, such as missing links or faulty display of images and videos.

3.3 Evaluation of the DigiCulture Courses on the Mobile Application

For the mobile application testing, the authors used the following testing methods: User Observation Session, Error testing method and Focus group. All the sessions were organized remotely using Zoom, on the Unicampus mobile platform (Fig. 2) that is available both on Android[2] and iOS[3].

---

[2] https://play.google.com/store/apps/details?id=ro.upt.unicampus.

[3] https://apps.apple.com/us/app/unicampus/id1397170089.

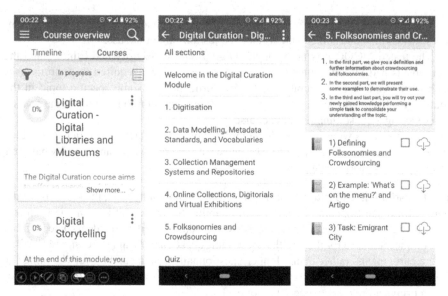

Fig. 2. Homepage of the DigiCulture platform on the UniCampus Android app

User Observation Session. The user observation method was organized with 3 student-participants. They had to complete tasks such as creating an account within the mobile application, logging in, accessing the files and the Digiculture courses in Romanian language, opening the inbox and sending a message to a contact in the friends list. Also, they had to change the language from the settings menu.

After the session ended, the students completed a post questionnaire evaluating the whole experience they had while using the DigiCulture mobile application.

The most important remarks were related to difficulties in creating a new account on the learning platform through the mobile app.

Error Testing Method. The methodology here was the same as for the web platform, but the participants reviewed only the "digital management in culture" course in the mobile app. The encountered issues were related to a faulty display of some learning elements, such as quizzes and videos, in the mobile app.

Focus Group. For the focus group, 20 students were asked to walk through some of the digiculture courses using the mobile application but also the website. We acted as moderators of the discussion and asked questions to direct the conversation to specific aspects of the platform and get out as many remarks as possible from the participants.

This method allowed us to gather more in-depth insights regarding what the participants enjoyed and what they found problematic. Reported issues were diverse, both related to the platform structure and navigation and to the learning content itself.

The issues reported during the focus group, but also through the other evaluation methods, will be detailed in the following section.

4 Results and Recommendations

Several usability problems were derived after applying all these usability evaluation methods. Severity ratings were used to prioritize the issues that affect most the user experience.

According to Jakob Nielsen [18], there are three factors that should be taken into consideration when analyzing a usability problem: frequency ("is it common or rare?"), impact ("will it be easy or difficult for the users to overcome?") and persistence ("is it a one-time problem that users can overcome once they know about it or will users repeatedly be bothered by the problem?").

Jakob Nielsen also proposed a four-step scale to rate the severity of usability problems, as it follows [18]:

0 = The problem is not a usability issue.

1 = "Cosmetic problem only": it does not have to be fixed unless extra time is available on project.

2 = "Minor usability problem": as the issue is not severe it should be solved only after major problems are solved.

3 = "Major usability problem": fixing this kind of issue should be a high priority because it affects the user experience.

4 = "Usability catastrophe": the platform should not be released until this kind of issue is resolved.

In Table 1, we present the severity rating for every major usability problem that was encountered and some recommendations to overcome each problem.

Table 1. Discovered usability problems, assigned severity ratings, and issued recommendations.

Usability problem	Severity rating	Recommendation
The "enroll in this course" button is hard to find. Test participants reported that it is way too small and looks more like ordinary text	4	Enrolling in a course is a crucial action for the success of the learning experience. The button needs to stand out immediately, through color and size
Some of the quizzes and videos are not displayed properly. Test participants had issues viewing or acting on them	4	The learning platform needs to be thoroughly checked for this type of issues, on all major web and mobile platforms, and these issues need to be corrected immediately
Marking an activity as checked is confusing. Test participants reported that this functionality sometimes worked and sometimes not, so they were unable to progress to 100% and complete the course	3	Along with checking for possible bugs, visible instructions on how this feature works needs to be displayed on the platform

(continued)

Table 1. (*continued*)

Usability problem	Severity rating	Recommendation
Some course modules lack navigation buttons. Test participants wondered why they needed to go back to the homepage of the course just to find the next module	3	All the modules in the courses need to be checked for missing navigation items. Proper navigation is very important for the user to make sense of where he/she is at the moment and where he/she could go next
The sidebar menu is too cluttered. Test participants complained that there are too many links and options in the sidebar menu, that it is too narrow, and that text is hard to read	3	The sidebar menu, which contains actions that can be done inside a course, needs to be decluttered by keeping only what is essential for the students. This can be determined by further usability studies and usage analytics
The table of contents of some courses is inconsistent with the actual content. Test participants were surprised that the contents did not match with what was advertised	2	For a proper user and learning experience, all the table of contents need to be checked and, if necessary, recreated, to eliminate confusion
The design of the platform is inconsistent. Test participants reported feeling confused because identical functionalities have slightly different designs throughout the platform	2	The platform needs to implement a design system in order to keep designs consistent across devices, screens, and functionalities
Course content is too segmented. Test participants remarked that some courses have too many mini pages of information, which leads to way too many navigation actions that are needed from their part	2	Courses need to be checked to keep a balance between information overload and number of screens
The tutors are hard to identify. Test participants reported that it is unclear who is tutorizing the course and how to contact them	2	Although contacting the tutor is less common in a MOOC, the details of who created the MOOC and his/her contact information, or a general contact information for the platform, need to be visible on the course page
Some external links do not open in a new browser tab. Test participants expected that links to external platforms, of which there are a lot in these courses, will open in a new tab	2	All the external links need to be checked to open in a new browser tab, so that students can easily return to the actual course content when finished
The progress bar is hard to notice. Test participants reported that they had issues in spotting the progress bar and that, sometimes, it does not seem to reflect the actual progress of the student inside a course	2	Along with checking for possible bugs in the functionality of the progress bar, this module needs to be made more visible, through location and design, in order to give the students a proper sense of how much work they still have to put in to finish the course

(*continued*)

Table 1. (*continued*)

Usability problem	Severity rating	Recommendation
Spelling mistakes within the courses. Test participants were bothered that the course content has not been thoroughly checked for typos	1	All the course content needs to be proofread again for spelling mistakes

Overall, despite the usability problems that the students reported, they appreciated the platform and they said that they would use the website and application again to enroll and learn.

5   Conclusions

This paper reported on a usability evaluation of the DigiCulture MOOCs, an Erasmus + project that aims to create a sustainable and efficient educational program dedicated to adult learners with low digital skills and low-qualified adults involved in the creative industries sector.

The evaluation was done as part of the Interactivity and Usability class of the Multimedia Technologies master's degree program at the Politehnica University of Timisoara (Romania), with 26 students with were involved as facilitators, observers and participants, under the supervision of the authors of this paper. All the usability evaluation methods were accomplished entirely remote, due to COVID-19 restrictions.

The evaluation was performed both for the website version of the DigiCulture courses and for the mobile application. The methods used for the testing of the website were the user observation session, the focus group, the questionnaire method, and the error testing method. For the mobile application, the methods used were the focus group, the error testing, and the user observation session.

This was the first usability evaluation for the DigiCulture courses, after the development process. Some of the most important problems encountered during the evaluation are: some important pieces of information, such as the enroll button, the tutor information and the progress bar are hard to find at first glance; some aspects of the course are defective, such as marking an activity as done or the display of some videos and quizzes; the course menu is too cluttered and almost unusable; some course content needs to be updated, such as the table of contents, and text needs to be proofread again; too much navigation required due to excessive segmentation of the content, while sometimes the navigation items are not implemented; and others.

Turning back to the research questions in the methodology, we found out that:

A1. The integration of the DigiCulture courses on the UniCampus platform is not finalized. Some modules, content, links, and navigation items are not properly working, and this can lead to unsatisfied users which will leave the platform.
A2. The initial experience of the students regarding the DigiCulture MOOCs is a positive one. They suggested several improvements, both in the interface of the platform and in

the content of the courses, but they graded the web and mobile platforms with *Good* on the SUS adjective rating scale and see themselves using the platform again in the future. This evaluation can serve as a user experience guide both for those implementing MOOC platforms and courses for the first time and for those wishing to run their own usability evaluation on this kind of platforms.

As further work, we intend to solve all the encountered usability problems and afterwards, we plan to organize another usability evaluation for the DigiCulture courses.

Acknowledgments. The current study has been carried out in the framework of the Erasmus+ Project "Digital Culture – Improving the Digital Competences and Social Inclusion of Adults in Creative Industries", Strategic Partnerships for higher education, (partially) founded by the European Union, Project Number 2018–1-RO01-KA204–049368.

References

1. Johansson, S., Frolov, I.: An Adaptable Usability Checklist for MOOCs: A Usability Evaluation Instrument for Massive Open Online Courses. Umeå University, Department of Informatics (2014)
2. Fernandez, A., Insfran, E., Abrahão, S.: Usability evaluation methods for the web: a systematic mapping study. Inf. Softw. Technol. **53**, 789–817 (2011). https://doi.org/10.1016/j.infsof.2011.02.007
3. Jakob Nielsen: Usability 101: Introduction to Usability. https://www.nngroup.com/articles/usability-101-introduction-to-usability/. Accessed 20 July 2020
4. Ramakrisnan, P., Jaafar, A., Razak, F.H.A., Ramba, D.A.: Evaluation of user interface design for leaning management system (LMS): investigating student's eye tracking pattern and experiences. Procedia. Soc. Behav. Sci. **67**, 527–537 (2012). https://doi.org/10.1016/j.sbspro.2012.11.357
5. Nielsen, J.: Usability Engineering. Morgan Kaufmann, Burlington (1994)
6. Holzinger, A.: Usability engineering methods for software developers. Commun. ACM. **48**, 71–74 (2005). https://doi.org/10.1145/1039539.1039541
7. Otaiza, R., Rusu, C., Roncagliolo, S.: Evaluating the usability of transactional web sites. In: 2010 Third International Conference on Advances in Computer-Human Interactions, pp. 32–37 (2010). https://doi.org/10.1109/ACHI.2010.27
8. Andone, D., Ternauciuc, A., Vasiu, R., Mihaescu, V., Vert, S.: DigiCulture - an open education environment for digital skills. In: Proceedings of the IEEE 20th International Conference on Advanced Learning Technologies (ICALT 2020), pp. 24–26 (2020)
9. Andone, D., Vasiu, R., Ternauciuc, A.: UniCampus: the first courses in a Romanian MOOC. In: 2017 IEEE Global Engineering Education Conference (EDUCON), pp. 1210–1215 (2017). https://doi.org/10.1109/EDUCON.2017.7943002.
10. Sauer, J., Sonderegger, A., Heyden, K., Biller, J., Klotz, J., Uebelbacher, A.: Extra-laboratorial usability tests: an empirical comparison of remote and classical field testing with lab testing. Appl. Ergon. **74**, 85–96 (2019). https://doi.org/10.1016/j.apergo.2018.08.011
11. Pappano, L.: The Year of the MOOC (2012). https://www.nytimes.com/2012/11/04/education/edlife/massive-open-online-courses-are-multiplying-at-a-rapid-pace.html
12. Korableva, O., Durand, T., Kalimullina, O., Stepanova, I.: Usability testing of MOOC: Identifying user interface problems. In: Brodsky, A., Hammoudi, S., Smialek, M., Filipe, J. (eds.) ICEIS 2019 - Proceedings of the 21st International Conference on Enterprise Information Systems, pp. 468–475. SciTePress, Portugal (2019)

13. Tsironis, A., Katsanos, C., Xenos, M.: Comparative usability evaluation of three popular MOOC platforms. In: 2016 IEEE Global Engineering Education Conference (EDUCON), pp. 608–612. IEEE (2016)
14. Andone, D., Vert, S., Mihaescu, V., Stoica, D., Ternauciuc, A.: Evaluation of the virtual mobility learning hub. In: Zaphiris, P., Ioannou, A. (eds.) HCII 2020. LNCS, vol. 12205, pp. 20–33. Springer, Cham (2020). https://doi.org/10.1007/978-3-030-50513-4_2
15. Lewis, J.R.: The system usability scale: past, present, and future. Int. J. Human-Comput. Interact. **34**, 577–590 (2018). https://doi.org/10.1080/10447318.2018.1455307
16. Rotaru, O.A., Vert, S., Vasiu, R., Andone, D.: Standardised questionnaires in usability evaluation. applying standardised usability questionnaires in digital products evaluation. In: Lopata, A., Butkienė, R., Gudonienė, D., Sukackė, V. (eds.) ICIST 2020. CCIS, vol. 1283, pp. 39–48. Springer, Cham (2020). https://doi.org/10.1007/978-3-030-59506-7_4
17. Bangor, A., Kortum, P., Miller, J.: Determining what individual SUS scores mean: adding an adjective rating scale. J. Usability Stud. **4**, 114–123 (2009)
18. Nielsen, J.: Severity Ratings for Usability Problems. https://www.nngroup.com/articles/how-to-rate-the-severity-of-usability-problems/. Accessed 23 Jan 2020

Self-assessing Teachers' Competences for Curricula Modernization Through MOOCs

Vlad Mihaescu[1]([⊠]) [iD], Rita Butkiene[2] [iD], Diana Andone[1] [iD], Cengiz Hakan Aydin[3] [iD],
Carlos Vaz de Carvalho[4] [iD], Olga Zubikova[5] [iD], Elif Toprak[3] [iD],
Evrim Genc-Kumtepe[3] [iD], Tim Brueggemann[5], and Sonja Intveen[5]

[1] Politehnica University of Timisoara, Timisoara, Romania
vlad.mihaescu@upt.ro
[2] Kaunas University of Technology, Kaunas, Lithuania
[3] Anadolu University, Anadolu, Turkey
[4] Polytechnic Institute of Porto, Porto, Portugal
[5] Fachhochschule Des Mittelstands, Bremen, Germany

Abstract. Massive Open Online Courses (MOOCs) paved the way for new instructional methods by and for academic early adopters, who shifted their traditional teaching in ways believed to improve the students experience and to provide more interactive learning opportunities. To analyze this impact in the education system, at different levels, we investigated the desired competencies of the academics who create, develop or integrate MOOCs in traditional higher education. For this purpose, a self-assessment tool for educators was created and this paper presents its pedagogical and technical design, its development and the main results from the first pilot evaluation with teachers from universities in different European countries.

Keywords: MOOC · eLearning · Curricula modernization · Teacher competences · Self-assessment

1 Introduction

The last decade has seen several changes in the approach of education delivery, several due to technologies, access to education and instructional design. Out of all the changes, one which was predicted to "disrupt" education, even since 2014, are the Massive Open Online Courses (MOOCs) [1], the non-formal, almost free and usually short, online educational courses [2].

Since the first MOOC creation in 2008, two essential educational paradigms were practiced for designing MOOCs. The cMOOCs were shaped by the theory of connectivism endorsed by George Siemens [3]. cMOOCs responded to the needs of the growing networked community in a digital era, promoted collaborative, socially situated learning, "…explored new pedagogies beyond traditional classroom settings and, as such, tended to exist on the radical fringe of Higher Education" [4].

© Springer Nature Switzerland AG 2021
A. Lopata et al. (Eds.): ICIST 2021, CCIS 1486, pp. 312–323, 2021.
https://doi.org/10.1007/978-3-030-88304-1_25

The connectivism approach competed with the instructional model of the MOOC design that followed behavioristic principles and came from organizations such as Coursera, Udacity or EdX. These xMOOCs were realized through instructional methods and supported with videos, quizzes and peer-graded assessment and were, in essence, "…an extension of the pedagogical models practiced within the institutions themselves…" [4].

Several studies indicate that MOOCs have created new instructional methods by and for the academics early adopters, who have shifted their traditional teaching in ways believed to improve the students experience and create more interactive learning opportunities [5, 6]. The latest trends in formal education deal with the integration of MOOCs into traditional curricula towards making them more flexible and engaging for higher education institutions (HEI) students [7, 8]. MOOC-based pedagogies are gradually becoming part of the formal curricula design [9]. Thus, HEI educators have to master new skills related to innovating their teaching practices with MOOCs. In this context, the needs of HEI teachers toward growing as MOOC designers should be clearly detected, emphasized and addressed within the still unresolved academic debate cMOOCs versus xMOOCs.

This attempt has been undertaken in the framework of the ongoing Erasmus+ project Curricular modernization by implementing MOOCs model[1]. The project aims at incorporating MOOC-based pedagogical approaches into formal curricula and focuses, inter alia, on the creation of supporting tools for HEI educators willing to introduce these approaches into teaching, such as 1) online-self assessment tool for the real-time diagnostics of the individual competence level in relation to MOOCs design; 2) open online training program for teachers on improving skills and competences needed for the MOOCs design and delivery. The project is composed of 5 HEIs which are Fachhochschule des Mittelstands (Germany), Kaunas University of Technology (Lithuania), Polytechnic Institute of Porto (Portugal), Polytechnic University of Timisoara (Romania), and Anadolu University (Turkey).

The present paper aims at demonstrating results obtained from the pilot implementation of the self-assessment tool for educators. It provides an overview of the pedagogical and technical design of the tool, portrays its innovative features, outlines the evaluation methodology for the piloting of the tool, and presents the analysis of the relevant evaluation insights followed by the final conclusions.

2 Development of the Self-assessment Tool

The intellectual output of the MODE IT project is the Open Online Teacher's Training Program for teaching staff at HEI with the aim to enable HEI teachers to develop and deliver MOOCs as well as to integrate MOOCs into formal curricula in a didactically sound manner. The training program is developed by applying the competence-based approach and implemented as a course in the Moodle virtual learning environment.

The MODE IT experts have identified 27 most relevant competences for the creation and delivery of MOOCs. These 27 competences were organized into 5 areas and became

---

[1] www.mode-it.eu.

a key factor for structuring not only the training program but also the self-assessment tool:

- Pedagogical competences for designing student-centred learning;
- MOOCs specific competences;
- Technology-related competences;
- Competences related to the theoretical foundations of MOOCs;
- Competences about MOOC integration into formal learning.

The self-assessment tool is developed as an integral part of the training program (Moodle course), allowing teaching staff at higher education institutions to assess their competence level in the design and development of MOOCs and to get immediate feedback for possible improvements.

The conceptual model used for the development of the self-assessment tool is presented in Fig. 1 (UML class diagram notation is used). Following a competence-based approach, our training program is composed of 5 learning modules:

- Foundation of online learning;
- MOOC course design;
- MOOC content production;
- MOOC delivery;
- MOOC in formal learning.

Each module (topic) covers at least one competence area and aims at at least 1 learning outcomes – competences of a particular level. For example, the module "Foundation of online learning" covers the competence area "Pedagogical competences for designing student-centred learning" in which competences are used to define learning outcomes of the module.

The purpose of the self-assessment tool is to assess the level of competence that each respondent has in each area and to provide an appropriate recommendation for further development, for example, to take a particular learning module. Instead of creating a single tool, encompassing all the areas of competences, a separate part of the tool for each area of competence was created, as it is reasonable to derive the overall level of competence based on the assessment of competences in that area. A generalized assessment of all competence areas is not as reasonable. Therefore, our self-assessment tool is modular and consists of 5 parts corresponding to the 5 identified competence areas. Each part of the tool is implemented as a separate multi-choice survey, including corresponding questions regarding the level of competences of that area. For example, the area "Pedagogical competences for designing student-centred learning" includes 6 competences, therefore, a relevant part of the tool has 6 corresponding questions.

During the self-assessment, a respondent is invited to assess the level of proficiency on each competence by indicating one of the statements that best characterizes the respondent's current competence level. We have used Bloom's taxonomy to formulate the statements of answer. Each set of possible answers consists of 7 statements. 6 statements correspond to 6 levels of the cognitive domain from Bloom's taxonomy. Statements of the same level in each question are formulated applying the same patterns and receive the

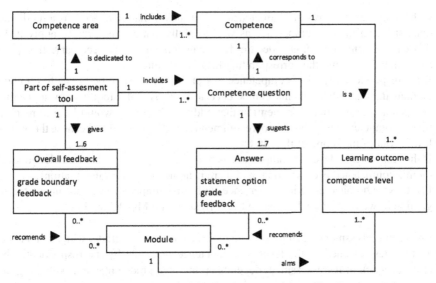

Fig. 1. A conceptual model used for development of the self-assessment tool.

same grade (Table 1). If the respondent does not have any experience with a particular competence, there is a possibility to tick the option "No statement applies to me". The grade for this option is 0.

Table 1. Patterns for statements in accordance with Boom's taxonomy.

Level of the cognitive domain	Patterns for statements of answer	Grade
1 (remember)	I **heard** about …	10%
2 (understand)	I can **explain** ideas and concepts related with …	20%
3 (apply)	I can **apply** methods and use them in new situations …	40%
4 (analyse)	I can **analyse** and organize testing on …	60%
5 (evaluate)	I can **justify** a stand or design according …	80%
6 (create)	I can **design** new original work on …	100%

For each selected statement, specific feedback is provided. A feedback of the same level statement is written by applying the same wording and logic:

– If the respondent's level of competence is 1 or 2 (according to Bloom), it indicates familiarity or knowledge with this competence. However, the level 3 (apply) is necessary if the respondent wants to be able to develop and deliver MOOCs, integrate them into formal curricula. Therefore, we recommend choosing the MOOC module that is assigned to the respective competence area and achieving the necessary level of competence.

– If the respondent's level of competence is 3, it means that he or she has a moderate understanding of this competence as well as skills that are required to apply it. In this case, the teacher should decide deeper understanding is necessary. If so, we recommend choosing the corresponding MOOC module.
– If the respondent's level of competence is 4 or 5, it means that he or she has a good or high understanding of this competence as well as skills required to apply this competence in practice. We mention that additional training would help to reach a higher competence level but do not recommend any MOOC module because the higher level is out of the scope of the MOOC.
– If the respondent's level of competence is 6, it means that his or her knowledge level on this competence is exceptional and there is no need for recommendations.
– For those who have no prior experience with this competence but are interested in gaining it, we recommend choosing the corresponding MOOC module.

After the assessment, each part of the tool returns the final grade, which is an average of grades assigned to the level of competence indicated by the respondent. The overall feedback of the assessment depends on the final grade obtained. Following the same principle, we specified 6 ranges for the overall grade and specified corresponding feedback. The meaning of each range feedback is close to the meaning of the level of cognitive domain defined in Bloom's taxonomy. It could be explained as follows:

– If the overall grade of self-assessment falls into the first range (0–5%) it means that probably all or most of the competences of the respondent are at the level 1 (remember) or the respondent does not possess particular competences at all. Therefore, we recommend choosing the MOOC module that is assigned to the respective competence area.
– If the overall grade falls into the second range (6–30%) it means that probably all or most of the competencies of the respondent are at the level 2 (understand). Despite that, some of them may be at a higher (3) level, so we also recommend choosing the MOOC module that is assigned to the respective competence area and achieving the necessary level of competences.
– If the overall grade falls into the third range (31–50%) it means that probably all or most of the competencies of the respondent are at the level 3 (apply). In this case, we highly suggest reviewing the specific feedback of each question, identifying competences that require improvement, and enrolling in the associated module.
– If the overall grade falls into the fourth, fifth or sixth range (51–70%, 71–90%, and 91–100% accordingly) it means that probably all or most of the competencies of the respondent are at the 4 (analyse), 5 (evaluate) or 6 (create) levels accordingly. However, some of them may be at a lower level. Therefore, we highly suggest reviewing the specific feedback of each question.

3   Self-assessment Tool Validation

This evaluation study proposed to explore the self-assessment tool participants' perceptions and perspectives regarding the effectiveness, efficiency, appeal and sustainability of the tool. More precisely, it intended to identify the participants' perceptions concerning:

- user friendliness of the tool,
- sufficiency of the User Guide,
- their satisfaction with the tool (user experience),
- effectiveness and usefulness of the tool,
- adequacy of the competences covered in the tool,
- appropriateness of the definitions of the competencies provided,
- adequacy of the use of Bloom's revised taxonomy as competence levels,
- satisfaction with the feedback received at the end of each competence area.

3.1 Data Collection

The data was collected during March-April 2021 from 64 voluntary participants coming from the 5 countries of the project partnership: Germany (15.6%), Lithuania (18.8%), Portugal (20.3%), Romania (21.9%) and Turkey (21.9%). In relation to gender, 60.9% of respondents were female, 34.4% were male and 4.7% preferred not to say. The age distribution of the participants was as follows: 9.4% under 30 years old, 34.4% between 30–39 years old, 34.4% between 40–49 years old, 14.1% 50–59 years old, 6.3% over 60 years old and 1.6% preferred not to say.

54.7% of the participants were teaching both face-to-face and online in a higher education institution, 28.1% were teaching mainly face-to-face in a higher education institution, 6.3% were teaching mainly online in a higher education institution, 3.1% were teaching mainly face-to-face in K12 school settings, 3.1% were teaching face-to-face and online in K12 school settings, 1.6% were teaching mainly online in K12 school settings and 1.6% were teaching face-to-face at a private institution.

Data was collected through an online evaluation form divided in four sections. A consent page, covering descriptions, instructions and statements about voluntarily participation, was also included.

In the first section of the form, the questions (Likert-type items) were related to the user friendliness of the tool (access and use), sufficiency of the User Guide, the participants' overall satisfaction with the tool, and effectiveness of the tool for helping to identify their strength and weaknesses regarding the competencies.

The second section consisted of 4 questions (Likert-type) about different aspects of the tool, such as effectiveness and usefulness of the tool, adequacy of the competences covered, appropriateness of the definitions of the competencies provided, and adequacy of the use of Blooms revised taxonomy. A text field was also provided for each question where the participants could indicate their insights about that aspect.

The third section covered the short version of the User Experience Questionnaire (UEQ-S) developed by Schepp, Hinderks and Thomaschewski [10]. The UEQ-S includes pairs of contrasting attributes that may apply to the self-assessment tool and participants are asked to express their agreement with each attribute.

The final section of the evaluation form included two open ended questions that asked participants to provide their thoughts, comments, and recommendations about the strength of the tool, and the areas that need improvement. The close-ended questions were related to the participants' demographics and previous teaching experiences.

The consistency of the pragmatic quality and hedonic quality scales was found reasonably high: Cronbach Alpha values were measured as 0.85 (pragmatic quality) and 0.81 (hedonic quality).

3.2   Results and Discussion

The first category of questions was related to "Access and Use" using a five-level Likert scale, with the options: Strongly disagree, Disagree, Neutral, Agree and Strongly Agree. The statements we chose for evaluation are:

- The registration procedure and the access to the tool is easy and well-navigated.
- The tool is easy to use.
- The tool itself is well-designed and appealing.
- The User Guide is well designed and provides sufficient information about access and use of the tool.
- The self-assessment results provide useful tips for improving my professional development.
- I can recommend this tool to my colleagues or students to identify their needs.
- I can use this tool in my courses.
- The results of the self-assessment accurately reflect my competency levels.

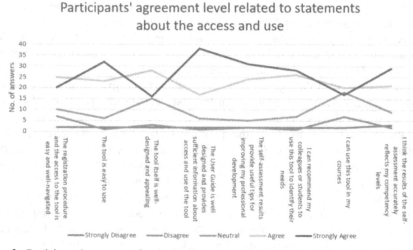

Fig. 2. Participants' agreement level related to statements about the access and use of the Self-Assessment tool.

Figure 2 presents the results we obtained. In general, a majority of positive scores (Agree and Strong agree) were chosen for all statements. However, we can draw some conclusions based on the differences. For example, the highest level of agreement was received by the development of the User Guide of the Self-Assessment tool, which shows the way in which the partnership designed it was very explanatory and useful. Another advantage of the tool is its easiness of use, as resulted from the answers offered by participants to the tool piloting phase. Almost identical scores were obtained by the statement related to the tips offered for improving professional development by the self-assessment results. We can also expect this tool to be recommended to other colleagues or students of our piloting group. Participants seem quite satisfied with the way in which the results reflect their competency levels. Even if the registration procedure and access to the tool navigation and easiness were rated with general positive remarks, the difference between this statement and the easiness of use, shows us that we can further improve this first step of the process, in order not to lose potential participants. Another place where some improvement could be in order is related to the design of the tool. The less agreed with statement was the "I can use this tool in my courses", which should further encourage us to find out the reasons for this answer, in our future research.

The next questionnaire section was related to Aspects of the Tool, using the same Likert scale presented earlier. The partnership decided to offer space for open remarks from participants in relation to each aspect taken into consideration. The aspects that we offered for evaluation are:

- The tool covers appropriate range of competencies regarding MOOCs, online learning and teaching.
- Descriptions of the competencies are precise and meaningful.
- Competency levels (based on Bloom's taxonomy) accurately represent users.
- Feedback provided at the end offers rich descriptions of the users' levels and prescriptive instructions about how to improve related competencies.

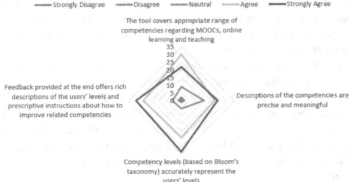

Fig. 3. Participants' agreement level related to statements about the aspects of the tool.

Figure 3 presents the graphic representation of the resulted answers. The scores received are positive in a large majority but there are again some slight differences. The statement "The tool covers appropriate range of competencies regarding MOOCs, online learning and teaching" is one which could be further improved, as some participants stated: "It should be more detailed in terms of technical competences and content design and creation", "Is missing netiquette or the Internet/on-line etiquette", "I think there should be a correlation between the salary of the teacher/assistant/professor, and the time needed to understand, implement and consolidate the most recent online teaching strategies. Also, the number of students that attend seminaries, laboratories, etc., compared to the number of teachers, greatly influences the quality of the classes. More students per teacher, means less time for each individual student, therefore downgrading the quality of the educational process", "Too many competences related to learning theories and not so many related to practical competences". Around 10% of participants did not feel that their knowledge about MOOCs was enough for them to correctly answer this question, choosing the *Neutral* option.

The aspect in which we should improve more according to our piloting participants is "Descriptions of the competencies are precise and meaningful". Here are some of the answers we received: "Could be simplified", "From Area 3 there are no more headings. I found them very helpful in Area 1 and 2!", "Some are not precise", "Some descriptions are not very clear", "Some definitions are too long and not too precise", "seem a bit confusing", "Descriptions are more technical… sometime is was difficult for me, to understand what I know and what I am doing… to answer the questions. Probably some examples will be nice", "somehow confusing", "some are too extensive", "The sentences are too long and complex. I had to read some of them three times before I understood the entirety. Better to formulate it shorter and in several sentences", "Designing online materials or finding/modifying online learning materials and licensing them appropriately is a pretty challenging task for many educators not only because of the task itself but also because of their lack of awareness. I believe the assessment tool should address this complexity", "The definition/description is detailed, but quite abstract. It is difficult for someone who has little knowledge/expression about/in the competencies to grasp exactly or to imagine what exactly is meant by the competency. (e.g. What exactly does it mean to be able to analyze or evaluate, to use MOOC content in a module or to ensure through interactive offers that the participants have reflected on the content)". All these comments prove that we need to reformulate the descriptions of the competencies, making them shorter and easier to understand.

The best results in this section were received by the statement "Competency levels (based on Bloom's taxonomy) accurately represent the users' levels". Here are some of the comments received: "very nice and suggestive", "Good idea to use Bloom's taxonomy" (2 persons). There were some opinions on improvement as well: "It is sometimes very difficult to differentiate between the answers because they are close together. In addition, in my opinion, they often belong together. However, this is not clear from the answers", "Some of the levels (especially the upper ones) may not accurately represent the users' levels".

Second in order of positive answers was the statement "Feedback provided at the end offers rich descriptions of the users' levels and prescriptive instructions about how to improve related competencies". Valuable comments were offered here for us as well: "should be more precise" (2 persons), "If you receive a very good grade, but not 10, the feedback says that you can take a course to perfect your skills, but it does not say which course", "I have not seen any feedback", "Feedback at the end is not rich in descriptions. It must explain more about the user's level and competencies", "It would be nice if feedback was offered in my own language", "I believe that in the absence of specific tasks instead of general descriptions, may lead the participants to overrate their capabilities", "There was feedback for each competence cluster. I found it nice to have a general overview that not only reports of the total value (the point value made no sense to me here) and the level in the five competence areas. In addition, there is feedback after the individual questions about which courses would be suitable for me. At the end of the self-assessment, it would be great to receive a list/overview of which courses are now recommended to me. Otherwise, the information from the intermediate feedback will be lost".

The next section in our questionnaire referred to Attributes. We presented pairs of contrasting attributes that may apply to the self-assessment tool participants completed. They were asked to express their agreement with each line of attributes. A scale was offered from 1 to 7, where 1 means full agreement with attribute 1 of the pair and 7 means full agreement with attribute 2 of the pair. We present the results of this section in Table 2.

Table 2. Evaluation of attributes related to the self-assessment tool.

Attribute	1	2	3	4	5	6	7	Attribute
Obstructive	1.6%	1.6%	3.2%	6.3%	28.6%	28.6%	30.2%	Supportive
Complicated	1.6%	9.5%	7.9%	12.7%	12.7%	30.2%	25.4%	Easy
Inefficient	3.2%	0%	6.3%	7.9%	36.5%	25.4%	20.6%	Efficient
Confusing	4.8%	4.8%	12.7%	6.3%	22.2%	25.4%	23.8%	Clear
Boring	4.8%	3.2%	3.2%	28.6%	25.4%	14.3%	20.6%	Exciting
Not interesting	1.6%	4.8%	3.2%	6.3%	23.8%	34.9%	25.4%	Interesting
Conventional	4.8%	4.8%	7.9%	14.3%	20.6%	27%	20.6%	Inventive
Usual	1.6%	3.2%	11.1%	15.9%	33.3%	17.5%	17.5%	Leading edge

The last section of the questionnaire was related to overall evaluations and demographics. We first inquired about what the strength of this tool is and what the things participants liked about it were. Most positive aspects indicated by pilot participants for this tool are related to the clear formulations of statements (22% of participants), the self-assessment (21%), the feedback offered (16%), the easiness of use (9%), the concept or its relevance especially in these pandemic times (8%).

Here are some examples of the answers we received: "Very nice balance between information and survey. The information in the evaluations is precisely formulated", "The questions and list of answers are very well formulated and very comprehensive, making it very easy to self-assess the competencies", "I liked that it is designed based on Bloom's taxonomy and provides overall feedback", "thought of the unthinkable, motivating, creative, gathering", "The tool offers precise information regarding analyzed competence in on-line educational systems and methods", "The tool offers a real evaluation of the personal teaching skills in regard to the modern teaching strategies", "Being able to detect your deficiencies in both theory and practice is the strength of this tool. Explaining the theoretical terms in a very clear way is another strength of this tool".

We also asked participants to write if there any areas which need improvement, and what are the things they disliked. The conclusion we can draw from this is that the tool can be difficult to understand, especially for teachers who do not possess advanced competences and knowledge on MOOCs (17% of participants). Also, the repetitiveness in formulations and long phrasing is boring and annoying for some participants (17%). Easiness of use (12.5%), design (9%) and language barriers (9%) were also highlighted as points for improvement.

Here are some examples of statements received: "I think it would be interesting to integrate some practical/applied questions. For example, to present a certain situation and a list of possible answers on how to deal with the situation, each answer corresponding to a certain level of a competency", "I find it a little bit unappealing and hard to motivate myself to keep on going (not in a way that it is difficult)", "the tool could be standalone to facilitate its access by teachers - I understand that when the MOOC is available everything is connected but anyway…", "Sometimes, the explanations were too long and the separation of each answer was not easy to decide on. The mentioning of many adverbs was irritating", "I think you should create a section at the start of the questionnaire, which evaluates general information regarding the teachers that answer the questions. You could ask questions like age, years in the educational system as a teacher, the types of courses or seminars that one teach, the number of students that you need to teach and since when did the on-line teaching methods were implemented in the college", "The questions and answers are too long and complex so that the questionnaire takes a long time. There is no final evaluation, only after each competence cluster. It would also be helpful to be able to look at the recommendations in retrospect. If the test lasts so long, I may not feel like looking at the relevant content immediately afterwards but may have forgotten the recommendations until the next time. The registration process (including the terms and conditions) is too lengthy. The language changes over and over again. The video guide is difficult to understand due to the poor pronunciation", "The navigation is unfortunately poor, especially in registration and initiating the test. I prefer more intuitive designs without the need for a long user's guide. The scope of the tool was good, but there might be a need for more depth for a more realistic representation of competencies", "There are two areas which I believe that would need improvement: 1) Production of Didactic Material and 2) Accessibility. 1) I am aware of the complexities of these issues, however I believe all Universities need to build a team to professionally design and produce learning material. I'm talking about a staff of professional graphic designers, studio professionals, instructional designers, etc. 2) I've been wondering about the accessibility for deaf students in this MOOC. It would be extremely difficult for deaf students to attend this course and there's still little bilingual courseware available for this public".

4   Conclusions

The adoption of MOOCs paved the way for teachers in Higher Education to create and use different instructional methods namely by integrating them in their formal teaching practices. For this to be possible, HEI teachers need to master new skills therefore becoming MOOC designers and deliverers. In the scope of the MODE-IT project, we designed and implemented a self-assessment tool that allows teachers to identify gaps in their competences and skills and we presented the results obtained from the pilot implementation of the tool for educators.

In general, results were quite positive and show that the developed tool does provide a precise profile of the teacher's abilities to design and deliver a MOOC. Nevertheless, there are still improvements to be made, namely in the concise definition of the competences and on the statements that identify the ability level of the teachers. An exploratory sequential mixed method can provide a better insight about the participants' perspectives and perceptions.

Acknowledgment. This study is partly financed by the Erasmus+ program, through the project "Curricular modernization by implementing MOOCs model" (MODE IT), ref. 2019–1-DE01-KA203–005051.

References

1. Christensen, C.M., Weise, M.R.: MOOCs' disruption is only beginning - The Boston Globe. BostonGlobe.com. https://www.bostonglobe.com/opinion/2014/05/09/moocs-disrup tion-only-beginning/S2VlsXpK6rzRx4DMrS4ADM/story.html. Accessed 18 Apr 2021
2. Siemens, G., Downes, S.: MOOC Course: Connectivism and Connective Knowledge, 28 June 2008. https://web.archive.org/web/20080629220943/http://ltc.umanitoba.ca:83/connec tivism/
3. Siemens, G.: Connectivism: a learning theory for the digital age. Int. J. Instruct. Technol. Dist. Learn. Obtained through the Internet: http://www.idtl.org/journal/Jam_05/article01.html (2005). Accessed Feb 2021
4. Yuan, L., Powell, S.: MOOCs and open education: Implications for higher education (2013)
5. Gerber, J.: MOOCs: Innovation, Disruption and Instructional Leadership in Higher Education. UCLA (2014)
6. Andone, D.: Methods and models of MOOCs integration in traditional higher education. In: MOOCs in Europe EADTU (2016)
7. Bruff, D.O., Fisher, D.H., McEwen, K.E., Smith, B.E.: Wrapping a MOOC: student perceptions of an experiment in blended learning. J. Online Learn. Teach. **9**(2), 187 (2013)
8. Holotescu, C., Grosseck, G., CREȚU, V., Naaji, A.: Integrating MOOCs in blended courses. E learn. Softw. Educ. 1 (2014)
9. Andone, D., Vasiu, R.: MOOCs in Higher Education—Flipped Classroom or a New Smart Learning Model?. In: State-of-the-Art and Future Directions of Smart Learning, pp. 303–307 (2016)
10. Schrepp, M., Hinderks, A., Thomaschewski, J.: Design and evaluation of a short version of the user experience questionnaire (UEQ-S). Ijimai **4**(6), 103–108 (2017)

Visual Educational Simulator of Pandemic: Work in Progress

Pavel Boytchev[1](✉) and Svetla Boytcheva[2]

[1] Faculty of Mathematics and Informatics - KIT, Sofia University "St. Kliment Ohridski", Sofia, Bulgaria
boytchev@fmi.uni-sofia.bg

[2] Institute of Information and Communication Technologies, Bulgarian Academy of Sciences, Sofia, Bulgaria
svetla.boytcheva@iict.bas.bg

Abstract. This paper presents the design and development of a visual pandemic simulator, which is still a work in progress. The goal is twofold: to make a simulator capable of demonstrating various pandemic and social situations including the current COVID-19 outbreak; and to serve as a platform for activities for graduate and undergraduate education. The paper presents the main steps of building the simulator and the corresponding educational opportunities.

Keywords: Visual simulator · Pandemic · Education · Graphics · STEM

1 Introduction

The creation of educational software has several missions – to provide foundations for the acquisition of certain knowledge, skills and competencies in students. On the other hand, this software must be attractive enough to hold students' attention, as well as to provide an intriguing environment and challenges. Their role is to motivate the learners to complete the training to the very end and not get discouraged, bored or give up prematurely.

Instructional simulation provides both a Virtual Learning Environment (VLE), interdisciplinary education on specific domain, tools and activities for achieving the desired goal, and flexibility for exploration of different scenarios. Lacka et al. [13] discuss the impact of the VLE in Higher Education on goals achievement. Their findings show that there is some positive effect of VLE by supporting cognitive outputs and enhancing learning and knowledge transfer. However, there are also some negative implications like increased time, efforts and resources needed in this learning journey.

The research is partially supported by the National Scientific Program "Information and Communication Technologies in Science, Education and Security" (ICTinSES) financed by the Ministry of Education and Science; and by Sofia University "St. Kliment Ohridski" Research Science Fund project N80-10-19/19.03.2021 "Integration of competence-based learning in higher education by means of high-tech tools".

A. Lopata et al. (Eds.): ICIST 2021, CCIS 1486, pp. 324–337, 2021.
https://doi.org/10.1007/978-3-030-88304-1_26

Several simulators are used successfully for different domains like Business [8], STEM[1] (Science, Technology, Engineering, Mathematics), Social Sciences[2] for higher education and for long life learning; and serious games [20]. The most effective are simulators for modeling dynamic environment and behavior that can be not so easily illustrated in the traditional static classroom. Siddiqui et al. [19] propose scenario-based educational tool for introductory technology course.

Currently the hot topic is the COVID-19 outbreak. COVID pandemic sparks an acute famine for distance learning and educating the population about the spread of infectious diseases. Exponentially increased is the number of e-Learning tools developed for the last year. The largest share of these tools is for various pandemic simulators. They provide diverse computer simulation models [10] for the epidemic dynamics [11], COVID superspreading prediction [12], interventions [3], population simulations[3] and risk assessment [17] and calculation the risk of infection [15]. Some simulators focus on medical students education [6], while others are dedicated to predictive analytics for prevention and control of the public health [9], and improve the response to COVID-19 crisis [7] rather than being used for educational activities.

In our primary interest are simulators with educational purpose. The best approach for modeling dynamic behavior is multi agent-based models (ABMs) [2], taking into account different simulation scenarios – outdoor/indoor activities, mobility restrictions [14], temporal models, demographic data, etc. Chertkov et al. [5] propose a pipeline from data through ABMs to Graphic Models that explore different graphical models for monitoring and control of pandemics. Another major factor is the various mathematical models that play important role in exploration of different scenarios in simulators [4,18], as well as the number of features (parameters) for the population used in such models.

This paper presents our efforts in building a visual mass simulator of pandemic and other social events. The focus of our work is to support sufficient flexibility in the simulation model by providing a highly configurable environment. The other major goal is to implement a diverse set of techniques and approaches that can be used for educational activities. The target audience of this educational content are undergraduate and graduate students from Sofia University studying Computer Sciences, Computer Graphics and High-performance Computing. The simulator is a web-based application, written in JavaScript and using Three.js[4] for rendering 3D graphics in real-time.

Section 2 of the paper describes the methodology and the overall architecture. Section 3 is about the construction of simulated environment and its educational potential. Section 4 presents how the virtual people and their behaviors are defined, so that it is possible to simulate both pandemic outbreaks and social events. Section 5 lists some preliminary results. The last Sect. 6 contains a summary of our efforts and plans for future development.

---

[1] https://phet.colorado.edu/.

[2] https://www.historysimulation.com/.

[3] https://ictr.github.io/covid19-outbreak-simulator/.

[4] https://threejs.org/.

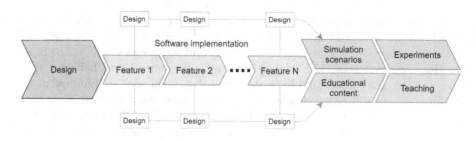

Fig. 1. Project workflow

2 Methodology and Architecture

The design and development of educational and educational-friendly software requires considering specific technological aspects and their impact on the educational goals. The goal of our project is two-fold: (1) to make a visual simulation for pandemic scenarios; and (2) to cover educational aspects providing sufficiently diverse learning opportunities for students.

The two-fold nature of the project makes significant change in the chosen methodology and the project workflow – Fig. 1. The initial phase is for the overall design of the software. The first and most important methodological decision in this phase is what type of simulation to implement and how to implement it, so that it provides multiple research and educational opportunities. A sufficient diversity of simulations is expected along with some level of unpredictability. The simulation should allow modeling a small neighborhood or a large metropolis.

From a visual point of view the simulation should generate rural and urban areas where virtual people live. The graphics should provide sufficient level of realism, but it is not expected to have photo realistic rendering.

The initial design phase is followed by successive implementations of specific simulator features described in Sects. 3 and 4. The implementation of these features generates research and educational topics to be used during the next phase of the project. Currently these topics are just slots of preliminary designs and some of them are also discussed in Sects. 3 and 4.

When the software implementation is complete the project splits into two interconnected development paths, each starting with its own design phase, that collects and aggregates the preliminary design slots. The result of these two parallel activities are designs of various simulation scenarios and designs of educational content. During the final phase the scenarios are used to obtain experimental results, while the educational content is reshaped and taught as university-level course. Several courses in the Faculty of Mathematics and Informatics at Sofia University are dedicated to teaching students design and development of software application and educational content. The simulator is expected to cover and rationalize many topics from these courses.

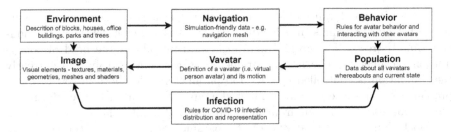

Fig. 2. Architecture of the simulator

The overall architecture of the simulator is presented in Fig. 2. Each block indicates a collection of simulator features. The links indicate the major data flow or data dependencies. *Environment* contains data structures supporting the simulation world – blocks, buildings, streets, parks, etc. *Navigation* describes the navigational network responsible for the motion of virtual people. *Population* defines physical and social properties of the virtual population. *Image* manages images of all objects in the simulated world, while *Vavatar* (virtual avatar) is responsible for animating people. Two blocks contain functionality to control the simulation – *Behavior* of virtual people and *Infection* model.

3   Simulated Environment

3.1   Ground Map and 2D Design

The topology of the simulation is based on *a ground map* constructed by recursive splitting. The typical result is presented in the top-left snapshot in Fig. 3. For a more realistic layout the algorithm is modified to support streets of various widths and orientations as shown in the top-right snapshot.

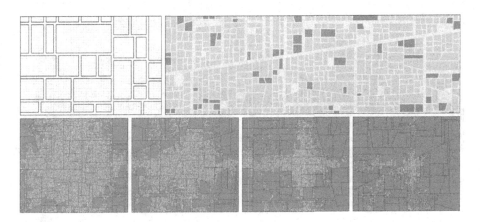

Fig. 3. Ground maps: original *(top-left)*, improved *(top-right)*; urban to rural *(bottom)*

The educational value of such map construction is to demonstrate recursive splitting algorithms and handling special cases and exceptions like non-orthogonal streets. The ground map algorithm introduces the need of configuration parameters. The list of parameters grows continuously and currently the simulation is controlled by over 130 parameters. The bottom row of Fig. 3 presents several procedurally generated maps. The parameters conform the ground map to any layout from megalopolis to a small village or even a single block. The educational role of the parameters is to make the code self-explanatory with names like GROUND_SIZE, STREET_WIDTH, TREE_HEIGHT, etc.; and to demonstrate techniques for supporting different setups within the same code.

3.2   Buildings and 3D Design

The transition from 2D ground map to 3D skyline requires the introduction of other techniques. One of the most often used algorithm for terrain construction (besides fractals) is based on Perlin noise. However, the original noise leads to smooth surfaces, see Fig. 4, left. To achieve a more realistic skyline students should either modify the algorithm or implement a new one. The right snapshots in Fig. 4 show the result of a modified algorithm that increases the sharpness of the surface. The upper image is a rendering of a city, and the lower image is the modified Perlin noise wrapping surface. This approach can be used for a discussion with students about applicability of algorithms – sometimes the original algorithms could and should be modified to suit specific needs.

Important assets in the simulated world are the buildings – houses, apartment buildings and office buildings. Every day the virtual people go from their homes to their offices and then return in the evening. Houses supports simulation of low population densities, while apartment and office high-rise buildings are used to simulate high densities.

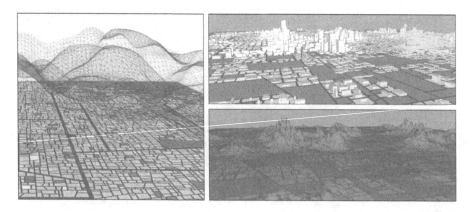

Fig. 4. Smooth Perlin noise surface *(left)*, realistic skyline *(top-right)* and its modified noise wrapping surface *(bottom-right)*

There are two approaches for making virtual buildings. The *manual design* relies on 3D collections, usually built by a digital artist or 3D scanned. The *procedural approach* uses software to generate the buildings. As all static assets in the simulation are procedurally generated, the buildings also follow this approach.

The number of buildings may become a performance challenge. To address this issue students can be introduced to several ways of managing large number of 3D objects. The most straightforward way is to define each building by itself. This is the simplest approach, but it is also the least efficient in terms of performance and allocated memory.

The second approach is to merge all buildings into a single 3D object, which provides a noticeable improvement in performance, but the memory consumption remains almost the same.

The most advanced approach is *instancing* – there is a definition of a single template building and all other buildings are its clones. The simulation world is a suitable playground for students to gain experience with instancing and its disadvantage – cloning generates exact copies.

Online 3D graphical systems use WebGL technology to send programs to the graphical processor. These programs are called shaders and are written in the special programming language GLSL (Graphics Library Shading Language). The making of variable clones will motivate the students to learn GLSL and shader programming. Small pieces of GLSL code are injected in the available shaders to transform the otherwise identical clones into individually shaped geometries. Some results of modified house buildings are shown in Fig. 5, left.

Modeling in 3D opens many opportunities for educational exploration. For example, the original shape of a tree in the simulated world is a cube, which is later sculptured into a tree with GLSL injection – see the right snapshot in Fig. 5. Graphical processors can execute hundreds of shader programs in parallel. This explains why instancing is the most performant approach compared to individual shapes or merged shapes.

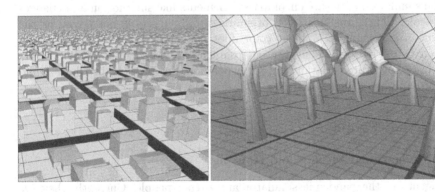

Fig. 5. GLSL injection into shaders allows variation in 3D clones – all houses are actually one house *(left)*, all trees are a single tree *(right)*

Fig. 6. Visual effects improve the natural appearance of the simulated world

3.3 Rendering

Some elements of the simulated environment have purely aesthetic value – trees, sidewalks, soft shadows are such elements, see Fig. 6. Their educational purpose is to demonstrate the main graphical effects techniques and to help students gain experience in graphical optimization. Visual effects are expensive, they cost a lot of processor time and resources. Finding the balance between visual appearance and performance is an important competence of digital artists.

The simulation of nature encompasses elements like sun motion and changes in sky color. The implementation of sunrises and sunsets is not trivial as the gradient of environment ambient color does not change as a linear transition between two colors. Modeling the environment provides possibility for future study of temperature variation, fog predisposition, fine particle distribution and other urban phenomena.

4   Virtual People

4.1   Navigational Meshes and Routing

The agents in the pandemic simulator are virtual people. Currently they are the only moving entities, besides the sun. To support population activities the simulator needs *a navigation mesh (navmesh)* – this is a special representation of interconnections in an area that allows navigation.

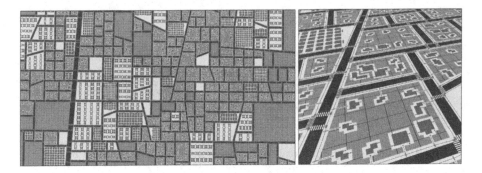

Fig. 7. A bird view and a close-up view of the navigation mesh

The simulator uses five types of navmeshes that define accessible areas inside and around houses; rooms, hallways and elevators in large buildings; sidewalks and pedestrian crossings. Figure 7 shows the global navmesh built by joining individual navmeshes. Accessible zones are indicated in red. The construction of a navmesh faces several challenges, like allocating pedestrian crossings, modeling vertical structures and traversing the navmesh. Each of these challenges can be turned into individual lesson as it may include discussions of possible solutions, their advantages and disadvantages.

The navmesh is the core data provider for the *route planner*. This is a collection of functions that build a path from one location to another. The navmesh is a graph and students know how to solve common graph problems, like traversing or finding a route. However, these solutions are not suitable in the context of the simulator. One particular example is the route planner – it finds a path that is *neither the shortest, nor the fastest*. The reason to implement suboptimal algorithm is to increase the level of natural behavior of virtual people (optimal algorithms always generate the same paths). This is a nice opportunity to show students some alternative approaches that generate less optimal, but more plausible solutions. Figure 8 presents a heatmap of generated routes between two fixed locations – the routes are random, but not too random.

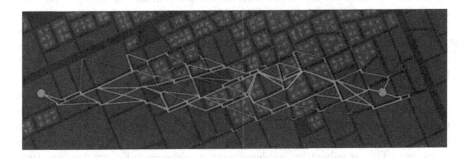

Fig. 8. A heatmap of multiple traversals between two locations

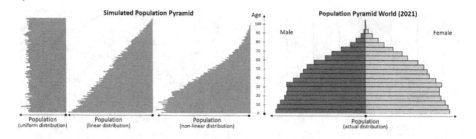

Fig. 9. Simulated *(left)* and real world *(right)* population distribution by age

4.2   Population Pyramid

The virtual people that walk in the simulation are generated at runtime. Each person is characterized by age and height, immune system, home and office locations, daily regime, etc. The behavior of a person is defined by 'simple' rules. This is another opportunity to show students how theoretical algorithms are modified to meet practical requirements. One example of such rule is the age distribution. Figure 9 presents three ways to simulate age distribution and the actual population pyramid for 2021 (source: U.S. Census Bureau, International Data Base, and The World Factbook 2021, [1]).

The simulator adopts the non-linear distribution. Its construction requires the students to design a modeling function that generates a specific curve. There are many possible solutions, like the average of three or more random samplings, the Gauss' normal distribution, and the cosine-based bell curve. Each of these solutions has its own advantages and disadvantages. Their common advantage, however, is that they could be profiled to model different population pyramids, including aging societies.

4.3   Body Shape and Motion

Although the focus of the simulator is not on photo-realistic rendering, the visual appearance of virtual people is essential to how users perceive the simulated environment. Instead of building own 3D model of the human body, the simulator uses predefined low-poly model.

There are many online repositories which provide 3D models of human bodies of different file format and licenses – some of these models are rigged, i.e. they have built-in skeletal system and can assume different poses or be animated; other models are static collection of vertices in 3D space.

Similarly to buildings and trees, we do not want to have a single body shape in the animation. When there is a crowd of people, they should have different body shapes and proportions. It is not just a matter of age (i.e. virtual children and adults), but people of the same age may have different heights, body-mass indices, etc. This is solved by implementing a more complex shader injection, which changes proportions of body parts.

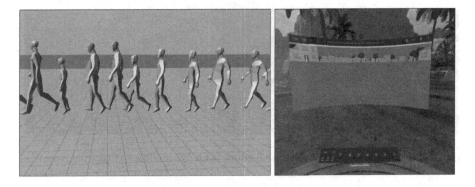

Fig. 10. Shader-rigged virtual people and simulator in Oculus Quest 2

Another challenge for the virtual people is their walking. Motion of body parts is done in the shader by multiplying vertices by rotation and translation matrices. This approach fits well in the provisioned educational activities by demonstrating how mathematical constructs are used to achieve biologically plausible motion – Fig. 10.

Under development is a special VR simulation mode. The right snapshot in Fig. 10 shows the simulation from the Oculus Quest 2 browser before entering VR mode. The VR mode will be used for future gaming in the simulator – the user will be one of the people in the city interacting with all other virtual people.

4.4 Infection Model

In Subsect. 4.2 we described how the population pyramid is defined by a custom curve. We use a similar approach for the viral shedding. The serial interval of COVID-19 infection is approximated in the simulator by a spline curve – see Fig. 11, left. The use of a spline allows easy modification of the curve profile, thus fine-tuning the simulation to different viral shedding patterns.

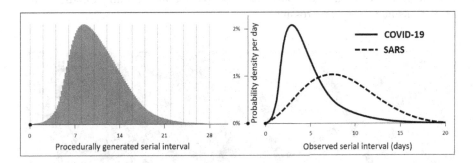

Fig. 11. Viral shedding curve – procedurally generated *(left)* and approximation of observed data *(right)* as reported in [16]

Fig. 12. Color-coding and overhead indicators of health condition (Color figure online)

The possibility to modify the shedding pattern can be 'advertised' to students as a feature supporting debugging and development. For example, testing the infection and healing process is faster if the timeline in Fig. 11 is shrunken from 28 days down to a few hours. This makes it possible to monitor the full cycle in a short period of time. To facilitate easier observation of how the pandemic is developing, the health status of virtual people could be color-coded and overhead indications could be added. Both techniques are demonstrated in the snapshots in Fig. 12. Bluish avatars represent healthy people, while reddish avatars are highly infectious people.

5   Preliminary Findings

When a new feature is implemented in the simulator it is tested individually and in combination with other features. A lot of interesting phenomena emerge during these tests. Such findings contribute to the creation new design slots, which will be used when the project splits into research and education paths.

One such phenomenon is the emerging self-organization when the number of virtual people increases to thousands or tens of thousands. For example, commuting people form human flow during morning rush hours. Figure 13 demonstrates two naturally occurring flow patterns – people streams around buildings and congestions at pedestrian crossings.

Fig. 13. Flow patterns around buildings *(left)* and at pedestrian crossings *(right)*

Fig. 14. A bug in GLSL injection scales roofs of buildings *(left)* and maps the shadows of trees over the building as if the ground is transparent *(right)*

An essential component of building a simulator as an educational activity is the high probability of introducing software bugs. Although most graduate and undergraduate computer science courses focus on how to avoid bugs, the building of the simulator embraces the bugs as a valuable educational asset. Carefully nurtured bugs may inspire students to pursuit other options and ideas.

Figure 14 shows two of the bugs. The left snapshot is caused by a bug in the GLSL injection. The shader calculates wrong scaling factors for roofs, which produces a medieval impression. The right snapshot presents a glitch in normal vectors that renders the ground transparent – the shadows of all trees and houses are projected onto the buildings, when the sun is below the horizon.

Of course, not every bug is worth showing. Most of them result in an empty screen or a grotesque pile of geometrical primitives. In spite of this, bugs provide excellent educational opportunities for students and teachers.

To debug navmeshes, routing and daily behavior of people, there is an enforced mode of the simulator – we can order everyone to go to a specific place, to stay at home, or to block elevators. Figure 15 shows a bird-view, a drone-view and a close contact with a group of people ordered to gather together in the park. This opens the software to simulating social events in the future.

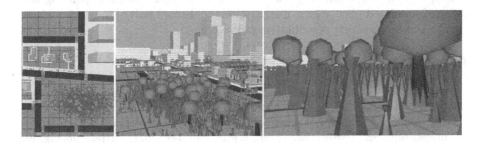

Fig. 15. Gathering a large group of people in the park

6   Conclusion

This paper presents a work in progress – the building of a visual simulator with focus on simulating pandemics and providing educational activities in a broad range of domains.

The simulator is highly configurable, flexible and applicable to different phenomena. The current implementation supports simulations from a single house to a large megalopolis, it can be fine-tuned to model infection spreading, but could be used to model social behavior including spreading rumors, gathering of large group of people, strikes, etc. The knowledge of designing configurability cannot be taught, but could be mastered by experience.

It might be considered controversial, but the building of a simulated world is an opportunity for the students to revisit and revise the algorithms they have studied in other disciplines. These algorithms focus on being optimal in terms of performance or allocated memory, while a simulated world needs suboptimal algorithms, which simulate the non-deterministic nature of humans.

The current status of the software development is finalizing its features – this is the software implementation phase in Fig. 1. The short-term plans for future development include the addition of more assets, like traffic lights, public and private transportation, new types of buildings (e.g. malls, schools, theaters, sport centers), more diverse behavior of virtual people and better VR support.

Our mid-term plans include the last two phases of the project – the development of a course for (under)graduate students, performing research experiments and opening the simulator for the public. Although the source code of the project is open[5], the simulator has no user interface for general users.

The long-term plans are focused on three orthogonal dimensions that span beyond the current project workflow from Fig. 1. The first dimension is upscaling the software by running the simulation engine on a supercomputer. This is in line with the just opened call Training and Education on High Performance Computing within the Horizon 2020 Framework Programme. The expectation is that such version of the software could simulate much larger populations at the scale of millions of virtual people. The second dimension is to develop deeper models by simulating interiors of buildings and rooms. The goal of this dimension is to provide more accurate model, because significant factor of pandemic development is the in-building infection. The third dimension is expanding the range of simulated phenomena, like smog, fog and small particles; winds and air circulation; temperature distribution and seasons.

References

1. The World Factbook 2021. Central Intelligence Agency, Washington, DC (2021). https://www.cia.gov/the-world-factbook/
2. Alsharhan, A.M.: Survey of agent-based simulations for modelling COVID-19 pandemic. Adv. Sci. Technol. Eng. Syst. J. **6**(2), 439–447 (2021). https://doi.org/10.25046/aj060250

---

[5] https://github.com/boytchev/COVID-19-SIM.

3. Barak, O., Gavish, N., Hari, L.P., Shohat, T.: Simulator of interventions for COVID-19 (2020). https://applied-math.net.technion.ac.il/files/2020/06/Covid_simulator.pdf
4. Burak, S., et al.: Mathemathical modelling and numerical simulations of COVID-19 spreading-example of Bosnia. Period. Eng. Nat. Sci. (PEN) **8**(3), 1566–1579 (2020)
5. Chertkov, M., et al.: Graphical models of pandemic. medRxiv (2021)
6. Cleto, C.R., Boulstridge, L., Stenhouse, C., Craig, D.: Using simulation training to introduce medical students to COVID-19 (2021)
7. Dieckmann, P., Torgeirsen, K., Qvindesland, S.A., Thomas, L., Bushell, V., Langli Ersdal, H.: The use of simulation to prepare and improve responses to infectious disease outbreaks like COVID-19: practical tips and resources from Norway, Denmark, and the UK. Adv. Simul. **5**, 1–10 (2020)
8. Fitó-Bertran, À., Hernández-Lara, A.B., López, E.S.: The effect of competences on learning results an educational experience with a business simulator. Comput. Hum. Behav. **51**, 910–914 (2015)
9. Ghaffarzadegan, N.: Simulation-based what-if analysis for controlling the spread of COVID-19 in universities. PLOS One **16**(2), e0246323 (2021)
10. Ghaffarzadegan, N., Childs, L.M., TÄuber, U.C.: Diverse computer simulation models provide unified lessons on university operation during a pandemic. BioScience **71**(2), 113–114 (2021)
11. Hsieh, J.L., Sun, C.T., Kao, G.Y.M., Huang, C.Y.: Teaching through simulation: epidemic dynamics and public health policies. Simulation **82**(11), 731–759 (2006)
12. Kurth, T., Brinks, R.: Predicting the pandemic (2020)
13. Lacka, E., Wong, T., Haddoud, M.Y.: Can digital technologies improve students' efficiency? Exploring the role of virtual learning environment and social media use in higher education. Comput. Educ. **163**, 104099 (2021)
14. Lima, L., Atman, A.: Impact of mobility restriction in COVID-19 superspreading events using agent-based model. PLOS One **16**(3), e0248708 (2021)
15. Loomans, M., Boerstra, A., Wisse, C.: Calculating the risk of infection. REHVA J. **2020**(5), 19–24 (2020)
16. Nishiura, H., Linton, N., Akhmetzhanov, A.: Serial interval of novel coronavirus (COVID-19) infections. Int. J. Infect. Dis. **93**, 284–286 (2020). https://doi.org/10.1016/j.ijid.2020.02.060
17. Peng, B., Pettit, R.W., Amos, C.I.: Population simulations of COVID-19 outbreaks provide tools for risk assessment and continuity planning. JAMIA Open **4**(3), 1–7 (2020). https://doi.org/10.1093/jamiaopen/ooaa074
18. Rubin, D.M., et al.: Facilitating understanding, modeling and simulation of infectious disease epidemics in the age of COVID-19. Front. Public Health **9**, 33 (2021)
19. Siddiqui, A., Khan, M., Akhtar, S.: Supply chain simulator: a scenario-based educational tool to enhance student learning. Comput. Educ. **51**(1), 252–261 (2008)
20. Zea, E., Valez-Balderas, M., Uribe-Quevedo, A.: Serious games and multiple intelligences for customized learning: a discussion. In: Brooks, A.L., Brahman, S., Kapralos, B., Nakajima, A., Tyerman, J., Jain, L.C. (eds.) Recent Advances in Technologies for Inclusive Well-Being. ISRL, vol. 196, pp. 177–189. Springer, Cham (2021). https://doi.org/10.1007/978-3-030-59608-8_9

Information Technology Applications-
Special Session on Language
Technologies

Generating Abstractive Summaries of Lithuanian News Articles Using a Transformer Model

Lukas Stankevičius[(✉)][iD] and Mantas Lukoševičius[iD]

Faculty of Informatics, Kaunas University of Technology, Kaunas, Lithuania
`lukas.stankevicius@ktu.lt`

Abstract. In this work, we train the first monolingual Lithuanian transformer model on a relatively large corpus of Lithuanian news articles and compare various output decoding algorithms for abstractive news summarization. We achieve an average ROUGE-2 score 0.163, generated summaries are coherent and look impressive at first glance. However, some of them contain misleading information that is not so easy to spot. We describe all the technical details and share our trained model and accompanying code in an online open-source repository, as well as some characteristic samples of the generated summaries.

Keywords: Summarization · Transformers · Natural language processing · Lithuanian language

1 Introduction

Recent innovations in deep learning models gave rise to new capabilities for natural language generation. Huge GPT-2 [21] and following GPT-3 [3] models attracted attention of the public with convincing stories from "new species of unicorns" to "colony of humans living in elevator shafts".[1] Even generation of realistic images from a written text prompt is now possible.[2]

Lithuanian language can not enjoy the same attention and application of innovations as English. There are only sparse records of text generation[3,4] which were more of creative projects with no scientific or technical details made public.

One practical application of text generation is summary writing. Now more than ever, growing amounts of information require thorough digestion and simplification. Currently, only extractive text summarization based on classical semantic analysis framework [29] is available for Lithuanian texts.[5]

---

[1] https://thenextweb.com/neural/2020/10/07/someone-let-a-gpt-3-bot-loose-on-red dit-it-didnt-end-well/.

[2] https://openai.com/blog/dall-e/.

[3] https://www.15min.lt/mokslasit/straipsnis/technologijos/lietuviskas-d-i-ne-dirbtin is-intelektas-o-dirbtinis-idiotas-646-748590 (in Lithuanian).

[4] https://ktu.edu/news/ktu-profesorius-saulius-keturakis-nuo-siol-lietuviu-literatu ra-kuria-ir-masinos/ (in Lithuanian).

[5] https://semantika.lt/Analysis/Summary.

© Springer Nature Switzerland AG 2021
A. Lopata et al. (Eds.): ICIST 2021, CCIS 1486, pp. 341–352, 2021.
https://doi.org/10.1007/978-3-030-88304-1_27

In this work we: (1) train the first Lithuanian monolingual transformer models on news articles summarization task; (2) explore different decoding options for the best summary generation; (3) share all the technical details and code for reproduction. We hope that this work will give a boost to the Lithuanian language generation as well as useful experience transferable to other mid-resource languages.

2 Previous Related Work

2.1 From n-gram to Transformer Language Models

Before the success of neural language models, statistical ones were the most common. One example is the n-gram language model. For chosen n, it approximates the conditional probability of the next word w_i, given a word sequence of length $i - 1$ behind, by

$$P(w_i|w_{1:i-1}) \approx P(w_i|w_{i-n:i-1}). \tag{1}$$

In practice, this means collecting n-gram counts from the corpus and normalizing them to probabilities. The higher n-gram is used, the bigger improvements are expected. However, increasing history size is difficult as it requires a very large corpus to produce sufficient counts and suffers from sparsity. It also leads to computational overhead, requires a lot of memory.

Neural language models offer several advantages over statistical ones. Instead of using predictive distributions determined by counting, they use internal representation to perform a high-dimensional interpolation between training examples [7]. This way neural networks are better at generating real-valued data than exact matches. Finally, these models do not suffer from the curse of dimensionality.

The first neural networks successfully adopted for language modeling were Recurrent Neural Networks (RNNs) of Long Short-Term Memory (LSTM) type [7,9,26]. They were also one of the first to be employed for abstractive text summarization [24]. The recurrent nature of this architecture makes it very simple to feed sequential text of varying length, while enhancements over simpler RNN variants increase stability with the added memory. It was a huge improvement over the n-gram language models but had its own drawbacks nonetheless.

Computations with recurrent neural networks do not scale well, because inputs to the model must be passed sequentially. Each word in a sequence must wait for the computation of the hidden state of the previous word to complete. This limits the parallelization of the computations.

The other drawback is that information of all the previous inputs has to fit into the last hidden state. As a result, only recent inputs are usually sufficiently "remembered", and the model is unable to model long-range dependencies between inputs. This was only partially addressed by deeper processing of the hidden states through specific units (LSTM), using Bi-directional models, and employing attention mechanisms [2].

Almost all of the above issues of neural language models were solved by the current state-of-the-art Transformer architecture [28]. The whole sequence now can be fed to a model at once, while added positional embeddings preserve the order information. Large data and computation resources can now be fully utilized. Additionally, due to the attention mechanism, each input word can attend to any other in any layer, thus producing contextualized word vectors.

As of now, there exist multiple Transformer type models. Many implementations can be found in the Huggingface Transformers library [31]. Although there are efforts [30] to use models trained on masked words predictions [4], usually the ones trained on language modeling (predicting the next word) are best suited for text generation. Specifically for the summarization task, the more notable Transformer models are: T5 [23], BART [15], PEGASUS [33], and ProphetNet [20].

2.2 Decoding Algorithms

Given a dataset $D = \{x^1, \ldots, x^{|D|}\}$, current state-of-the-art text generation models [22] train a neural network with parameters θ to minimize the negative log-likelihood

$$\mathcal{L}(D) = -\sum_{k=1}^{|D|} \log \prod_{i=1}^{|x^k|} p_\theta(x_i^k | x_{<i}^k), \tag{2}$$

where x_i^k is the i-th word of the k-th text in the dataset D.

After this kind of training, candidate word probabilities can be inferred for all words in a vocabulary. The chosen word can later be appended to conditional input to predict the next one. The process repeats for the desired output sequence length or until the special token (i.e., <eos> for T5) is reached. Also, additional words can be added to condition the model more specifically [11,23].

Below we will describe various decoding algorithms for choosing the next word from given probabilities of all the words in a vocabulary.

Maximization-Based Decoding. These are greedy, deterministic decoding methods. They assume that the model assigns higher probabilities for higher-quality text.

The most simple decoding is called **greedy search**. It selects the next word as the one with the highest probability. This simplicity makes it very fast, albeit not optimal.

Another popular, heuristic expanding the one above, is **beam search** decoding. Instead of choosing only one word with the highest probability at a time, a defined number of word sequences with the highest overall probabilities are kept. This way, a single low-probability word would not shadow a high-overall-probability sequence.

A natural way to improve beam search is to use a higher beam size. An obvious drawback is that the computation intensifies. A second disadvantage, as noticed in [12,27] for translation tasks, is that increasing beam size reduces BLEU score (mentioned in Sect. 2.4). This is explained by higher beam sizes generating shorter sequences. This effect is especially strong when beam sizes are in the range of 100–1 000. According to [17], low beam sizes produce more on-topic but nonsensical text, while the high ones converge to a correct and generic, but less relevant response.

Sampling. As argued in [10], human language does not follow a distribution of high probability next words, in contrast to what greedy decoding methods do. This issue is alleviated by stochastic decoding methods.

In the most basic form, sampling is used to randomly select the next word according to its conditional probability distribution. Instead of sampling from the distribution of all vocabulary words, **Top-K** sampling was proposed in [6]. Here K most probable next words are selected and the probability mass is redistributed among only those words.

Later **Top-p** (nucleus) sampling [10] was suggested to adapt to different initial probability distributions. Here the most probable words are selected such, that the sum of their probabilities is not greater than p. This way an adaptation to sharp or flat probability distributions is implemented.

2.3 Additional Techniques

During language modeling, the last neural network layer produces output for each word in vocabulary. These outputs are raw values called "logits". To convert them into probabilities, commonly a softmax function is used:

$$\text{softmax}(y_i) = \frac{\exp(y_i)}{\sum_j \exp(y_j)}. \tag{3}$$

One technique to rebalance the probabilities is a softmax temperature parameter τ. Then the probability of word i given all vocabulary logits $\mathbf{y}$ is

$$P_i = \text{softmax}(y_i/\tau) = \frac{\exp(y_i/\tau)}{\sum_j \exp(y_j/\tau)}. \tag{4}$$

Then $\tau > 1$, the probability distribution becomes more uniform, and more diverse outputs are expected. Otherwise, the probability concentrates on a smaller number of top words.

2.4 Evaluation Methods

It is very difficult to evaluate the quality of abstractive summarization. Even if one has reference summaries, alternative correct summaries can be easily produced using different words, their order, sentence length, emphasis, etc. The most accurate evaluation thus would be done by humans. Yet it is very expensive and slow, conducting it effectively is difficult. Due to these reasons, automatic evaluation metrics are widely used.

ROUGE. Introduced by [16] and abbreviated from Recall-Oriented Understudy for Gisting Evaluation (ROUGE), they are word-overlap-based metrics. The following ROUGE metrics are regularly used for summary evaluation.

ROUGE-n. Let p be "the number of common n-grams between the candidate and the reference summaries", and q be "the number of n-grams extracted from the reference summary only" [1]. Then the recall score is computed as

$$ROUGE\text{-}n = \frac{p}{q}. \tag{5}$$

The precision score is divided by "the number of n-grams extracted from the generated summary only" instead, and F-score combines the precision and the recall. We report F-scores in our results. Typically, n values of 1 and 2 are used.

ROUGE-L. This metric calculates the length of the longest common subsequence between the candidate and the reference summaries.

For example, on English news dataset CNN/Daily Mail [8,18], the highest ROUGE scores using abstractive summarization currently are reported at ROUGE-1 = 45.94, ROUGE-2 = 22.32, and ROUGE-L = 42.48 [5].

Other Evaluation Metrics. One of the attempts to capture the overlap between meanings instead of exact words is to compare word vectors. BERTScore [34] is a model-based metric that uses a pretrained BERT [4] model to produce contextualized embeddings and matches words in the candidate and reference sentences by cosine similarity. Compared to ROUGE, however, this evaluation method is more compute-intensive and lacks the simple explainability.

In machine translation, BLEU [19] is considered the standard evaluation metric. BLEU is based on precision, while ROUGE can be based more on recall and thus is more suitable for the summarization task.

3 Data

We crawled news articles with summary and the main text (body) parts from the most popular Lithuanian news websites. We filtered data so that summary > 10 and the main text > 100 characters in length. As the goal of summarization is to produce a shorter text than the original, we used only the articles where the main text length in characters was at least twice the summary length.

We want our models to learn abstractive summarization and avoid copying. Due to this reason, for each summary and main text pair, we found the longest matching string sequence and calculated the overlap as a ratio of this sequence and the summary lengths. We left only pairs with this overlap ratio less than 0.2. This criterion is similar to summaries not having very high ROUGE-L scores compared to the main texts.

The final filtered dataset consists of 2 031 514 news articles. Detailed statistics are depicted in Table 1. We put random 4 096 articles from this set aside from training for validation.

Table 1. Our data corpus statistics

Website	Article count	Time period	
		From	To
15min.lt	767 182	2007-07-09	2020-09-23
lrytas.lt	522 519	2017-03-30	2020-09-24
delfi.lt	436 487	2000-01-27	2020-09-25
lrt.lt	181 356	2012-05-25	2020-09-24
technologijos.lt	66 867	2007-02-22	2020-09-24
bernardinai.lt	25 250	2004-03-30	2020-04-29
kasvyksta.lt	18 781	2012-03-15	2020-09-25
panele.lt	11 587	2007-03-07	2020-09-24
kaunodiena.lt	1 485	2002-08-05	2014-06-25

4   Methods

We used SentencePiece [14] to encode text as unigram [13] subwords. A tokenizer was trained on 10^6 samples of our text corpus and was set to have a vocabulary size of 32 000 (the same size as the English tokenizer from [23]).

We used T5 base [23] transformer model implementation from [31]. This library also contains methods we used in this work for text generation. The model was trained for 350 000 steps with batches of 128 text-summary pairs (achieved by 32 gradient accumulation steps), both truncated to 512 tokens. Using mixed precision and GeForce RTX 2080 Ti GPU it took approximately 500 h and consisted of 22 passes through the dataset (epochs). We used Adafactor [25] optimizer with 10 000 warm-up steps followed by inverse square root internal learning rate schedule.

We initialized the weights with a pretrained English *t5-base* model, as it showed a faster convergence compared to random weight initialization (see Fig. 1). We do not use a pretrained multilingual *mt5-base* model [32] because: (1) due to shorter tokens, tokenized sequences are on average 1.49 times longer and (2) it has 580 M parameters versus our used 220 M mainly due to the bigger multilingual vocabulary embedding matrix. These reasons made training multilingual *mt5-base* 4 times slower than a monolingual model based on *t5-base* and higher ROUGE scores were faster reached with the latter.

We decided that the generated sample is repetitive if any constituent word count, except the stop word "ir" ("and" in Lithuanian), is greater than 7. We also calculated a generated text length fraction as a ratio of the generated text to the target summary character counts. ROUGE scores were calculated for stemmed texts.

5   Results

In this section, we first report results with a model trained for 65 000 steps and then see the changes continuing the training further.

5.1   Repetition

We found out that the best way to avoid repetition is to obstruct the repeated generation of 2-grams by setting `no_repeat_ngram_size` parameter value to 2. This way 36 repetitive samples (out of 4 096) of greedy beam search with beam size 10 were reduced to 0.

5.2   Reshaping Probability Distribution

To our surprise, greedy methods gave quite decent results. Any attempt to reshape probability distribution favored tokens with the top probabilities. For sampling, we tried temperatures τ values 0.8, 0.6, 0.4, 0.2, 0.1, and 0.05, with the last one yielding the best scores, ROUGE-2 = 0.132. We also experimented with Top-p sampling trying p values of 0.9, 0.8, 0.6, 0.4, 0.2, and 0.1, with the last one also yielding the best scores, ROUGE-2 = 0.131. Both decoding methods had all metrics approximately the same as greedy search. Top-k similarly resulted in best $k = 5$ (tried 50, 40, 30, 20, 10, 5), ROUGE-2 = 0.109.

5.3   Best Decoding Methods

The best results were obtained with beam search decoding (see Table 2). There was no significant difference between greedy and Top-k ($k = 50$) beam searches. Though the latter is expected to be more diverse due to its stochastic nature. Increasing beam size from 10 to 20 only increased the generation time to more than 3 h and did not benefit ROUGE scores.

Training the model longer is beneficial. After 250 000 steps, mean ROUGE-2 reached 0.148 for greedy, 0.163 for greedy beam search, and 0.161 for Top-50 beam search decoding (see Fig. 1). We use ROUGE-2 as the main metric here, as it seems to be the hardest of the three to get high values. Training even further, we observe overfitting: the validation loss begins to ascent, and ROUGE metrics deteriorate (note, however, the log-scale of the x-axis).

We discuss the qualitative analysis of the generated summaries in the next Sect. 6 and provide some illustrative generated summaries in Appendix A.

Table 2. Text generation performance metrics on 4 096 validation articles of model trained for 65 000 steps. For ROUGE F-scores are given. All methods use `no_repeat_ngram_size` = 2, ten beams for beam searches.

Decoding method	Performance metric: mean (standard deviation)			
	ROUGE-1	ROUGE-2	ROUGE-L	Length fraction
Greedy search	0.298 (0.154)	0.132 (0.137)	0.233 (0.147)	0.79 (0.40)
Greedy beam search	0.303 (0.162)	0.140 (0.146)	0.238 (0.155)	0.82 (0.39)
Top-50 beam search	0.306 (0.156)	0.138 (0.143)	0.235 (0.152)	1.07 (0.67)

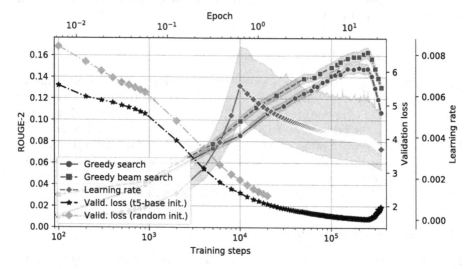

Fig. 1. ROUGE-2 mean F-score, learning rate, and validation loss dependency on model training steps. Shadow areas correspond to confidence interval of 95%. ROUGE-2 and learning rate are shown for model trained with *t5-base* initialization.

6   Conclusion and Discussion of Results

We trained the first reported monolingual Lithuanian transformer model and compared various decoding algorithms for abstractive news summarization. We used a moderately-sized modern universal transformer model T5, because of the computational requirements as well as the availability of training texts. We still observe that the model tends to overfit if trained for too long.

The best configuration we achieved is the model trained for 250 000 steps and greedy beam decoding with 10 beams. It achieved ROUGE-2 = 0.163.

Mostly all the generated summaries were coherent and made the first impression of being professionally written. Some of them successfully collected important information from various parts of the input text and summarized the main idea of the text quite impressively.

However, a closer examination of the generated samples reveals some chaotic and misleading summaries. There were a lot of text samples with minor factual mistakes, such as a mistaken number, abbreviation, name, day of the week, that can often be identified only by reading the main body text carefully or comparing with the target summary. Sometimes irrelevant information was added to the generated summaries, likely the one too often seen during the training. An example dynamic of summaries generated of a single text during the training is depicted in Appendix A.2. While all the summaries above 0 steps sound convincing, completely factually correct summaries are only at 175 000 and 300 000 steps, others have small errors.

A lot of high-ROUGE samples were finely combined multiple excerpts from the main text and learned templates repeating in our target data. On the other hand, there were also very good abstractive summaries with ROUGE scores just above zero. This emphasizes both the need for thorough data preparation and better evaluation of the summary quality. The latter could be covered with more resource-intensive scores like BERTScore [34] or manual human evaluation.

Overall, our trained model is good for generating fiction but makes trusting the generated news summaries problematic. Thus, for real-world applications, a more substantial human intervention is needed for quality assessment/control.

We hope that this work will boost adopting transformers for the Lithuanian language. We make our trained model and code available at https://github. com/LukasStankevicius/Generating-abstractive-summaries-of-Lithuanian-news-articles-using-a-transformer-model.

A   Text Sample Generation Dynamics

A.1   Reference Summary

Kai Lietuva dar buvo okupuota ir mūsų šalies krepšininkai privalėjo žaisti TSRS rinktinėje, keli jų buvo ryškūs lyderiai.[6]

A.2   Generated Summaries

0 steps, R-1 = 0.136, R-2 = 0, R-L = 0.091 Lietuvos krepšinio legenda pelnė po 13,6 taško per 84 mačus. Dešimtuke taip pat yra, ir

25 000 steps, R-1 = 0.182, R-2 = 0, R-L = 0.136 Lietuvos krepšinio federacijos (LKF) sudarytame geriausių visų laikų rezultatyviausių krepšininkų sąraše – Arvydas Sabonis ir Modestas Paulauskas.

---

[6] The original article and summary are available at https://www.15min.lt/24sek/naujiena/lietuva/tarp-penkiu-rezultatyviausiu-tsrs-rinktines-visu-laiku-zaideju-trys-lietuviai-875-1380030 (in Lithuanian).

75 000 steps, R-1 = 0.130, R-2 = 0.022, R-L = 0.109 Legendinis Lietuvos krepšininkas Arvydas Sabonis pirmadienį socialiniame tinkle pasidalijo statistika, kuri viršūėje yra Arvydo Sabonio. 1982 metais debiutavęs 222 cm ūgio vidurio puolėjas su raudona apranga sužaidė 52 rungtynes, per kurias rinko po 15,6 taško. Tai pats aukščiausias rezultatyvumo vidurkis tarp visų sovietų komandai atstovavusių žaidėjų, skaičiuojant tuos, kurie sužaidė ne mažiau nei 50 rungtynių.

100 000 steps, R-1 = 0.169, R-2 = 0.049, R-L = 0.145 Lietuvos krepšinio legenda Arvydas Sabonis pirmadienį socialiniame tinkle pasidalijo statistika, kurios viršūnėje yra A.Sabonis. 1982 metais TSRS rinktinėje debiutavęs 222 cm ūgio vidurio puolėjas su raudona apranga sužaidė 52 rungtynes, per kurias rinko po 15,6 taško. Tai pats aukščiausias rezultatyvumo vidurkis tarp visų SSRS komandai atstovavusių žaidėjų.

125 000 steps, R-1 = 0.360, R-2 = 0.083, R-L = 0.320 Lietuvos krepšinio federacijos (LKF) prezidentas Arvydas Sabonis ir buvęs Kauno "Žalgirio" krepšininkas Rimas Kurtinaitis tapo rezultatyviausiais visų laikų TSRS rinktinės žaidėjais.

150 000 steps, R-1 = 0.318, R-2 = 0.095, R-L = 0.227 Arvydui Saboniui ir Šarūnui Marčiulioniui – rezultatyviausi visų laikų Tėvynės sąjungos (TSRS) rinktinės krepšininkai.

175 000 steps, R-1 = 0.207, R-2 = 0.036, R-L = 0.172 Lietuvos krepšinio federacijos (LKF) prezidento Arvydo Sabonio rezultatyvumo vidurkis yra aukščiausias tarp visų Sovietų Sąjungos rinktinėje atstovavusių žaidėjų, skaičiuojant tuos, kurie sužaidė bent po 50 oficialių rungtynių.

200 000 steps, R-1 = 0.197, R-2 = 0, R-L = 0.131 Legendinis Arvydas Sabonis yra vienas geriausių visų laikų Lietuvos rinktinės krepčininkų, sužaidęs bent po 50 oficialių rungtynių nacionalinėje komandoje. Jis yra pirmas pagal rezultatyvumo vidurkį tarp visų sovietų komandoje atstovavusių krepšininkų.

225 000 steps, R-1 = 0.296, R-2 = 0.077, R-L = 0.185 Legendinis Lietuvos krepšininkas Arvydas Sabonis yra pirmas pagal rezultatyvumą tarp visų Sovietų Sąjungos rinktinės žaidėjų, kurie sužaidė bent po 50 oficialių rungtynių Lietuvos rinktinėje.

250 000 steps, R-1 = 0.136, R-2 = 0, R-L = 0.136 Lietuvos krepšinio federacijos (LKF) generalinis sekretorius Mindaugas Špokas pirmadienį socialiniame tinkle "Facebook" pasidalino statistika, kurios viršūėje yra Arvydas Sabonis. Tai pats aukščiausias rezultatyvumo vidurkis tarp visų sovietų komandai atstovavusių žaidėjų.

300 000 steps, R-1 = 0.175, R-2 = 0.036, R-L = 0.175 Lietuvos krepšinio legenda Arvydas Sabonis yra geriausias visų laikų rezultatyviausias krepšininkas tarp visų sovietų rinktinei atstovavusių žaidėjų, skaičiuojant tuos, kurie sužaidė ne mažiau nei 50 oficialių rungtynių.

350 000 steps, R-1 = 0.364, R-2 = 0.038, R-L = 0.255 Buvęs Lietuvos krepšinio rinktinės vidurio puolėjas Valdis Valteris ir buvęs Kauno "Žalgirio" krepšininkas Rimas Kurtinaitis yra tarp rezultatyviausių visų laikų Lietuvos rinktinės žaidėjų.

References

1. Allahyari, M., et al.: Text summarization techniques: a brief survey. arXiv preprint arXiv:1707.02268 (2017)
2. Bahdanau, D., Cho, K., Bengio, Y.: Neural machine translation by jointly learning to align and translate. arXiv preprint arXiv:1409.0473 (2014)
3. Brown, T.B., et al.: Language models are few-shot learners. arXiv preprint arXiv:2005.14165 (2020)
4. Devlin, J., Chang, M.W., Lee, K., Toutanova, K.: BERT: pre-training of deep bidirectional transformers for language understanding. arXiv preprint arXiv:1810.04805 (2018)
5. Dou, Z.Y., Liu, P., Hayashi, H., Jiang, Z., Neubig, G.: GSum: a general framework for guided neural abstractive summarization. arXiv preprint arXiv:2010.08014 (2020)
6. Fan, A., Lewis, M., Dauphin, Y.: Hierarchical neural story generation. In: Proceedings of the 56th Annual Meeting of the Association for Computational Linguistics (Volume 1: Long Papers), pp. 889–898 (2018)
7. Graves, A.: Generating sequences with recurrent neural networks. arXiv preprint arXiv:1308.0850 (2013)
8. Hermann, K.M., et al.: Teaching machines to read and comprehend. arXiv preprint arXiv:1506.03340 (2015)
9. Hochreiter, S., Schmidhuber, J.: Long short-term memory. Neural Comput. **9**(8), 1735–1780 (1997)
10. Holtzman, A., Buys, J., Du, L., Forbes, M., Choi, Y.: The curious case of neural text degeneration. In: International Conference on Learning Representations (2019)
11. Keskar, N.S., McCann, B., Varshney, L.R., Xiong, C., Socher, R.: CTRL: a conditional transformer language model for controllable generation. arXiv preprint arXiv:1909.05858 (2019)
12. Koehn, P., Knowles, R.: Six challenges for neural machine translation. arXiv preprint arXiv:1706.03872 (2017)
13. Kudo, T.: Subword regularization: improving neural network translation models with multiple subword candidates. In: Proceedings of the 56th Annual Meeting of the Association for Computational Linguistics (Volume 1: Long Papers), pp. 66–75 (2018)
14. Kudo, T., Richardson, J.: SentencePiece: a simple and language independent subword tokenizer and detokenizer for neural text processing. In: Proceedings of the 2018 Conference on Empirical Methods in Natural Language Processing: System Demonstrations, pp. 66–71 (2018)
15. Lewis, M., et al.: BART: denoising sequence-to-sequence pre-training for natural language generation, translation, and comprehension. In: Proceedings of the 58th Annual Meeting of the Association for Computational Linguistics, pp. 7871–7880 (2020)
16. Lin, C.Y.: Rouge: a package for automatic evaluation of summaries. In: Text Summarization Branches Out, pp. 74–81 (2004)

17. Manning, C., See, A.: Stanford CS224N: NLP with deep learning—winter 2019—lecture 15 – natural language generation (2019). https://youtu.be/4uG1NMKNWCU

18. Nallapati, R., Zhou, B., dos Santos, C., Gülçehre, Ç., Xiang, B.: Abstractive text summarization using sequence-to-sequence RNNs and beyond. In: Proceedings of The 20th SIGNLL Conference on Computational Natural Language Learning, pp. 280–290 (2016)

19. Papineni, K., Roukos, S., Ward, T., Zhu, W.J.: BLEU: a method for automatic evaluation of machine translation. In: Proceedings of the 40th Annual Meeting of the Association for Computational Linguistics, pp. 311–318 (2002)

20. Qi, W., et al.: ProphetNet: predicting future n-gram for sequence-to-sequence pre-training. In: Proceedings of the 2020 Conference on Empirical Methods in Natural Language Processing: Findings, pp. 2401–2410 (2020)

21. Radford, A., Wu, J., Child, R., Luan, D., Amodei, D., Sutskever, I.: Language models are unsupervised multitask learners. OpenAI Blog 1(8), 9 (2019)

22. Raffel, C., et al.: Exploring the limits of transfer learning with a unified text-to-text transformer. arXiv preprint arXiv:1910.10683 (2019)

23. Raffel, C., et al.: Exploring the limits of transfer learning with a unified text-to-text transformer. J. Mach. Learn. Res. 21, 1–67 (2020)

24. Rush, A.M., Chopra, S., Weston, J.: A neural attention model for abstractive sentence summarization. In: Proceedings of the 2015 Conference on Empirical Methods in Natural Language Processing, pp. 379–389 (2015)

25. Shazeer, N., Stern, M.: Adafactor: adaptive learning rates with sublinear memory cost. In: International Conference on Machine Learning, pp. 4596–4604. PMLR (2018)

26. Sundermeyer, M., Schlüter, R., Ney, H.: LSTM neural networks for language modeling. In: Thirteenth Annual Conference of the International Speech Communication Association (2012)

27. Tu, Z., Liu, Y., Shang, L., Liu, X., Li, H.: Neural machine translation with reconstruction. In: Proceedings of the AAAI Conference on Artificial Intelligence, vol. 31, no. 1, February 2017. https://ojs.aaai.org/index.php/AAAI/article/view/10950

28. Vaswani, A., et al.: Attention is all you need. arXiv preprint arXiv:1706.03762 (2017)

29. Vitkutė-Adžgauskienė, D., Utka, A., Amilevičius, D., Krilavičius, T.: NLP infrastructure for the Lithuanian language. In: Proceedings of the LREC 2016: 10th International Conference on Language Resources and Evaluation, Portorož, Slovenia, 23–28 May 2016. European Language Resources Association, Paris (2016)

30. Wang, A., Cho, K.: BERT has a mouth, and it must speak: BERT as a Markov random field language model. arXiv preprint arXiv:1902.04094 (2019)

31. Wolf, T., et al.: Transformers: state-of-the-art natural language processing. In: Proceedings of the 2020 Conference on Empirical Methods in Natural Language Processing: System Demonstrations, pp. 38–45. Association for Computational Linguistics, October 2020. https://www.aclweb.org/anthology/2020.emnlp-demos.6

32. Xue, L., et al.: mT5: a massively multilingual pre-trained text-to-text transformer (2020)

33. Zhang, J., Zhao, Y., Saleh, M., Liu, P.: PEGASUS: pre-training with extracted gap-sentences for abstractive summarization. In: International Conference on Machine Learning, pp. 11328–11339. PMLR (2020)

34. Zhang, T., Kishore, V., Wu, F., Weinberger, K.Q., Artzi, Y.: BERTScore: evaluating text generation with BERT. arXiv preprint arXiv:1904.09675 (2019)

How to Improve E-commerce Search Engines? Evaluating Transformer-Based Named Entity Recognition on German Product Datasets

Sergej Denisov[✉] and Frederik S. Bäumer

Bielefeld University of Applied Sciences, Bielefeld, Germany
{sergej.denisov,frederik.baeumer}@fh-bielefeld.de

Abstract. The quality of e-commerce search engines often suffers from data that online retailers poorly maintain. This situation can be observed on consumer-to-consumer marketplaces as well as on business-to-consumer platforms. One way to improve search quality is to perform linguistic enhancement of the product data. In this case, Named Entity Recognition is primarily used to identify important content and give it a higher weighting in the search. Our approach detects e-commerce entity types, such as products, brands, and various product attributes. Because of the low availability of existing resources and linguistic complexity identifying these entity types is challenging. Therefore, we acquire data from two online e-commerce marketplaces to build six German datasets based on product titles and descriptions. For these datasets, we evaluate the NER performance of the state-of-the-art models BERT, RoBERTa, and XLM-RoBERTa. The best performance archived the XLM-RoBERTa model with an F1 score of 0.8611 averaged over all datasets.

Keywords: Transformer · Named entity recognition · E-commerce

1 Introduction

Online marketplaces, such as Amazon or eBay, each offer millions of products on their platform. The products, which different sellers usually offer, vary significantly in the product description quality. While some sellers (e.g., professional retailers) provide extensive and structured descriptions of the products supplied, most sellers offer only unstructured descriptions [12]. For this reason, and due to the high number of products on offer, marketplace vendors need to ensure that customers can quickly search for the products on offer and obtain the best possible results. If the search results do not provide the customer's desired products, this can lead to the customer substituting the marketplace with different alternatives. Therefore, optimizing the search engine and ensuring a satisfactory user experience is essential for marketplace providers.

The Information Extraction (IE) [5] research area deals with identifying in-formation from free texts and the intention to structure them. It includes e.g., unstructured product information data. A subfield of IE is Named Entity Recognition (NER) [31], which

© Springer Nature Switzerland AG 2021
A. Lopata et al. (Eds.): ICIST 2021, CCIS 1486, pp. 353–366, 2021.
https://doi.org/10.1007/978-3-030-88304-1_28

deals with the extraction of entities from texts. The traditional approaches of NER deal with the identification of people, location information, and organization [31]. This work presents a NER approach for extracting entities from product titles and descriptions for the German e-commerce domain. With such a system, it is possible to classify tokens from search queries, product titles, and descriptions into predefined entities, e.g., brand and product. Identifying these entities can help a search engine retrieve relevant products and give the customer a pleasant shopping experience.

Our approach consists of two subtasks. For the first subtask, we acquire product titles and descriptions from two German online marketplaces. We then apply several preprocessing steps to the acquired HTML documents to improve the quality of the documents. After that, we analyze the preprocessed data to ensure the data's quality and diversification within the categories. Lastly, three sub-samples of 1,000 product titles and descriptions are taken and annotated with the Prodi.gy[1] framework. The second subtask consists of evaluating the state-of-the-art transformer models BERT [9], RoBERTa [16], and XLM- RoBERTa [7]. We use the created datasets for fine-tuning the models and apply the Weights & Biases library for hyperparameter search.

The paper's structure is as follows: In Sect. 2, we provide an overview of the related work. Then, we give information about the acquired data, preprocessing it and the resulting datasets (Sect. 3). We present the models for performing NER on the created datasets in Sect. 4. After that, we evaluate and discuss the models' weaknesses and strengths to determine the best model for our use case (Sect. 5). Finally, we summarize our results in Sect. 6.

2   Related Work

In the following, we provide a brief overview of NER, the synergy effects of NER and Information Retrieval (IR), and existing datasets.

NER and IR are two strongly related research areas. On the one hand, NER can help improve IR's resulting quality (e.g., through disambiguation). On the other hand, IR methods can help to detect named entities. As early as 1997, it was demonstrated by Thompson and Dozier (1997) that names appear conspicuously often in search results and that a particular search function for this purpose turns out to be highly effective [30]. Li et al. (2011) have also developed an IR system that searches based only on recognized entities. The system can compete with established methods in evaluation [15]. Research in this area is also referred to as NERQ or Named Entity Recognition in Query.

Guo et al. (2009) were able to detect named entities in 70% of the search queries examined in a commercial search engine. However, certain patterns and features are missing in search queries, causing conventional NER techniques to produce poor results. For example, they are often written in lower case and contain only the most necessary terminology [4, 10]. In this regard, Guo et al. (2009) take query log data as training data for a semi-supervised method that allows them to recognize and classify named entities. For example, in "harry potter walkthrough", "harry potter" is recognized as a named entity and "Game" is recognized as the most likely entity class. "Movie" and "Book"

---

[1] Available at https://prodi.gy/, last accessed 2020–03-11.

are less likely but possible, while "Music" is eliminated as a class. Finally, the term "walktrough" gives a decisive clue to the class "Game". A similar approach is followed by Pantel et al. (2012), who additionally consider the user intention behind a query. Caputo et al. (2009) can also demonstrate the benefit of NER for IR with their SENSE (SEmantic N-levels Search Engine) system, in which they extend a keyword-based search with semantic levels [4].

However, NER also benefits from this symbiosis. For example, Rued et al. (2011) use search engines to search known entities with context words and use the resulting alternative search suggestions to extend, evaluate, and improve their system [28]. Furthermore, query log files provide information about word constellations that are conducive to recognition and disambiguation.

As for the NER model architectures, Collobert et al. (2011) presented the first unsupervised learning approach based on neural networks [6]. Thereafter, the most popular techniques for NER models relied on Recurrent Neural Networks (RNN), and Long Short-Term Memory (LSTM) networks [11, 14, 19]. Based on these architectures, approaches like Flair [1], and ELMo [25] were released and archived outstanding results in NLP-tasks. Recently, several language models have been published based on the Transformer architecture, such as BERT, RoBERTa, and XLM-RoBERTa. These models benefit from the pre-training and fine-tuning techniques and archive state-of-the-art performance for a wide range of NLP-tasks. One close approach to our work is to improve NER based on Distributed Word Representations [12]. They created an e-commerce dataset consisting of titles from different product categories from eBay and evaluated NER performance with a Conditional Random Field (CRF) model. In recent years, various deep learning approaches have been evaluated for NER in the e-commerce domain. Two papers use CRF models to perform NER for search queries and product titles in the e-commerce domain [8, 23]. Two newer publications study the performance of Bidirectional LSTM and LSTM-CRF models for the equivalent research area [20, 33]. Recently, Zhang et al. (2020) present a bootstrapped NER approach for the e-commerce domain, which uses a combination of BERT and a Bi-LSTM [35]. As for evaluating NER in the German language, we identified three publicly available datasets. The two most popular datasets are CoNLL 2003 shared task [31] and GermEval 2014 shared task [2]. The third dataset is based on articles from historic newspapers [24]. The NER performance for these three datasets has been evaluated with two CRF-based models and one BiLSTM model [27].

We dedicate ourselves to this topic because product information and titles are getting worse as sellers offer more products than ever before and have less time to maintain the unique content. Simultaneously, NER methods are becoming more powerful through transformer-based methods and can be a solution to compensate for the deficiencies in search.

3   Data Acquisition and Dataset

For the German language in the context of e-commerce, we did not find any datasets in the NER domain that are suitable for the research question of this paper. For example, our research question differs from the usual requirement for training data. We are explicitly looking for dirty data that also occurs in reality but is often filtered in training data or linguistic resources. For this reason, we have created our own datasets.

Amazon and a small German online marketplace (from now on referred to as Online-Shop) were our sources for the necessary datasets to train and evaluate the models. We first present the acquired data and the data preprocessing (Sect. 3.1). We then explain the choice of tagging scheme as well as entities for our annotations, and then present the annotated datasets (Sect. 3.2).

3.1 Data Cleansing and Preprocessing

For data acquisition, we used Scrapy[2] to collect the data (s. Table 1). We acquired a total of 1,871,200 product details for 74 different categories from Amazon and a total of 16,159 product details from the Online-Shop. Content at the Online-Shop is professionally maintained, while at Amazon, sellers publish the content according to their quality standards. We collected the data from Amazon between October and December 2019 and the Online-Shop data in April 2020.

Table 1. Corpus overview.

	Amazon	Online-Shop
No. of documents	1,871,200	16,159
No. of documents with a title	1,871,200	16,159
No. of documents with a short description	1,694,353	16,159
No. of documents with a long description	1,108,234	16,159

The most frequent categories are "Kitchen", "Sports", "Apparel", and "Jewelry". Because online marketplaces organize their products into a category structure to create a good user experience, the goal was to obtain data from as many categories as possible. To learn more about the acquired data, we took a closer look at the long descriptions, short descriptions, and titles. However, preprocessing was necessary for this and in preparation for annotation. It became obvious that Amazon products are subject to higher competitive pressure and that retailers use search engine optimization techniques to appear at the top of search engine results. The optimization technique leads to significantly longer titles, often only a mere collection of search terms. Furthermore, there are many very similar titles which we need to identify and ignore when selecting training data. Table 2 shows the resulting descriptive statistics for the acquired data.

---

[2] Available at https://scrapy.org/, last accessed 2020–03-11.

Table 2. Descriptive statistics for the acquired data.

	Amazon	Online-Shop
No. of unique titles	1,681,848	12,796
No. of unique short descriptions	929,326	16,159
No. of unique long descriptions	601,939	16,159
Avg. No. of tokens for titles	15.20	7.37
Avg. No. of tokens for short descriptions	94.64	12.40
Avg. No. of tokens for long descriptions	81.32	46.34
Max. No. of tokens for titles	87	19
Max. No. of tokens for short descriptions	1,687	84
Max. No. of tokens for long descriptions	1,687	562
No. of unique tokens for titles	1,254,473	11,671
No. of unique tokens for short descriptions	2,252,716	8,687
No. of unique tokens for long descriptions	2,477,740	41,964
No. of bigrams for titles	26,610,616	106,241
No. of bigrams for short descriptions	104,788,269	155,714
No. of bigrams for long descriptions	60,309,593	540,247
No. of trigrams for titles	24,929,421	93,554
No. of trigrams for short descriptions	103,859,469	144,480
No. of trigrams for long descriptions	59,708,755	530,811

We used the following heuristics to preprocess the acquired data for the annotation process with Prodi.gy:

- We extracted textual data from the HTML documents with BeatifulSoup[3].
- We cleaned up the extracted text by removing all newline and tabstop characters and unescaping all HTML-entities.
- We removed duplicate entries for product titles and descriptions.
- We discarded product descriptions with fewer than two sentences.
- We discarded product titles with less than one token.
- We used langdetect[4] to filter out product descriptions and titles that were not classified as German with a probability of higher than 0.999.
- We applied Cosine Similarity product titles and descriptions.
- We selected the most diverse German product titles and descriptions.

We use sklearn[5] for calculating pairwise Cosine Similarity. This function compares each document's similarity with all the documents present in the corpus. The documents are sorted in ascending order of similarity. We then randomly sample 1,000 documents from the top 5,000 documents to create the datasets.

---

[3] Available at https://pypi.org/project/beatifulsoup4/, last accessed 2020–03-11.

[4] Available at https://pypi.org/project/langdetect/, last accessed 2020–03-11.

[5] Available at https://scikit-learn.org/, last accessed 2020–03-11.

3.2 Annotated Datasets

The two most common tagging schemes are BIO, and BILOU [26]. The BIO tagging scheme assigns the labels Beginning, Inside, and Outside to text segments. The BILOU scheme expands the BIO scheme with the labels Last and Unit. A tagging scheme's choice plays a significant role in a model's results, and it has been shown that the BILOU scheme produces better results than the BIO scheme [26]. Therefore, we choose the BILOU tagging in our work.

During the annotation phase, we focused on the two diverse categories computer and automotive and choose the following e-commerce entities: "Brand", "Product", "Model", "ItemNo", "Quantity", "Color", "Size" and "Attribute". In Table 3, examples referring to each entity for the computer dataset are shown.

Table 3. Examples of entities for the computer dataset.

Entity	Example
Brand	Amer Networks, Canon, Kyocera
Product	Keyboard, Flash-/Programmiermodul (*Flash/programming module*), RP-SMA-Stecker (*RP-SMA connector*)
Model	MX 440, GXT5, FX3
ItemNo	253-375BK, 7660–0318-01-P, SS310GRFAN
Quantity	2PCS, 2X, 2 Stück (*2 piece*)
Color	Grün transparent (*Green transparent*), Schwarz (*Black*), grau/anthrazit (grey/anthracite)
Size	250 GB, 3,7 m × 3,7 m, A4
Attribute	multifunktional (*multifunctional*), gebraucht (*used*), halogenfrei (*halogen-free*)

We have annotated several product attributes, which do not belong to the chosen categories. The idea is that the datasets can be expanded with more entities, e.g., new entity "State" for "gebraucht" (used). The tag distribution across the eight entities for every product title and description dataset is shown in Figs. 1 and 2.

Figures 1 and 2 indicate that the distribution of entities is uneven. The title datasets contain more entities than the description datasets. For the titles and description datasets, the most frequent entity is "Attribute". Besides that, "Size", "Product", and "Model" appear quite frequent. In contrast, the entities "Quantity", "Color", and "ItemNo" occur less frequently.

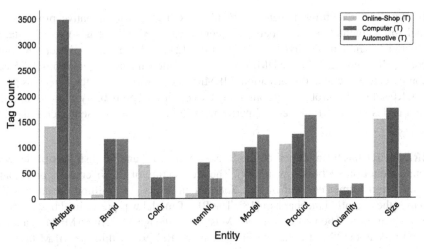

Fig. 1. A figure caption is always placed below the illustration. Short captions are centered, while long ones are justified. The macro button chooses the correct format automatically.

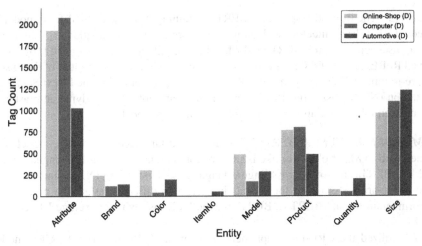

Fig. 2. A figure caption is always placed below the illustration. Short captions are centered, while long ones are justified. The macro button chooses the correct format automatically.

4 Transformer-Based NER

Pre-training a language model needs immense computing power and a sizable amount of data [9]. The training will typically take several days to weeks due to the model's complexity and numerous trainable parameters. Lately, many different pre-trained models based on the transformer architecture have been released. These models have proven to archive state-of-the-art results in down- stream NLP-tasks, such as NER [17]. In this work, we used a CRF model [13] as our baseline approach and compared it with BERT, RoBERTa, and XLM- RoBERTa on the previously created datasets (Sect. 3).

CRF Baseline. Conditional Random Fields (CRF) is a discriminative probabilistic model for segmentation and labeling sequence data [13]. CRF has some advantages compared to Hidden Markov Models (HMMs) [21] and Maximum Entropy Markov Models (MEMMs) [22]. While HMMs make strict independence assumptions, CRF can accommodate any context information. MEMMs are suffering from the label bias problem. CRF solves this problem by computing the conditional probability of global optimal output nodes [13]. CRF model still performs well in Sequence-to-Sequence tasks [29, 34].

BERT. BERT has been trained on the BooksCorpus [36] and English Wikipedia, with a total amount of 3.3 billion words [9]. The architecture of BERT consists of 12 bidirectional transformer encoder blocks, 768 hidden layers, 110 million parameters [9], and uses the Attention mechanism [18]. The BERT model was pre-trained based on two pre-training tasks. The first task is the "Masked Language Modeling (MLM)", and the second task is the "Next Sentence Prediction (NSP)" [9]. Within the MLM task, the model predicts 15% of random masked words from a sentence. In the second task, the model gets pairs of sentences as input and predicts if the second sentence in the pair is the original document's subsequent sentence.

RoBERTa. The Robustly Optimized BERT Pretraining Approach (RoBERTa) model is based on BERT's architecture with an improved pre-training technique [16]. Liu. et al. (2019) discovered that the BERT model had been significantly undertrained [16]. They trained RoBERTa on 160 GB of text, utilizing nearly ten times the amount of data used for pre-training BERT. They improve the pre-training by removing the "Next Sentence Prediction (NSP)" task from BERT's pre-training and introducing dynamic masking. The masked token continuity changes for every training epoch.

XLM-RoBERTa. XLM-RoBERTa is a multilingual language model. The model was trained with an MLM objective like BERT on monolingual data from 100 languages [7]. XLM-RoBERTa improves cross-lingual language understanding (XLU) and achieves state-of-the-art performance for various languages in different tasks. The model outperforms multilingual BERT (mBERT) for the NER-task with an average F1 score of 2.4%.

We utilized the CRFsuite implementation for the CRF model[6]. The CRF model makes use of the following features: word identity, word suffix, word shape, word POS tag and information from nearby words. We applied the following hyperparameters for training the CRF model: gradient descent with the L-BFGS method and a maximum of 100 iterations. The coefficients for L1 and L2 regularization are fixed to $c1 = 0.4$ and $c2 = 0.0$. We did not specifically optimize the hyper- parameters for the CRF model [13], as this model served as a baseline for all further experiments.

For fine-tuning the transformer models, we worked with the Python Simpletransformers library[7]. It is based on the Transformers library by Hugging Face [32]. It has

---

[6] Available at https://pypi.org/project/sklearn-crfsuite/, last accessed 2020–03-11.

[7] Available at https://github.com/ThilinaRajapakse/simpletransformers, last accessed 2020–03-11.

been observed that for Transformer models, large data sets (e.g., more than 100.000 labeled training examples) are far less sensitive to hyperparameter choice than small data sets [9]. Since our datasets are small, finding the best performing hyperparameters is essential. For hyperparameter search and the experiment tracking, we applied the Weights & Biases Framework [3]. It supports running Sweeps for the model optimization. We conducted Bayes searches to determine optimized hyperparameters for the BERT, RoBERTa, and tXLM-RoBERTa models. We also experimented with the uncased version of the two BERT models, but these performed a lot worse than the cased version. We used the following values for each model to determine the optimal hyperparameters (Table 4).

Table 4. Values used for the hyperparameter optimization with weights & biases.

Model	Epochs	Learning rate	Learning rate
mBERT (*bert-base-multilingual*)	2, 3, 4, 5	5e−5, 3e−5, 2e−5	8, 16, 32
GermanBERT (*bert-base-german-dbmdz-cased*)	2, 3, 4, 5	5e−5, 3e−5, 2e−5	8, 16, 32
RoBERTa (*roberta-large*)	2, 4, 6, 8, 10	5e−5, 3e−5, 2e−5	8, 16, 32
XLM-RoBERTa (*xlm-roberta-large*)	2, 4, 6, 8, 10	5e−5, 3e−5, 2e−5	8, 16, 32

After running the hyperparameter optimization on our datasets, we discovered that a batch size of 8, a learning rate of 5e−5, and 4 training epochs produced the highest F1 scores for the mBERT and GermanBERT model. For RoBERTa and XLM-RoBERTa, the highest F1 score was achieved with the same batch size and learning rate but 10 training epochs.

5 Results and Discussion

We conducted an 80/20 split for the training and evaluation datasets. For measuring the performance, we utilized the precision, recall, and F1 scores. We use a micro-averaged calculation to account for the imbalanced distribution of the entity types since it depends on each entity type's frequency. In Table 5, the results for the five models and all datasets are shown.

As seen in Table 5, the four transformer-based models outperform the CRF model. For every dataset, the transformer-based models archive higher precision, recall, and F1 scores than the CRF model. Specifically, the results display that the XLM-RoBERTa model yields the highest F1 scores for every dataset. Furthermore, the mBERT, GermanBERT, and RoBERTa models produce similar results. GermanBERT is slightly outperforming mBERT and RoBERTa.

Table 5. Micro-averaged precision, recall, and F1 score results of individual model for all datasets. Bold text indicates the highest F1 score for the dataset. OS, A, and C designate Online-Shop, Automotive, and Computer dataset. T and D indicate the title or description dataset, respectively.

	OS-T	A-T	C-T	OS-D	A-D	C-D	Avg.
CRF							
Precision	0.8320	0.7082	0.7387	0.7572	0.7471	0.6901	0.7456
Recall	0.8354	0.7394	0.7394	0.7621	0.7050	0.6758	0.7360
F1-Score	0.8337	0.7182	0.7390	0.7596	0.7255	0.6828	0.7431
mBERT							
Precision	0.9106	0.8396	0.7682	0.8396	0.7923	0.7476	0.8164
Recall	0.9195	0.8625	0.8019	0.8697	0.8617	0.7635	0.8465
F1-Score	0.9150	0.8509	0.7847	0.8544	0.8544	0.7555	0.8310
GermanBERT							
Precision	0.9333	0.8282	0.7757	0.8227	0.7821	0.7463	0.8147
Recall	0.9390	0.8700	0.8111	0.8615	0.8686	0.7984	0.8581
F1-Score	0.9362	0.8486	0.7930	0.8416	0.8231	0.7715	0.8357
RoBERTa							
Precision	0.9150	0.8211	0.7879	0.8267	0.8065	0.7429	0.8167
Recall	0.9317	0.8435	0.8127	0.8550	0.8548	0.7674	0.8442
F1-Score	0.9233	0.8321	0.8001	0.8406	0.8299	0.7550	0.8302
XLM-RoBERTa							
Precision	0.9468	0.8542	0.8340	0.8481	0.8201	0.7817	0.8475
Recall	0.9549	0.8733	0.8574	0.8729	0.8824	0.8120	0.8755
F1-Score	**0.9508**	**0.8637**	**0.8455**	**0.8603**	**0.8501**	**0.7965**	**0.8611**

The conducted experiments have shown that the Online-Shop datasets achieve better results than the Amazon datasets. These results conclude that the quality of the data heavily influences the performance of the individual models. The Amazon data contains mostly unstructured and inaccurate titles and descriptions, while the Online-Shop data has a specific structure because the content is professionally maintained. Moreover, the Amazon product titles and descriptions contain several errors. The most critical ones are spelling and grammatical errors. Furthermore, there are products in the wrong category with incorrect information. Besides that, text formatting errors like missing spaces are present.

As we analyzed the different entities' performance, it was evident that the distribution of the entities within the dataset should be as balanced as possible for better results. The entity types with a small number of entities primarily performed poorly. Hence, optimization towards more annotations for entity types with few examples is essential.

Also, we trained all models with a smaller amount of data of one dataset. Therefore, we used the Online-Shop (T) dataset with 25%, 50%, and 75% data. The primary purpose was to determine if we have annotated enough data and if larger datasets would perform more effectively (Fig. 3).

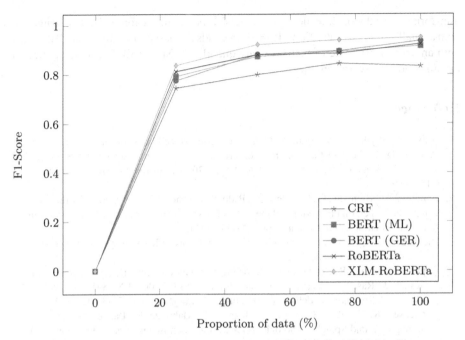

Fig. 3. Micro-averaged F1 scores of individual models for Online-Shop title dataset.

With only 25% (250 examples) of the Online-Shop title dataset, the CRF model achieves an F1 score of 0.7452, and the transformer-based models an F1 score between 0.7759 and 0.8376. It can be observed that XLM-RoBERTa reaches an F1 score of 0.9219 with a portion of 50% (500 examples) from the datasets. Furthermore, using more than 50% of the datasets only results in a slight increase of the F1 score.

6 Conclusions

For cases where online marketplaces' search function does not find the desired products for the customer or does not find any products, we investigated the possibility of optimizing the search function applying NER. In this work, we created six German e-commerce NER datasets from product titles and descriptions. We then used these datasets to evaluate a CRF model and four state-of-the-art transformer-based models. Our experiments indicate that entity distribution and data quality is the essential point for model results.

For the best possible optimization of product search, entities' distribution should be as even as possible. Therefore, the most rarely occurring entities must be complemented with further annotations. For our datasets, it is also possible to get additional entities from the "Property" entity. It would lead to a more balanced distribution of the entity types. Furthermore, the created datasets expose that online marketplaces have different quality standards for publishing product titles and descriptions. Therefore, the application of data preprocessing should improve the quality of data.

Overall, our experiments demonstrate that with the support of NER, entity identification and classification are reliable for German product titles and descriptions. The transformer-based models achieve excellent NER performance for the German language with a small amount of data. XLM-RoBERTa yields the best performance for all datasets with an average F1 score of 0.8611. Consequently, XLM-RoBERTa can be applied to optimize product search engines.

References

1. Akbik, A., Blythe, D., Vollgraf, R.: Contextual string embeddings for sequence labeling. In: Proceedings of the 27th International Conference on Computational Linguistics, pp. 1638–1649. ACL, Santa Fe, New Mexico, USA, August 2018. https://www.aclweb.org/anthology/C18-1139
2. Benikova, D., Biemann, C., Kisselew, M., Padó, S.: Germeval 2014 named entity recognition: companion paper. In: Proceedings of the KONVENS GermEval Shared Task on Named Entity Recognition Hildesheim, Germany, pp. 104112 (2014)
3. Biewald, L.: Experiment tracking with weights and biases (2020). https://www.wandb.com/softwareavailablefromwandb.com
4. Caputo, A., Basile, P., Semeraro, G.: Boosting a semantic search engine by named entities. In: Rauch, J., Raś, Z.W., Berka, P., Elomaa, T. (eds.) ISMIS 2009. LNCS (LNAI), vol. 5722, pp. 241–250. Springer, Heidelberg (2009). https://doi.org/10.1007/978-3-642-04125-9_27
5. Carstensen, K.-U., Ebert, C., Ebert, C., Jekat, S.J., Klabunde, R., Langer, H. (eds.): Computerlinguistik und Sprachtechnologie. Spektrum Akademischer Verlag, Heidelberg (2010). https://doi.org/10.1007/978-3-8274-2224-8
6. Collobert, R., Weston, J., Bottou, L., Karlen, M., Kavukcuoglu, K., Kuksa, P.: Natural language processing (almost) from scratch. J. Mach. Learn. Res. **12**, 2493–2537 (2011)
7. Conneau, A., et al.: Unsupervised cross-lingual representation learning at scale. In: Proceedings of the 58th Annual Meeting of the ACL, pp. 8440–8451. ACL (2020). https://doi.org/10.18653/v1/2020.acl-main.747. https://www.aclweb.org/anthology/2020.acl-main.747
8. Cowan, B., Zethelius, S., Luk, B., Baras, T., Ukarde, P., Zhang, D.: Named entity recognition in travel-related search queries. In: Proceedings of the Twenty-Ninth AAAI Conference on Artificial Intelligence, pp. 3935–3941. AAAI Press (2015)
9. Devlin, J., Chang, M., Lee, K., Toutanova, K.: BERT: pre-training of deep bidirectional transformers for language understanding. CoRR abs/1810.04805 (2018)
10. Guo, J., Xu, G., Cheng, X., Li, H.: Named entity recognition in query. In: Proceedings of the 32nd International ACM SIGIR Conference on Research and Development in Information Retrieval, pp. 267–274. SIGIR 2009, ACM, New York, NY, USA (2009)
11. Huang, Z., Xu, W., Yu, K.: Bidirectional LSTM-CRF models for sequence tagging. CoRR abs/1508.01991 (2015). http://arxiv.org/abs/1508.01991
12. Joshi, M., Hart, E., Vogel, M., Ruvini, J.D.: Distributed word representations improve NER for e-commerce. In: Proceedings of the 1st Workshop on Vector Space Modeling for Natural Language Processing, pp. 160–167. ACL, Denver, Colorado (2015). https://doi.org/10.3115/v1/W15-1522. https://www.aclweb.org/anthology/W15-1522
13. Lafferty, J.D., McCallum, A., Pereira, F.C.N.: Conditional random fields: probabilistic models for segmenting and labeling sequence data. In: Proceedings of the Eighteenth International Conference on Machine Learning, pp. 282–289. ICML 2001, Morgan Kaufmann Publishers Inc., San Francisco, CA, USA (2001)
14. Lample, G., Ballesteros, M., Subramanian, S., Kawakami, K., Dyer, C.: Neural architectures for named entity recognition. In: Proceedings of the 2016 Conference of the North American Chapter of the ACL: Human Language Technologies. pp. 260–270. ACL, San Diego, California (2016). https://doi.org/10.18653/v1/N16-1030

15. Li, X., Dai, G., Lai, S., Dai, H.: Neos: a pure named entity oriented search engine. In: 2011 IEEE International Conference on Signal Processing, Communications and Computing (ICSPCC), pp. 1–4 (2011)

16. Liu, Y., et al.: Roberta: a robustly optimized BERT pre training approach. CoRR abs/1907.11692 (2019). http://arxiv.org/abs/1907.11692

17. Lothritz, C., Allix, K., Veiber, L., Bissyande, T.F., Klein, J.: Evaluating pre trained transformer-based models on the task of fine-grained named entity recognition. In: Proceedings of the 28th International Conference on Computational Linguistics, pp. 3750–3760. International Committee on Computational Linguistics, Barcelona, Spain, December 2020

18. Luong, T., Pham, H., Manning, C.D.: Effective approaches to attention-based neural machine translation. In: Proceedings of the 2015 Conference on Empirical Methods in Natural Language Processing, pp. 1412–1421. ACL, Lisbon, Portugal, September 2015

19. Ma, X., Hovy, E.H.: End-to-end sequence labeling via bi-directional LSTM-CNNS-CRF. CoRR abs/1603.01354 (2016). http://arxiv.org/abs/1603.01354

20. Majumder, B.P., Subramanian, A., Krishnan, A., Gandhi, S., More, A.: Deep re- current neural networks for product attribute extraction in ecommerce. CoRR abs/1803.11284 (2018). http://arxiv.org/abs/1803.11284

21. Manning, C.D., Schutze, H.: Foundations of Statistical Natural Language Processing, 1st edn. MIT Press, Cambridge (1999)

22. McCallum, A., Freitag, D., Pereira, F.C.N.: Maximum entropy Markov models for information extraction and segmentation. In: Proceedings of the Seventeenth International Conference on Machine Learning, pp. 591–598. ICML 2000, Morgan Kaufmann Publishers Inc., San Francisco, CA, USA (2000)

23. More, A.: Attribute extraction from product titles in ecommerce. CoRR abs/1608.04670 (2016). http://arxiv.org/abs/1608.04670

24. Neudecker, C.: An open corpus for named entity recognition in historic newspapers. In: Proceedings of the Tenth International Conference on Language Resources and Evaluation (LREC 2016), pp. 4348–4352. European Language Resources Association (ELRA), Portoroz, Slovenia, May 2016. https://www.aclweb.org/anthology/L16-1689

25. Peters, M., Neumann, M., Iyyer, M., Gardner, M., Clark, C., Lee, K., Zettlemoyer, L.: Deep contextualized word representations. In: Proceedings of the 2018 Conference of the North American Chapter of the ACL: Human Language Technologies, vol. 1, (Long Papers), pp. 2227–2237. ACL, New Orleans, Louisiana, June 2018

26. Ratinov, L., Roth, D.: Design challenges and misconceptions in named entity recognition. In: Proceedings of the Thirteenth Conference on Computational Natural Language Learning (CoNLL-2009), pp. 147–155. ACL, Boulder, Colorado, June 2009. https://www.aclweb.org/anthology/W09-1119

27. Riedl, M., Padó, S.: A named entity recognition shootout for German. In: Proceedings of the 56th Annual Meeting of the ACL (vol. 2, Short Papers), pp. 120–125. ACL, Melbourne, Australia, July 2018. https://doi.org/10.18653/v1/P18-2020. https://www.aclweb.org/anthology/P18-2020

28. Rüd, S., Ciaramita, M., Müller, J., Schütze, H.: Piggyback: using search engines for robust cross-domain named entity recognition. In: Proceedings of the 49th Annual Meeting of the ACL: Human Language Technologies, pp. 965–975. ACL, Portland, Oregon, USA, June 2011. https://www.aclweb.org/anthology/P11-1097

29. Sutskever, I., Vinyals, O., Le, Q.V.: Sequence to sequence learning with neural networks. In: Proceedings of the 27th International Conference on Neural Information Processing Systems – vol. 2, pp. 3104–3112. NIPS 2014, MIT Press, Cambridge, MA, USA (2014)

30. Thompson, P., Dozier, C.C.: Name searching and information retrieval. In: Second Conference on Empirical Methods in Natural Language Processing (1997). https://www.aclweb.org/anthology/W97-0315

31. Tjong Kim Sang, E.F., De Meulder, F.: Introduction to the CoNLL-2003 shared task: language-independent named entity recognition. In: Proceedings of the Seventh Conference on Natural Language Learning at HLT-NAACL 2003, pp. 142–147 (2003)

32. Wolf, T., et al.: Huggingface's transformers: state-of-the-art natural language processing. CoRR abs/1910.03771 (2019)

33. Wu, C.Y., Ahmed, A., Kumar, G.R., Datta, R.: Predicting latent structured intents from shopping queries. In: Proceedings of the 26th International Conference on World Wide Web, pp. 1133–1141. WWW 2017 International World Wide Web Conference Steering Committee, Republic and Canton of Geneva, CHE (2017)

34. Yang, X., et al.: Bidirectional LSTM-CRF for biomedical named entity recognition. In: 2018 14th International Conference on Natural Computation, Fuzzy Systems and Knowledge Discovery (ICNC-FSKD), pp. 239– 242 (2018). https://doi.org/10.1109/FSKD.2018.8687117

35. Zhang, H., Hennig, L., Alt, C., Hu, C., Meng, Y., Wang, C.: Bootstrapping named entity recognition in e-commerce with positive unlabeled learning. In: Proceedings of the Third Workshop on e-Commerce and NLP. Annual Meeting of the ACL (ACL-2020), ECNLP 3, ACL 2020, July 9, Seattle, USA. ACL (2020)

36. Zhu, Y., et al.: Aligning books and movies: towards story-like visual explanations by watching movies and reading books. In: 2015 IEEE International Conference on Computer Vision (ICCV), pp. 19–27 (2015). https://doi.org/10.1109/ICCV.2015.11

Rule-Based Chatbot Integration into Software Engineering Course

Mikas Binkis[(✉)], Ramūnas Kubiliūnas[(✉)], Rima Sturienė[(✉)], Tatjana Dulinskienė[(✉)],
Tomas Blažauskas[(✉)], and Vitalija Jakštienė[(✉)]

Kaunas University of Technology, Kaunas, Lithuania
{mikas.binkis,ramunas.kubiliunas,rima.sturiene,
tatjana.dulinskiene,tomos.blazauskas,vitalija.jakstiene}@ktu.lt

Abstract. A Chatbot refers to software that can perform services based on commands or answers given by a user during an online conversation. The Chatbots are applied in different areas ranging from pure entertainment solutions to learning support systems. In this article, we investigate Chatbot systems as a way to support learners during educational video sessions. We propose a rule-based Chatbot system that uses speech recognition and synthesized answers for increased immersiveness and for supporting the learners with different sensual perceptions. We introduce the design methodology we followed while creating a Chatbot system, explain the Chatbot behavior from learner and teacher perspectives and describe the system structure. The system was validated using the System Usability Scales (SUS) methodology. It shows that the current implementation has an average usability score; therefore, it needs improvement. On the other hand, the survey shows a positive learners attitude towards the proposed system.

Keywords: Virtual assistants · Chatbots · Learning systems · SUS · SCORM

1 Introduction

The virtual assistant, intelligent virtual assistant and a chatbot refer to software that can perform services based on commands or answers given by a user during a conversation. The term "chatbot" usually refers to online virtual assistants because they enrich online chat applications. The application area of the chatbots is large - from pure entertainment applications, home automation systems, online shopping assistants to the applications supporting learning. Virtual assistants are known since the last century, but nowadays, they can play a bigger role as speech recognition technologies become mature. Also, there is a need for such emerging technologies as virtual reality. In this case, users can not use the usual user interfaces, and virtual assistants' usage seems like a natural choice.

Chatbots can be categorized by the underlying development techniques [1]:

1. The rule-based conversation is a simple Chatbot development method, which relies on defying a set of rules that the bot follows depending on the user's answers. While the rule set can be quite extensive, the main drawback of this technique is

© Springer Nature Switzerland AG 2021
A. Lopata et al. (Eds.): ICIST 2021, CCIS 1486, pp. 367–377, 2021.
https://doi.org/10.1007/978-3-030-88304-1_29

that Chatbots cannot work outside the defined scenarios, thus limiting the ability to respond accurately.

2. The deep learning approach uses Machine Learning algorithms to understand the context and generate answers to questions in a more human-like response form. The main advantages of artificial intelligence-based Chatbots are continuous improvement, based on gathered data, and better decision making when it comes to more complex queries. Nevertheless, their success heavily depends on their training, so it is crucial to provide large amounts of meaningful data to implement Chatbot's starting version properly.

3. Ensemble methods are a combination of previously mentioned techniques, which inherit the best qualities of each method to provide even more naturally sounding answers to a very wide array of user queries.

4. Domain-specific Chatbots is an approach where Chatbots are created for a particular domain, such as Education, Sales, Healthcare & others. While previously mentioned techniques are employed in order to create a specialized Chatbot, this allows it to cover the particular field more extensively, thus providing increased effectiveness and better-perceived usability for the end-user [2].

5. Chatbot builder is an approach, which relies on Chatbot development tools that offer the creation of Chatbots with little or even without actual coding. Modern Chatbot builders (such as MobileMonkey, DialogFlow, BotCore.ai, etc.) provide extensive configuration options, rule-based machine learning, neural-language processing capabilities, and integration into well-known chat platforms [3, 4].

Chatbot technology applications in education vary from simple, supportive questions regarding learning material to support complex individualized feedback. In most cases, the actual usefulness of a Chatbot and practical application in an educational context heavily relies on the answering success rate.

In one case, M. Verleger & J. Pembridge from Embry-Riddle Aeronautical University present their created application of AI-based Chatbot "EduBot" as an aid for introductory programming course [5]. The most notable takeaway from the experiment was that students were quickly dissatisfied with the tool if their questions were answered inaccurately or no answer was found—this lead to using existing information sources, such as Google or integrated help directory.

Another study by Y. Lin & T. Tsai presents an application of a Chatbot based on IBM Watson Assistant and Facebook Messenger [6]. The experiment hints that students are more likely to use the conversational assistant software in larger class. In those cases, the teachers have rather limited time for one-to-one interactions.

Gaglo et al. stress the importance of Chatbots during the Covid pandemic. It provides the means for teachers to detect early knowledge deficiencies in students and the opportunities for students to catch up without the fear of being judged or mocked [7].

It is worth noting that the use of Chatbots can be extended to common such administrative situations/questions as class scheduling, scholarships, student welfare, thus improving overall Chatbot application in the whole educational process, especially higher education [8].

For our approach, we use a rule-based Chatbot because it allows an easy authoring of the chatbot conversations. Also, it is sufficient for the task of supporting learners in watching educational videos. The proposed chatbot uses speech recognition and synthesized answers for increased immersiveness and for supporting the learners with different sensual perceptions.

2 Chatbot Design Methodology

During the "Softaware" project [9], we have created tens of videos as learning resources. The duration of the video range from 5 to 15 min. Despite the videos being short, students expressed the opinion that many videos are still too long, boring, and too many concepts are being presented. Therefore we decided to introduce the chatbot to support the presentation of video material. Initially, we designed the guidelines in the form of requirements that governed the creation of the chatbot:

- the chatbot shall be unobtrusive, and the learner should be able to disable the chatbot at any moment;
- the learner shall be able to invoke the chatbot at any given moment;
- the chatbot shall present the table of contents to guide the learner when watching video;
- the chatbot shall have a help system and introduce the ways it can be used;
- the chatbot shall implement the self-assessment system and provide feedback;
- the chatbot shall interact with the learner using visual, audio, and text conversation forms to support learners with different learning styles;
- the chatbot shall indicate different states, such as talking/writing, waiting for a response, being idle.

As one can see from the requirement, different system parts need to be designed before starting the implementation. The methodology which we follow while designing a chatbot is depicted in Fig. 1.

Fig. 1. The design methodology of the chatbot

First, we design the help system because the help system needs to be consistent with other parts of the system, and it should be available at any given moment. Normally - it is a one-time job because the help system can be reused in other chatbots. Sometimes the chatbot help systems will differ a bit if different interactions are planned for chatbots. The help system also includes the table of content.

Next, we design a learning path. It is a pedagogical activity. A video has a sequential nature as the presenter introduces concepts progressively. Therefore, in most cases, the introduction of the concepts will be sequential. However, we need to establish the video's concepts, the interactions related to the concepts, and the related interruption events at this stage. We designed two types of interactions: informational conversation and quiz-type conversation. The informational conversation aims to stimulate the learner, motivate him or just provide a piece of information. The quiz is related to a conversation when a chatbot has the purpose of asking self-assessment questions. Finally, designing the interruption events means designing a sequence of timeline events that tell when specific conversations need to happen during video playback.

Having a learning path in place, we can design the conversations or dialogs. It means we need to create the sentences the chatbot needs to speak (and write) and the responses to learner answers. In our case, we use a rule-based chatbot. Therefore it is necessary to define the rules for sentence selection.

After designing the conversations, the evaluation system should be designed. We may evaluate different aspects of the learning activity: answers to the chatbot questions and the viewed video parts. All the assessed activities will be available for the teacher to review in a learning management system.

Finally, we find it necessary to include gamification and create gamification rules to increase the motivation to do the learning activities using a chatbot. The creation of the gamification rules happens inside a learning management system using a chosen gamification plugin.

3   Chatbot Implementation

One of the important aspects of the chatbot system was the seamless integration requirement with major learning management systems so that the learners and teachers could use their ordinary tools along with a chatbot. Figure 2 depicts learner use cases.

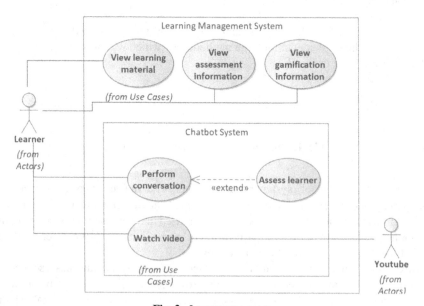

Fig. 2. Learner use cases

It is important that the learner can view additional learning material before or after using a chatbot. The learner can use the chatbot to watch a video and to communicate with a chatbot. A chatbot may ask questions to assess the learner. The learner can later review assessment information and related gamification information such as received badges, ladders, and similar.

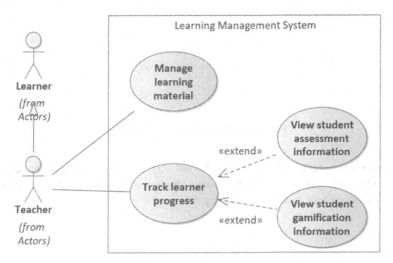

Fig. 3. Teacher use cases

The teacher can do all the things a learner can do (see Fig. 3). Additionally, he has the tools to manage the learning material and track the learner's progress. He can view the detailed activity and assessment information as well as the gamification information. All the necessary tools reside inside a learning management system.

Figure 4 depicts system deployment. The chatbot is provided as a SCORM package in the form of a zip file. In our case, we used the Moodle learning management system, but it can be any learning management system that supports the SCORM standard. The learning management system also should support gamification itself, or some gamification plugin needs to be used. In our case, we use the "LevelUP" plugin. The chatbot system uses youtube services to reduce the chatbot package's size and reduce the LMS server's possible load. Therefore the video should be deployed on youtube first.

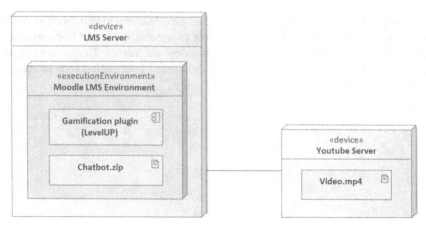

Fig. 4. Chatbot deployment diagram

The chatbot system was implemented from scratch using javascript language for implementing the system and implementing chatbot story scripts. The implemented system consists of four main parts (see Fig. 5).

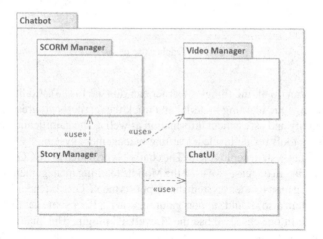

Fig. 5. Chatbot system package diagram

The SCORM Manager implements the necessary functionality to interact with the learning management system, providing a self-assessment evaluation. The video manager implements the Youtube video's playback and provides a video observer object for realizing interruption events such as pausing a video to start the conversation. The ChatUI package is responsible for providing a user interface and interactions with a learner. The package provides graphical and audio interfaces. The conversation is depicted using avatars and texts (see Fig. 6). The texts are spoken by the chatbot character (an owl). The input is implemented using spoken language processing and providing the answer options in the form of buttons.

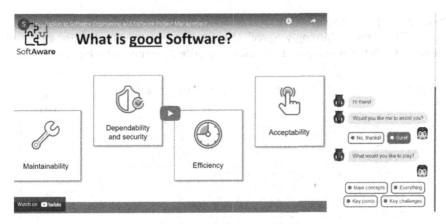

Fig. 6. Chatbot user interface

4 Experiment

The video "Introduction to software engineering" [10] from "SoftAware" project videos was chosen to demonstrate the chatbot capabilities. The video was split into four parts: introduction, main concepts, key challenges, and summary. You can see the corresponding topics provided by the chatbot in Fig. 6. The learning path we implemented was straightforward: learners have to watch the separate sections of the video and after each section answer one question related to the content provided in that section. Figure 7 depicts this scenario:

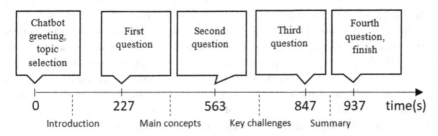

Fig. 7. Chatbot scenario used for the experiment

The implemented chatbot was used in the course "Software Engineering". This course is dedicated to second-year undergraduate students at Kaunas University of Technology at the Faculty of Informatics.

The aim of the experiment was to assess the usability of the chatbot and to explore the possibilities to use it in the learning process.

The System Usability Scale (SUS) methodology was used to achieve the goal. This methodology is widely used to determine the usability of software for its simplicity, shortness, and reliability, even with a small sample size [11]. A closed questionnaire is provided to system users. It is based on the original SUS questionnaire and consists of

10 statements [12]. Statements are rated on a 5-point (Likert type) scale from "Strongly Disagree" (1 point) to "Strongly Agree" (5 points). Odd statements describe a positive attitude towards the system; even statements describe a negative one (Fig. 8).

		Srongly Disagree 1	2	3	4	Srongly Agree 5
1	I think that I would like to use this system.	O	O	O	O	O
2	I found the system unnecessarily complex.	O	O	O	O	O
3	I thought the system was easy to use.	O	O	O	O	O
4	I think that I would need the support of a technical person to be able to use this system.	O	O	O	O	O
5	I found the various functions in this system were well integrated.	O	O	O	O	O
6	I thought there was too much inconsistency in this system.	O	O	O	O	O
7	I would imagine that most people would learn to use this system very quickly.	O	O	O	O	O
8	I found the system very cumbersome to use.	O	O	O	O	O
9	I felt very confident using the system.	O	O	O	O	O
10	I needed to learn a lot of things before I could get going with this system.	O	O	O	O	O

Fig. 8. SUS questionnaire

Overall SUS score. Overall SUS score is calculated using the formula provided in the methodology [13]. A result is a number between 0 and 100, but it is not a percentage. There are three SUS score ranges: 0–64 (the system is not acceptable), 65–84 (the system is acceptable), 85–100 (the system is excellent). The average SUS score is 68.

Twenty-four students in the "Software Engineering" course responded to the online questionnaire. The collected data and the calculated SUS scores are presented in the table (Fig. 9). A heat-map with a positive and a negative reaction is obtained in the table by combining different reaction colors. The calculated score for each student is given in the right-hand column of the table. The score for each question is given in the bottom row of the table. The overall SUS score of the Chatbot implementation is 69,8 out of 100. This means that the system is acceptable but could be improved.

The result is easier to interpret when SUS scores are converted to percentiles ranks and grades (A-F). The grading scale on a curve obtained by Lewis and Sauro was used.

The result in this study corresponds approximately to the 56th percentile and the letter grade C (see Fig. 10). The calculated SUS score (69,8) is a higher score than 56% of all applications tested.

Learnability and Usability. The learnability sub-scale is based on items 4 and 10, the usability sub-scale - on the other eight items. Sub-scales obtained in this study are presented in Fig. 11.

Student	Q1	Q2	Q3	Q4	Q5	Q6	Q7	Q8	Q9	Q10	Score
1	5	5	5	1	4	1	5	1	5	1	87,50
2	3	3	3	3	3	3	3	3	3	3	50,00
3	1	4	3	2	2	3	2	3	2	2	40,00
4	4	2	4	1	4	2	5	3	5	1	82,50
5	5	5	5	1	5	1	5	1	5	1	90,00
6	4	5	3	4	4	3	4	5	4	4	45,00
7	1	2	5	2	4	3	3	3	4	2	62,50
8	5	3	5	2	5	2	5	2	4	2	82,50
9	3	2	5	1	3	3	4	2	5	1	77,50
10	4	4	4	4	4	4	3	3	3	5	45,00
11	3	3	5	3	3	3	5	5	5	3	60,00
12	5	1	5	1	5	1	5	1	5	1	100,00
13	4	4	4	5	4	5	4	5	4	4	42,50
14	4	2	4	2	4	2	3	1	5	2	77,50
15	4	2	4	1	4	2	4	3	4	1	77,50
16	3	3	4	1	4	2	4	2	3	1	72,50
17	1	2	4	1	1	4	4	3	1	1	50,00
18	5	1	5	1	5	2	5	3	4	1	90,00
19	4	2	5	1	3	2	5	3	4	1	80,00
20	4	2	3	2	3	1	2	1	3	2	67,50
21	3	2	4	2	3	4	3	3	4	2	60,00
22	3	2	5	2	3	2	4	3	4	2	70,00
23	4	2	5	1	4	2	4	1	4	2	82,50
24	4	1	4	1	4	2	5	3	4	1	82,50
Score	64,58	58,33	82,29	78,13	66,67	63,54	75,00	59,38	72,92	77,08	

Average score: 69,79

Recommended ranges:
Not Acceptable = 0-64
Acceptable = 65-84
Excellent = 85-100

Positive Response - Agree or Strongly Agree for positive questions, Disagree or Strongly Disagree for negative questions
Neutral -neither Agree nor Disagree, or unable to answer
Negative Response - Agree or Strongly Agree for negative questions, Disagree or Strongly Disagree for positive questions

Fig. 9. SUS heat-map

The respondent's learnability score is higher than the usability score in most cases (see Fig. 11). The average learnability score (77,6) is also higher than the average usability score (67,8). Sauro [14] notes that the structure of learnability and usability depends on certain circumstances. Several students reported technical glitches in communicating with Chatbot. Problems may have been due to insufficient technical capacity: "…something feels off. But I like that it is engaging", "…it froze when I answered Yes", "…it asks

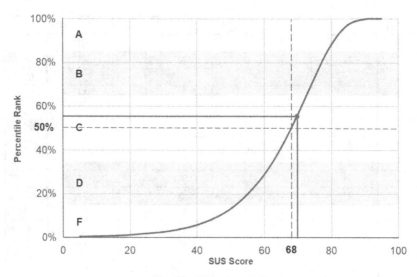

Fig. 10. SUS score [14]

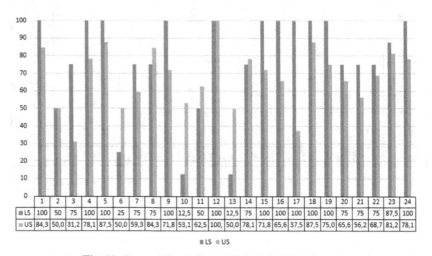

Fig. 11. Learnability (LS) and Usability (US) Sub-scales

a question and you have no way of answering it". Respondents confirmed a positive attitude towards the system by answering the additional question, "Would you recommend this system to a colleague or other stakeholders?". 17 respondents out of 24 answered this question in the affirmative.

5 Conclusions

Chatbots nowadays are applied in many areas ranging from pure entertainment solutions to learning support systems. We proposed a rule-based Chatbot system that uses speech recognition and synthesized answers for increased immersiveness and for supporting the learners with different sensual perceptions. The aim of this system is to support learners during educational video sessions.

The system was validated using the System Usability Scales (SUS) methodology. It showed that the current implementation has an average usability score, which hints at the need for improvement. The survey also showed a positive learners attitude towards the proposed system. Therefore we see the importance of enhancing the Chatbot usability and availability. This is vital for emerging learning technologies, such as virtual reality environments, which do not have usual support systems.

References

1. Singh, S., Thakur, H.K.: Survey of various AI Chatbots based on technology used. In: 2020 8th International Conference on Reliability, Infocom Technologies and Optimization (Trends and Future Directions) (ICRITO), pp. 1074–1079 (2020). https://doi.org/10.1109/ICRITO 48877.2020.9197943
2. Liu, Q., Huang, J., Wu, L., Zhu, K., Ba, S.: CBET: design and evaluation of a domain-specific chatbot for mobile learning. Univ. Access Inf. Soc. **19**(3), 655–673 (2019). https://doi.org/10.1007/s10209-019-00666-x
3. Pérez-Soler, S., Juárez-Puerta, S., Guerra, E., de Lara, J.: Choosing a chatbot development tool. IEEE Softw. **38**, 94–103 (2021). https://doi.org/10.1109/MS.2020.3030198
4. Top 20 Best Chatbot Builders For Big and Small Business (2021). https://www.chatbots.org/best-chatbot-builders. Accessed 16 Apr 2021
5. Verleger, M., Pembridge, J.J.: A pilot study integrating an AI-driven Chatbot in an introductory programming course, pp. 1–4 (2018). https://doi.org/10.1109/FIE.2018.8659282
6. Lin, Y.-H., Tsai, T.: A conversational assistant on mobile devices for primitive learners of computer programming. In: 2019 IEEE International Conference on Engineering, Technology and Education (TALE), pp. 1–4 (2019). https://doi.org/10.1109/TALE48000.2019.9226015
7. Gaglo, K., Degboe, B.M., Kossingou, G.M., Ouya, S.: Proposal of conversational chatbots for educational remediation in the context of covid-19. In: 2021 23rd International Conference on Advanced Communication Technology (ICACT), pp. 354–358 (2021). https://doi.org/10.23919/ICACT51234.2021.9370946
8. Cordero, J., Toledo, A., Guamán, F., Barba-Guamán, L.: Use of chatbots for user service in higher education institutions. In: 2020 15th Iberian Conference on Information Systems and Technologies (CISTI), 1–6 (2020). https://doi.org/10.23919/CISTI49556.2020.9141108
9. SoftAware Project (2021). https://softaware-project.eu/. Accessed Apr 19 2021
10. Blažauskas, T.: Introduction to Software Engineering and Software Project Management (2021). https://www.youtube.com/watch?v=uN8-BKTzFGo. Accessed Apr 17 2021
11. Tullis, T., Stetson, J.: A Comparison of Questionnaires for Assessing Website Usability (2006)
12. Brooke, J.: SUS – a quick and dirty usability scale, pp. 189–194 (1996)
13. Lewis, J., Sauro, J.: Item benchmarks for the system usability scale. J. Usabil. Stud. **13**, 158–167 (2018)
14. Sauro, J.: 5 ways to interpret a SUS score. MeasuringU, 19 Sep 2018

Speech Synthesis Using Stressed Sample Labels for Languages with Higher Degree of Phonemic Orthography

Arnas Radzevičius[1]([⊠]), Aistis Raudys[2]([⊠]), and Pijus Kasparaitis[2]([⊠])

[1] AAI Labs, Suopių g. 21, Riešė 14265, Lithuania
arnas@aai-labs.com
[2] Institute of Informatics, Vilnius University, Naugarduko 24,
03225 Vilnius, Lithuania
{aistis.raudys,pijus.kasparaitis}@mif.vu.lt

Abstract. Introducing neural networks into the field has improved the performance of speech synthesis systems significantly. Most research was done on the English language which has substantial speech data resources, however, a low degree of grapheme-phoneme correspondence. Other, low resource languages pose different challenges that may be overcome using different approaches to text embeddings. In the present paper we present the results of using stressed text labels in speech datasets to train a speech synthesis model for a low speech data resource language - Lithuanian. Nvidia's implementation of the Tacotron 2 system and the Lithuanian language speech dataset (corpus) with stressed text labels were used to train speech synthesis models. By introducing accentuation into sample labels, we show a significant improvement in speech naturalness as measured by MOS.

Keywords: Speech synthesis · Neural networks · Datasets · WaveGlow · Tacotron 2 · Phonemic orthography

1 Introduction

A phonemic orthography is an orthography in which the graphemes (written symbols) correspond to the phonemes (spoken sounds) [1]. Some languages have a higher degree of grapheme-phoneme correspondence. This means that words are pronounced very similarly to the way they are spelled. Finnish, Albanian, Georgian, and other languages are good examples of that. Other phonemic orthographies can be defective (e.g., English), or slightly defective (e.g., Lithuanian, which will be used as an example throughout this paper). This information is important to the implementation of a speech synthesis system. A lot of research was carried out to convert graphemes to phonemes in highly non-phonemic languages, such as English [2–4]. The converted graphemes are then used to train a deep neural network to synthesize speech. Without this conversion, some neural networks struggle to ensure correct pronunciation of synthesized speech [5].

© Springer Nature Switzerland AG 2021
A. Lopata et al. (Eds.): ICIST 2021, CCIS 1486, pp. 378–387, 2021.
https://doi.org/10.1007/978-3-030-88304-1_30

However, the opposite may be the case for languages with higher grapheme-phoneme correspondence. In such languages, most of the letters are pronounced the way they are spelled. For example, the majority of letters in the Lithuanian language correspond to the same phoneme regardless of the context of a sentence. Still, it is not a complete phonemic orthography, since the vowels are not fully distinguished [6]. Nevertheless, the phonemic complexity is lower as compared to that in the English language; this facilitates the task of preparing the text for neural network training.

In the Lithuanian language, the same word often has more than one pronunciation. It depends on the accentuated (stressed) letter, e.g., the word "pastato" is pronounced differently in the following two sentences: "eikite tiẽsiai iki pãstato gãlo", "Jìs pastãto dáiktą añt stãlo.". The morphological analysis can help to determine the stress position in the word of the sentence [7]. Another approach is to use stressed text data to train a neural network that can put accents on appropriate words in a sentence. The latter is more preferable for a neural network TTS system application.

Since the main problem that sets the Lithuanian language apart from a phonemic orthography is that some of its vowels are not fully distinguished (the same letter can be used for the short and long vowels, e.g., "a", "e"), using a stressed-label speech dataset may be sufficient to train a neural network to synthesize speech. This eliminates (or replaces) the need for pronunciation dictionaries [8] which are not publicly available for many languages and are hard to compile. This is especially important to the languages that have low speech data resources.

To leverage all that, we will use Nvidia's implementation of Tacotron 2 as an acoustic model and a WaveGlow vocoder. It is possible to use raw text as dataset sample labels to train the Tacotron 2 model, however, our experiments show that this has a negative impact on the performance of a speech synthesis model. The results also show the advantages of using the stressed text as sample labels. Further work may include modifying TTS systems where input text embeddings originally are phonemes. An example of such a system is Microsoft's FastSpeech 2 [9], in which the vocabulary of phonemes is used to train the model. We could experiment to discover whether the stressed text would work equally well for the languages with a higher degree of a phonemic orthography.

2   Background

In the present section, we are going to review briefly the background of this work, including the Tacotron 2 and WaveGlow neural networks, Lithuanian speech corpus stressing, the TTS system evaluation by MOS, and, finally, a brief history of other Lithuanian text-to-speech synthesizers.

2.1   Tactoron 2 and Nvidia

Tacotron 2 is a neural network architecture for speech synthesis directly from the text [10]. Like most TTS (text-to-speech) systems, the TTS synthesis process takes place in two steps [11–13]. First, the input character embeddings are converted to a mel-scale spectrogram using a recurrent sequence-to-sequence feature prediction network that is based on encoder-decoder architecture with an autoregressive decoder. Such a system is typically called an acoustic model. The outputs of the acoustic model are then fed into the WaveNet [12] model (that was modified to accept mel-spectrograms as inputs) which uses the spectrogram to synthesize a time-domain waveform. WaveNet is called a vocoder model since it can synthesize audio from a given sequence of features. It generates audio by sampling one frame at a time and is conditioned on the previously generated frames. To summarize, the original Tacotron 2 system uses two main components - a Tacotron acoustic model and a WaveNet vocoder - to synthesize speech. The present authors claim that the quality of speech synthesis done by the model rivals that of a real human speaker. The main disadvantage of the system, however, is that the inference time is much slower than real-time because WaveNet generates each audio frame sequentially; consequently, it cannot be deployed in a real-world application.

In this paper, Nvidia's implementation of Tacotron 2 [14] is used to train a Lithuanian speech synthesis model. Nvidia's Tacotron 2 differs from the system described in the original paper in that it uses WaveGlow [13,15] instead of WaveNet [12] as a vocoder. This greatly speeds up inference time. WaveGlow is a generative model that generates audio by sampling from the distribution of audio samples conditioned on a mel-spectrogram [13]. With the help of Tacotron, a trained WaveGlow model can sample a good quality waveform from a mel-spectrogram much faster than in real-time. The MOS score provided by the authors of the WaveGlow paper shows that the vocoder synthesizes audio quality similar to that generated by WaveNet.

2.2   Text Stressing

Instead of using raw text embeddings to train the Tacotron 2 model as it was done in the original paper and Nvidia's implementation when training the English language speech synthesis model, we will use a Lithuanian language speech dataset where each sample label (sentence) is stressed. The program that uses the algorithm based on the morphological analysis [7] was used to semi-automatically stress the speech corpus sample labels. The program runs through dataset sample labels, stresses each word and marks the words that can be stressed in multiple ways or the words that were not stressed. Then the user of the program can choose appropriate stressing of the words from the proposed options or put the accents manually.

This program was used to stress 91-h Lithuanian speech corpus sample labels. Each accent (stress mark) is actually a UTF-8 combining character [16] that is combined with a previous letter in a character sentence, e.g., two UTF-8 symbols 'a' and \u0300 are combined into 'à'. We used three combining characters (accents) as character embeddings when training a TTS model: \u0300 (grave), \u0301 (acute), and \u0303 (tilde). Using these character embeddings, a neural network can learn which letter in a word should be accented, thus improving naturalness of synthesized speech. See Sect. 3.1 for more details on the Lithuanian speech corpus stressing.

2.3   Mean Opinion Score

The mean opinion score (MOS) [17] is a subjective evaluation metric of text-to-speech systems. It is calculated by collecting the results of a subjective listening test. Subjective listening tests are generally regarded as the most reliable and definitive way of assessing speech quality and naturalness [18]. In general, subjective quality measures require that:

- there are enough listening subjects of sufficient diversity to produce statistically significant results;
- experiments are conducted in the controlled environment with specific acoustic characteristics and equipment;
- every subject receives the same instructions and stimuli.

In the MOS test, the listeners evaluate randomly selected samples from a pool of speech samples (either signals or utterances). In the case of TTS MOS, the pool of speech samples usually contains audio samples generated by multiple TTS systems and ground truth (real human speech samples). The MOS score is calculated for each of the sources. Also, the limitation is that the same listening test should never contain two samples created from the same utterance.

At the beginning of the test, listeners are asked to use headphones to achieve better results because by using loudspeakers people have a smaller discrimination capacity. They are also provided with the MOS score table, like that in Table 1.

Table 1. Mean opinion score table [18]

Rating	Quality	Distortion
5	Excellent	Imperceptible
4	Good	Just perceptible, but not annoying
3	Fair	Perceptible and slightly annoying
2	Poor	Annoying, but not objectionable
1	Bad	Very annoying and objectionable

2.4   Other Lithuanian Text-to-Speech Synthesizers

The synthesis of the Lithuanian speech has a history of about 30 years. A comprehensive review was published 5 years ago [19]. The first Lithuanian commercial format speech synthesizer Apollo was developed by Dolphin systems Inc. in 1994. Later, concatenative synthesizers, mainly based on diphones, were developed and refined for a long time. In 2013–2016, a significant breakthrough in terms of voice quality was achieved with the development of unit selection synthesizers. In recent years, statistical-parametric synthesis using the Merlin neural network package has been mastered and this method has been shown to outperform unit selection synthesis [20].

3   Experimental Setup

3.1   Dataset

To train a neural network, a 91-h one-speaker Lithuanian speech dataset was created. The first stage in creating the dataset was to collect multiple audiobooks narrated by Vytautas Radzevičius and their e-book counterparts. Then the text and audio speech were aligned using Aeneas, an open-source tool [21]. This process is called forced alignment [22] and it results in a sync-map that contains the start and end timestamp of each sentence in the audio. Then, using this sync-map, the audio was cut into samples of the length ranging from 2 to 14 s. Finally, the data was structured as a set of audio sample and label (transcription) pairs.

Nevertheless, the quality of the dataset is relatively poor. That is because the Aeneas aligning tool is not perfect and makes mistakes even after trying out multiple configurations. Another drawback is that the speaker does not always narrate the same words as in the corresponding e-book due to a human factor. Some manual work was done to correct the dataset as well as possible, but the audio-text pairs are still not completely accurate (correct). This affected the quality of the model, which is reflected in MOS (see later Sections).

After building the audio and text pair dataset, each sample label (text sentence) was automatically stressed using the program described in Sect. 2.2. The stressed text labels were manually reviewed and fixed by a professional philologist to ensure correctness. The stressed-text speech corpus was later used in model training.

3.2   Model Configuration

To train both Tacotron 2 and WaveGlow, the same hyperparameters as in corresponding papers were used. Only the batch sizes were reduced (from 64 to 16 for Tacotron 2 and from 24 to 12 for WaveGlow) because of a lack of computational resources. The hyperparameters for Tacotron 2 and WaveGlow are summarized in Tables 2 and 3, respectively. Other details can be found online.

3.3   Training Setup

We carried out the experiments on Google Virtual Machine with an 8-core CPU, 1 x Nvidia Tesla T4 GPU and 30 GB of RAM. We used publicly available pre-trained models published by Nvidia for both Tacotron 2 and WaveGlow. We used them to fine-tune the models on our data to save computational resources.

Table 2. Tacotron 2 hyperparameters [14].

Hyperparameter	Value
Character embedding dimension	512
Encoder kernel size	5
Encoder number of convolutions	3
Encoder embedding dimension	512
Decoder number of frames per step	1
Decoder RNN dimension	1024
Decoder pre-network dimension	256
Max decoder steps	1000
Decoder gate threshold	0.5
Pre-attention dropout	0.1
Pre-decoder dropout	0.1
Attention RNN dimension	1024
Attention dimension	128
Attention location number of filters	32
Attention location kernel size	31
Mel-post processing network embedding dimension	512
Mel-post processing network kernel size	5
Mel-post processing network number of convolutions	5

Table 3. WaveGlow hyperparameters [15].

Hyperparameter	Value
Mel-spectrogram channels	80
Coupling layers	12
Invertible 1×1 convolutions	12
Coupling layer dilated convolutions	8
Residual connections	512
Skip connections	256
Early channel output after every N layers	4
Number of early channer outputs	2
Batch size	12

The fine-tuning of the vocoder is of especial importance as the authors of the paper state that they used 8 Nvidia GV100 GPU's to train for 580000 iterations with a batch size of 24, and such resources are expensive.

4   Results

The WaveGlow vocoder was fine-tuned on our speech corpus first. It took 111 h to train the model for 84000 iterations (42 epochs). Then the Tacotron 2 model was trained for 18 h to reach 24000 iterations (24 epochs). We conducted a MOS survey to evaluate the following four acoustic model - vocoder model combinations:

- A Tacotron model trained on a dataset without stressed text labels and a pre-trained WaveGlow model. (NP)
- A Tacotron model trained on a dataset without stressed text labels and a finetuned WaveGlow model. (NF)
- A Tacotron model trained on a dataset with stressed text labels and a pre-trained WaveGlow model. (SP)
- A Tacotron model trained on a dataset with stressed text labels and a fine-tuned WaveGlow model. (SF)

The survey also contained ground-truth (GT) samples. There were 6 survey participants. The participants were familiarised with the purpose of the survey, given instructions on how to complete the survey, and were asked to use headphones throughout the whole survey process to achieve more reliable results [18]. Each participant had to rate 75 audio samples generated by 5 sources (NP, NF, SP, SF, and GT) on a scale from 1 to 5. To avoid response bias, the participants were not informed on which sample was generated by which source. The rated utterances (samples) contained no numbers or abbreviations, but they did have punctuation. The shortest utterance duration was 1.5 s (2 words), while the duration of the longest sample was 9 s (18 words). The participants were provided with the MOS table (like that in Table 1) for reference. The MOS evaluations were calculated with 95% confidence intervals (CI) computed from the t-distribution.

The MOS results are provided in Table 4. As we can see, the system that has a Tacotron model trained on the stressed text and a fine-tuned WaveGlow vocoder perform significantly better than the systems that have either a Tacotron model that is not trained on the stressed text or that uses a pre-trained WaveGlow model. On the other hand, there is a fairly big gap between the best-performing speech synthesis system and the ground truth. This may be due to several reasons. The first reason, as mentioned in Sect. 3.1, is a poor audio-text correspondence between the dataset samples, which has a negative impact on the performance of the synthesizer. Another reason may be that the MOS survey was not conducted completely correctly, as it contained multiple signals (utterances) generated by each of the 5 sources (models, ground-truth). This practice is not recommended

Table 4. The MOS evaluation with 95% confidence intervals (CI) computed from the t-distribution comparison between the ground-truth (GT), the model that was trained on non-stressed text labels (NF) and the model that was trained on stressed text labels (SF).

Model	MOS ± CI
NP	2.267 ± 0.638
NF	2.612 ± 0.442
SP	2.619 ± 0.870
SF	3.525 ± 0.573
GT	4.786 ± 0.336

[18]. Another reason may be that there were not enough survey respondents - confidence intervals are quite big for each source.

Nevertheless, the trained speech synthesis model (SF) shows fairly good results in terms of speech naturalness and pronunciation. The model responds to the punctuation and can synthesize various (difficult) sentences. The observed disadvantages were that the synthesis might fail in very short or very long sentences. It also breaks when attempts are made to synthesize two sentences separated by a dot. This might be again the fault of the poor-quality dataset, as this behavior usually is not observed in Tacotron models.

5   Future Work

5.1   Speech Corpus

The next natural step in limproving the quality of synthesized speech is to fix the errors in the Lithuanian speech corpus. This has the potential of solving the above-described multiple currently encountered synthesis problems.

5.2   Automatic Stressing Model

The stressed dataset sample labels were generated by using a semi-automatic tool (program) that still requires human expert intervention. Currently we are working on a completely automated text-stressing neural network model. This may provide high stressing accuracy results and thus remove the need for human expert work. It would be extremely useful in creating new stressed datasets and training of new models with different voices. Also, it would ease the inference process, since now the user himself needs to put accents on the words in the sentence he wants to synthesize. A high accuracy stressing neural network model may work as a pre-processor for speech synthesis model input.

Currently, we are creating multiple high quality speech datasets narrated by different speakers. Quality checks are done by human listeners to ensure the correctness of the audio-text correspondence between the dataset samples. Since the quality of these datasets will be better than that used for the experiments in this paper, a speech synthesis model of better performance is expected to be trained by applying transfer learning to the model described therein. These multiple speaker datasets may also stimulate further research into multi-speaker speech synthesis for languages with higher orthographic degree.

6   Conclusions

In the present paper we proposed to use the stressed text for speech dataset sample labels for languages with a higher degree of a phonemic orthography. The main problem we tried to solve was an incorrect pronunciation of synthesized speech. We used the UTF-8 combining characters \u0300, \u0301, \u0303 (accordingly, grave, acute and tilde) as character embeddings to allow the Tacotron model to learn to pronounce words when explicitly specified by accents. Our experimental results show that the use of stressed dataset sample labels significantly outperforms the TTS models trained on a dataset with raw (not stressed) sample labels. Hence, by using stressed text sample labels for languages with a higher degree of a phonemic orthography, it is possible to replace the hard to create phoneme vocabulary necessary in some speech synthesis neural networks to achieve high quality speech.

Although the proposed approach is a relatively small modification to the usual speech synthesis model training workflow, this study may be useful to the developers whose aim is to train a text-to-speech model for a low resource language that has a higher orthographic degree.

References

1. Sgall, P.: Towards a Theory of Phonemic Orthography. John Benjamins, Amsterdam (Philadelphia) (1987)
2. Berndt, R.S., Reggia, J.A., Mitchum, C.C.: Empirically derived probabilities for grapheme-to-phoneme correspondences in English. Behav. Res. Methods Instrum. Comput. 19(1), 1–9 (1987)
3. Bisani, M., Ney, H.: Joint-sequence models for grapheme-to-phoneme conversion. Speech Commun. 50(5), 434–451 (2008)
4. Rao, K., Peng, F., Sak, H., Beaufays, F.: Grapheme-to-phoneme conversion using long short-term memory recurrent neural networks. In: 2015 IEEE International Conference on Acoustics, Speech and Signal Processing (ICASSP), pp. 4225–4229. IEEE (2015)
5. Ren, Y., et al.: FastSpeech: fast, robust and controllable text to speech. arXiv preprint arXiv:1905.09263, 2019
6. Balode, L., Holvoet, A.: The Lithuanian language and its dialects. In: Circum-Baltic Languages: Typology and Contact, pp. 41–80 (2001)
7. Kasparaitis, P.: Automatic stressing of the Lithuanian text on the basis of a dictionary. Informatica 11(1), 19–40 (2000)
8. Wells, J.C., Hung, T.T.N.: Longman pronunciation dictionary. RELC J. 21(2), 95–97 (1990)

9. Ren, Y., et al.: FastSpeech 2: fast and high-quality end-to-end text to speech. arXiv preprint arXiv:2006.04558 (2020)
10. Wang, Y., et al.: Tacotron: towards end-to-end speech synthesis. arXiv preprint arXiv:1703.10135, 2017
11. Oord, A., et al.: Parallel WaveNet: fast high-fidelity speech synthesis. In: International Conference on Machine Learning, pp. 3918–3926. PMLR (2018)
12. van den Oord, A., et al.: WaveNet: a generative model for raw audio. arXiv preprint arXiv:1609.03499 (2016)
13. Prenger, R., Valle, R., Catanzaro, B.: WaveGlow: a flow-based generative network for speech synthesis. In: ICASSP 2019–2019 IEEE International Conference on Acoustics, Speech and Signal Processing (ICASSP), pp. 3617–3621. IEEE (2019)
14. Tacotron 2 (without wavenet). https://github.com/NVIDIA/tacotron2. Accessed 23 Apr 2021
15. WaveGlow: a flow-based generative network for speech synthesis. https://github.com/NVIDIA/waveglow. Accessed 23 Apr 2021
16. Yergeau, F.: UTF-8, a transformation format of ISO 10646. Technical report, STD 63, RFC 3629, November 2003
17. ITUT Recommendation. Telephone transmission quality subjective opinion tests. A method for subjective performance assessment of the quality of speech voice output devices (1994)
18. Ribeiro, F., Florêncio, D., Zhang, C., Seltzer, M.: CROWDMOS: an approach for crowdsourcing mean opinion score studies. In: 2011 IEEE International Conference on Acoustics, Speech and Signal Processing (ICASSP), pp. 2416–2419. IEEE (2011)
19. Kasparaitis, P., et al.: Lietuviško balso sintezatoriu kokybės vertinimas. Kalby studijos (28), 80–91 (2016)
20. Kasparaitis, P., Beniušė, M.: Statistical parametric speech synthesis of lithuanian, p. 43 (2019). http://lki.lt/26-oji-tarptautine-moksline-jono-jablonskio-konferencija
21. Aeneas. https://github.com/readbeyond/aeneas. Accessed 23 Apr 2021
22. Moreno, P.J., Joerg, C., Van Thong, J.-M., Glickman, O.: A recursive algorithm for the forced alignment of very long audio segments. In: Fifth International Conference on Spoken Language Processing (1998)

Author Index

Printed in the United States
by Baker & Taylor Publisher Services